IF YOU'RE SO SMART, WHY AREN'T YOU HAPPY?

IF YOU'RE SO SMART, WHY AREN'T YOU HAPPY **?**

Raj Raghunathan

PORTFOLIO / PENGUIN

PORTFOLIO / PENGUIN
An imprint of Penguin Random House LLC
375 Hudson Street
New York, New York 10014
penguin.com

Photograph credits
Page 81: Nina Leen / Getty Images
201 (left): Steve Granitz / Getty Images
201 (right): Walter McBride / Getty Images

ISBN: 978-1-10198-073-6
International edition: 978-0-399-56439-0

Printed in the United States of America
10   9   8   7   6   5   4   3   2   1

Set in Warnock Pro with Avenir Next LT Pro
Designed by Daniel Lagin

To the Sign

If

If you can keep your head when all about you
Are losing theirs and blaming it on you,
If you can trust yourself when all men doubt you,
But make allowance for their doubting too;
If you can wait and not be tired by waiting,
Or being lied about, don't deal in lies,
Or being hated, don't give way to hating,
And yet don't look too good, nor talk too wise:
If you can dream—and not make dreams your master;
If you can think—and not make thoughts your aim;
If you can meet with Triumph and Disaster
And treat those two impostors just the same;
If you can bear to hear the truth you've spoken
Twisted by knaves to make a trap for fools,
Or watch the things you gave your life to, broken,
And stoop and build 'em up with worn-out tools:
If you can make one heap of all your winnings
And risk it on one turn of pitch-and-toss,
And lose, and start again at your beginnings
And never breathe a word about your loss;
If you can force your heart and nerve and sinew
To serve your turn long after they are gone,
And so hold on when there is nothing in you
Except the Will which says to them: "Hold on!"
If you can talk with crowds and keep your virtue,
Or walk with Kings—nor lose the common touch,
If neither foes nor loving friends can hurt you,
If all men count with you, but none too much;
If you can fill the unforgiving minute
With sixty seconds' worth of distance run,
Yours is the Earth and everything that's in it,
And—which is more—you'll be a Man, my son!

Rudyard Kipling

FOREWORD

What does it take to lead a happy and fulfilling life?

W hat does it take to lead a happy and fulfilling life? Over the past four decades I have had the privilege of working with over 150 major CEOs, including Alan Mulally (CEO of the Year when he was at Ford), Dr. Jim Kim (president of the World Bank), and Ian Read (CEO of Pfizer). At Johnson & Johnson I did a huge leadership development project involving Ralph Larsen (then CEO) and their top 2,000 leaders. Every single one of the leaders whom I have taught or coached has pondered this question. And since you are reading this book, I'll assume that you, too, have spent considerable time on it.

The answer to the question, it turns out, is both a little simpler and a little more complicated than you might think. It's simpler because, ultimately, it doesn't take that much more than what you already have to be happy. As you'll learn toward the end of this book, beyond basic necessities and adequate health, it takes just three things to be happy: (1) great social relationships, (2) a sense of purpose (doing something meaningful), and (3) a "positive" attitude toward life—an attitude that lets you feel a sense of being in control even in challenging times. That's all it takes to be happy.

The answer to what it takes to be happy is a little more complicated than that for three reasons. First, being the smart and successful person that you are, you aren't going to be satisfied with knowing just *what* it takes to be happy; you will also want to know *why* it takes these things to be happy. That makes the answer more complicated because figuring out the answer to the "why" question means delving deep into happiness research, which takes work. Second, as I know from personal experience and as I have discussed in my book, *Triggers*, simply knowing what it takes to be happy, and why, isn't enough. It's also important to know *how* you are going to achieve those things that you need to be happy. You need to have a *plan* that will work, and then you need to execute this plan well. Figuring out a plan that's both compelling in theory and feasible in practice complicates the answer to the question.

The final, and I think most important, reason that the answer is complicated has to do with self-awareness—or lack of it. If you are like most smart-and-successful people I know, you have a dream. The dream goes something like this:

> I'm incredibly busy right now. Given pressures of work and home, and new technology that follows me everywhere and e-mails and voice mails and global competition, I feel about as busy as I ever have. Sometimes I feel overcommitted. I don't tell others this, but every now and again my life feels just a little bit out of control. But I'm working on some very unique and special challenges right now. And I think the worst of this is going to be over in two or three months. And after that I'm going take two or three weeks to get organized and spend time with the family. And I'm going to begin my new "healthy and happy" life program. And everything is going to be different. And it won't be crazy anymore.

How many years have you had this dream? And for how long are you going to continue to have it? If you aren't careful, you could have this dream forever!

What does it take to lead a happy and fulfilling life? It takes self-awareness to realize that leading a happy and fulfilling life is more important than anything else that you have done or will do. Self-awareness is crucial because from it comes the all-important decision to *not postpone the decision to lead a happy and fulfilling life*. Developing such self-awareness can be difficult, particularly if you are overcommitted, tired, and depleted. This is the third reason that makes the answer to the question complicated.

But you are in luck. If there's one guy who can uncomplicate things for you, it's Raj. Raj makes being happy simple in three ways. First, he makes it easy to understand and assimilate the scientific findings on happiness. How? By using a structure—7 "sins," 7 "habits," and 7 "exercises"—that's simple to comprehend, and infusing it with just the right mix of interesting anecdotes and relevant research. Second, he has done the hard work of identifying the most powerful happiness-enhancing exercises, so you don't have to. All you need to do is understand *why* the exercises work, and execute them to the best of your ability.

Finally, this book offers the most compelling set of arguments for why you need to give the goal of leading a happier and more fulfilling life—a goal that, I might add, almost every spiritual leader and philosopher, from Aristotle and Buddha to Maya Angelou and Zorba the Greek, has sought—your highest priority. The desire for happiness may appear to be self-centered, but follow Raj and dig a little deeper. You'll find that there's perhaps no goal that's more noble. The determinants of happiness are also those of developing into a nicer—kinder and more compassionate—human being. If that weren't enough, the things that lead to happiness also lead to success.

How important do I think it is for you to read this book? Let me just say that if you are smart and successful and yet feel that you aren't as happy as you could—or want to—be, I wouldn't just recommend that you read this book. I would say that you *owe it to yourself to drop everything else you are doing and start reading the book now!*

Life is good.

Marshall Goldsmith, Spring 2016

CONTENTS

——————

Introduction

WHAT LED ME TO TEACH HAPPINESS, AND HOW THIS BOOK IS STRUCTURED

E ven until just a few decades back, if you happened to lose touch with a childhood friend—because, for example, your family moved from one city to another—you had little hope of reconnecting with that friend. That aspect of life has changed now, thanks mainly to Facebook. And so it happened that I met a close friend after losing touch with him for nearly thirty years. As it turned out, although we had moved to different corners of India after we had last met there, we were practically neighbors now. My friend lives in Houston, Texas, while I live in Austin—a mere 170 miles separating us.

As we caught up over drinks, I got to do something that only those lucky enough to meet a close friend after a significant passage of time can do: reconnect with my *own* past self. My friend reminded me of how I was known, all those years back, for my easygoing and lighthearted nature. He recalled the time when we had an important impending exam, one for which my friends—and their mothers, literally—were planning to pull an all-nighter. As for me? I went to bed at my regular time and got my full quota of ten hours of sleep, thank you! He also reminded me of the time when we had a formal dinner party for which everyone else showed up in spiffy blue blazers and khaki slacks. I, on the other hand, sauntered in, unabashed, in a parrot-green shirt and sunflower-yellow bell-bottoms (it was the seventies, after all). My friend recalled that everyone had made fun of me at the party, but I took the ribbing in good spirit. So unflappable was I, recalled my friend, that I was definitely the go-to person if anyone needed cheering up.

Listening to these stories, I couldn't help but feel wistful about my past self. I would like to believe that I am relatively easygoing even today but have to acknowledge that I've become less "chilled out" with age.

What had become of the person I once was? When and how did I lose my "innocence"?

Happiness Across the Life Span

As I thought about this question, I realized that the past might seem rosier than it actually was. If you have maintained a journal for some length of time, you know that the past wasn't any more hunky-dory than is the present. We remember the past as having been more pleasant for two main reasons. First, we tend to cope better with the big negative events than we expect to; so the impact of a romantic breakup or of the failure to get a dream job seldom lingers as long as we think it will. Second, we tend to give the negative events from our past a positive spin over time; thus, the heartbreak from being rejected for a prom date or the embarrassment from failing an important exam become, in due course, stories that make our life more colorful, rather than ones that cast a dark shadow on it. It is precisely because past negative events become more positive in our memory that women agree to go through a second childbirth and authors agree to write a second book.

That said, it does appear that most of us were happier as kids than we are as adults, as the graph on page 3 suggests.

The graph confirms, among other things, that one of the most trying periods in our lives is adolescence: not only do we look and behave awkwardly then, we also feel our worst. The graph also confirms the so-called midlife crisis: our most miserable days as an adult typically occur between the ages of forty and fifty.

The fact that we were happier as kids than we are as adults raises an important question: what did we know as kids that we forget as adults? Or, more to the point: what do we know now, but did not as kids, that is hurting our happiness?

I got my first glimpse into the answer to this question in the spring of 2009.

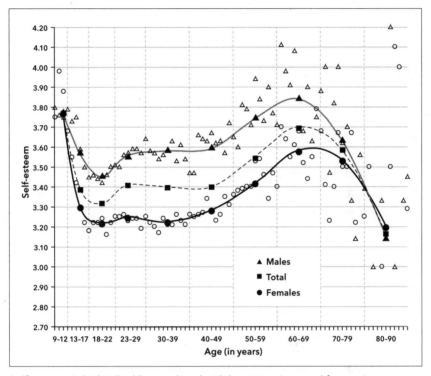

Self-esteem (which is highly correlated with happiness) across life span*

---

* The graph, from Robins et al. (2002), is of self-esteem, rather than of happiness, across the life span. I have taken a little poetic license here in equating self-esteem to happiness. However, this poetic license is justified in light of the following three reasons. First, findings show that self-esteem is highly correlated with happiness (Steel et al. 2008) and as such is a good proxy for it. Further, the S-shaped pattern of self-esteem across life span appears to be the most common pattern with happiness as well (e.g., Deaton 2007; Blanchflower and Oswald 2008; Baird et al. 2010). Finally, I wished to show that people are generally happier as kids than as adolescents or adults; this point does not come across in the happiness surveys, which tend to exclude participants below sixteen years of age. B. M. Baird, R. E. Lucas, and M. B. Donnellan (2010), "Life Satisfaction Across the Life Span: Findings from Two Nationally Representative Panel Studies," *Social Indicators Research* 99(2): 183–203; D. G. Blanchflower and A. J. Oswald (2008), "Is Well-being U-shaped over the Life Cycle? *Social Science & Medicine* 66(8): 1733–49; A. Deaton (2007), *Income, Aging, Health and Well-being Around the World: Evidence from the Gallup World Poll* (no. w13317), National Bureau of Economic Research; the paper can be accessed at: http://www.nber.org/papers/w13317; P. Steel, J. Schmidt, and J. Shultz (2008), "Refining the Relationship Between Personality and Subjective Well-being," *Psychological Bulletin* 134(1): 138–61.

My Course on Happiness

By that time, I had been teaching at the McCombs School of Business at The University of Texas at Austin for more than eight years. Over these years, I had begun to feel increasingly uneasy about the usefulness and relevance of the courses I was teaching, such as "Customer Insights" and "Consumer Behavior." It's not that I thought these courses weren't helping my students advance their careers or their organizations' goals. Rather, my uneasiness was rooted in issues that were simultaneously more philosophical and practical: *I wasn't sure that I was helping my students lead happier, more fulfilling lives.*

I knew that academic and career success don't automatically translate into happiness and fulfillment, and to me, it seemed obvious that the primary purpose of education ought to be to help people lead happier, more fulfilling lives. If our education system doesn't ultimately lead to better quality of life for all concerned, how good is it? I doubted that my courses—or for that matter, most courses offered at business schools—were helping students lead happier and more fulfilling lives, and this troubled me. (If you are wondering what happiness means and whether it can be reliably measured, hold on to your horses. I'll get to this topic toward the end of the chapter.)

So after wallowing in this worry for a few years (until I made tenure, basically), I decided to do something about it. I put together a course with the objective of giving students the opportunity to discuss one of life's most important questions: *What are the determinants of a fulfilling and happy life?* I knew I didn't have all the answers, but nevertheless felt that it would be better to give the students an opportunity to discuss this question than to do nothing.

When I first offered my course, I wasn't sure how successful it would be. Many of my colleagues felt business-school students are too hard-nosed, mercenary, and self-centered to find the topic of happiness and fulfillment attractive. However, from the start, my course has been oversubscribed. Indeed, the very first time I taught the course, I was honored with a university-wide "professor of the month" award. The next year I was nominated for the "professor of the year" award, and soon I was getting the best ratings I had ever obtained for any course I have taught. Once word got out about the course, I started getting invitations to give talks at corporations. I am currently one of the faculty members at Whole Foods' Academy for Conscious Leadership.

Up to the summer of 2015, I had taught just over 1,000 students from the McCombs School of Business and from the Indian School of Business in Hyderabad. By the end of 2015, that number grew by several orders of magnitude, reaching an incredible 100,000 students on January 1, 2016! The reason for this astronomical growth was the launch of an online version of the course on June 15, 2015, on the world's most popular MOOC (massive open online course) platform: Coursera. Since its launch, the course has consistently figured in the top-ten list of Coursera courses and was recently rated as *the top* MOOC of 2015 by class-central.com (a third-party information portal for MOOCs). To this day, I regularly get e-mails from students in the course thanking me for offering it. One recently wrote, "I started the course all over again last week. Not because the first time around was difficult, but because there is so much information packed into the course that a second round seems imperative," and then went on, "To simply say 'The course is very useful' is an understatement." Another wrote, "The Happiness Course is possibly one of the best things that happened to my life—and I kid you not! I was enthusiastic about life in general, but after this course, I immediately started to feel so much difference in how I live every single day of my life." Yet another student said, "This engaging and often profound course takes the wisdom of many great teachers, researchers, and philosophers and puts these truths into an accessible, logical, and workable program to create increased personal happiness and meaning." The course has been so successful because of a combination of several factors, including a deep hunger to understand the determinants of happiness and fulfillment, and recent advances in our scientific understanding of what it takes to lead a happy and fulfilling life—thanks in no small part to the field of positive psychology. An equally important reason, I believe, is that many of the students in my class have experienced an actual improvement in their happiness levels by taking the class.

When I first offered my course, my objective wasn't anything as lofty as improving students' happiness levels; I merely wished to give them the opportunity to discuss one of life's big questions: what are the determinants of a happy and fulfilling life? In the beginning, even this modest aim seemed out of reach because there was no standard textbook on happiness. Indeed, I wasn't even sure *what* to include in the course.

It was with the aim of figuring out the course content that I decided to sit in on a class along similar lines being offered by Professor Srikumar Rao, who, at that time, was teaching at Columbia University. It was through one of the exercises that Srikumar had us undertake—an exercise called "Mental Chatter"—that I got a glimpse into why I myself had become less easygoing over time. This, in turn, gave me crucial insights into both course content and structure.

Insights from the Mental Chatter Exercise

The mental chatter exercise calls for maintaining a brutally honest record, on a daily basis for a period of two weeks, of one's naturally occurring thoughts. (You can read the instructions for the exercise on the book's website: www.happysmarts.com/book/exercises/mental_chatter.) To successfully participate in the exercise, it is important to not steer your thoughts in a more positive direction when recording them, and to resist the tendency to find closure or meaning in interpreting the day's events. This makes the mental chatter exercise very different from the more familiar practice of maintaining a journal. The mental chatter exercise requires that you maintain a full record of your negativity, because the spontaneously occurring negative thoughts are not meaningless, irrelevant thoughts that are randomly produced by the mind. Rather, they are rooted in deep-seated goals, desires, and values. Attempting to override negative chatter with positive thinking is akin to popping peppermints to smother bad breath: it may address the symptom but will not address the cause. In other words, if one aspires not just to enhance one's well-being but to sustain this enhancement, it is necessary to gain a deeper understanding of the goals, desires, and values that are responsible for the negative mental chatter.

In the course of completing the mental chatter exercise, I discovered something quite startling. I discovered that my mental chatter was far more negative than I had expected it to be. I hadn't realized that beneath my outward positivity lurked a cesspool of negativity. Although this negativity—which manifested itself, among other things, as anxiety about whether others respected me enough or as frustration with my inability to get my kids to behave like I wanted them to—had always been there, it wasn't until I did the mental chatter exercise that I became aware of its scope and intensity.

As I brooded about the negativity of my mental chatter ("Do I really feel *so* concerned about what others think of me? Am I really *that* frustrated with my kids?"), I wondered if my case was unique. Perhaps, I thought hopefully, I was so positive otherwise that my mental chatter seemed particularly negative in contrast. But what if—God forbid—my mental chatter was in fact more negative than that of others? (Being a normal human being, I naturally wanted others to be just as miserable as I was.)

I couldn't wait for Professor Rao's next class, so that I could compare notes with other students. To my relief, the other students were in the same boat: their mental chatter was just as negative. Later, once I began teaching my own course on happiness, I got the opportunity to inflict, if that's the word, the mental chatter exercise on my students. And, as you may have guessed, the theme that had emerged in Professor Rao's class was replicated among my students.

What Ails the Smart-and-the-Successful

Over the past five years, I have had the privilege of subjecting close to 1,500—mostly the smart-and-the-successful—people to the mental chatter exercise. I decided to focus on the unhappiness of the smart-and-the-successful (henceforth, the S-and-S) mainly because I find their lack of happiness to be particularly intriguing. The S-and-S, by definition, have superior IQ, greater drive, superior critical-thinking ability, a better work ethic, and so on. As a result, one would expect them to be better at achieving goals, especially important ones. Thus, given that happiness is one of our most important goals, one would expect the S-and-S to be happier and more fulfilled. And yet, as numerous findings show, the S-and-S aren't any happier than their less smart or successful counterparts. Those with a university degree, for example, are not much happier than those without a degree; indeed, beyond a basic undergraduate degree, the more educated you are, the less happy you are likely to be. Even the trait that one might consider to be the quintessential one of the S-and-S, or at least the smart—intelligence—has only a spotty relationship with happiness, leading some researchers to conclude that intelligence is virtually unrelated to happiness. Likewise, although there is a small positive relationship between wealth and happiness, it is not as significant as one might expect it to be. Fame too, has little effect on happiness, findings show.

Why aren't the S-and-S as happy as they could—or should—be?

My colleagues Hyunkyu Jang, a PhD student at UT Austin, and Robin Soster, a professor of marketing at the University of Arkansas, obtained some important insights into this question by administering the mental chatter exercise to a number of S-and-S students. We discovered that almost every student is surprised by how much more negative their mental chatter is than they expect it to be. On average, somewhere between 50 and 70 percent of the average student's spontaneously occurring thoughts are negative. This is in sharp contrast to what they expect: they expect 60 to 75 percent of their thoughts to be positive. The fact that students' mental chatter is more negative than they expect it to be is, however, only part—and in my opinion, the less interesting part—of the story. The more interesting part has to do with the *content* of negativity.

The negative mental chatter of the students falls into three main categories:

- Thoughts related to inferiority
- Thoughts about lack of love and connectivity with others
- Thoughts about lack of control

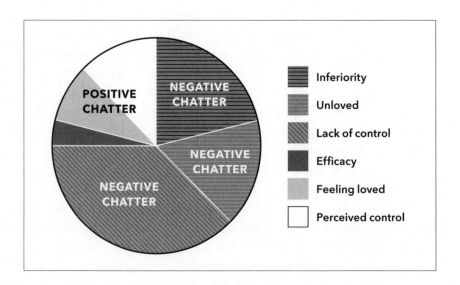

As I surveyed this list of reasons for the unhappiness of the students, I realized that no existing book on happiness tackled them head-on. And yet, there was a lot of research on these topics. Much of this research explored the behaviors, goals, and values in which the three categories of mental chatter are rooted. Thoughts related to inferiority, for example, are rooted in the tendency to engage in social comparisons (e.g., "keeping up with the Joneses"), which, in turn, is rooted in the desire for superiority. Thoughts about lack of love and connectivity are, likewise, rooted in insecurities about relationships, manifested through either "neediness" (or relationship anxiety) or "avoidance." Similarly, thoughts about lack of control are rooted in the desire for control, and in the tendency to be a "maximizer"—someone who has an irrepressible urge to make things better.

Poring over these findings helped me gain a deeper understanding of why I myself had, over the years, evolved into a less happy version of my former self. I realized that, although the behaviors, goals, and values that produce the negative mental chatter are detrimental to happiness, most of us, particularly the S-and-S among us, are unwilling to let go of them. Why? Because we believe that they are critical determinants of something else that we value deeply: success. Many of us believe, for example, that the need for superiority—the desire to be the wealthiest, fastest, strongest—is a very important determinant of success. Likewise, we believe that the ability to be an "island"—emotionally unaffected by others—is a defining feature of strong leaders, and that success comes to those who seek to control others and the environment. In fact, however, evidence does not support any of these beliefs. For example, although the need for superiority may motivate us to pursue goals, it is, overall, more a hindrance than a help when it comes to achieving them. Likewise, the world's best leaders are not emotionally distant, but rather are compassionate and kind. The need for control, too, has its limits, and being overly controlling is not the optimal way to succeed.

So in other words, I discovered that it's best to let go of the behaviors, goals, and values that were fueling our negative mental chatter and replace them with the other behaviors, goals, and values that are more productive. Doing so would not only improve our happiness levels, but also improve our odds of success.

Structure of the Book: The Seven "Sins," "Habits," and "Exercises"

I refer to the behaviors, goals, and values that fuel our negative mental chatter and deflate our happiness as the "deadly happiness sins." I use the word "sin" not to connote a moral transgression; rather, I use it in a tongue-in-cheek way to refer to the idea that our unhappiness is often the result of our own doing. One way to enhance happiness levels, then, is to get rid of the seven deadly sins. A complementary way is to nurture what I call the "habits of the highly happy." There are seven such habits, one corresponding to each of the seven "sins."

The book is thus structured along the seven pairs of "sins" and "habits," as shown in the table below. Each chapter consists of two parts—one (part "A") that discusses a "sin" and another (part "B") that discusses the corresponding "habit."

BOOK CHAPTERS AND THEIR TITLES		
CHAPTER NUMBER	**CHAPTER NAME**	**CONTENT**
Chapter 1A	Devaluing happiness	The 1st sin
Chapter 1B	Prioritizing—but not pursuing—happiness	The 1st habit and exercise
Chapter 2A	Chasing superiority	The 2nd sin
Chapter 2B	Pursuing flow	The 2nd habit and exercise
Chapter 3A	Desperation for love	The 3rd sin
Chapter 3B	The need to love (and give)	The 3rd habit and exercise
Chapter 4A	Being overly controlling	The 4th sin
Chapter 4B	Gaining internal control	The 4th habit and exercise
Chapter 5A	Distrusting others	The 5th sin
Chapter 5B	Exercising "smart trust"	The 5th habit and exercise
Chapter 6A	Passionate/indifferent pursuit of passion	The 6th sin
Chapter 6B	Dispassionate pursuit of passion	The 6th habit and exercise
Chapter 7A	Mind addiction	The 7th sin
Chapter 7B	Mindfulness	The 7th habit and exercise

In addition to the "sins" and "habits," I also review seven "happiness exercises," which are discussed in conjunction with the habits, in part B of the chapters. These exercises are designed to nurture the habits while mitigating the sins.

The Importance of Open-mindedness and Diligence

If the experiences of my students are anything to go by, you will find that you are able to relate, at an intuitive level, to most of the seven sins and habits. That is, you will find the discussions of why the sins lower happiness levels and why the habits enhance them to be instinctively appealing. That's not to say that you won't disagree with anything in the book. Indeed, it's very likely that not only will you disagree with at least some sections of the book, but that they will make you uncomfortable. The reason for this is that we are so deeply conditioned to exhibit certain traits and behaviors (e.g., pursuit of superiority) that we find it disturbing if their validity is questioned. When you experience such discomfort, I urge you to be as open-minded as you can. That is, in the event that you feel skeptical about a particular concept, I ask that you do not immediately dismiss it. In particular, I request that you take the exercise associated with each sin/habit as seriously as you can. If it helps, imagine that you have been ordered by your boss or your spouse (which can sometimes be the same thing) to complete each exercise. Later, once you have finished the book, you will be in a better position to assess the value of various concepts and exercises.

That said, I should mention that not all the concepts and exercises in this book will work equally well for you. As Professor Sonja Lyubomirsky notes in *The How of Happiness*, there is such a thing as a "happiness strategy fit." Depending on your traits and lifestyle, certain concepts and exercises are likely to be more relevant for you than others. To help you figure out the concepts and exercises that work best for you, I recommend that you maintain a journal for the duration of your time reading this book, starting today. Because the book is structured along seven main topics, I recommend that you take seven weeks to complete the exercises, at the rate of one exercise a week. On my website (www.happysmarts.com/book/exercises/journal) you'll find a link that takes you to a password-protected online journal template. One advantage of using this online journal is that you will automatically receive a daily e-mail reminder to make an entry. Of course, if you prefer not to make entries online, but would still like to use the template I have created, you can download a hard copy from the website. Alternatively, if you prefer to maintain your journal elsewhere—for example, in a notebook—that's fine too.

Whichever avenue you choose, you can find the instructions for the journal on the same website. The website also contains instructions for several other happiness exercises, including the seven central to this book. If an important reason you are reading this book is to experience a boost in happiness levels, I urge you to complete the seven exercises diligently. The combination of open-mindedness and diligence, I have discovered, is crucial for experiencing a boost in happiness levels. In the classes that I've taught, over 70 percent of students who attend all classes and complete all exercises show an improvement in happiness levels. By contrast, among those who aren't as diligent, only 25 percent show an improvement.

The First Happiness Measurement

Even if your interest in this book is purely academic—that is, you aren't necessarily interested in improving your happiness—I imagine that you would be curious about the effect that exposure to the concepts in the book is having on your happiness. To help you in this endeavor, I have included something called the "Satisfaction with Life Scale" which you can fill out at three points in the book. (You can also fill out this scale on the book's website, at www.happysmarts.com/book/scales/satisfaction _with_life/first_measurement.) The first point is now; you'll find the scale on page 14. The second point is at the end of chapter 3B—close to the middle of the book. The final point is at the end of the book, after the last chapter. As you will see, the type of happiness this scale measures isn't ephemeral mood; rather, it's a reflective assessment of how well your life is going, all (or at least most) things considered. As it turns out, the type of happiness measured by this scale correlates significantly, and in the expected direction, with (a) neurological correlates (like serotonin and cortisol levels), (b) others' assessments of one's happiness levels, and (c) other behavioral measures, including stability of marital relationships.* Thus, the satisfaction with life scale seems quite reliable and, as a testament to this, the paper in which this scale originally appeared has been cited more than ten thousand times!

I hope you'll find that your happiness levels improve because of this book. And not just that; I hope you'll discover something else that I find to be one of the most gratifying aspects of seeking a life of happiness and fulfillment: *the things that lead to happiness and fulfillment are the things that make us not just better—more kind and compassionate—but also more successful.* That is, the recipe for happiness is also a "win-win-win" recipe, a topic that I will revisit in the concluding chapter.

With that uplifting thought, allow me to wish that you have as enjoyable a time reading this book as I had writing it.

Happy reading!

Raj Raghunathan
January 15, 2016
Austin, Texas

---

* For excerpts from an interview with Professor Ed Diener on the validity of the satisfaction with life scale, see the following video from my Coursera course: https://www.coursera.org/learn/happiness/lecture/zzsHz/week-1-video-2-happiness-is-a-balloon.

SATISFACTION WITH LIFE SCALE

Note: This scale was developed by Professor Ed Diener—aka "Dr. Happiness"—and his colleagues. Since the article in which the scale appeared was first published (in 1985), it has been cited more than ten thousand times, attesting to the scale's reliability. One reason the scale is so reliable is because it doesn't just measure momentary swings in mood, but rather measures overall satisfaction with life. Note that you may find you are dissatisfied with some of the items in the scale (particularly the last item), and you may even feel that you aren't 100 percent sure about how to interpret some items. If this happens, set your dissatisfaction aside and try to interpret the items in the way that makes the most sense to you, keeping in mind that the scale is trying to measure how satisfied—or happy and fulfilled—you are with your life overall.

For each of the five items below, circle a number from 1 through 7, where 1 = "strongly disagree" and 7 = "strongly agree." (You can also fill out the scale online by going to www.happysmarts.com/book/scales/satisfactionwithlife/first_measurement.) Once you have responded to all five items, total up your rating for each item to come up with your overall satisfaction with life score. On the next page, you'll find an explanation of what your score means.

	STRONGLY DISAGREE				STRONGLY AGREE	
In most ways, my life is close to my ideal	1	2	3	4	5	6	7
I am satisfied with my life	1	2	3	4	5	6	7
The conditions of my life are excellent	1	2	3	4	5	6	7
So far, I have the important things I want in life	1	2	3	4	5	6	7
If I could live my life over, I would change almost nothing	1	2	3	4	5	6	7

INTERPRETING YOUR SATISFACTION WITH LIFE SCORE

IF YOUR SCORE IS . . .	YOU ARE . . .	WHICH MEANS . . .
32–35	Extremely happy	This book may not improve your happiness levels any further, but it can help you understand why you are as happy as you are.
28–31	Very happy	This book can help you sustain your already high happiness levels.
23–27	Happy	This book can definitely help you increase your happiness levels even further.
18–22	Not-so-happy	There is definitely scope for improvement in your happiness levels and this book can definitely help.
13–17	Unhappy	Your happiness levels can do with a big improvement and this book can definitely help.
12 and below	Potentially depressed	This book can help, but you may also wish to get some professional help (e.g., by seeing a therapist).

Chapter 1A

THE FIRST DEADLY HAPPINESS "SIN": DEVALUING HAPPINESS

├───┤

n a typical month, I attend anywhere between two and four parties—all for the purely academic reason of keeping up with the latest marketing trends, of course. And when I am at a party, the question I am most frequently asked is: "What do you consider to be your most interesting research finding?"

When someone asks me this question, I tell them that the best way for me to answer it is by posing a question of my own. I then pose "The Genie Question" to them. It goes like this:

> *Imagine that a Genie appears in front of you and grants you three wishes. Before making your wishes, assume that the Genie is all-knowing and all-powerful. So don't limit yourself in any way; imagine that the Genie has the power to grant you any wish you make.*
>
> *What three wishes would you make?*

(Note to my dear reader: I urge you to take a minute or two to jot down your wishes. Doing so, I promise, will help you relate much better to this chapter's content.)

Wish # 1: _____

Wish # 2: _____

Wish # 3: _____

Most people have little trouble in answering the Genie Question, and their wish list usually reads something like this:

Wish #1: A great deal of money—enough to cover any and all expenses
Wish #2: Stupendous success and its accoutrements: fame, power, and respect
Wish #3: Great/fulfilling relationships, especially with family and friends

A few people, usually the ones who consider themselves smarter than average, make only one wish: that the Genie grants them all their future wishes. I tell these overambitious types that, although their wish makes sense, it isn't suitable for our purposes. I tell them that the Genie Question isn't merely an intellectual exercise; rather, it's an exercise designed to reveal some important insights into how people sabotage their own happiness. So I ask them to pat themselves on the back for being smart, but to go back and answer the Genie Question again.

Surprise, Surprise!

Over the years, several hundred people have answered the Genie Question. Sometimes their responses are amusing. One woman wished to marry a cross between Michael Jackson and Paul McCartney. Another wished that he could travel back in time to 1969 so that he could lie in wait for Neil Armstrong and Buzz Aldrin to land on the moon and shout "Boo." But mostly, people's responses are more surprising than amusing. What's surprising is that happiness is missing from their wish list. Most psychologists, and even many economists, think that happiness is our main goal in life. Even the Declaration of Independence affirms happiness as one of our most cherished goals. And yet, hardly anyone asks the Genie for happiness. Why?

One reason, you may think, is that people ask for those things that *lead* to happiness: strong relationships, money, status, and so on. But why not ask for happiness directly? After all, if you wished to travel from New York to New Delhi, why get a ticket to a place (e.g., London) that happens to fall on the way? Why not head to New Delhi directly? And so it is with the

Genie too. Why ask the Genie for the *means* to happiness when you could ask for happiness itself?

One may wonder if people don't ask the Genie for happiness because, despite what psychologists and economists claim, happiness isn't such a high priority for them. Along with my two trusty colleagues Sunaina Chugani from the City University of New York and Ashesh Mukherjee from McGill University, I investigated this possibility. We administered a survey to respondents from various walks of life—from students and housewives to white- and blue-collar workers and retirees. The survey presented respondents with sixteen important "life goals" and asked them to rank these goals in descending order of importance. Among the goals were "being rich," "career success," "physical health," "great/fulfilling relationships," "being happy," etc.

As the table below reveals, "being happy" emerged as people's most important goal—on par, statistically speaking, with "great/fulfilling relationships." In other words, psychologists and economists are not only in agreement with each other (for once!), they are also right: happiness *is* a very important goal for most people.

But while this is reassuring to know, we are still left with the question: *Why don't people ask the Genie for happiness?*

S. NO.	GOAL	AVERAGE RANK
1	Great/fulfilling relationships	3.19
2	Being happy	3.31
3	Great career success	4.78
4	Being rich	5.46
5	Being a good person; helping others	6.23
6	Being free to do as you please	7.44
7	Job satisfaction	8.12
8	Physical health	8.86
9	Being famous	9.45

S. NO.	GOAL	AVERAGE RANK
10	Respect/admiration of peers	9.56
11	Spiritual growth	10.19
12	Being really good at something/achieving mastery	11.23
13	Figuring out the meaning of life	11.34
14	Finding your purpose in life	11.79
15	Physical attractiveness	12.22
16	Being powerful	12.67

Sixteen "Life Goals" and Their Average Rank Across Respondents

As it turns out, there's an intriguing reason why people don't ask the Genie for happiness. But before I get to that reason, allow me to tell you a story.

The Fundamental Happiness Paradox

It was a warm and sultry afternoon in mid-September when my cousin and I strolled into a salad bar in Austin. It was a typical salad bar with many vegetarian options (onions, tomatoes, lettuce, olives, chickpeas) and some nonvegetarian ones (bacon crumbles, ham pieces, grilled chicken). You could take what you wanted, and pay for it by the pound.

My cousin, like many people, was price sensitive. He recognized that, pound for pound, the nonvegetarian items were more expensive than the vegetarian ones. This would tempt him to load his plate with the nonvegetarian items. But doing so would come at a cost to his enjoyment of the salad. He didn't eat bacon and didn't care for grilled chicken; he liked his chicken fried, not grilled. And I knew that he loved chickpeas.

So what would he do? Would he maximize value for money and go for more grilled chicken, or would he maximize enjoyment and go for more chickpeas? The suspense was killing me, but thankfully, I didn't have to wait for long. He loaded his plate with more grilled chicken than chickpeas. Value for money had trumped enjoyment.

As my cousin sat at the table, I turned to him and said without a hint of sarcasm—well, maybe just a *tiny* hint of it—"I hope you enjoy your salad."

My cousin had exhibited what I call the *fundamental happiness paradox*.

The paradox refers to the idea that, although happiness is one of our most important goals, people often forget this and get distracted by other goals—goals like "value for money."

Consider results from a study inspired by my cousin's experience. Participants in the study were asked to read the following scenario first.

Scenario 1: Salad Bar

Imagine that you are at the salad bar at a restaurant that charges you by the pound. You fill your plate with whatever you want, and you pay $5.99 per pound. There are many things you can add to your salad, and you know that certain things (e.g., mushrooms) are more expensive than certain other things (e.g., chickpeas). Imagine that you enjoy the less expensive items more than you enjoy the more expensive ones. For example, you find chickpeas to be tastier than mushrooms.

Once participants had read this scenario, we asked them to respond to the following question:

Which of the following two options would make you happier?

Option A: Adding more mushrooms to your salad so that you get your money's worth

Option B: Adding more chickpeas to the salad so that you derive greater enjoyment from it

---

The purpose behind this study was to figure out which benefit—enjoyment of the salad or value for money—people consider to be more important for happiness. If people believe that value for money is more important than enjoyment for happiness, then they should pick Option A. If, however, they believe that enjoyment for happiness is more important than value for money, they should pick Option B. Results confirmed what we intuitively knew. Enjoyment of salad turned out to be more important for happiness: an overwhelming majority (98 percent) picked Option B.

Having confirmed that Option B is the happiness-maximizing one, we turned next to testing whether people would in fact pick this option if given a choice between the two. So we exposed another set of participants to the same scenario, but instead of asking them to choose the option that would make them happier, we asked them to select one of the two options for personal consumption. If maximizing happiness is more important than is maximizing value for money, one would expect 98 percent of these participants to choose Option B. But in fact, only 76 percent chose Option B. So 22 percent of respondents in this study (or about one in five) appeared to be willing to sacrifice happiness for the sake of value for money.

Now, you could argue that those who chose Option A were also maximizing happiness in their own way. Perhaps value for money was a more important determinant of happiness than enjoyment of the salad was for them. But this argument doesn't hold water because, as we saw from our first study, an overwhelming majority (98 percent) thought Option B was the happiness-maximizing option. So to the extent that the second group was similar to the first—and there's no reason to suspect otherwise—a similar proportion should have preferred Option B. The fact that 22 percent of the respondents in the second group didn't choose this option indicates that they weren't maximizing happiness, but rather, were maximizing something else: value for money.

Consider another example that suggests a similar propensity to sacrifice happiness for something else.

Scenario 2: Happy or Right?

Imagine that you are in a very satisfying romantic relationship with a wonderful boyfriend. However, there is one area in which you want him to improve: lose weight. You give him good advice on how to lose weight, but he never follows your advice. This continues for several months. Then one day, he comes home very excited and tells you that he has met someone who has motivated him to adopt a new lifestyle—a lifestyle that will enable him to lose weight. As he tells you about this new lifestyle, you recognize that it is actually very similar to the one that you had been recommending to him all along! Your partner appears to have been persuaded by another person to make the very changes that you have been asking him to make.

What would you do?

Option A: Point out (angrily!) to him that the other person has not told him anything new.

Option B: Congratulate him for having figured out how to achieve his goal.

In this scenario, a majority of participants (85 percent) reported that Option B was better suited for enhancing happiness than Option A. These people recognized that in relationships, you can often either be right or happy—not both. And yet, when we asked a different set of participants to choose one of the two options for themselves, only 72 percent selected Option A. So 13 percent (or about one in eight) seemed willing to sacrifice happiness for the sake of "being right."

Another quick study showed that one in six would sacrifice happiness for the sake of fame and beauty. These findings suggest that the fundamental happiness paradox is quite prevalent.

The Job Selection Scenario

One limitation of the scenarios I have discussed thus far is that they all involve making simple, hypothetical choices. So you could ask whether the fundamental happiness paradox occurs in more real-world and important contexts.

Would, for example, people sacrifice happiness in contexts involving job choice?

To find out, my coauthors and I gave students at the McCombs School of Business the following scenario.*

Scenario 3: Intrinsically Motivating vs. Extrinsically Motivating Job

Imagine that you have two job offers:

Job A is high paying, and accepting this job will make you rich. This job will also set you on the path to a successful professional career. However, you have been told by former students who have taken up this job that the work is very uninteresting, stressful, and involves long hours. Further, the people who work at this job are known to be difficult to get along with.

Job B, on the other hand, does not pay as well as Job A; in fact, it pays only about half as much. While this salary is sufficient for a decent life, it won't make

---

* You can watch my collaborator on this project, Professor Chugani, describe this and other studies at: https://www.coursera.org/learn/happiness/lecture/Rr8sv/week-1-video-7-devaluing -happiness-in-job-choice.

you rich. However, the work will be much more to your liking than the work in Job A, and the people who work at this job are easy to get along with and genuinely nice.

Which job would you pick?

As usual, we asked one group of students to pick the option better suited for enhancing happiness. A majority (78 percent) picked Job B, the intrinsically motivating job with lower pay. So if happiness is students' most important goal, a similar proportion should choose Job B. And indeed, contrary to what we had seen in previous studies, that's what we found: 74 percent of the students—a proportion very close to 78 percent—chose this option!

Why were the results from this study different? Could it be that people make happiness-enhancing decisions in contexts that are more important?

At first glance, that's what the results would appear to suggest. But something about the results did not sit well with me—or, indeed, with my collaborators. The more we thought about the results, the more we started having doubts about it. If you know Business-school students as well as I do, you can guess what was bothering us. The typical B-school student is more interested in making money than in pursuing intrinsic interests. Having graduated from a B-school myself, I knew that this reputation—of being money-minded—is, well, well earned. And yet, a majority of the students in our study had chosen the intrinsically motivating job. How come? Were these students somehow different? Or could it be that they were *unwilling* to admit their true preferences so as to present themselves as non-money-minded souls?

My collaborators and I hatched a plan to find out.

When psychologists want to ferret out from people something to which they won't freely admit, they use a trick called the *projective technique*. The technique involves asking people their opinions of what *other* people think about the sticky issue, rather than asking them what they themselves think. The technique works because people care much more about their own reputation than they do about that of others. In the job selection scenario, for example, students may not be willing to admit to their own money-mindedness, but most will have little hesitation in "admitting" to the money-mindedness of their peers. The projective technique is as effective as it is simple, and as a result, has had a long history of use in research.

Here's a simple example of how you could use the projective technique in your own life. Say you want to know how many people pee in swimming pools. (Why wouldn't you?) You would get a much better estimate if you asked people to answer the question "How many *other* people do you think pee in pools?" than if you asked them "How often do *you* pee in pools?" If they answer "most people," you can rest assured (in a manner of speaking) that peeing in pools is very common.

A Pilot Test of the Job Selection Scenario

The next time I was in the MBA classroom, I gave students the descriptions of the same two jobs (Job A and Job B) and asked them to assume that they had both offers. I then asked, "How many would choose Job A—the unmotivating job with the high pay?"

A few hands—about five out of forty—went up.

I then asked, "How many of you would choose Job B—the low-paying, but intrinsically motivating job?" Many more hands, around twenty this time, went up. This pattern was similar to the one we had obtained earlier: a larger proportion seemed to prefer the low-paying, intrinsically motivating job over the high-paying-and-less-motivating job.

I feigned surprise and said, "Interesting! One would think that MBAs are more money-minded than you guys appear to be. How come?"

"We're different," one of the students said after a pause. "We are less interested in making money and more interested in following our passion."

"What about MBAs from other schools?" I asked. "How many of them would have chosen the high-paying job?"

"Definitely a lot more than in our school," said another student, looking around at her classmates for support, which they readily provided.

"How about the undergraduates from our own school?" I asked next. "Are they more like you or are they more like MBAs from other schools?"

"Definitely more like MBAs from other schools," said yet another student, with a grunt of disdain. "As an undergrad, all you care about is making money. It's only after you have worked a few years that you realize money isn't everything."

Hmmm . . . I said to myself, *I would love to find out what the undergrads think.*

I soon got the opportunity. I did the same exercise with them, and you can guess what I found. The undergrads believed that they were far less money-minded and far more interested in following their passion than were the MBAs.

So our hunch appeared to be right. The students did seem to have a desire to hide their true preferences in job selection contexts.

How could we get around this desire for self-presentation to show more *direct* evidence that our students—and by extension, other people—exhibit the fundamental happiness paradox even in relatively important contexts such as job choice?

This is the task to which we turned next.

Evidence for the Fundamental Happiness Paradox in a Job Selection Scenario

I knew, having gotten an MBA myself, that students' money-mindedness is most likely to be on display during the job interview season. So in our next study, my colleagues and I simulated the conditions of a job interview. Here's what happened. Students took part in a "test" that involved answering twelve questions on various topics. The idea was to get the students to experience some "competitive stress"—the type of stress they typically experience during the job interview season. We did this to see whether getting students to marinate in stress would help us get around their desire to self-present. We expected that putting them under stress would have this effect, but we also felt that the *type* of stress would matter. Specifically, we felt that the more the stress resembled the type of stress they experienced during the job interview season, the more likely they would be to choose the extrinsically motivating (higher-paying) job. To test for this, we told one set of participants that their performance in the test would reveal how well they would do in job interviews. The remaining students were told that their performance in the test would reflect their "personality type." Then both sets of students were exposed to the same two job descriptions (Job A and Job B) and asked to choose one. In both groups, we expected a proportion higher than 26 percent—which, as you may recall, was the proportion that chose the extrinsically motivating job when there was no stress—to choose the higher-paying job. We also expected that the proportion would be higher among those in the "job stress" group than among those in the "personality stress" group. Our expectations were confirmed: 55 percent of students in the "job stress" group, and 44 percent of those in the "personality stress" group, chose the extrinsically motivating job.

What these results show is that the more a situation induces stress, and the more this stress resembles the type of stress associated with interviewing for jobs, the more one is likely to sacrifice happiness and choose the extrinsically motivating job.

This study provides more direct evidence for the fundamental happiness paradox, but we weren't done yet. We wanted to document evidence for it in an actual, real-world, job-selection context.

Our final study was run in two stages. In stage one, which took place about two months before the actual job interview season, MBAs were given a list of nine industries (e.g., packaged goods, investment banking, retailing) and asked to pick three in which they would be interested in applying for a job. Then the students were given two job descriptions in each of the three industries they picked. (The two descriptions in retailing, for example, were for jobs with Whole Foods and Walmart.) The job descriptions contained enough information to allow the students to figure out both the intrinsic worth (e.g., alignment with values) and the extrinsic worth (e.g., pay) of each job. Then the students were asked to indicate their relative preference between the two jobs in each of the three industries they picked. Subsequently, students were asked to rank-order all of the six jobs that they had seen.

This is what we found. In this—the first—stage of the study (which took place well before the interview season), intrinsic motivation proved to have a bigger impact on job preference than extrinsic motivation. The intrinsically motivating jobs (such as the one with Whole Foods) got a higher rating and ranking than the extrinsically motivating ones. Results also showed that the majority of students (73 percent) considered the intrinsically motivating job with lower pay (Job B) to be better suited for enhancing happiness than the less-motivating job with the higher pay (Job A). In other words, before the interview season had begun, students seemed to be indicating a preference for the happiness-maximizing alternative.

In the second stage of the study, which took place closer to the job interview season, we had the students repeat what they had done in stage one. That is, they first picked three of the nine industries to apply to, and then rated the two jobs in each industry in terms of intrinsic and extrinsic rewards. They then indicated their relative preference between the two jobs in each of the three industries, and then ranked the six jobs in order of preference. Our prediction was that the students' preferences would have shifted between stage one and stage two toward extrinsic rewards and away from intrinsic ones.

And that's exactly what we found. Whereas the average ranking of the three extrinsically motivating jobs was 3.58 in stage one, it was 3.25 in stage two. (Note that lower ranking means more preferred.) Likewise, while the average ranking for the three intrinsically motivating jobs was 3.41 in stage one, it was 3.79 in stage two.

Why Do People Exhibit the Fundamental Happiness Paradox?

What do these findings imply?

The most straightforward implication is that, although happiness is a very important goal for most people—as we saw from the happiness surveys—they also seem to *devalue* it as they go about their lives. That is, people seem to routinely sacrifice happiness for the sake of other goals.

One may argue that this is not the only interpretation of the results. Specifically, one could say that the participants in our studies were maximizing happiness in their own way. For example, the MBA students in the job-choice study may have been trying to maximize "future happiness" over "present happiness." Jobs with higher salaries, after all, provide greater potential for paying off loans and for saving for a rainy day. But note that, if this explanation were true, those with higher outstanding loans should have shown greater preference for the higher-paying jobs. But that's not what we found. We found, instead, that outstanding loan amounts had little effect on preference for jobs; students with low outstanding loans were just as likely to prefer the higher-paying jobs as those with high outstanding loans. Yet another result rules out the explanation that students in the job-choice study were trying to maximize future happiness. Recall that the students' preferences changed over time. Specifically, preference for the extrinsically motivating jobs became more pronounced in stage two (versus stage one). This should not have happened if the students were trying to maximize future happiness across both stages. So the best explanation for our results is that the students were sacrificing happiness for the sake of another goal—the goal, perhaps, of impressing others—in this study. The fact that a similar pattern of results was obtained across a variety of other scenarios—such as the "salad bar" and "relationships" scenarios—suggests that the fundamental happiness paradox is quite prevalent.

How Significant Is the Fundamental Happiness Paradox?

When I present these results to people, many of them agree that the fundamental happiness paradox seems quite prevalent. But they also feel that it is not such a big deal. After all, only a small proportion—somewhere in the range of 15 to 20 percent—seem to exhibit it in any given context.

To those who arrive at such a conclusion, I sound a cautionary note. I tell them that the fundamental happiness paradox is likely much more prevalent in the real world than our studies seem to indicate. Why? Because few people would be willing to freely admit to being petty, superficial, or money-minded. So our studies likely *underestimate* the prevalence of the fundamental happiness paradox. Findings from some follow-up studies in which we used the projective technique support this conjecture; in these studies, the proportion who exhibit the fundamental happiness paradox was roughly *double* that which I reported earlier in this chapter. Another reason why the paradox is more significant than it would seem at first blush is that we make hundreds, if not thousands, of decisions each day. So even if we exhibit the fundamental happiness paradox in only a fraction of the decisions we make, we would still be leaving a lot of happiness on the table.

If the fundamental happiness paradox is as prevalent as it seems, then an important question arises: *Why* do people devalue happiness—a goal that, by their own admission, is all-important?

That's the question to which I'll turn in the next chapter.

Chapter 1B

THE FIRST HABIT OF THE HIGHLY HAPPY: PRIORITIZING–BUT NOT PURSUING–HAPPINESS

Here's a popular story that you've likely heard before. A rich American banker was once vacationing in a small Mexican fishing village. One day, he found himself sitting on the dock next to a fisherman from the village and they got talking. The banker soon figured out that the fisherman was quite sharp—sharp enough, in fact, to be a successful banker on Wall Street.

"You know," said the American at one point, "you are really smart. I bet you could easily be a very successful investment banker on Wall Street."

"But why would I want to be an investment banker?" asked the fisherman.

"So that you could earn some big bucks," said the banker, flashing his Rolex watch for emphasis.

"And then?" asked the fisherman innocently. "What would I do with all the money?"

"Why," said the American excitedly, "you could retire early! And who knows, if everything works out well, you could even dream of settling down in a small Mexican village like this one here and do nothing but fish all day!"

"But . . ." began the fisherman, but he didn't have to complete the sentence. The American realized that the fisherman was already living his dream.

There are a couple of reasons why I like this story, but before I get to them, I should quickly mention the one reason I *don't* like it: it seems to suggest that short-term happiness is always more important than long-term happiness. Clearly, it's not so simple. On some occasions, long-term happiness may be more important than short-term happiness. I'll get to when it is worth sacrificing short-term happiness for long-term happiness in Chapter 2B. For now, let me get back to the story of the Mexican fisherman. One reason I like the story is because it is a neat example of the fundamental happiness paradox in action. Despite having clarity on what will make him happy—a relaxed life involving a lot of fishing—the rich American couldn't help but be distracted by other goals. Another reason I like the story is because it exemplifies how easy it is to fall prey to the fundamental happiness paradox. If you are like most people, you can easily relate to the rich American, which means that you realize how easy it is to forget all about happiness and sacrifice it for other goals as we go about our lives.

I have been studying the fundamental happiness paradox for several years now, and yet I find myself prone to it on occasion. Just the other day, I was shopping for a pair of glasses and found out that there was a promotion going on: buy one pair and get another of equal or lesser value for half off. I soon found a great-looking pair for $120 and decided to buy it. Then, to take advantage of the promotion, I started looking for another pair and found a nice one. This pair was better-looking than all the other options. I was about to select it when I noticed that it was worth only $70. Because the original pair was $120, I felt that I was losing $50 by choosing the $70 pair. But at the same time, I knew that none of the other pairs of glasses was as good-looking as the $70 one. What was I to do? Select the good-looking pair that was worth only $70 or select a worse-looking pair that would give me more value for money?

It was only after I'd spent a good ten minutes mulling over this question that I realized how close I had come to falling prey to the fundamental happiness paradox! Once that realization sank in, I quickly selected the $70 pair and walked out feeling happy. But the experience taught me that overcoming the tendency to devalue happiness would be a long and tricky process, one that would involve getting to the bottom of why we devalue happiness.

Why We Devalue Happiness

So why *do* we devalue happiness—a goal that, by our own admission, is an all-important one?

The Genie Question, it turns out, is useful for answering this question. I typically follow up the Genie Question with another question. I ask those who do not wish for happiness to explain the absence of happiness from their wish list. The explanations that people come up with reveal three main reasons why we devalue happiness.*

First, many people think happiness is too "abstract," particularly when compared with money, fame, and status. As one of my students put it, "I wouldn't ask the Genie for happiness because I don't know what I would get in return if I did; in contrast, I know *exactly* what I would get if I asked for money, fame, status, or physical attractiveness." In other words, a big reason why we devalue happiness is because we don't have a clear and concrete idea of what happiness is. This makes perfect sense if you consider findings from research on what's called the *fluency effect*. These findings show that we tend to devalue things when they are abstract, ambiguous, or otherwise difficult to understand.

Another reason we devalue happiness is because of some negative beliefs that we harbor about it. These negative beliefs make happiness less attractive than it would otherwise be. A common negative belief is that happiness will make us lazy. As one of my students put it, "I wouldn't ask the Genie for happiness because, if I am happy, why would I work? I would turn lazy!" I suspect that a major reason why many of us feel that we'd become lazy if we are happy is because, at the frenzied pace at which we lead our lives, the only moments in which we feel relaxed and happy are when we have time on our hands—like when we are on vacation. So we come to associate happiness with "chilling out." But as it turns out, the notion that we'd turn lazy if we are happy isn't true. Here's a sampling of findings on the impact that happiness has on productivity and success:†

---

* For the comprehensive set of reasons people come up with (for not asking the Genie for happiness), see the book's website: www.happysmarts.com/book/The_Genie_Question/Reasons.

† I had the pleasure of interviewing Professor Ed Diener—"Dr. Happiness"—himself about the functionality of happiness for my Coursera course. You can watch excerpts from this interview at: https://www.coursera.org/learn/happiness/lecture/mSNAw/week-1-video-8-

- Happy employees are likely to perform objectively better on tasks (including tasks that involve leadership and creativity).
- Happy employees earn more.
- Happier (optimistic) CEOs foster a more positive work climate, which in turn improves organizational productivity.
- Happier CEOs receive higher performance ratings from chairpersons of their boards and head companies with greater returns on investment.

and my favorite:

- Happier batsmen in cricket have higher batting averages.

Another negative belief that many of us harbor about happiness is that it will make us selfish. This, again, turns out to be a misconception. Findings show that we are likely to be kind and caring when we are happy. Here, again, is just a small sample of findings on the topic:

- Happy people volunteer more.
- Happy people are also more likely to judge others favorably, and are more willing to share their good fortune with others more equitably.
- People in happy moods (versus those in sad or neutral moods) contribute more money to charity; people in happy moods are also more likely to donate blood;

and my favorite:

- Happy people are more likely to volunteer for an extra experiment.

Yet another negative belief about happiness is that it is fleeting. As one respondent to the Genie Question put it, "Why should I ask for something that I know won't last for long?" The respondent has a point. As we know from personal experience, positive feelings tend not to last long; even a

---

three-negative-misconceptions-about-happiness. The same video also features an excerpt from an interview with Professor Barbara Fredrickson on why we are likely to be more productive when we feel happy.

small negative intrusion—like bad weather or an unpleasant interaction—can spoil our mood. That doesn't mean, however, that some types of positive states can't last longer than others. As we will see later in this chapter, there is reason to believe that certain types of positive states have the potential to last much longer than other types.

In addition to believing that happiness is too "abstract" and to harboring negative beliefs about happiness, there's a third reason why we devalue it: it simply doesn't occur to us that what we ultimately want out of life—why we do anything and everything we do—is to lead a happier, more fulfilling life.

I got my first hint of this when administering the Genie Question to my students one time. After I posed the question to them, but before they could answer it, I accidentally reminded them that they could ask for "anything and everything—including happiness."

Guess what I found? That's right! The proportion who asked for happiness shot up—from a mere 6 percent (which is what I normally find) to about 18 percent: a threefold increase!

This result—which, incidentally, is my most interesting research finding to date—suggests that an important reason why people don't have happiness on their Genie wish list is because *it simply doesn't occur to them to ask for happiness.* This result also explains why happiness is rated as a very important goal in happiness surveys. In these surveys, happiness is explicitly listed as one of the goals; so people have little trouble rating or ranking it as a top goal.

The fact that people forget all about happiness when responding to the Genie Question *unless* they are reminded of it is quite consistent with findings on something called "medium maximization." Medium maximization refers to the propensity to forget all about the end goal that one wants to achieve, and to pursue, instead, the *means* (or mediums) to that end goal. In a clever experiment that documented medium maximization, one group of participants was told that they could choose to engage in either a short (twenty-minute) or a long (twenty-five-minute) task in return for a reward. If they chose the short task, participants were told that they would receive one pound of Snickers bars in return. If they chose the long task instead, they were told that they would receive the option of choosing between one pound of Snickers bars and one pound of Almond Joy bars. Another group of participants in the experiment was given the same two (long versus short) tasks to choose from, but with a twist: a "medium" was introduced. Participants were told that engaging in the short task would give them 60 points, which they could use to procure one pound of Snickers bars, whereas engaging in the long task would give them 100 points, which they could use to procure either one pound of Snickers or one pound of Almond Joy.

As it turned out, a majority of participants in both groups favored the Snickers bar to the Almond Joy bar. So participants in both groups would have been better off choosing the short (versus long) task. However, the introduction of the medium changed their preference. When there was no medium, participants chose the short task, but when the medium was introduced, participants favored the long task. Why? Because the medium distracted them from what they ultimately wanted (which is enjoyment of the candy) and made them focus, instead, on maximizing the medium (points).

Think about what these findings imply for money—the most common medium. They suggest that people can get so caught up in chasing money that they forget all about why they wanted the money in the first place.

Findings from studies on the fundamental happiness paradox are, of course, entirely consistent with medium maximization. What they also show is that money is not the only medium that distracts us from happiness; other goals—like the desire to be right, and to have beauty, fame, or prestige—can too.

If the fundamental happiness paradox is as prevalent as it appears to be, and if the tendency to devalue happiness is rooted in a variety of sources—from being unclear about what happiness means and harboring negative misconceptions about happiness to medium maximization—a question that naturally follows is: how can we mitigate the first deadly happiness sin?

Prioritizing—but Not Pursuing—Happiness

That's the question my colleagues—Kelly Goldsmith from Northwestern University, David Gal from the University of Illinois at Chicago, and Lauren Cheatham from Stanford University—and I mulled over at length one summer. One strategy that appeared to hold some promise was the simplest of them all: reminding oneself, as I did in the glasses store, to prioritize happiness over other goals. Recall "my most interesting finding" to date—the finding that the likelihood of happiness being on people's Genie wish list shoots up when they are reminded about happiness. This finding suggested to us that simply reminding people to make happiness-enhancing decisions could lower their tendency to be distracted by other goals and hence help them overcome the sin of devaluing happiness.

But could such a simple strategy actually work in real life?

To find out, Kelly, David, Lauren, and I conducted a study in which we asked more than three hundred employees from seven different Fortune 500 companies to keep track of their happiness levels on a daily basis for a period of a week. We divided the employees into two groups. One group received an e-mail every day for a whole week. The e-mail gently reminded them to make happiness-enhancing decisions. The second group did not receive any such e-mail. Then we asked both groups to tell us how happy they were at the end of the week. We found that those who received the daily e-mail reminders were far happier by the end of the week than those who didn't. Our findings also showed that the reason they were happier was because they made happiness-enhancing choices such as going to a kids' baseball game, rather than sitting at home and watching TV, when they received the e-mail reminders. We replicated these results in two other controlled laboratory experiments.

So it seems that the simple strategy of reminding people to make happiness-enhancing decisions can indeed help them overcome the first deadly sin. But although the strategy is simple, it comes with an important caveat: reminding oneself to make happiness-enhancing choices can improve happiness levels, but it's important not to *pursue* or chase happiness. Why? Because when one pursues happiness, one is likely to compare how one feels with how one would *ideally* like to feel, and since we generally want to feel happier than we currently do, we are likely to feel unhappy about being unhappy if we pursue happiness! So while it is a good idea to prioritize happiness, it is not a good idea to pursue it, as several studies have found.

So the question is: how does one pull off this delicate balancing act—of prioritizing, and yet not pursuing, happiness?

One way is to consider how we pursue some other important goals in life that, like happiness, cannot be pursued too directly. Consider sleep. Constantly watching out for the moment when you fall asleep and telling yourself, "There! I almost fell asleep right there!" is, as several insomniacs have discovered, a better recipe for staying awake than it is for dozing off. A better way to get a good night's sleep is to take some steps—like eating a light dinner, working out, and perhaps most important, not getting into a heated argument with one's spouse about which TV channel to watch— that increase the odds of falling asleep, but then, having taken these steps, not monitor whether one is about to fall asleep. That's the way to prioritize, but not pursue, sleep. And in much the same fashion, the way to prioritize, but not pursue, happiness is to take some steps that increase the odds of being happy.

That brings us to the two steps for increasing the odds of experiencing happiness on a more regular basis: **(1) Defining happiness** and **(2) Incorporating happiness**.

Defining happiness means figuring out what happiness means to you. This step is obviously important if you are to prioritize happiness because, without knowing what happiness means to you, it's difficult to give it greater priority. The problem, however, is that happiness can be very difficult to define. One reason for this is that, as Daniel Kahneman—the Nobel laureate and professor of psychology and public affairs emeritus at Princeton University—has noted, there are two types of happiness that most of us care about, and it turns out that these two types of happiness do not always go together. One type of happiness has to do with immediate, visceral feelings—for example, how pleasant or unpleasant you feel at this moment. The other type of happiness has to do with a more holistic assessment of how satisfied you are with your life. The former type of happiness has to do with your immediate life circumstances (e.g., whether you are feeling sick today or have just had a sumptuous meal), while the latter has more to do with the "bigger picture" (e.g., your bank balance or the quality of your relationships). So one could feel "happy" or "satisfied" with one's life overall (because things look good in the "big picture") and yet be unhappy at the level of immediate emotions—or vice versa. Another reason why happiness is so difficult to define is because people differ in what makes them happy. For example, the thing that terrifies one person (sailing) may be the very thing that floats someone else's boat.

But even though happiness may be difficult to define, it turns out that all of us have an implicit understanding of what it means—which is why almost no one is confused when asked, "How happy are you?" If people didn't have an implicit understanding of what happiness means to them, they wouldn't be able to answer this question. This suggests that people intuitively associate "happiness" with some type of positive emotion. This in turn means that, if we want to figure out what people mean by "happiness," all we would need to do is get at the emotion with which they implicitly associate the term. As it turns out, there's a relatively easy way to do this. It is to simply ask people to "recall a recent event that made you happy." People's responses to this question can then be used to figure out the emotions with which they associate the term "happiness."

My colleagues and I have successfully used this approach to get at people's definition of happiness. In one survey, we asked 188 respondents to recollect and write about a recent event that made them "happy." Then, with the help of two research assistants, we analyzed the content of their responses. Our findings revealed that people predominantly associate the word "happiness" with four types of emotions: love/connection, joy, authentic pride, and hubristic pride.

Here's how these emotions may be defined:

- **Love/connection** is the feeling associated with being in an intimate relationship. Although love/connection is usually felt in connection with another person or a pet, it can also be felt with an activity (e.g., playing tennis), an event (e.g., a concert), or an object (e.g., a pen).
- **Joy** stems from the feeling that life is going well—one feels safe and secure—and that it is okay to let one's guard down and be playful or even silly.
- **Authentic pride** is the feeling associated with having achieved something important and worthwhile, such as making a great presentation or helping others achieve a goal.
- **Hubristic pride** is the feeling that arises from recognizing that "I am special, superior"; hubristic pride involves either an implicit or an explicit comparison with another person, and is accompanied by the perception of one's own superiority over the other.

These are, of course, not the only emotions with which people associate "happiness." Barbara Fredrickson from the University of North Carolina at

Chapel Hill and her colleagues have found that there are at least seven other "positive emotions" that people experience regularly, and each of these emotions could easily be associated with the word "happiness." These emotions include serenity, awe, inspiration, interest, and hope.

Harmony and Abundance as Definitions of Happiness

In addition to these emotions, there are two others that, in my opinion, merit attention. Let's call these emotions **harmony** and **abundance**.

- **Harmony** is the feeling that arises from not wanting to be somewhere else, doing something else.

In this definition of happiness, one is happy so long as one isn't feeling or thinking something that one doesn't want to feel or think. So for example, one could feel angry *and* yet be happy (or at least not be unhappy) at the same time—providing the anger doesn't feel unwanted or unwarranted. In the unlikely event that you have ever been treated unfairly by a customer service agent (I am being sarcastic here, of course), that's how you might have felt. Likewise, one could feel nervous (e.g., while riding a roller coaster) or sad (e.g., while watching a play) *and* be "happy" at the same time.

Here's the other definition of happiness—happiness as "abundance":

- **Abundance** is the feeling that results from the belief that one has enough—indeed, more than enough—of anything and everything that one could want from life: money, love, good fortune, and the like.

Abundance stems from the belief that, no matter how dire a situation might be, every little thing will be all right in the end. When we are feeling abundant, life seems like a cozy mess: perfect despite its imperfections. The term "cozy mess" evokes a particular image in my mind that I think you may find useful. When my daughter was about two, she would surround herself with blankets and pillows—and anything else that she could lay her hands on (soft toys, a cardboard box, a toy laptop, etc.)—and promptly fall asleep in the middle of it. My wife and I felt impelled to clean up the disorganized "mess" in which we found our daughter. But to our daughter, the mess wasn't uncomfortable at all—it was *cozy*! In a similar way, to someone feeling abundant, life's challenges and problems are what make life *interesting*—not threatening. This is why a person feeling abundant feels fully engaged with *everything* life has to offer, including its challenges.

Although both harmony and abundance are characterized by complete acceptance of whatever one is experiencing, they are both different from a state of apathy—which is also characterized by complete acceptance of everything one is experiencing. The main difference is that, while apathy is characterized by the feeling of helplessness, harmony and abundance are characterized by optimism. As such, when feeling harmonious or abundant, one is likely to want to change things for the better even as one is completely comfortable with everything one is experiencing.

The idea that one would want to change something that is already perfect may seem like a contradiction in terms, but it isn't. Consider the following example as an illustration. Imagine that you have had a good night's rest, and that you are feeling fresh and energetic. It's a crisp and beautiful sunny morning and you have a challenging game of tennis awaiting you. You feel energized by the prospect of playing the game and, hopefully, emerging a winner.

In this example, although you are feeling great and life is "perfect," you would still want to engage your opponent and win against him. Indeed, it's precisely because you have an interesting challenge to overcome that life is "perfect." This doesn't mean, of course, that life would be perfect only if one is constantly challenged. In a state of harmony and abundance, one is fully accepting of situations in which one isn't facing challenges; such situations provide the opportunity to experience serenity—or joy.

It is this rare combination of two seemingly contradictory traits—full acceptance *and* full engagement (including the desire to change things)—that makes harmony and abundance so alluring as definitions of happiness. In addition, there are at least two other features that make them both worthy candidates as definitions of happiness. First, recent research by Michaël Dambrun and his colleagues suggests that happiness need not be fleeting if it is defined along the lines of harmony or abundance. Why? Because both harmony and abundance have less to do with external circumstances and more to do with internal ones. They both hinge on the capacity to—as the authors put it—"*deal with whatever comes his way in life.*" Meaning that, if one were to define happiness as harmony or abundance, one would retain the keys to one's happiness in one's own hands and thus one's happiness wouldn't be as subject to the vagaries of life as it otherwise might. Second, although very few (typically less than 2 percent) spontaneously equate "happiness" with either harmony or abundance in our surveys (in which, as you may recall, we ask people to recall a recent event that made them "happy"), almost everyone can relate to both definitions once they are articulated to them. This suggests that both harmony and abundance are at least somewhat familiar to people, which means that most people can entertain either as a definition of happiness.

Incorporating Happiness

Defining happiness—that is, having a relatively concrete idea of what happiness means to you—is the first of the two steps in the first happiness exercise. The second step is to figure out the set of things that makes you feel happy in the way that you have defined it. This step involves recalling previous occasions when you felt happy in the way that you have defined it, and making a list of things—activities, people, objects, experiences, and so on—that triggered that positive feeling. For example, if you choose to define happiness as love/connection, you would think back to previous occasions in which you felt this emotion and identify its determinants (e.g., hanging out with friends, vacationing with family). Likewise, if you defined happiness as harmony, you would list the things (e.g., going for a run, practicing mindfulness) that made you experience that emotion. In other words, the second step involves creating a "portfolio" of things (pictures, songs, people, and activities) that you believe are reliable determinants of happiness as you have defined it.

The First Happiness Exercise

To summarize, the first happiness exercise involves the two steps for enhancing happiness levels: defining happiness and incorporating happiness. As with the other happiness exercises discussed in this book, you will find the detailed instructions for both steps on the book's website (www .happysmarts.com/book/exercises/Defining_incorporating_happiness) and the abridged instructions in the appendix for this chapter. Before you get to the instructions, however, it will be useful to quickly discuss *why* the two steps in this exercise can help you overcome the first deadly happiness sin, the sin of devaluing happiness.

Recall that one reason we devalue happiness is because we don't have a concrete idea of what happiness means to us. The first step in the happiness exercise, defining happiness—which involves coming up with a concrete idea of what happiness means to you—obviously addresses this reason. Another reason we devalue happiness is because of the negative beliefs we harbor about it, such as "happiness will make me lazy," or "happiness will make me selfish," or "happiness is fleeting." Depending on how one defines happiness, the happiness exercise can help address this reason too. Defining happiness as "authentic pride" (the feeling when we believe that we have achieved something worthwhile) can help us overcome the belief that happiness is associated with laziness, because achieving something worthwhile isn't possible without concerted effort. Likewise, equating happiness to love/connection can help us overcome the belief that happiness makes us selfish. Similarly, by equating happiness to harmony or abundance, we can overcome the belief that happiness is fleeting.

The final reason we devalue happiness is because of medium maximization—the tendency to focus on the means to happiness, rather than on happiness itself. One reason we fall prey to medium maximization is because we don't consciously consider the implications of our judgments and decisions for our happiness. Both steps in the first happiness exercise help address this problem. By taking the effort to define happiness, we give it greater prominence; as we saw earlier, we give greater importance to things that are more concrete and easier to process. And by identifying the set of things that lead us to feel happy, we recognize the types of judgments and decisions we need to be making in order to enhance our happiness levels.

One last thing before you rush off to start the first happiness exercise. Note that overcoming the tendency to devalue happiness will likely take a lot of time and conscious effort on your part. One reason for this is that most of us are conditioned to devalue happiness right from childhood. I can recall an event involving my son in which I *almost* caught myself "coaching" him to devalue happiness. When my son was about three, he saw a kid in the neighborhood riding around in one of those cute little toy cars and, naturally, wanted one for himself. He managed to persuade us to buy him one. We ordered it online, and soon enough it arrived in a big brown box. My son was understandably ecstatic about his new toy and was totally into it . . . for all of three days. After that, all he wanted was to play with the *box* in which the car arrived! Why? Because he was infatuated with this cartoon character called Hamilton the Pig who apparently lived in a box. So he wanted to do the same thing.

I remember being quite upset about this. I wanted my son to play with the car because (*dammit!*) it cost more. But then it suddenly struck me that here I was, trying to get my son to give greater priority to value for money than to happiness. I realized that it really shouldn't matter to me *how* my son was having fun so long as he was. I also realized that it is precisely because we tell our children what to value—money, value for money, status, beauty, power, etc.—that they learn to lose sight of what makes them truly happy. Once I realized this, not only did I let my son continue to play with the box to his heart's content, I told myself that I would try to do the same myself—that is, not get distracted from making happiness-enhancing decisions.

Now, I must hasten to add that, although I managed to avoid instilling the first deadly happiness sin in this instance, I am sure there were many other instances in which I failed to do so. Plus, I recognize that I am not the only one from whom my son learns the "rules for living"—he learns them from other sources too. So to the extent that the tendency to devalue happiness is prevalent—and it is, as we will see in the chapters to come—it is likely that he too, like the rest of us, will grow up to be conditioned to devalue happiness.

This just means that, to lead a life of happiness and fulfillment, it will take more than merely figuring out the determinants of happiness; it will take becoming increasingly aware of when, how, and why we tend to devalue happiness, and will also take nurturing the first habit of the highly happy: prioritizing, but not pursuing, happiness.

Chapter 2A

THE SECOND DEADLY HAPPINESS "SIN": CHASING SUPERIORITY

A s a three-year-old toddler, my son went to a local day care near our house. One day, after dropping him off, I was merrily on my way to work when I noticed that I had failed to leave behind his lunch box. Swearing under my breath (what is it about repeating a task that gets my goat?), I made a U-turn and drove back to the day care. Just as I was about to enter his class, I noticed through the glass pane on the door that all the kids, including my son, were sitting in a circle around the music teacher. I decided to observe what was going on. The teacher, with a guitar in hand, was strumming the chords to a well-known song, encouraging the kids to join in. Like typical three-year-olds, most of the kids were horsing around, tickling one another and making funny noises. I was gratified to notice that my son, along with a few other kids, was paying full attention to the teacher.

The teacher was good, both musically and in terms of motivating the kids. He nodded enthusiastically at the kids who were singing and patiently attempted to get the other kids involved as well. Within minutes, however, it was clear that he wasn't able to maintain the attention of the kids who were goofing off. He started focusing, through eye contact and smiles, on the kids who were singing. It was at this point that I noticed something a little more subtle beginning to unfold. Among the kids who were singing, one was particularly good. (It wasn't my son.) I noticed how this kid's (let's call him Ben) superior singing ability was beginning to affect the teacher's response toward him. Although the teacher made eye contact with all the kids who were singing, I could see that he was paying particular attention to Ben. The teacher's eyes lingered a little longer on Ben. Ben also got a few more smiles, and the smiles grew bigger over time. Ben soon began noticing the teacher's favorable response to him and started putting even more effort into his singing, reinforcing a virtuous cycle. Within minutes, the other kids, including my son, noticed this development. One of the kids tried to emulate Ben, but alas, the talent just wasn't there. As for my son, he became progressively quieter and eventually, by the end of the session, began horsing around like some of the other kids. In the few minutes that I observed this drama unfold, it was relatively obvious that Ben had emerged as the "teacher's pet": the most important kid in class.

Even as children, we are exposed to feedback that, in subtle or not-so-subtle ways, pegs us as superior or inferior to others around us.* In the story that I just recounted, the stakes weren't high. My son wouldn't have been denied food or otherwise punished for singing badly. Nevertheless, the teacher's preferential treatment of Ben had a significant impact on him: he felt deflated enough to stop singing. Later that evening, my son told me that he wasn't interested in singing because "I am no good at it, Daddy." One can thus easily imagine the emotional impact that others' judgments can have on us in situations in which the stakes are, in fact, high. Think, for example, of the impact that teachers' and parents' judgments have on high school kids who fail to get good grades. Or consider the impact of failing to acquire a girlfriend or boyfriend when everyone else has one (or more). Is it any surprise that self-esteem is at its lowest among high school kids? And is it any surprise, too, that middle age—which is when many of us are forced to acknowledge that we haven't achieved as much as some of our peers have—is such a rough time?

---

* I am not suggesting here that children or, for that matter, adults shouldn't be given feedback on how well (or poorly) they stack up to others. For societies to function efficiently, it is imperative to assess the relative prowess of people and organizations; otherwise, we would collectively suffer. What I am suggesting here instead—as will become clear in the pages to come—is that we need to give our children the capacity to sever the link between their relative standing (with respect to others) and their self-worth and emotional well-being.

Reasons We Seek Superiority

The second deadly happiness sin is chasing superiority—a sin that is at least partly the result of being socially conditioned to be better than others. We are conditioned by our parents, teachers, mentors, media—virtually everyone in society—to be the "best" (better than everyone else) at whatever we do.

But exactly why does everyone goad us to be superior? What's in it for parents if their son or daughter is the best at spelling bees or basket weaving?

One reason is that, in our evolutionary past, superiority served a critical role: it enhanced our chances of survival. "Superior" people—those who were bigger, faster, stronger, or wealthier—were more likely to survive. When a marauding tribe attacked a village, it was the fastest runner who had the best chance of surviving. Likewise, in times of famine and scarcity, it was the one with the most power and resources who had the best chance to survive. So a big reason why everyone seeks superiority is because everyone is hardwired to do so. This also explains why our parents and caretakers push us to pursue superiority. As our "well-wishers," they want us to have the best chance of surviving.

Of course, it's not just from our parents that we learn about the importance of superiority; we learn about it from our teachers and employers too. We learn that valedictorians get better scholarships, CEOs get higher wages, and top entertainers get better deals and more magazine covers. We also learn about the importance of superiority from TV and magazines, which selectively cover stories of successes rather than failures.

One consequence of being conditioned, especially by those about whom we care a lot, to pursue superiority is that we come to tether our self-esteem to being superior. When we learn that the amount of love and attention we get from others depends on how well we stack up to our peers, we internalize the need for superiority to such an extent that we seek it even if the others aren't around to judge us. So although we start seeking superiority as toddlers and kids to measure up to others' standards, we end up seeking it later in life as adolescents and adults to measure up to our *own* standards. Thus, the need cuts into the very core of our being.

The need for superiority is also rooted in our desire to figure out whether we are making adequate progress toward cherished goals. As humans, one of our most important goals is *mastery*—the desire to become increasingly competent or effective at something. One way we can figure out whether we are getting better at something is by comparing ourselves with others. If we do something better than others, we feel we must be making progress; if, on the other hand, we do something worse than others do, we feel we must be regressing or stagnating. So apart from the desire for others' approval and the desire for self-esteem, the need for mastery is another reason why we seek superiority.

There is yet another important reason that we seek superiority: being "superior" gives us the *autonomy* or freedom to be who we are; findings show that higher-status individuals don't feel the need to watch what they say or otherwise restrict their behaviors. Those of lower status, by contrast, feel the pressure to be more accommodating.

Thus, superiority is not just about survival. It is about many other things too. It is about the need for approval. It is about self-esteem. It is about mastery, and about autonomy. So chasing superiority is not some shallow or superficial trait that only those with an unusually big "ego" or with a narcissistic personality exhibit. Rather, it is a deep-seated need that almost all of us pursue.

The Many Manifestations of the Need for Superiority

The pursuit of superiority manifests itself in myriad ways, some of which can be simultaneously funny and poignant. Consider the desperate attempts of those well past their prime, particularly as entertainers or athletes, to cling to the spotlight—a theme that is well exploited in Billy Wilder's classic movie *Sunset Boulevard*. Or consider how Facebook "friends" tom-tom their achievements or selectively upload only their most flattering images. Unsurprisingly, findings show that exposure to such friends' updates on Facebook triggers more negative feelings than positive ones. This is sad because most people presumably want to feel happy for their good-looking and successful friends, yet they can't help but feel jealous and envious of them.

The need for superiority seems alive and well even in contexts in which the whole point is to curb this need. If you have ever been to a meditation session, you surely recognize the "beatific one"? This is the person with the soft eyes and cherubic smile who pronounces in a cloyingly sonorous voice after the session that it was "awesome beyond words." The subtle message of the beatific one is: *I am better at meditation than you, pal, so don't even think of competing with me on spirituality!* The need for superiority is also manifested in the tendency to affiliate oneself with those who are superior. As you may know, the propensity among students to wear their university's jersey is higher when the university team has won a game than when it hasn't. Why? Because it feels good to be associated with the "superior" team!

Does Being Superior Make You Happier?

If chasing superiority is so prevalent, surely being superior boosts happiness levels, right? Indeed it does. Consider results from one study in which, as participants were given feedback that made them feel superior or inferior to others, researchers observed their facial expressions. Findings showed that participants made to feel superior displayed more positive expressions, while those made to feel inferior displayed more negative ones. So at least immediately after getting feedback, it seems that being superior feels good.

But what about in the long run? Are superior people happier over time? For example, are bosses happier than their subordinates?

This is a difficult question to answer for many reasons, including that people's happiness depends on a number of factors other than superiority—such as lifestyle, opportunities, and responsibilities. There's also the problem of reverse causation. Happy people are generally more successful; so if findings show that bosses are happier than their subordinates, it may be because they were happier to begin with.

Even with all of these problems that make it difficult to ascertain the true relationship between superiority and happiness, it appears that being superior does enhance happiness levels. Perhaps the most convincing evidence of this relationship comes from one of the most influential sets of studies in all of psychology, the famous "Whitehall" studies.

Imagine that you are a lowly clerk working for the government of the United Kingdom. (Yes, life sucks.) On your paltry income, all you can afford is regular British food—meat and potatoes (*not* tandoori chicken). The good news is that you have a lift in your flat, and your rent is paid by the government. Imagine further that the government also takes care of your medical expenses, which means that, should you be able to afford all the warm ale you want, your liver would be covered. And finally, imagine that although most of the other government employees are higher up in the hierarchy than you—and consequently draw higher wages—you and your family receive the same medical attention they do because all government employees are covered by the same medical plan. In other words, although you are materially worse off than most others in your organization, your basics are covered and the medical attention you receive is no different from that which your superiors receive.

Is your health likely to be just as good as that of your superiors?

The answer, it turns out, is no. You are likely to be in poorer physical and emotional health. In a set of studies that commenced in the 1960s and continue to be conducted to this day, known as the Whitehall studies, researchers found that, despite receiving identical medical attention, those lower in status are more prone to falling sick, are sick for longer periods of time, have shorter life spans, and suffer more emotional negativity than those higher in status. For example, even after controlling for lifestyle (e.g., amount of sleep) and habits (such as smoking), employees in the lowest grade had a mortality rate two times higher than that of men in the highest grade. The Whitehall studies have been replicated across multiple countries, including Finland and Australia.

Why are those higher in status more physically and emotionally healthy?

Clearly, it can't be because they have a better chance of survival—participants in these studies were not struggling to meet basic needs. Researchers have conducted a number of follow-up studies to find out exactly why status improves health and happiness, and their results reveal that status matters because of two main reasons. Self-esteem is one of them. Those higher in status enjoy better self-esteem and, as a result, are happier. The other reason is control—or autonomy. Those higher in status perceive themselves to have greater autonomy and control over their own decisions and this makes them happier.

Pursuit of Superiority and Materialism

Given everything I have discussed thus far, it would be tempting to arrive at the conclusion that, to maximize happiness, one should pursue superiority. However, as it turns out, although being superior makes one happy, the pursuit of superiority is likely to lower happiness levels. This is such an important point to note that I think it's worth repeating: although *being superior* enhances happiness levels, it turns out that the *pursuit of* superiority lowers happiness levels. Or, put in more technical terms, *controlling for one's current status, the greater the need for superiority, the lower the happiness levels*. This means that regardless of how wealthy, famous, powerful, or attractive you are compared with others, the more you strive for superiority, the less happy you will be.

To delve into why this contradiction occurs, allow me to share with you a short—and real-life—story.

I was recently on a cruise ship, soaking up the warm waters of a perfectly calibrated hot tub on the ship's main deck, and drifting gradually off into la-la land, when I was rudely awoken by the announcement that the "Hairy Chest Contest" was about to begin. Although I wasn't interested in participating in this contest—being, er, somewhat deficient on a critical dimension—I could hardly pass up the opportunity to witness it. So I shook off my stupor, slicked back the hair on my head (of which I continue to possess an adequate quantity), put on my shades, and got ready to observe the heroics of the hirsute. As it turned out, my time was well spent. The South African grandpa (a cofinalist) gave the red-haired Irish milkman (another cofinalist) a run for his money. Although the latter "won"—based on an informal polling of the audience—it was by no means a cakewalk.

Later that evening, I had the good fortune of sitting next to the South African grandpa at one of the many bars on the ship. After stealing a quick glance at his chest to confirm his identity, I casually let him know that, as far as I was concerned, he was the winner of the contest. I didn't expect much more than an acknowledgment of my support from him, but the loss to the Irish milkman had apparently cut him to the quick.

"*Thank you!*" he said, clasping my hand and shaking his head in disappointment. "Thank you *so* much. I too thought I should have won. But what can you do? I guess the *audience* gets to decide who the winner is!" he said with contempt. Clearly, it had been a bad hair day for the Springbok.

"There, there," I said in return, patting his well-padded back. I could empathize with the man's pain, having often experienced the feeling that I had "won" something—such as a debate on whether the soul exists—only to realize, based on the reaction of onlookers, that my opponent had trounced me. The point of the story is that, even with something as seemingly easy to measure as the hairiness of the chest, it can be difficult to figure out who the winner is. This problem gets even hairier, so to speak, in contexts in which the yardsticks are even more ambiguous.

Consider the following examples:

Who's the best drummer of all time?

My pick would likely be Stewart Copeland, but I could just as easily be persuaded to pick Neil Peart, who arguably has better "groove." Other people—the more technically inclined—may prefer Steve Smith or Buddy Rich, while those who favor an expanded definition of drums may pick an exponent of the mridangam, djembe, or steel drum.

Who is the best cricketer ever?

Well, maybe this one is not such a good example because the answer is obvious, especially if you are Indian. (Most Indians, especially of my generation, are fanatical fans of a certain Sachin Tendulkar, and consider him to be the best cricketer ever.)

Who's the best-ever marine engineer? The best-ever gardener? Businessman? Cook?

You get the point. The fact is, it is difficult—if not impossible—to come up with objective yardsticks for assessing one's standing relative to others in almost any domain. Indeed, it is the dearth of such yardsticks that permits people to hold an overly exalted view of themselves in relation to others—a phenomenon known as the "better-than-average" effect. Almost everyone believes that they are better than the average person on positive traits such as professionalism, warmth, and kindness when clearly, by definition, no more than half the people can be better than average and some people must therefore be deluding themselves.

As an astute reader, you must have noted that the dearth of objective yardsticks for assessing one's standing relative to others poses a serious problem for those seeking superiority. If the metrics for assessing one's superiority over others are subjective and ambiguous, how in the world is one to proceed?

Given this seemingly intractable problem, you would think that people would have long given up on chasing superiority. But the desire for superiority is apparently so strong that we don't give up so easily. Instead of comparing ourselves with others on ambiguous—but relevant—yardsticks, we do the next best thing: we compare on yardsticks that are less ambiguous, even if these yardsticks are not relevant for assessing the original dimension of interest to us. I am talking here, of course, of extrinsic yardsticks—money, power, and fame. These yardsticks allow us to assess our standing relative to others even in areas that have little to do with money, power, or fame. Thus, for example, to gauge whether Bill Gates is a better leader than, say, Steve Jobs, we use their relative net worth as a proxy for leadership skills, the logic being that the richer person must be the better leader. Likewise, to assess whether Stewart Copeland is a better drummer than Neil Peart, we look at the number of Facebook fans they have, or compare the prices that tickets to their concerts command.

The problem—or benefit, depending on your point of view—of using these proxy yardsticks is that they allow comparisons *across* domains. For instance, I could, as a professor, judge my standing relative to someone who has nothing to do with the profession of professing. How? By assessing how much more (or less) wealthy, powerful, or famous he appears to be compared with me. I say *appears to be* because it is often difficult to know exactly how wealthy, powerful, or famous someone else is, which is why we use signals of wealth (e.g., brand of car owned), power (e.g., position in the company), or fame (e.g., number of Twitter followers) as proxy measures for actual wealth, power, and fame.

As it turns out, the proxy yardsticks of wealth, power, and fame, while offering the benefit of being quantifiable, come saddled with a very heavy problem: they make us focus on accumulating extrinsic—or materialistic—rewards, and such a materialistic focus, it turns out, is one of the biggest happiness killers.

Why Materialism Lowers Happiness

I can distinctly recall how elated I felt when I took up my position at the McCombs School of Business. Before joining McCombs, I was earning a paltry stipend as a PhD student, and I was being offered six times that amount as an assistant professor. I literally couldn't figure out what I would do with so much money. Even after budgeting liberal amounts for all conceivable expenses, my calculations told me that I would be worth a million dollars in a few short years. I called up my parents to convey the good news, and bought a bottle of bubbly to celebrate. But as you may have guessed, I rejoiced too soon. Despite receiving reasonably good raises in each of the fifteen years that I have worked at McCombs, I am still short of achieving my target (so contributions are welcome!).

The catch with earning more is that expenses, seemingly magically, catch up with earnings. This is one reason why earning more doesn't enhance happiness levels. But there's a related, and even more compelling, reason why more money doesn't usually buy more happiness: the psychological boost that one derives from higher earnings wears off quickly, and one needs a new increase to experience the same psychological boost. The tendency to adapt to new levels of money—or, for that matter, any other metric of superiority, including power, fame, or beauty—is so prevalent that adaptation could be considered one of the most fundamental aspects of human nature. It is the tendency to adapt, for instance, that is responsible in part for the intriguing and well-known finding that a mere two years after the event, lottery winners are no happier than nonwinners. The fact that we adapt to new levels of wealth, power, and fame—and other materialistic proxies for superiority—means that, if we were to tether our happiness to the need for superiority, we would need to become increasingly wealthy, powerful, and famous over the course of our lives to maintain high levels of happiness. You don't have to be a genius to know that this is very unlikely.

Adaptation, then, is a big reason why materialism diminishes happiness levels in the long run. A related reason is the unrealistically high expectations that people have of materialistic things to bring happiness; these high expectations, findings show, are a major reason for the discontent of materialistic people. Yet another reason why materialism lowers happiness is that it promotes self-centeredness and lowers compassion, making others less likely to cooperate with materialistic people, leading them to be less happy in the long run. Perhaps as a result of lower compassion, materialistic people are more likely to compromise on things that actually bring joy and happiness—things like hanging out with friends and family or contributing to society—in favor of money, power, and fame.

Confirming these conclusions, a study in which researchers followed twelve thousand college freshmen for a period of nineteen years (from when they were eighteen, in 1976, to when they were thirty-seven, in 1995) showed that those for whom "making money" was the primary goal were far less happy with their lives two decades later. Other findings reveal that compared with nonmaterialistic people, materialistic people are more likely to suffer from mental disorders.

Given the significance of being materialistic for happiness, you may be curious to assess your own levels of materialism, and to help you do so, I have included a materialism scale at the end of this chapter.

Other Reasons Why Chasing Superiority Lowers Happiness

In addition to materialism, there are several other reasons why the pursuit of superiority lowers happiness. Tethering one's self-worth (or self-esteem) to being better than others can lead to obsessing about the implications of failing to achieve this goal, making one more vulnerable to depression. Further, our perceived sense of superiority is affected more by how we believe our *acquaintances*—rather than our close friends or family members—perceive us. This makes the foundations of our sense of superiority shaky and unstable. Further, the need for superiority has been shown to lead to the "better than average" effect that I mentioned briefly earlier—the tendency to perceive oneself as more positive than one actually is—leading one to become blind to one's foibles and failings. Thus, those with a high need for superiority may end up sacrificing long-term learning and growth for the sake of short-term boosts in hubristic pride.

Yet another reason why the pursuit of superiority lowers happiness is because of the detrimental effect it has on the quality of relationships. Those who pursue superiority tend to be "takers," according to Adam Grant, author of *Give and Take*, and takers aren't well liked. In one study, people were asked to express their willingness to cooperate with the suggestions of either a "taker" or a "giver," and findings showed that people were much more likely to cooperate with givers. One reason why takers aren't well liked may be because they tend to get angry and aggressive toward others, particularly when they don't get the respect they think they deserve. Unsurprisingly, takers have been shown across a number of studies to be less happy than givers.

Finally, and perhaps most important, the need for superiority instills the tendency to compare oneself with others, and this tendency has been shown to lower happiness levels. Specifically, findings show that the less attention you pay to how much better or worse than others you are, the happier you are likely to be; or conversely, the more you compare yourself with others, the less happy you will be.*

Mitigating the Need for Superiority

The discussion thus far may be summarized as follows:

- Not only is the need for superiority hardwired in us, but most of us are also socialized to pursue it.
- Although being superior makes one happier (and less stressed), pursuing superiority lowers happiness.

To lead a happier life then, it is clear what we need to do: mitigate the need for superiority—but without jeopardizing the chances of being successful at what we do. Doing so will, for all the reasons that we have discussed, almost certainly enhance happiness levels.

But how can one mitigate the need for superiority without jeopardizing the chances of succeeding?

The first thing to do would be to get rid of a prevalent misconception about the need for superiority. From teaching my class on happiness, I have discovered that many of us believe the need for superiority is an important

---

* For a short interview with Professor Tom Gilovich of Cornell University on this topic, see https://www.coursera.org/learn/happiness/lecture/JsKhm/week-2-video-2-effects -of-chasing-superiority-on-happiness.

determinant of success. As a result, we fear that mitigating this need will make us less successful. As it turns out, the belief that the need for superiority is a determinant of success is wrong—or to be more accurate, *mostly* wrong. It's not as if the need for superiority doesn't play any role in motivating us to accomplish things; it can light a fire under our backside to get things done. However, once we start a task, the need for superiority is more of a hindrance than a help, particularly in the kinds of jobs that you and I have—cognitive, intellectual (rather than menial) jobs. The idea that the need for superiority can be a hindrance to success may seem counterintuitive at first, but as we will see soon—in the very next chapter, in fact—results from several studies provide compelling evidence that the need for superiority undermines success.

Apart from getting rid of the misconception that the need for superiority is a determinant of success, it will help to watch out for situations that make us feel insecure—because it is when we feel insecure that we are more likely to seek superiority. Consider results from one study in which participants were asked to take a test and given either a blow to their self-esteem or a boost to it via feedback on their performance in the test. (The feedback was bogus; regardless of how well they actually performed, participants were made to feel that they had done well or poorly.) These participants were then asked to evaluate either members of their own group or those of an outside group on both positive and negative traits. Findings showed that participants who were told that they had performed badly on the test were much more likely to derogate out-group members than those who had been told that they did well. Findings from several other studies confirm that our need for superiority is more pronounced when we feel insecure.

One other factor that heightens the need for superiority is, ironically, material success. Exposure to symbols of material success—such as luxury goods—it turns out, makes us more self-centered and materialistic. This suggests that people with greater access to resources—that is, the smart-and-the-successful among us—may be more prone to seeking superiority. There is support for this idea; even though Americans enjoy never-before-seen levels of material prosperity, the desire for material success has reached an all-time high. Findings from the American Freshman surveys show, for example, that while less than 40 percent of freshmen mentioned material success as their most important goal in the 1970s, that figure was over 80 percent in 2014.

In addition to being on the lookout for situations in which the need for superiority is more pronounced, there are at least two other things that one could do to tamp down this need. I will get to these things in the next chapter.

MATERIALISM SCALE

This eighteen-item materialism scale (which can also be accessed and completed on the book's website, at www.happysmarts.com/book/scales/materialism) was developed by Richins and Dawson (1992), and has three "subscales," one each for "success," "acquisition centrality," and "happiness" (more on that shortly). For each item, indicate your extent of (dis)agreement by picking a number from 1 to 7, where 1 = "strongly disagree," and 7 = "strongly agree."

1. I admire people who own expensive homes, cars, and clothes.
2. Some of the most important achievements in life include acquiring material possessions.
3. I don't place much emphasis on the amount of material objects people own as a sign of success.*
4. The things I own say a lot about how well I'm doing in life.
5. I like to own things that impress people.
6. I don't pay much attention to the material objects other people own.*
7. I usually buy only the things I need.*
8. I try to keep my life simple, as far as possessions are concerned.*
9. The things I own aren't all that important to me.*
10. I enjoy spending money on things that aren't practical.
11. Buying things gives me a lot of pleasure.

12. I like a lot of luxury in my life.
13. I put less emphasis on material things than most people I know.*
14. I have all the things I really need to enjoy life.*
15. My life would be better if I owned certain things I don't have.
16. I wouldn't be any happier if I owned nicer things.*
17. I'd be happier if I could afford to buy more things.
18. It sometimes bothers me quite a bit that I can't afford to buy all the things I'd like.

Scoring Scheme

Add up the scores for these items first: 1, 2, 4, 5, 10, 11, 12, 15, 17, and 18; then reverse score the items with an asterisk, items 3, 6, 7, 8, 9, 13, 14, and 16 (the simplest way to do this is by subtracting the score you gave yourself on each of these items from 8; so, for example, if you gave yourself a "5" on item #3, then the actual score would be 8 - 5 = 3 and so on). Then, add up both sets of scores to arrive at your final "materialism" score.

If your score is greater than 72, then you are more materialistic than not; a score of about 99 or more would indicate higher-than-optimal levels of materialism.

Item numbers 1 through 6 tap into the "success" dimension of materialism, which refers to the extent to which conventional (or materialistic) success (wealth, power, etc.) matters to you; a score of 24 or greater means you are more materialistic than not on this dimension, and a score of 33 or more would indicate higher-than-optimal levels of materialism on this dimension. Item numbers 7 through 13 tap into the "acquisition centrality" dimension, which refers to the importance materialists attach to acquiring more possessions, which allows acquisitiveness to function as a life goal for them; a score of 28 or more indicates you are more materialistic than not on this dimension, and a score of 38 or more would indicate higher-than-optimal levels of materialism on this dimension. Item numbers 14 through 18 tap into the "happiness" dimension, which refers to the extent to which you believe that you have the things you need in order to be happy; a score of 20 or greater means you are more materialistic than not on this subscale, and a score of 27 or more would indicate higher-than-optimal levels of materialism on this subscale.

Chapter 2B

THE SECOND HABIT
OF THE HIGHLY HAPPY:
PURSUING FLOW

├─────────────────────────────────────┤

I magine that you have a task to do—say, write a book chapter. You arrive at your office to get in a full day's work, but for reasons best known to you, begin dilly-dallying. You surf the Web, indulge in some idle office gossip, and drink a large mug of coffee. Finally, when you have run out of excuses to dawdle further and begin to feel a mixture of guilt and panic welling up, you settle in front of your computer, crack your knuckles, and begin writing.

You find the going tough, just as you had all of last week. The right words—the *mots justes*, as the French might call it—aren't coming to you, but you persevere doggedly. Finally, after a full hour of striving, you wonder why this chapter is proving so difficult to write. More out of desperation than hope, you revisit an old document containing the chapter outline, and as you review it, you have an epiphany. You realize that the story line has a problem and that needs to be fixed in order to make progress. You are simultaneously frustrated and elated by this discovery. You're frustrated because this means that you'll need to start the chapter from scratch. You're elated because you are confident that the revised story line will work. You spend the next few minutes fighting the lethargy to restart the chapter, and finally take the plunge after a quick bathroom break.

During the next hour, your office buddies come knocking to see if you'd like to join them for coffee. You decline. You are also interrupted by several phone calls and e-mails. You attend to these interruptions cursorily before getting back to work. It's only when you register a sharp pang of hunger that you realize you have been working, nonstop, for three hours! You wonder where the time went and how you could have gone on for so long without being interrupted. You look over at the phone and discover, to your surprise, that it's off the hook; you turn to your e-mail and find that it's been closed. You realize that you must have taken the phone off the hook and closed the e-mail at some point, although you have no recollection of doing either.

Before you head out to a late lunch, you review what you have written and realize, with immense satisfaction, that you have accomplished more in three hours than you did all of last week.

Flow

Most of us have experienced, at one point or another, what the leading psychologist Mihaly Csikszentmihalyi calls *flow*—the kind of experience in which you get so absorbed that you lose track of time. Mihaly (pronounced Me? High!, but without the question or the exclamation marks) Csikszentmihalyi (cheek-sent-me-high-yee) first documented the phenomenon back in the 1970s.

In one of his best-known studies, Csikszentmihalyi gave his participants a beeper and a journal to carry with them over the course of a week.* He programmed the beepers to go off at random times during these days. And whenever the beeper went off, participants were instructed to stop what they were doing, and describe, in the journal that they were given, both what they were doing and how they felt while doing it. Thus, had you been a participant in the study and the beeper had gone off while you were writing the book chapter, you would have stopped typing, taken out your journal, and described what you were doing ("writing chapter 2B of my book"), and also described how you felt while doing it ("frustrated *and* elated!").

At the end of the journal-keeping period, Csikszentmihalyi gathered up the journals from all the participants and began poring over what they had written. Csikszentmihalyi was after the same thing that scores of philosophers

---

* You can watch excerpts from my interview with Professor Csikszentmihalyi at https://www.coursera.org/learn/happiness/lecture/0EBz1/week-2-video-4-flow-is-discovered.

and mystics from the past, from Aristotle to the Buddha, had been after: the recipe for happiness.

Csikszentmihalyi's Question

Put yourself in Csikszentmihalyi's shoes for a moment. Imagine that you are going through the journal entries of hundreds of respondents from various walks of life.

What would you have found?

What you would have found, I believe, would have depended on the questions you asked yourself as you were going over the journals. Had you asked, "Are certain jobs more satisfying than other jobs?" you might have found that artists are better off than janitors. If, instead, you had asked, "Are people happier at work or elsewhere?" you might have found that people are happiest when socializing, not so happy at work, and least happy when commuting. These findings, while interesting, wouldn't have been nearly as insightful as those that Csikszentmihalyi found.

The genius of Csikszentmihalyi lay in the question that he posed, a question no scientist before him had tried to answer. His question was: Is there something common to the experiences that people from various walks of life—from the plumber and the artist to the businessman and the scientist—find meaningful? And, if so, what is it?

In posing this question, Csikszentmihalyi made an implicit assumption that, although people may differ in *what* they find meaningful (e.g., a musician may find more meaning in composing a sonata than in sprinting a hundred meters, while the reverse may be true for an athlete), there is something common to the experiences that people, no matter what their background, find meaningful. And by seeking to identify that which is common to these diverse experiences, Csikszentmihalyi was after a *general* recipe for happiness, a recipe that could work just as well for the factory foreman as it does for the makeup artist. It could well have turned out, of course, that there is nothing common to the experiences that people from different walks of life find meaningful. If so, Csikszentmihalyi would have hit a dead end and that would have been that. But, as it turns out, there *is* something common across the experiences that everyone, regardless of their background, finds meaningful. And to understand what this common thing is, it is useful to get a deeper understanding of the concept of flow.

Features of Flow

So what exactly is flow?

Csikszentmihalyi found that flow experiences are characterized by certain common features. One important feature has to do with the perception of time. Paradoxically, time appears to both slow down *and* speed up when experiencing flow.

Consider the following as an illustration. Imagine that you are playing tennis. As you prepare to receive the next serve, you feel that you are caught in a bit of a time warp: everything seems to be happening in slow motion. You are able to see the ball much more clearly than you normally would—so clearly, in fact, that you can see the strands of fur on the ball as it hurtles toward you. And because time seems to have slowed down, you feel like you have more time on your hands to execute your shots. You find that you are able to reach balls that you normally couldn't. Further, although you are moving faster and covering more ground than you normally would, you don't feel exhausted—because your movements are efficient. Indeed, your movements are not just efficient, they are *fluid*, like that of a dancer. In other words, you feel a bit like the character Neo from *The Matrix*: time seems to be moving so slowly that you feel like you can dodge bullets. And yet—here's the paradoxical bit—when the game is over and you glance at your watch, you realize that the game took far longer than you imagined.

A second defining feature of flow is the lack of self-consciousness. When experiencing flow, people report being so absorbed in the activity that they do not have any leftover attentional capacity to evaluate how well—or poorly—they are performing the activity. In other words, being in flow takes all the psychic energy that one has. It is only when the flow activity has ended or some external trigger (such as a beeper going off) interrupts flow that people are able to step back and evaluate their performance.

A third feature of flow, a feature that, well, flows from the other two, is that of "being in the moment." When experiencing flow, people report being acutely focused on the task at hand. Or more precisely, they report being fully engrossed in achieving the next immediate *sub*goal of the task. As an illustration, imagine that you are climbing up a rock face and that your plan is to have a picnic lunch with your buddy after reaching the summit. If you are experiencing flow, this ultimate goal—of having a picnic lunch with your friend—would recede from your focus. Instead, your focus would be on the next crevice or ledge to hold on to. Or, it might be on the dampness of your fingers or the presence of prickly shrubs on your path. In other words, your focus would be on those things that have immediate relevance for your task at hand. Your focus wouldn't be on what you plan to do once you reach the summit. This is not to say that you would actively push away thoughts of future plans during flow; rather, your focus on the immediate task at hand would be a natural by-product of your absorption in the flow-inducing activity.

Pursuing Flow: The Second Habit of the Highly Happy

Chances are, you were able to relate to all three features of flow. This is because you, like most others, have experienced flow. The fact that all of us have experienced flow suggests that flow isn't the prerogative of one person or profession. Flow is available to all. I find this—that something as seemingly esoteric and mysterious as flow can be experienced by anyone and everyone—to be incredible.

What I find to be even more incredible, however, is that everyone, universally, finds flow to be meaningful and satisfying. Think about it. Some of us are brought up in capitalist societies; others, in socialist ones. Some of us grow up in rural settings; others, in urban dwellings. Many of us are citizens of democracies; others, of autocracies. And yet, despite our vast differences, we all share this seemingly quirky trait—of finding flow experiences to be deeply meaningful. This suggests that the desire to be absorbed—or to "get lost"—in flow is a fundamental need.

What's important about the need for flow is that, unlike the second deadly happiness sin—chasing superiority—it has the potential to enhance not just our own happiness levels, but also the happiness levels of others around us. And as if that weren't enough, pursuit of flow is arguably a more reliable determinant of success than is the pursuit of superiority, which is why pursuing flow is the second habit of the highly happy.

But before I tell you why flow enhances happiness, let's take a look at one last feature of flow.

Match Between Available and Required Abilities

Imagine, one more time, that you are playing tennis against someone. When are you likely to experience flow: When your opponent is far better or far worse than you?

Csikszentmihalyi's findings suggest that you are *not* likely to experience flow in either situation. When your opponent is far better than you, you are likely to be anxious; when he is far worse than you, you are likely to be bored. Csikszentmihalyi found that flow happens in the sweet spot between anxiety and boredom. In other words, flow is most likely when your skill levels are matched by the skill levels of your opponent. In fact—this is what makes flow particularly intriguing—even a perfect match of skill levels is not ideal; flow is most likely when your opponent's skills are *just*, ever so slightly, higher than your own skills.

So imagine that you are an intermediate-level tennis player with, say, a USTA rating of 4.0. You are most likely to experience flow when you are playing against someone who is just above your level—someone with a rating of 4.5 or, better yet, a rating of 4.1. Consider what happens when your opponent is just a little better than you. To win against this opponent, you can't rely on your *current* skill level alone; you would need to up your skill level. However, you wouldn't have to up it by much: you would only need to do it by a little bit. In other words, flow is most likely when you are challenged, but not by too much or too little. Such situations, in which you are challenged to just the right level, ensure that you are learning and growing even as you are engaged in the activity.

The fact that so long as you are able to put yourself in a situation in which your current skill levels are just a little bit lower than the skill levels required of you, you are likely to experience flow means that you can manufacture flow more or less at will. So for example, you could experience flow in chess by playing against someone (or a computer program) that is just a little bit better than you are. Likewise, you could experience flow in crossword or Sudoku by doing a puzzle that is just beyond your current capabilities.

Now, interestingly, not all situations in which there is a match between available and required abilities will result in equally absorbing or meaningful flow experiences. To understand why, put yourself back on a tennis court one last time. Imagine that you are a beginner, playing against another beginner. Given the low skill levels, both you and your partner will likely hit the ball out of the court (or into the net) far more often than you will put it into play. Even on the occasions in which one of you manages to put the ball into play, chances are that the other (you or your partner) can't reach the ball because it's been accidentally hit too hard or too far from you. Thus, whatever flow you experience is likely to be disrupted by long intervals of nonflow (picking up the ball from the net, retrieving the ball from out of court, etc.).

Contrast that with a scenario in which both you and your opponent are experts, with USTA ratings of 6.0 or higher. At this exalted level of skills, you and your opponent are likely to sustain flow for far longer durations. Your rallies are likely to last several seconds and, in the course of these rallies, both of you are likely to be stretched to the limits of your capabilities. Thus, the higher up you are in terms of available ability, the greater the chance that you will be able to sustain flow.

Why Flow Enhances Happiness

We'll return to the differences between high and low flow experiences shortly. But before I do that, let me turn to why flow experiences enhance happiness levels. The most obvious reason, of course, is that flow experiences are enjoyable in the moment. In one study, students were asked to perform either a high-flow activity or a low-flow activity for one hour. Then the happiness levels of these participants were measured. Findings showed that students in the former group were significantly happier than those in the latter.

Another reason flow experiences boost happiness levels has to do with mastery. As just discussed, flow experiences occur when you are challenged to improve and grow. As a result, if you are able to string together a sufficiently large number of flow experiences in some domain (say juggling), *you can't help but improve your skills in that domain.* And if you manage to string together a *critical* number of flow experiences in a domain, you will, willy-nilly, *have* to master that domain—or at least make significant progress toward it. And because the need for mastery is one of our most deep-seated needs—as I mentioned in chapter 2A—flow enhances happiness levels by enabling us to progress toward this important goal.

Yet another reason why flow enhances happiness levels has to do with *others'* happiness. As mentioned earlier, flow experiences have the potential to enhance not just our own happiness, but also the happiness of others around us. Why? Because, very simply, people are inspired by seeing others in flow. Imagine being at a rock concert in which the band is, well, rocking. Or imagine listening to a nerdy—but passionate—professor deliver a lecture on his favorite topic.

The fact that others derive inspiration from our flow suggests that pursuing flow is a much more sustainable source of happiness than is chasing superiority. Recall that, when you pursue the need for superiority, others do not look kindly upon it. There is a good reason why people are supportive of others' flow but aren't supportive of their need for superiority. Unlike the yardsticks for superiority—like wealth, fame, or power—*flow isn't finite or scarce*. That is, one person's flow doesn't have to come at the cost of another's. By contrast, because extrinsic rewards are limited, an increase in one person's wealth, power, or fame has to come at the cost of another's.*

What Disrupts Flow

Think of any invention—from airplanes and computers to Scotch tape and Zipcars—and you can bet that flow was involved in all of them. And yet, many of us are unaware of this fact. Instead, we believe that our achievements are due to our drive to be successful or superior. That is, we tend to attribute our achievements to the desire for worldly success when, in fact, flow is the real hero. The irony is that, far from improving our chances of achieving success, the desire for worldly success often *lowers* it. So in many ways, we have it backward: although it is flow that determines success, we believe that it is the desire for worldly success—and the associated need for superiority—that determines it.

This is not to say that the need for superiority has no role to play in our achievements. Often, we embark on the pursuit of a goal or persist with it because of the desire for superiority. However, this need plays a limited role: although it can keep us motivated in goal pursuit, the need for superiority

---

* This idea was expressed to me by Professor Csikszentmihalyi during my interview with him (for my Coursera course). You can watch an excerpt of this interview at https://www.coursera.org/learn/happiness/lecture/hMLNh/week-2-video-7-why-flow-enhances-happiness.

won't lead us to success if it isn't complemented by flow. Indeed, once we start a task, thoughts of worldly success or of besting someone else hinder, rather than help, us in making progress on the task. The reason for this is that our processing capacity is limited; so the more of it we allocate to thoughts of wealth, fame, power, or other yardsticks of superiority, the less capacity we will have to devote to the task at hand. It is when we forget about extrinsic rewards and focus on the task at hand that we are likely to make the most progress.

This fact is well known to anyone who has attempted to achieve a lofty goal. Think, for example, of Olympic athletes. Although these athletes have as strong a competitive streak as anyone, they are also masters at being able to keep thoughts of superiority (success or failure) at bay. In fact, as most sports psychologists know, the factor that differentiates the truly great athletes from the merely good ones is not physical or technical ability; rather it is a *mental* ability—the ability to forget what just happened, to not think of what might happen in the future, and to pay attention, instead, to what's happening right now. Without this ability to be in the moment, the great athletes wouldn't have what it takes to get into flow.

In case you are wondering whether flow is crucial only in highly competitive domains such as sports, think again. Across a series of well-designed studies, the behavioral economist Dan Ariely and his colleagues have shown that the desire for worldly success gets in the way of doing well in almost any domain. In one study, participants were challenged to solve thirteen sets of three anagrams each, like the ones below:

1. SUHOE
2. TAUDI
3. GANMAAR

For eight of the thirteen sets, participants worked on the anagrams by themselves in a private cubicle. For the rest, participants were asked to walk up to the front of the room and solve the anagrams under the public gaze of the other participants. Participants were paid the same amount for solving the anagrams—regardless of whether they did it in private cubicles or in public. So the monetary incentives were the same across the two conditions. However, as you can imagine, there was much more pressure to perform in the "public" condition. In which condition would the participants solve more anagrams—when they have more pressure on them or less?

The findings showed that the participants performed far worse when they were under social pressure than when they were not. Ariely and his colleagues conducted several other studies to assess the impact that incentives have on performance. Across all these studies, a consistent pattern emerged: participants performed better when they didn't have the pressure of a monetary reward hanging over their heads like Damocles' sword.*

These findings are, of course, broadly consistent with those from the classic studies (conducted in the 1980s) on intrinsic motivation. As those studies showed, extrinsic rewards and incentives—carrots and sticks—worsen (rather than improve) performance. The reason why extrinsic rewards hurt our performance is because they distract us from getting into flow; when we are rewarded or punished based on *outcome* of goal pursuit, we lose the ability to focus on the *process* of goal pursuit.

Getting Flow Back into Your (Work) Life

If flow is a critical determinant of both happiness and success, then it follows that finding flow at work is important, as we spend the bulk of our "waking life" at work. However, most of us do not find work to be as meaningful or satisfying as we should—or could. A recent worldwide survey revealed that about twice as many employees are dissatisfied with their jobs as are satisfied. This wasn't always the case. In the 1970s and 1980s, job satisfaction in the United States was much higher than it currently is.

Most people recognize that it's a shame to find work meaningless and unfulfilling. Which is why, as Herminia Ibarra, author of a book called *Working Identity*, notes, so many of us dream of quitting our jobs one day and doing something more meaningful. But then it remains a dream forever because we are too afraid to actually take the plunge and quit the meaningless job and pursue a meaningful one instead. So we end up leading a discontented life and postpone finding "real enjoyment and happiness" till after retirement. And by the time retirement rolls around, we

---

* You can watch my interview with Professor Dan Ariely on this topic on my Coursera course at http://www.coursera.org/learn/happiness/lecture/q2fSM/week-2-video-3-is-need -for-superiority-important-for-success.

either have no energy left or we have not spent enough time cultivating the skills needed to experience high flow on a regular basis. So we basically end up postponing leading a fulfilling and meaningful life until it's too late.

The good news is that it doesn't have to be that way. There are some things that you can do right away to get more flow into your life. The first and most obvious thing you can do, if you aren't already doing it, is to re-connect with a hobby. This is because hobbies are a great way to experience flow, particularly since many of them are relatively easy to pick up even after a long hiatus. But hobbies can go only so far to instill meaning into life. What is far more impactful is to find flow at work.

What could you do to more regularly experience flow at work?

I recently asked Professor Steven Tomlinson, a very well-respected business school professor who currently teaches at the Acton School of Business, this question.* His advice was that one should try to do two

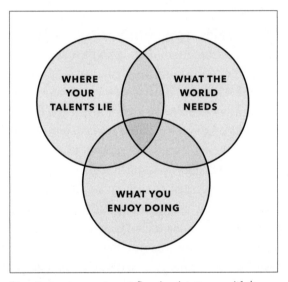

Figuring out a way to get flow back into your life†

---

* You can watch excerpts from my interview with Professor Tomlinson on my Coursera course at https://www.coursera.org/learn/happiness/lecture/oMQFr/week-2-video-9-getting -flow-back-into-your-life.

† To these three circles, one might add a fourth: what the world will pay you for. Although chasing money for its own sake is clearly not good for happiness (or success), all things being equal, more money is better, at least up to a point.

things. The first is to start identifying where one's talents lie and try to nurture those talents in one's current job. If this means taking on more responsibility or bending one's job description, so be it. This might take some courage and hard work, but it will be worth it. Second, identify the things that the community—city, country, or even the whole world—needs, and try to find ways to meet those needs.

So Steven's suggestion is to first gain clarity on things that lie in either of the top two circles in the figure on page 70—and ideally, the things that lie at their intersection—and then attempt to incorporate those things into your existing job.

To Steven's advice, I would add one more thing: get to do more of the things that you *enjoy* doing at work (which is the third—bottom—circle). The reason is because it's often easier to answer the question "What do I enjoy doing?" than to answer the questions "What am I really good at?" or "What does the world need?" According to research by Professor Robert Vallerand of Université du Québec à Montréal, a vast majority of us (85 percent) know where our passion lies, which suggests that most of us already know what we enjoy doing. And if we enjoy doing something, then there's a good chance that it will also induce flow and thereby foster creativity and success. As Csikszentmihalyi finds in his research, contrary to the popular myth, it is not the depressed and lonely who are more creative; rather, it is those who lead a relatively happy and stable life.

Choosing Flow Doesn't Mean Sacrificing Long-term Happiness for Short-term Happiness

Prioritizing enjoyment over other—particularly extrinsic—goals isn't the same thing as sacrificing long-term happiness for short-term happiness. Even if one enjoys doing something, like writing, or designing products, building expertise takes dedication and effort. It takes what Angela Duckworth, a professor in the department of psychology at the University of Pennsylvania, calls "grit." In other words, the process of building expertise is often painful in the short run, but this is the type of pain that's worth enduring, because it is in the service of something larger, and more meaningful—the goal of building expertise which, as we saw earlier, is essential to experiencing "high flow."

This brings me to a topic I broached earlier, in chapter 1B—about when it is worth sacrificing short-term happiness for long-term happiness. In my view, other than occasions when a minimal sacrifice of short-term happiness will likely yield substantially higher levels of long-term happiness, it's only worth doing so in two main contexts: (1) when one's basic necessities haven't yet been met, and (2) when the sacrifice of short-term happiness improves the odds of experiencing flow-inducing, or otherwise meaningful, activities. In all other contexts, including the most prevalent one of seeking greater wealth, power, fame, or control than one needs, it isn't worth sacrificing short-term happiness for long-term happiness. I say this on the basis of two main themes to emerge from the discussion thus far: (1) pursuing flow is a far better approach for enhancing not just short-term and long-term happiness, but also success, than is pursuing extrinsic rewards, and (2) we are likely to be less productive when we take on the additional pressure of pursuing extrinsic rewards than we otherwise would be, particularly in intellectual/creative tasks.

The "Slow and Organic" Path to a Career Shift

Getting back to what you could do to improve the odds of experiencing more flow at work, what if your current job doesn't lend itself to exercising your strengths or pursuing your purpose or passion? For example, what if you are in a sales job and your interests lie in writing computer code? What could you do then?

One option is to consider quitting your job and taking up one that you think will offer you the opportunity to nurture your talents or passion. Depending on your life circumstances, this could be a tough choice to make. Say you are middle-aged and have a family that depends on your income for support. It won't be easy to take the risk to quit your current job to try out something totally different. At the same time, however, you may be convinced that there's no way to make your current job more meaningful; so trying out a new job or career path may be the only option you have.

If this is your situation, you should consider making the bold move to change your job, but do it in a way that reduces the associated risk. Herminia Ibarra, author of *Working Identity*, has interviewed several dozen people who transitioned from one job to another, and her work suggests that often, the best strategy may be to retain your currently unsatisfying job as you try to figure out something more meaningful to do. Specifically, she finds that those who spend a few hours every week exposing themselves to people and activities involved in the job that they think would be more meaningful are often better off than those who, one fine day, quit their current job to take up another one.

Let's say that you are an accountant and you find your job unsatisfying. You believe that what you would really enjoy doing—and where your talents lie—is in owning a scuba diving shop. If so, you could spend a few (two to three) hours every week finding out more about what it would be like to operate a dive shop. For example, you could volunteer your services for free at a local dive shop. You could man the register at the shop, help out with refilling the tanks, or earn a teacher's license to help beginners work toward certificates. Over time, as you gain experience working at the dive shop, you will discover whether, in fact, what you thought was your passion is indeed your passion—or whether it was just one of your fantasies. If you end up discovering that operating a dive shop isn't, after all, your cup of tea, you will be happy that you didn't quit your day job to find this out. Conversely, if you find out that operating a dive shop is everything you dreamed it would be, your time volunteering would be well spent—you would have developed some important contacts with people in that line of business and also gained important knowledge on what it takes to operate a dive shop. Further, you would not have upset the applecart at home; your family wouldn't be unhappy with you for quitting your job and disrupting their lives.

So almost any way you look at it, the "slow and organic" path to transitioning from your current and unsatisfying job to a more meaningful one may be a better strategy than that of jumping ship one fine day.

A Plan for the "Best Possible Life"

The "slow and organic" path may be a better one than suddenly quitting your job and taking up a new one, but in order to execute it, you first need to know where your passion lies. As I mentioned earlier, Robert Vallerand's research suggests that most of us (85 percent) know what we are passionate about. However, as I have discovered from teaching my class on happiness, many of us also believe that our passion can't be our career because it can't make us money. One of my students, who was specializing in finance, voiced this concern in class one day. "My passion is origami," she said. "I can spend *hours* making figures out of paper and get completely lost in it. But I don't think I could support myself—let alone a family—making paper figures." She wondered how she could possibly shift from an investment banking job (which is what she expected to get) into one that involved origami.

There are no easy answers to such questions, of course, but the one thing that can definitely help is to visualize what your life would be like if everything worked out perfectly. In other words, visualizing your "best possible life" and then articulating it on paper will increase the chances that you actually get to lead it. Findings show that, when you visualize a goal, you automatically become more attuned to events, people, and activities that are relevant for achieving that goal. Indeed, this effect—whereby you become more attuned to goal-relevant stimuli—happens *subconsciously* such that, when you have clarity on what you want to achieve, you start doing things that, even if you aren't aware of it, enhance your chances of achieving it.

Now, the end result may not be exactly how you visualized it, but your life will be much closer to your ideal than it would otherwise be. My student—the one interested in origami—discovered this for herself. She started the "best possible life" exercise without much confidence in it, but as she started putting pen to paper, she got into it. In the course of completing the exercise, she realized that her "best possible life" needn't necessarily involve origami; she discovered that what she was ultimately passionate about was *art* in any form. So she ended up visualizing a life in which she was somehow involved with the art world, and she eventually ended up in a job that involves pricing artwork (mainly paintings). Pretty cool, huh? She definitely thinks so, because she loves her job and feels that she wouldn't have landed it if not for the "best possible life" exercise.

On the book's website, you will find instructions for the "best possible life" exercise (www.happysmarts.com/book/exercises/best_possible_life). The exercise is obviously designed to help you find and nurture the second habit of the highly happy: pursuing flow. So if you happen to be in the lucky position of already finding your work meaningful and enjoyable, you may wonder whether there is something else you could do instead, to enhance your happiness levels. There is. Or, to be more precise, there are *two* things you could do: exhibit self-compassion and express gratitude. Both, for reasons I will get to shortly, serve to mitigate the need for superiority and thereby enhance happiness levels.

Self-Compassion: A Practice for When Things Aren't Going Well

Imagine that you work as a salesperson and that you failed to achieve your target last month. Or imagine that you are a student and failed to get a good grade. Or maybe you are a parent and were too harsh on your kid. In such situations, as Professor Kristin Neff, a colleague of mine at the University of Texas at Austin, argues, most of us are prone to beating ourselves up. Professor Neff finds that we are often our own worst enemies when we haven't achieved as much as, or behaved like, we wanted to.* As a result, our self-esteem suffers, leading us to chase superiority because, as I mentioned in the previous chapter, we are more likely to seek superiority when we feel insecure.

One reason we engage in negative self-talk is because we feel that it will motivate us to do better next time. However, in reality, the negative self-talk just gets us down, makes us feel miserable, and actually demotivates us. A far better way to deal with failures, according to Professor Neff, is to exhibit what she calls *self-compassion*. In brief, self-compassion involves three components:

1. Self-kindness
2. Common humanity
3. Mindfulness

The first component (self-kindness) involves treating yourself as you would a close friend or family member. One way to exhibit self-kindness is to think of what you would say to someone else who comes to you for

---

* I interviewed Kristin Neff on the topic of self-compassion for my Coursera course. You can watch excerpts from this interview at https://www.coursera.org/learn/happiness/lecture/8OmBu/week-2-video-10-a-practice-for-when-things-are-not-going-well-self-compassion.

support after experiencing a failure, and saying those very things to yourself. As you can imagine, self-kindness makes you feel less insecure. The second component, common humanity, involves recognizing that failures are a part of life and that everyone experiences them. That is, it involves realizing that failure is an unavoidable part of being human and that nobody is perfect. This component also makes one feel less insecure by affirming that one is not alone or separate from others. The final component is mindfulness, which involves being fully aware of what one is experiencing without denying or rejecting it, but in a kind and compassionate way. As we will see closer to the end of this book, perhaps somewhat counterintuitively, being mindful *lowers* stress levels and improves positivity, thereby making one less insecure. Because all three components of self-compassion make one feel more secure, they mitigate the propensity to chase superiority. On the book's website you will find more details on what self-compassion is and how to practice it (www.happysmarts.com/book/exercises/self-compassion).

Expressing Gratitude: A Practice for When Things Are Going Well

Another exercise that's equally potent in lowering the propensity to chase superiority is expressing gratitude. This is an exercise for when things are going well. Although we are less likely to chase superiority when we aren't feeling insecure, we can nevertheless reinforce the need for superiority even when things are going well—for example, by feeling hubristic pride and taking all credit for the success.

Let's say that you just got promoted. Or that you just aced a test. Normally, most of us can't help but feel a tinge of hubristic pride when this happens. Even if we are modest when talking about the success to others, we are usually patting ourselves on the back in private, telling ourselves, "Raj, there's no one quite like you!" or "Raj, you are the best; no one but you could have done it!" This might feel good in the moment, but in the long run, what it does is strengthen our need for superiority.

Now, instead of patting ourselves on the back and feeling hubristic pride—or in addition to doing that—imagine doing something else. Imagine that you think of someone else who played a critical part in your success. Maybe it was the tireless work staff who kept the coffee flowing—without which you couldn't have pulled all those all-nighters that led to the success. Or maybe it was your spouse who took care of the kids while you were pulling long hours at work. You could even go back in time and think of all the people who may have played an indirect role in your success, such as your high school teacher who encouraged you to aim high, or your grandma who had faith in you when everyone else had doubts.

The gratitude exercise hinges on the idea that no one achieves anything just by themselves. All of us, at one point or another, had to depend on others. And the realization that you could not have achieved what you did without support from others is typically accompanied by a sense of gratitude for those who helped you. Notice what happens when you feel grateful. You think of those who helped you in positive terms. This, in turn, makes you feel connected to them. As a result, you might pick up the phone to talk to them; or you might talk to them more pleasantly and listen to them more intently when you do talk to them. Or, you might say good things about them to someone else. And by doing these things, you will set in motion a chain of events that will strengthen the bond between the two of you.

There are several studies that show that expressing gratitude strengthens social bonds. One study showed that freshmen sorority sisters who expressed gratitude to their seniors for giving them a gift were more likely to subsequently befriend them. Another study showed that, compared with materialistic youth, grateful youth were more likely to flourish—they had better grades, higher life satisfaction, a richer social life, and lower levels of envy and depression. So one way to think of gratitude is that it acts as a bridge between hubristic pride and connection. It takes you from a self-centered positive feeling—the feeling of hubristic pride—to an *other-centered* positive feeling: the feeling of love or connection. In this way, it takes you away from a type of happiness that doesn't typically last very long to one that has the potential to last longer. And in that process, it helps mitigate the need for superiority by making you feel less isolated and more connected with others.

But that's not the only reason why gratitude helps boost happiness levels. It also helps in a number of other ways, which is why Professor Sonja Lyubomirsky of the University of California at Riverside calls gratitude a "meta-strategy"—meaning it helps boost happiness in many different ways.* This is why I have chosen expressing gratitude as the exercise for this chapter. As with all the other exercises in this book, you can look up the detailed instructions for the "expressing gratitude" exercise on the book's website (www.happysmarts.com/book/exercises/expressing_gratitude) and the abridged instructions in the appendix for this chapter.

---

* You can catch my interview with Professor Lyubomirsky in which she lists her reasons for calling gratitude a meta-strategy at https://www.coursera.org/learn/happiness/lecture/Tx8Zm/week-2-video-13-summary-of-week-2.

Chapter 3A

THE THIRD DEADLY HAPPINESS "SIN": DESPERATION FOR LOVE

I n a movie that I cut school to watch as a teenager (sorry, Mom, I'll never do it again!), a pregnant lady, whose innocent and peace-loving husband is killed by an evil villain, gives birth to a child whom she raises to be tough and hardy. She loves the child dearly but subjects him to various kinds of harsh treatment, including dangling him in cold rain, denying him food, and letting him cry himself to sleep—all with the purpose of turning him into a sturdy, independent lad. The ploy works! The boy, who grows up to be a spitting image of his dad (a common occurrence in Bollywood movies), avenges his father's death by bashing the villain's head against a rock, and everyone lives happily thereafter.

The movie capitalizes on a seemingly prevalent lay belief, namely, that adversity—even extreme adversity—is good for kids. This belief was prevalent in the early part of the twentieth century, particularly among a breed of psychologists called behaviorists. Indeed, the behaviorists believed that showering love and affection on infants by cuddling, nuzzling, or holding them would make them weak, lazy, and overly dependent. We now know that the behaviorists were wrong. To grow up into healthy adults, children need love and nurturance as much as they need food and nutrients. Of course, most parents (except the ones in bad movies) know this instinctively, but there was little scientific support for this theory until Harry

Harlow, a newly minted PhD from Stanford University, joined the faculty at the University of Wisconsin in 1930.

Harlow's Monkeys

Harlow didn't set out trying to prove that love and nurturance are just as important as food and nutrients for human beings. He was out to prove something else, namely, that living beings aren't the machines that the behaviorists had made them out to be. But that's a story for another day. In order to test his thesis about love, Harlow needed monkeys, and back in the 1940s, monkeys were in short supply in the United States. So Harlow did something that had never been done before: he raised his *own* monkeys by letting the adult monkeys in his lab mate with one another. Harlow understandably wished to raise healthy monkeys, and in order to improve the odds of doing so, he had the baby monkeys separated from their mothers soon after they were born. These baby monkeys were placed in separate cages so as to prevent the spread of disease. Thus, ironically, it was with the aim of raising healthy monkeys that Harlow denied the babies the opportunity to be cuddled and held by their mothers.

As you may have guessed, contrary to what Harlow and his team expected, the lab monkeys grew up to be psychologically damaged. Healthy monkeys, when put in a cage together, are curious about one another and soon start to play—much the way healthy human infants do. Further, after spending time together, healthy monkeys form bonds with one another and resist separation. But the monkeys raised in Harlow's lab were different. When put in a cage, they were either uninterested in others or openly hostile. They were particularly averse to being touched by other monkeys, or, for that matter, by the researchers; if someone got too close, they became so aggressive as to cause bodily harm. Many of the monkeys also routinely inflicted injury on themselves—by chewing on their own limbs. Several of them also rocked themselves incessantly and stared emptily into space with indifference. Later, René Spitz, a researcher working with orphaned humans, would find that human infants deprived of love and nurturance also exhibit similar symptoms.

Initially, Harlow and his team didn't realize that they were raising mentally unhealthy monkeys. It took an outsider in the form of John Bowlby, a British psychoanalyst, to notice it. But once he did get the suggestion from

Bowlby, Harlow began investigating the role that love plays in the growth and development of monkeys.

The Need for Love in Primates

In one of their best-known experiments, Harlow and his team directly pitted the need for love and nurturance against the need for food and nutrients. In this experiment, a bunch of baby rhesus monkeys were separated from their mothers soon after birth. These monkeys were then individually closeted in a cage with two inanimate figures, both roughly the size of an adult monkey. These inanimate figures were designed to be the baby monkeys' "surrogate mothers," and came complete with a mouth, eyes, and a body. However, as shown in the figure below, while one of the surrogate mothers was layered with foam and cloth, making it soft and cuddly, the other was made out of wire mesh, and was thus harsh to the touch.

To test the relative importance of love versus food, Harlow and his students did something very clever. For half the baby monkeys, they placed

The cloth and wire-mesh mother figures in Harlow's experiments

the source of food (a bottle with milk) in the body of the wire mesh figure, while for the other half, they placed this food source in the body of the foam and cloth figure. Thus, while the foam-and-cloth figure was the supplier of love and nurturance—or "contact comfort," as Harlow called it—for all baby monkeys and the supplier of food for half of them, the wire-mesh figure was the supplier of food for the rest of them. Harlow hypothesized that the need for contact comfort—the desire to cuddle and nuzzle with a soft and nurturing figure—was just as deep-seated a need as the desire for food. As such, he predicted that the baby monkeys would spend a signifi-cant amount of time with the cloth-and-foam figure *even when this figure did not carry the milk bottle*. (Behaviorists, on the other hand, would have predicted that the monkeys would spend *all* their time with the figure that carried the milk—even if it was the wire-mesh figure—because this figure held the rewarding stimulus: the milk).

Findings proved Harlow right. But even he could not have fathomed how intense the need for love and nurturance was for the baby monkeys. When the wire-mesh figure carried the milk bottle, the baby monkeys spent just enough time to derive the necessary nutrients from it and spent the rest of the time with the foam-and-cloth figure. In a typical twenty-four-hour period, the babies spent barely one hour with the wire-mesh figure, and *all* this time was spent sucking on the milk bottle; by contrast, they spent about eighteen hours with the foam-and-cloth figure. (The rest of the time in the twenty-four-hour period was spent elsewhere in the cage.) And when the foam-and-cloth figure carried the milk bottle, the baby monkeys spent absolutely *no* time with the wire-mesh figure. Thus, con-trary to what the behaviorists had proposed, namely, that babies develop attachment to mother figures solely because the mother figures are the source of food, Harlow's findings showed that attachments are based more on the need for love and nurturance than on the need for food.

In follow-up experiments, Harlow and his team provided additional evidence in support of their theory. In one experiment, baby monkeys were exposed to a threatening object, one that made loud clattering noises and resembled an aggressive adult monkey. When this object was introduced into the cage, the baby monkeys, which were naturally distressed, always sought out the cloth-and-foam (and not the wire-mesh) figure to cling to. In another experiment, Harlow and his team found that young monkeys reared with real (live) mothers and playmates easily learned to play and socialize with other young monkeys later in life. Those raised with the foam-and-cloth mothers were slower, but seemed to catch up socially by about a year. By contrast, monkeys raised with only the wire-mesh mothers became socially incompetent, and when older, were often unsuccessful at mating. Further, these unsocial adult females that did have babies were neglectful of them, indicating that the monkeys' capacity for love and nurturance depended on whether they themselves had been sufficiently loved and nurtured as babies.

The Need for Connection in Humans

Although Harlow's findings wouldn't surprise us now, they were surprising to the behaviorists at that time. They wondered whether the results would generalize to humans. Love may be critical for monkeys, but is it critical for humans?

For understandable reasons, replicating Harlow's results with human babies isn't possible. (Imagine separating human babies from their mothers for the sake of an experiment!) However, because some human babies are, for unfortunate reasons, separated from their parents at birth, we sometimes get a peek at how such separation affects their psychological well-being. René Spitz was one of the pioneers in documenting the psychological damage that being denied love does to human babies. In a series of videos that are easily available online, he documented the typical behaviors that infants separated from their mothers exhibit. He found that the behaviors such infants exhibit are chillingly similar to those that the baby monkeys in Harlow's studies did—including unfriendliness, listlessness, and a lack of curiosity.

Spitz's findings confirmed what John Bowlby—the British psychoanalyst we encountered earlier—had found when comparing the childhood experiences and psychological profiles of forty-four juvenile thieves with a control group of forty-four other "healthy" adolescents. Bowlby found that the juveniles were more likely to have been separated from their mothers for more than six months before they had turned five, and that they were also much more likely to exhibit "affectionlessness" or "detachment."

The need for love and nurturance is arguably at its most intense during infancy—for understandable reasons. Human babies are, after all, among the most helpless of any living things. But the desire for love and nurturance does not vanish in later years. As several scholars have noted, we continue to have an intense desire to develop and maintain relationships with others even as adolescents and adults. Indeed, the desire for romantic love is among the most defining features of the human experience, which is why it is the subject of so many books, movies, and folktales. The intensity of our desire for love is perhaps best captured in a Greek myth according to which, once upon a time, gods and humans existed together. Humans had four arms, four legs, and two heads at that time, and grew to be increasingly powerful as time went on. One day, the gods decided that the humans were getting too powerful, and seeking to wrest back control from them, cut the humans in half. Each human now had two arms, two legs, and one head. From that time onward, the main point of human existence became the search for the other half that would make them whole again. The search for romantic love, according to this myth, is nothing short of a quest to become complete and whole once more.

If you have ever been in love, you know that the Greek myth is onto something. When you are in love, it feels like nothing is more important than to be in close proximity to your partner. And indeed, at the height of passionate love, you feel that nothing and no one can stop you from wanting to merge with your partner. And when that feeling is reciprocated, no challenge seems insurmountable. Being in love, in other words, feels positive, potent, and powerful all at once, and unsurprisingly, therefore, is universally rated as one of our most cherished experiences.

The Many Manifestations of the Need for Connection

A central feature of human existence, then, is that of seeking emotional connection with others. The desire for connection is often exhibited in interesting ways, as demonstrated in an early study by a psychologist named Solomon Asch. In this study, participants were shown a line of a certain length (such as the "target line" below), and asked to judge which among three other lines is the closest in length to the target line.

Target line: _____

Options: a) _____   b) _____   c) _____

In this example, line b is clearly closest in length to the target line, and few people would, under normal circumstances, fail to identify it as the correct option. But under social pressure, people are prone to pick the wrong answer—even if they realize at some level that the answer is wrong. Consider the following scenario as an illustration. Imagine that you have signed up for a study about "visual perception." As you enter the lab, you see that there are six other participants in the study. The experimenter introduces the study as an exploration of people's ability to judge line lengths and then asks participants to take part in a task similar to the one I just described. Specifically, the experimenter projects four lines—one target line and three options—onto a screen, and asks the other six participants to voice their opinion before turning to you. Now imagine that *all* of these other participants pick option c as their answer. That is, imagine that all of the other participants choose the option that is patently wrong. Now it's your turn to answer.

What would you do? Would you pick the option that you privately know to be the correct one (option b)? Or would you pick the option that everyone else seems to think is the correct one (option c)? Most people believe they would pick the correct answer (option b)—even if others have picked a different answer. But in fact, Asch found that most people pick the answer that the others have picked. (As you might have guessed, Asch hired confederates—people who were paid to act like real participants—to play the role of the "other participants" in his study.) Asch's findings, which have since been replicated in several other experiments, suggest that people have a "herd mentality": we feel compelled to agree with others even if we know that they are wrong. The pressure to conform to others is driven, in large part, by the desire to form and maintain bonds with others.

In a set of experiments that my coauthor Kim Corfman and I conducted, we took a leaf out of Asch's book and paired real participants with a confederate. We asked each participant-confederate pair to watch three short videos. One set of pairs watched videos that were entertaining, while another set watched videos that were boring. In the course of watching these videos, the confederates in half the cases behaved in a way that conformed to the participants' reactions to the videos. For example, when it was clear that the participants were enjoying the videos, the confederates made statements or gestures that suggested they too were enjoying them. In the rest of the cases, the confederates behaved in a way that disconfirmed the participants' reactions to the videos. For example, they made statements or gestures that suggested they found the entertaining videos to be boring.

Our objective was to get at the following question: what would have a bigger impact on participants' enjoyment from participating in the experiment—the quality of the videos they were watching or the extent of agreement with the confederates about the videos? One would think that the quality of the videos—that is, whether the videos were entertaining or boring—would be the primary driver of enjoyment, but our results showed this wasn't the case. We found that perceived agreement with the confederate was a much more potent driver of enjoyment. So for instance, viewing the boring videos was more enjoyable when the confederate agreed with them (and seemed to find the videos to be boring) than was viewing the entertaining videos when the confederate disagreed with them (and seemed to find the videos to be boring).

These findings suggest that we care a lot more about whether others agree or disagree with us than we do about the "objective" quality of our shared experiences. An important reason why we care so much about whether others agree with us, it turned out in our studies, is because of our deep-seated desire to forge a bond with others. The more we believe that others agree with us, the better we feel are our chances of forging a bond with them, and this makes us feel good. When others disagree with us, we feel pessimistic about forging a bond with them, and this makes us feel sad.

Perhaps the most powerful evidence in support of the need for connection comes from findings on loneliness. John Cacioppo, a researcher who has spent a considerable part of his impressive career exploring the effects of feeling psychologically separated from others, finds that feeling lonely is perhaps the single biggest determinant of a host of psychological and physiological illnesses, ranging from depression and insomnia to obesity and diabetes. Interestingly, it is perceived (and not actual) loneliness that matters, and given its significance for happiness, I have included a loneliness scale at the end of this chapter. You can fill it out if you are curious about your perceived loneliness levels.

Connection Increases Happiness

Numerous studies confirm that a sense of connection with others is one of our most important needs. One study explored what differentiated the top 10 percent of the happiest people from the rest of the participants in the study. They found that *every single one* in the happiest group had at least one intimate relationship. This finding indicates that if you wish to belong to the very happiest group, having a strong relationship is not a luxury—it's a necessity. Similar results were obtained in another, more exhaustive, study that tracked 268 men from entering college in 1938 to the late 2000s. Results showed that the strength of social relationships was the *only* characteristic that distinguished the happiest 10 percent from the rest. In another study, participants were asked to recall the activities in which they had engaged on the previous day and to report how happy they had felt while engaging in those activities. Results showed that, of the twenty-five categories of activities (like eating, commuting, etc.), the *top two* happiest categories involved human connection—"intimate relations" and "socializing." Findings from another study with 1,600 Harvard students revealed a correlation of 0.7—an incredibly high number—between connectedness and happiness.

If being in relationships is important for happiness, then feeling isolated should be associated with the opposite of happiness: depression. And that's indeed what findings show. As already mentioned, Cacioppo and his colleagues have found that feeling lonely triggers a host of psychological and physiological problems. This is not surprising, because findings show that being socially excluded activates the same parts of the brain that get activated when we are physically hurt. In a study that documented this, participants were invited to play a computer game called "cyber ball" in which they were led to believe that they were partnering with two other participants. In reality, participants were partnered with a computer program that was rigged. The game involved passing a ball to one of the other participants in the study. For one set of participants, the game was a pleasant experience: they got the ball passed to them just as often as it was to the two other "participants." For the other set of participants, however, the game was far less pleasant: once they passed the ball to one of the other participants, the ball never got back to them. Thus, participants in this condition were made to feel isolated. Brain scans of these participants revealed that the experience of being isolated activates the same parts of the brain that being physically hurt does.

The Third Deadly Happiness Sin

Long story short, the need for love and connection—or, as some psychologists call it, *the need to belong*—is not just an important need for human beings, it is a critical need. Armed with this insight, most people are likely to conclude that "if love and connection are so critical to being happy, then I better grab as much love as I possibly can!"

And judging by how prevalent the need to be loved is, this is precisely how many of us approach relationships; we are often desperate for love and connection. But as critical as being loved is for being happy, the pursuit of this desire is also the cause of much misery and suffering. This is because there is a thin line separating a *healthy* desire for love and connection and an unhealthy desire for it. A healthy desire for connection is manifested in what researchers call a "secure attachment" style. Those who exhibit secure attachment strike a fine balance between seeking love and connection and not being desperate for it. As such, they are comfortable seeking intimacy and not feeling threatened by others' attempts at seeking it. Those who exhibit an unhealthy desire for connection, by contrast, either become desperate in their desire for intimacy—a tendency that may be referred to as "neediness"—or feel threatened when others seek intimacy with them—a tendency that may be called "avoidance." In other words, an unhealthy attitude toward relationships is exhibited through one of two extremes: neediness or avoidance. Neediness and avoidance may appear to be the opposite ends of the spectrum—and in terms of behavior, they are—but they share an important commonality: they are both rooted in deep-seated insecurities about relationships. This is why *desperation for love*, which is rooted in insecurities about relationships and is the source of both neediness and avoidance, is the third deadly happiness sin.

———

It is through a series of studies conducted by Mary Ainsworth (a Canadian psychologist and a student of John Bowlby's) and her colleagues in the 1970s and '80s that we know that both neediness and avoidance are rooted in insecurities about relationships. Ainsworth and her colleagues found that it is the babies who feel insecure about their worthiness because they aren't given enough, or the right type of, love and nurturance by their parents who exhibit either neediness or avoidance. By contrast, babies who feel secure about their worthiness exhibit secure attachment. Later, two researchers—Cindy Hazan and Phillip Shaver—built on Ainsworth's findings to show that the attachment tendencies we exhibit as infants and children carry over into our adulthood.

The fact that neediness and avoidance are triggered by our childhood experiences and subsequently affect our behaviors as adults might appear to suggest that it is impossible to overcome the attachment styles we develop as infants. However, as we will see shortly, this is not the case; through the use of some strategies, we can overcome neediness and avoidance and steer ourselves toward a secure attachment style. But before I get to those strategies, it will be useful to discuss why neither neediness nor avoidance is good for happiness.

Why Neediness and Avoidance Lower Happiness Levels

Let's start with the findings on the unhappiness of the needy. Results from one study involving ninety-nine older adults and ninety-six younger adults from the same community showed that, across both age groups, needy adults were far less happy than the secure. Results from another study showed that needy individuals are much more likely to suffer from depression and anxiety than secure dependents.

Why are the needy less happy than the secure?

There are several reasons for this. Being needy, as many of us have discovered the hard way, is not an attractive trait. In other words, you turn people off when you are needy. One reason for this is that the needy are often too easily available and people are programmed to devalue things that are easily available. Another reason why neediness lowers happiness levels is because it triggers loneliness—perhaps because people tend to avoid the needy. This, in turn, triggers a vicious cycle, whereby the needy become even more desperate for connection. Yet another reason why neediness lowers happiness is because of the story you tell your-self about who you are when you are needy. The story you tell yourself is, "I am incomplete, fragmented, and broken, and I desperately need a companion to complete me." An important subtext of this story is this: "I feel insecure about what I have to offer and about my overall attrac-tiveness to others. I fear that I am undeserving and unworthy of others' love and attention." As you can tell, such a story is not conducive to happiness.

If neediness lowers happiness, one might assume that the opposite of neediness—avoidance—would enhance happiness. But that's not the case. The discomfort that avoidants feel with intimacy spoils the quality of their relationships. This is a problem that avoidants face both in romantic and in workplace settings. For instance, avoidants experience lower job satisfac-tion than do either the needy or the secure. Avoidants are also prone to being less satisfied with the help they get from others, and this in turn makes them less likely to engage in healthy collaboration with others. Un-surprisingly, therefore, avoidants aren't very effective as leaders. A final rea-son why being avoidant lowers happiness is because, like neediness, it leads to loneliness. Although avoidants view themselves as strong and indepen-dent, it turns out that this self-view is mostly a façade. At a deeper level, avoidants too are just as eager for love and connection as the needy. But unlike the needy, they want *others* to take the initiative to connect with them. And when such initiative from others isn't forthcoming—which is often the case, because being avoidant isn't endearing—the avoidants find themselves isolated and bereft of meaningful connections. Thus, just like the needy, avoidants too feel frustrated about not being in intimate rela-tionships, which lowers happiness.

Overcoming Neediness and Avoidance

If it's best to feel secure to feel happy, what can those who exhibit neediness or avoidance do? This is a particularly important question for those who may not have received sufficient love and nurturance as infants. Fortu-nately, it turns out that attachment style can be altered. One study showed that mere exposure to words that connote intimacy, such as "love" or "hugs," can at least temporarily boost feelings of relationship security. Similarly, another study showed that being asked to recall instances from one's childhood in which one experienced love and nurturance can, at least temporarily, make one feel more secure.

Of course, while the fact that there are ways to temporarily boost feelings of security is reassuring, what would be more desirable is a lasting impact. Are there strategies for sustaining a secure attachment style? It turns out there are. Before I get to these strategies, however, it may be useful for you to get a good idea of where you stand in terms of your attachment style. In the appendix to this chapter, you will find a short, twelve-item scale called "Experiences in Close Relationships" (or ECR). (You can also find the scale at www.happysmarts.com/book/scales/ECR.) Filling out the scale will give you a good idea of your current attachment style, and if it turns out that you have a tendency to be either needy or avoidant, it will help to practice the three strategies I discuss below.

Strategies for Promoting Secure Attachment

The first strategy for mitigating neediness is expressing gratitude. Findings show that those who express gratitude enjoy a richer social life. This may be because expressing gratitude leads to friendships and this can, in turn, mitigate neediness/avoidance and foster a sense of security. Researchers are calling gratitude the "find, remind, and bind" emotion. "Find," because gratitude allows one to find or identify people who could turn out, later, to be good friends or even life partners. (This happens because grateful people are, unsurprisingly, better liked by others.) "Remind," because it reminds us of our friends' or partners' strengths. And "bind" because, well, expressing gratitude helps bind the people in the relationship.

Another practice that has immense potential for mitigating neediness and avoidance is self-compassion. As you may recall, an important component of self-compassion is common humanity, which involves recognizing that *everyone* experiences hardships and failures. This recognition can help you feel more connected with others and therefore enhances feelings of security and mitigates both neediness and avoidance. Another way by which the practice of self-compassion enhances relationship security is by deactivating the "threat system," which is associated with feelings of insecurity and defensiveness, and activating instead the

"self-soothing" system, which is associated, among other things, with secure attachment.

In addition to expressing gratitude and self-compassion, there is yet
another strategy for fostering security and mitigating neediness/avoidance.
This strategy is rooted in the main focus of the next chapter, the third habit
of the highly happy: the need to love (and give).

LONELINESS SCALE

Instructions*

This scale, developed by Daniel W. Russell (1996), has twenty items and can be accessed on the book's website at www.happysmarts.com/loneliness _scale. Simply circle one of the four numbers next to each item to indicate how often you feel this way, 1 being "never" and 4 being "almost always." Note that about half the items (more on this shortly) are worded in a way that probes what you feel is missing from your life, while the other half probe what you feel is present.

	NEVER			ALMOST ALWAYS
1. How often do you feel that you are "in tune" with the people around you?	1	2	3	4
2. How often do you feel that you lack companionship?	1	2	3	4

---

* I've borrowed these instructions from J. T. Cacioppo and W. Patrick, *Loneliness: Human Nature and the Need for Social Connection* (New York: W. W. Norton & Company, 2008).

	NEVER			ALMOST ALWAYS
3. How often do you feel that there is no one you can turn to?	1	2	3	4
4. How often do you feel alone?	1	2	3	4
5. How often do you feel part of a group of friends?	1	2	3	4
6. How often do you feel that you have a lot in common with the people around you?	1	2	3	4
7. How often do you feel that you are no longer close to anyone?	1	2	3	4
8. How often do you feel that your interests and ideas are not shared by those around you?	1	2	3	4
9. How often do you feel outgoing and friendly?	1	2	3	4
10. How often do you feel close to people?	1	2	3	4
11. How often do you feel left out?	1	2	3	4
12. How often do you feel that your relationships with others are not meaningful?	1	2	3	4
13. How often do you feel that no one really knows you well?	1	2	3	4
14. How often do you feel isolated from others?	1	2	3	4
15. How often do you feel you can find companionship when you want it?	1	2	3	4
16. How often do you feel that there are people who really understand you?	1	2	3	4
17. How often do you feel shy?	1	2	3	4
18. How often do you feel that people are around you but not with you?	1	2	3	4
19. How often do you feel that there are people you can talk to?	1	2	3	4
20. How often do you feel that there are people you can turn to?	1	2	3	4

Scoring Scheme

Add your score on the following items first: 2, 3, 4, 7, 8, 11, 12, 13, 14, 17, 18; then reverse code your score (by subtracting it from 5) for the following items, and then add them up: 1, 5, 6, 9, 10, 15, 16, 19, 20. Then add up both sets of scores to arrive at your final loneliness score.

Score Interpretation

High loneliness is defined as scoring 44 or higher. Low loneliness is defined as scoring 28 or lower. A score of 33–39 implies middle of the spectrum (neither lonely nor not lonely).

ECR (EXPERIENCES IN CLOSE RELATIONSHIPS) SCALE AND SCORING SCHEME

├─────────────────────────┤

Instructions

The following statements, which form the ECR scale that can be accessed at www.happysmarts.com/ECR_scale, concern how you feel in romantic relationships. We are interested in how you generally experience relationships, not just in what is happening in a current relationship. Respond to each statement by indicating how much you agree or disagree with it. Mark your answer using the following rating scale:

	STRONGLY DISAGREE				STRONGLY AGREE		
1. It helps to turn to my romantic partner in times of need.	1	2	3	4	5	6	7
2. I need a lot of reassurance that I am loved by my partner.	1	2	3	4	5	6	7
3. I want to get close to my partner, but I keep pulling back.	1	2	3	4	5	6	7
4. I find that my partner(s) doesn't want to get as close as I would like.	1	2	3	4	5	6	7

	STRONGLY DISAGREE				STRONGLY AGREE		
5. I turn to my partner for many things, including comfort and reassurance.	1	2	3	4	5	6	7
6. My desire to be very close sometimes scares people away.	1	2	3	4	5	6	7
7. I try to avoid getting too close to my partner.	1	2	3	4	5	6	7
8. I do not often worry about being abandoned.	1	2	3	4	5	6	7
9. I usually discuss my problems and concerns with my partner.	1	2	3	4	5	6	7
10. I get frustrated if romantic partners are not available when I need them.	1	2	3	4	5	6	7
11. I am nervous when partners get too close to me.	1	2	3	4	5	6	7
12. I worry that romantic partners won't care about me as much as I care about them.	1	2	3	4	5	6	7

Scoring Scheme

Add up the scores for anxiety (or neediness) items: 2, 4, 6, 8 (reverse—that is, subtract from 8; e.g., if you gave yourself a 5 on item #8, your final score for that item would be 8 - 5 = 3 and so on.), 10, 12; add up the scores for the avoidance items: 1 (reverse), 3, 5 (reverse), 7, 9 (reverse), 11. If your score is over 25 on either, you have that tendency; if both scores are below 25, you are secure. Note that a small percentage of the population (about 5 percent) turns out to be both anxious (needy) and avoidant.

SELF-COMPASSION EXERCISE

Take out a sheet of paper and answer the following questions:

1. First, think about times when a close friend feels really bad about him- or herself or is really struggling in some way. How would you respond to your friend in this situation (especially when you're at your best)? Please write down what you typically do, what you say, and note the tone in which you typically talk to your friends.
2. Now think about times when you feel bad about yourself or are struggling. How do you typically respond to *yourself* in these situations? Please write down what you typically do, what you say, and note the tone in which you talk to yourself.
3. Did you notice a difference? If so, ask yourself why. What factors or fears come into play that lead you to treat yourself and others so differently?
4. Please write down how you think things might change if you responded to yourself in the same way you typically respond to a close friend when you're suffering.

Why not try treating yourself like a good friend and see what happens?

Chapter 3B

THE THIRD HABIT OF THE HIGHLY HAPPY: THE NEED TO LOVE (AND GIVE)

D uring a recent trip to Las Vegas, my wife and I got to experience something rather interesting. About an hour into the flight, we heard the following announcement by a flight attendant: "We apologize for the interruption, but if there are any doctors on board, could you please make your way to the front of the aircraft? Thank you!"

"Someone must be sick," my wife said to me, and she was right. A second announcement confirmed that a fellow passenger had had a heart attack, and that the crew was looking for someone on board with a medical background. Our flight must have been an unusual one, for there were as many as three doctors and two nurses on it. As I watched these good Samaritans head to the front of the aircraft to assist the patient, I couldn't help but feel a warm glow. I was heartened that so many people were willing to volunteer their services to help someone totally unknown to them.

This episode hinted at something that I had long suspected: people have an innate desire to help others. Of course, a cynic might argue that the doctors and nurses were willing to help only because they were bored, or because they wanted to be seen as heroes by other passengers. Fair enough. But consider this: had they decided not to help unless they were paid for it, they could have made a killing (both literally and figuratively). The fact that they not only volunteered, but did so with genuine enthusiasm, suggests that their actions were spontaneously well intentioned.

The question, of course, is why don't doctors and nurses—and more generally, most humans—exhibit altruistic behaviors on a more regular basis? For example, why don't doctors routinely treat their patients for free? Why don't educators offer their courses for free? And why don't authors publish their books for free?

These are interesting questions, and ones I will get to toward the end of the chapter. For now, let me turn to a more fundamental question: Which is a more accurate depiction of human nature: selfishness or selflessness? Are people hardwired for generosity or for greed?

Prosocial Behavior Makes Us Happy

Imagine that you are sauntering along from your parking garage to your office one day, and you stumble upon a $5 bill on the road. After looking around to make sure that no one has seen you spotting the bill, you do what any decent and self-respecting person would do: you swoop down on the bill and pocket it. You are, of course, pleased to have found free money and decide to give yourself a treat at the local Starbucks. As you are about to enter the coffee shop, however, you notice an intriguing headline in the local newspaper: "New study shows that spending money on others makes you happier!" The headline gives you pause and makes you ponder whether you'd indeed be happier if you spent the $5 on someone else rather than on yourself. After considering the idea for precisely three seconds, however, you dismiss it as unworthy of further consideration. A few minutes later, you are seen slurping an iced strawberry Frappuccino, a wide smile adorning your face. But even as you sip the drink, you can't help but wonder if the newspaper headline may have been right. Would you in fact have been happier had you spent the money on someone else rather than on yourself?

Most people think not. In a survey that posed a similar question, 63 percent (or close to two thirds) of respondents predicted that they would be happier if they spent the money on themselves than on someone else. And yet, thanks to some wonderful new research, we know that these respondents are wrong. You would, in fact, have been happier if you had spent the money on someone else.

Consider results from one study conducted at the University of British

Columbia.* As students were rushing to their classes at eight o'clock one morning, a researcher stopped them in their tracks and asked them if they'd be willing to participate in a study. If the student agreed, the researcher gave him (or her) an envelope that contained either a $5 or a $20 bill. One group of participants was instructed to spend the money on themselves, while the other group was instructed to spend the money on someone else. After confirming that the participants had understood these instructions, the researcher asked them to provide a phone number at which they could be reached. Later that evening, the researcher contacted the participants to check if they had followed the instructions. Most had. The researcher then posed the question of central interest: "How happy do you feel?"

Here's what they found. Contrary to what you might think, participants who received $20 weren't happier than those who received $5. (This may seem surprising at first, but remember that students who got $5 weren't aware that other students got $20, and both groups were, of course, pleased to receive free money.) More important, participants who spent the money on others had become significantly happier than those who spent the money on themselves. Specifically, compared with how happy they were that morning, the mood of those who spent money on someone else improved significantly compared with that of participants who spent it on themselves.

I know what you're thinking. You're wondering whether these results would have been obtained if the participants had spent *their own* money instead of the experimenter's. It stands to reason, of course, that it is easier to be happier after spending someone else's money than one's own. You may also be wondering about the validity of students' self-reported happiness levels. You may feel that participants in the "spend money on others" condition may have reported a higher level of happiness than they actually felt. Who, after all, would want to report being unhappy after being told to be nice to others—especially on someone else's dime? Another concern is whether the results would have been obtained if the participants had been hard up for money. Participants in the study were students from a prestigious

---

* I had the pleasure of interviewing Harvard professor Michael Norton on this and related studies, for my Coursera course. You can watch excerpts from it at https://www.coursera .org/learn/happiness/lecture/VKRt2/week-3-video-7-evidence-for-the-need-to-love-and -give.

university in a rich country. Would people from a poorer country—say, Uganda—have derived a similarly higher level of happiness after spending money on others?

These are valid questions of course, and unfortunately, not all of them can be answered through experiments. For example, it would be difficult to ask participants to donate some of their *own* money to charity in an experiment. (Participants would likely stage a walkout!) Still, to the extent that we can tell from surveys and findings, it appears that the link between prosociality and happiness is robust.

Consider the following—seemingly incredible—finding from a survey. Using data from a worldwide poll involving more than 200,000 respondents across 136 countries, researchers examined the correlation between altruism (specifically, whether the respondent had donated to charity in the past month) and self-reported life satisfaction. Results revealed that, in 120 of these 136 countries (which translates to 90 percent of countries worldwide), those who donated to charity reported a higher level of life satisfaction than those who didn't. The effect of charity on life satisfaction wasn't a trivial one either: it had the same effect as *doubling* household income! Given that most countries in this sample were poor (with a per capita GDP of less than $1,000 per year), these results suggest that altruism leads to happiness not just in rich countries, but even in poor ones.

The problem with this type of worldwide data is, of course, that one can't infer causality from it. It would be difficult to conclude from the data that altruism leads to happiness; it could just as easily be that happiness leads to altruism. (As you may remember from chapter 1B, happy people are more altruistic.) To circumvent this problem, researchers conducted a study using participants from only two countries—Canada and Uganda. Canada, of course, is one of the most developed nations in the world, with a per capita GDP of $51,964, making it the 15th richest nation in the world; Uganda, by contrast, ranks a lowly 176th—with a per capita GDP of a mere $657.37. Participants from both countries were asked to recall a recent event in which they had spent a small sum of money (about $20 Canadian or its Ugandan equivalent—about 10,000 shillings) either on themselves or on someone else. Then they were asked to recall how happy they had felt after doing so. Confirming results from other studies, findings revealed that participants who spent money on others were significantly happier than those who had spent it on themselves. Of course, Canadians and Ugandans differed on *what* they spent their money on; whereas Canadians generally spent it more on luxuries (e.g., a scarf), Ugandans spent it on necessities (e.g., medical supplies). However, in both countries, the overall pattern was the same: spending money on others made people happier.

Are We Hardwired for Altruism?

The positive effects of altruism on happiness have been documented across so many studies now that it would be difficult to argue that human beings are essentially or always selfish; it appears that we have at least a sliver of altruism in us. This desire to exhibit altruism—a desire that I refer to as *the need to love (and give)*—manifests itself in many different ways, including in the fondness for mollycoddling a cute puppy or for pinching the cheeks of a chubby-faced baby. Researchers refer to this type of desire, the desire to "gently hurt" cute animals or babies, as *cute aggression*. The reason for this seemingly bizarre desire is the yearning to express love—albeit in a somewhat warped way—for the object of one's affection.

If people have a need to love (and give), a few important questions arise. Is this need innate or is it socially conditioned? And if it is innate, is there evidence in support of it? For example, do toddlers who have not yet been socialized exhibit the need to love (and give)?

These are important questions because the answers to them have significant implications for what we can expect from our fellow humans. If the need to love is innate—and even toddlers exhibit it—it would mean that the potential we have for love and compassion is immense. By exposing people to the right set of messages, we could hope to build societies in which people exhibit never-before-seen levels of kindness and compassion. If, on the other hand, the need isn't innate but is "merely" socialized, it would be an uphill battle to enhance people's altruistic tendencies beyond what they already are.

Until recently, we had little data on whether, and to what extent, toddlers exhibit altruism. But researchers have recently explored this topic quite a bit, and the results from their studies are as heartening as they are surprising. In one study, twenty toddlers—all just shy of their second birthday—were introduced to a monkey puppet who, they were told, "liked treats." Soon afterward, an experimenter gave these toddlers treats—eight pieces of either Teddy Grahams or Goldfish crackers. Then the experimenter did one of the following: (1) found another treat and gave it to the monkey while the toddler watched, (2) found another treat, gave it to the toddler, and asked him or her to give it to the monkey, or (3) asked the toddler to share one of his or her own treats with the monkey. Independent observers rated the toddlers' happiness in these three scenarios.

If toddlers are more selfish than selfless, they should be happiest when they are given these snacks for personal consumption. If, on the other hand, toddlers are more generous than selfish, they should be happier when the monkey is given the snacks. Particularly strong evidence in support of generosity would be obtained if the toddlers derived greatest enjoyment when parting with their *own* stash of snacks, rather than when they were being generous with the experimenter's stash. And that's exactly what the researchers found: as can be seen from the figure below, toddlers were happy to be given the snacks, even happier when asked to feed the monkey from the experimenter's stash, and happiest when asked to give away from their own stash. The fact that "costly giving" evokes the greatest level of happiness suggests that children do not need much encouragement to be kind.

As it turns out, these are not the only findings that suggest that humans have an innate desire for altruism. Several other studies have confirmed it too.

"Costly giving" enhances happiness the most among young children

Why the Need to Love (and Give) Improves Happiness

If the need to love is a hardwired need, then it follows that being generous and kind is going to make us happy—and as we saw earlier, it does. But exactly why does being kind and generous make us happier?* One reason is that it takes the focus away from one's own worries and problems and toward *others'* worries and problems. Consider findings from one study in which researchers followed five women, all of whom had multiple sclerosis (MS), over a three-year period. These women were selected to act as peer supporters for other MS patients and were trained in providing compassionate care. They were instructed to call each of their patients for fifteen minutes each month for the three-year period. Findings showed that the benefit that these five women volunteers derived was seven times larger than that experienced by the patients they were serving!

Another reason why being kind and generous boosts happiness is because of reciprocity: people are, as you might expect, grateful when you are kind and generous to them, and this in turn boosts their happiness levels. In one study, researchers measured how helpful participants had been to others over a ten-week period, and also measured the extent to which their helpfulness generated gratitude in those that they had helped. Findings showed strong evidence that being generous elicits gratitude—via, for example, smiles and thank-yous—and that this, in turn, boosts happiness levels.

Yet another reason why being kind and generous boosts happiness is because, remarkably, it improves overall health. Findings show that, even after controlling for other factors like income and mobility, people who provide support to others report better overall physical health. In an interesting study that examined the link between giving and physical health, participants were given $10 and told that they could share as much or as little of it with another person who hadn't received any money. Results showed that the greater the amount of money the participants decided to give to the other person, the happier they felt. And not just that, the stress

---

* Watch excerpts from my interview with Professor Michael Norton on this topic at https:// www.coursera.org/learn/happiness/lecture/ABiEE/week-3-video-8-why-the-need-to-love -and-give-enhances-happiness.

levels of the participants who gave away more money—measured by the amount of cortisol in their saliva—was also lower.

The final and perhaps most compelling reason why being generous boosts happiness levels is because of the story we tell ourselves about who we are. When we are nice to others, we tell ourselves the story that we are kind and big-hearted—along the lines of "I am a king" or "I am a queen." In other words, when we help others, we feel more capable, effective, and *abundant.* What's truly remarkable about this is that we don't need to be extravagantly generous in order to feel abundant—even a small gesture of generosity will do. In one study, participants received an envelope with $1 and were asked to either donate the money or keep it for themselves. Findings showed that those who chose to donate the money felt wealthier even though, objectively speaking, those who donated the money were slightly poorer (because they had given their money away).

The Need to Love (and Give) as a Source of . . . *Success!*

Many of my students are surprised that generosity has such a big effect on happiness. (I have to confess that I too didn't realize it till I tried it out for myself.) What they find to be even more surprising, however, is its effects on *success.*

Most people think that to be successful—particularly in corporate settings—it is necessary to be mean and unethical. This is because we believe that being compassionate makes us "soft" and that being soft in the dog-eat-dog world of business is tantamount to rolling over and asking people to use you as a doormat. However, as Adam Grant, author of *Give and Take,* argues on the basis of an impressively large number of findings, it is those who are kind and generous—the "givers," as Grant calls them—who are most likely to succeed, *even in the world of business.* Consider the following remarkable finding: although people who earn more money are slightly more generous (unsurprisingly), those who are more generous earn significantly more. The economist Arthur Brooks has explored both directions of causality, and he finds that the effect of generosity on income is greater than the effect of income on generosity. In one study, he analyzed data from more than thirty thousand Americans, and found that, for every extra dollar earned, giving to charity went up by 14 cents (or 14 percent). By contrast—are you ready for this?—for every dollar donated, *income went up by as much as $3.75*—a whopping 375 percent!

There is evidence from several other sources that givers are more likely to succeed in their careers than "takers." (Takers, as the term suggests, are primarily interested in their own welfare and not in that of others.) In one study, researchers categorized people into one of two groups: "work altruists" or "work isolators." Work altruists are those who are there for others—colleagues, family, friends—when the others need them. Work isolators, on the other hand, are those who look for help from others. In other words, work altruists are the givers in organizations and provide as much as twenty times more support to others than do work isolators, who are the takers. Findings from the study showed that work altruists are *six times* as likely to be promoted as are work isolators. In summarizing these results, Shawn Achor, one of the researchers involved in the project and author of *The Happiness Advantage,* notes: "It turns out that giving feels better, does more for you, and provides greater returns in the long run, than getting ever does."

The Three Essential Rules for Giving

So far, I have reviewed evidence to suggest that being kind and generous is one of the most reliable sources of both happiness and success. Does this mean that the more you give, the happier and more successful you will be? The answer is clearly no, and the reason is that, although being kind and generous can make you happier and more successful (for all the reasons I discussed), it also takes energy and resources. So giving beyond a point is likely to burn you out. In other words, there *is* such a thing as being "generous to a fault." This is why, if you ever had to take care of someone 24/7, you were likely not a happy camper. One study showed that caretakers of Alzheimer's patients are three times as likely to be depressed as the average person. Being *too* loving and giving can also lower success. Although studies show, as I mentioned earlier, that givers are most likely to succeed in their careers, what's also true is that they are the *least* likely to succeed. This is not a contradiction. It turns out that there are two categories of givers, and only one of them rises to the top; the other category flounders.

Adam Grant uses the term "selfless givers" to refer to those who give so indiscriminately that they burn out and end up at the bottom, and the term "otherish givers" to refer to those who are smart about how they practice generosity and often rise to the top.* Otherish and selfless givers share an important common feature: they are both equally well intentioned. They both want to improve the welfare of others. However, the thing that differentiates them is that otherish givers aren't indiscriminately generous. They are better at identifying when, how much, how, and to whom to give. This might seem like a strike against otherish givers, but it really isn't. As Adam Grant points out, it is the otherish givers who have a bigger beneficial impact on others in the long run.

There are two main strategies that otherish givers use to keep themselves from burning out. The first strategy is that they *contain their cost of giving*. In other words, they try to maximize the positive effects of their generosity. If they find that four or five people need the same type of help (e.g., coaching in calculus), they address their needs at the same time, rather than individually. If they believe that someone else would be a better source of help, they put help seekers in touch with these other people. And so on. In sum, otherish givers are efficient in practicing their generosity.

The second strategy that otherish givers use is *value expansion*. In short, this strategy refers to managing one's own emotional resources in order to not burn out. So for instance, otherish givers take (authentic, not hubristic!) pride in the beneficial ripples that their actions generate. They also feel grateful to be in a position to be kind and generous, which energizes them to continue to give.

"Containing the cost of giving" and "value expansion" are such important elements in the otherish giver's arsenal that they could be considered part of the "essential rules for giving." To these rules, I would add a third: *get to see the impact of your giving*. Several findings confirm that those who get to witness the impact of their generosity derive the biggest boost in happiness. In one study, researchers handed out a $10 Starbucks gift card

---

* Although I wasn't able to interview Adam Grant himself on these topics (since he was busy writing his second book), he was kind enough to introduce me to Reb Rebele, one of his collaborators. You can watch my interview with Reb on a number of topics, including (a) findings on how otherish givers are more successful than takers, matchers, or selfless givers, and (b) the strategies that otherish givers use to enhance everyone's (including their own) well-being at https://www.coursera.org/learn/happiness/lecture/LWoDi/week-3-video-9 -the-rules-for-giving-when-does-giving-enhance-happiness-and.

to two groups of participants. One group was instructed to use the gift card for themselves, while another group was instructed to give it to someone else. Those asked to give the card were, in turn, split into two subgroups. One subgroup was asked to accompany the recipient of the gift card as they used it, while another was asked to not be present when the card was being used. Here's what the researchers found. Those asked to give the gift cards away were happier than those who were asked to use it themselves. (This finding shouldn't surprise you by now.) What's more interesting, those who were present when the gift card was used were happier than those who were not present. Why? Because seeing the impact of one's generosity on the beneficiary matters.

Why Isn't Generosity More Prevalent?

We have covered quite a bit of ground so far, so a quick recap is in order:

- We all have a deep-seated desire to be kind and generous—something that I call the need to love and give.
- Being loving and giving can boost not just our happiness, but also our chances of success—but only if done right (i.e., when we follow the three essential rules for giving).
- The three essential rules for giving are: (1) contain the cost of giving, (2) use value-enhancing strategies, and (3) get to see the impact of your giving.

Based on this recap, it would appear that the answer to a question I had raised earlier—which is a more accurate depiction of human nature: selfishness or selflessness?—is "both." To most people, it isn't news that we are capable of selfishness. We observe greed and self-centered behavior all the time. However, what we don't notice as much is how robust the need for kindness and generosity is. Most of us think of others, particularly strangers, as more selfish than selfless—even though one could quite easily argue that it is the other way around. Consider this. People routinely leave larger-than-expected tips for waiters and waitresses. (I'm sure you too are "guilty" of this "crime.") People open doors and smile at strangers all the time. At baggage carousels in airports around the world, people fall over themselves to retrieve someone else's bags. On the streets in every corner of the world, people routinely help disabled pedestrians cross the road. People appear to be particularly nice to children and the elderly. Just the other day, a store owner gave free lollipops to my kids. On subways and buses, it's not unusual for people to get up and offer their seats to the elderly. On airplanes, doctors and nurses jump to the assistance of sick passengers with unexpected alacrity. I could go on, but you get the point: there is little doubt that there's a *lot* of kindness and generosity in the world—much more so than you would expect if human nature were essentially selfish.

Why then is it that most of us believe greed and selfishness, rather than generosity or selflessness, to be a more accurate depiction of human nature? One reason has to do with what's covered in the media. As the saying goes, "if it bleeds, it leads"—meaning that negative stories are favored over positive ones in newspapers and on TV. Constant exposure to negative stories, as you can imagine, leaves us feeling there's more negativity in the world than there is positivity. But the fact that the media favor negative stories only begs another question: why do people prefer negative stories? The media, after all, cater to what people demand; if people preferred positive stories to negative ones, the media would be only too happy to oblige. The reason people prefer negative stories is that such stories are more relevant for increasing our chances of survival. Simply put, those who notice others' negative behaviors are more likely to survive than those who do not. Here's how Jonathan Haidt makes this point in *The Happiness Hypothesis*. Imagine that you were designing the mind of a fish. Would you have it respond just as strongly to opportunities (say, the opportunity to eat a yummy-looking fish) as you would to threats (say, a dangerous-looking fish)? No way! As Haidt puts it, "The cost of missing a cue that signals food is low; odds are there are other fish in the sea, and one mistake won't lead to starvation. The cost of missing the sign of a nearby predator, however, can be catastrophic."

In other words, it is more *adaptive* to pay greater attention to others' negative behaviors than to their positive ones. This may be why, as several researchers have documented, negative stimuli have a bigger psychological impact on us than do positive ones of equal magnitude—a phenomenon that some researchers have referred to as "bad is stronger than good." For instance—as we will see in more detail in a future chapter—it takes as many as five positive remarks from a significant other to compensate for one negative remark from them! Likewise, it takes three positive experiences to compensate for a negative one.

What all of this suggests is that we need to critically reexamine what many of us have taken to be an inalienable truth about human nature—that it is basically selfish and greedy. If we do, I believe that we will start noticing many more acts of selflessness and generosity than we might have imagined were possible. For instance, we would notice that many more doctors offer their services for free than we may have thought. (Check out www.doctors withoutborders.org.) We would also notice that lots and lots of top scholars—many more than we may have thought possible—offer their courses for free. (Check out www.coursera.org or www.edx.org; both are online platforms offering more than five thousand courses collectively on a variety of topics—from astronomy and calculus to dieting and, yes, happiness—absolutely free.) So the question I raised earlier—why don't doctors treat their patients for free? why don't educators offer their courses for free?—was really a trick one. It turns out that numerous doctors and educators—and indeed, people from a wide range of other professions, including lawyers and tax accountants—do routinely offer their services for free. It's just that most of us are too busy focusing on others' negative behaviors to notice their positive ones.

If the discussion in the previous section didn't convince you that there's more positivity in the world than most of us realize, that's okay. That wasn't the main point. Rather, the main point I wanted to make is this: *the need to love (and give) is a much more reliable determinant of happiness and success than is the need to be loved.* Of course, you may not be fully convinced of this point either. But I hope that reading about all of those studies has made you willing to at least experiment with generosity to assess whether it has a positive impact on your happiness and success.

That brings me to the third happiness exercise, one I call "creative altruism." This exercise is all about practicing generosity—but with strict adherence to the three essential rules for giving.

Practicing Generosity: The Creative Altruism Exercise

The "creative altruism" exercise, as the name suggests, is all about being creative and having fun while being kind and generous. The instructions for the exercise (available at www.happysmarts.com/book/exercise/creative_altruism; see abridged instructions in the appendix for this chapter) call for you to play an altruistic prank on someone. I use the word "prank" here deliberately. We have all played pranks as kids, and typically when we do, only we derive mirth from it; the victim of our prank is usually worse off. In the case of the creative altruism exercise, however, you won't be having your fun at someone else's expense; rather, both you and the "victim" of your prank will enjoy it.

There are two main "creative constraints" in this exercise. First, you will need to expend some resources (effort, time, money) in perpetrating your prank. So for example, merely watching a heartwarming act of kindness on YouTube won't suffice. Second, it is best if the "victim" of your prank is someone totally unknown to you—a complete stranger. The reason for this constraint is to put the findings on generosity to a stiffer test. Discovering that being kind and generous to those we already know makes us happy wouldn't be all that noteworthy. But if being kind and generous to a perfect stranger makes us happy, it would be noteworthy—particularly if we didn't expect to meet the stranger ever again, as it would suggest that we are hardwired for generosity.

If you are concerned that you can't think of any creative ways to be altruistic, don't fret. You'll find a long list of ideas on the book's website (www .happysmarts.com/book/exercises/creative_altruism). On the same site, you'll also find useful tips on how to go about perpetrating your act. Before you go to the website to read the instructions and embark on your creative altruism project, however, do remember to adhere to the "three essential rules for giving." First, make sure to contain your cost of giving. For example, if you want to distribute water to runners on a trail, make sure to position yourself at a place where you are likely to encounter enough runners. Second, be sure to use value-enhancing strategies. In the context of this exercise, this means: *don't forget to have fun.* As I have discovered from my students' experiences, this is a critical rule to follow because, if you aren't having fun doing the exercise, there's a good chance that you won't experience a boost in happiness. Finally, make sure that you see the impact of your generosity. For instance, if your idea is to distribute food to the homeless, stick around to receive feedback from them. There's nothing wrong with basking in the positivity you have generated. In fact, in many ways, it's an act of generosity to receive others' thanks gracefully.

Concluding Thoughts

Before concluding this chapter, I would be remiss if I did not touch on one question that I am sure is on your mind: given that I appear to be such a strong proponent of generosity and kindness, why am I not offering this book for free?

It's a long story, and there was a time when I did wish to offer the book for free, but as those who have published a book (or work for the publishing industry) know, offering a book for free after signing a publishing contract is not an option. So I have done what I believe to be the next best thing: I have offered the content I cover in this book for free on Coursera. The course is called "A Life of Happiness and Fulfillment" and can be accessed at www.coursera.org/course/happiness (or by simply Googling "Raj happiness course" and clicking on the first link that appears). I have also decided to use all of the advance that I received for the book to help defray the cost for those who can't afford to pay the full price. In short, if you (or someone you know) is interested in buying the book, but can't afford to pay the full price, you can go to the book's website (www.happysmarts.com/book) and click on the "pay it forward" link (or go to www.happysmarts.com/book/pay_it _forward). On the day that the book is launched, I will have deposited the advance I received for it into an account dedicated to this cause. On each occasion that someone orders my book through this link, the price of the book will be deducted from the account's balance. So long as there is a positive balance in the account, people will be able to buy the book for as little they want to offer (plus shipping and handling). Of course, needless to say, if some good Samaritan wishes to contribute to this cause so that someone else may be able to access the book for free, so much the better! (You can donate to this cause on the same—www.happysmarts.com/book/ pay_it_forward—link.) I am excited to find out how long the chain of paying it forward for this book lasts! But that's not the only thing I am excited about. I am also excited to find out if your happiness levels have improved since we last measured them. To find out, please fill out the "Satisfaction with Life Scale," which you will find on the next page, and, if you are up for it, share with us your score at www.happysmarts.com/book/scales/satisfaction _with_life/second-measurement.

THE SECOND HAPPINESS MEASUREMENT USING THE SATISFACTION WITH LIFE SCALE

For each of the five items below, circle a number from 1 through 7, where 1 = "strongly disagree" and 7 = "strongly agree." You can also fill out the scale online by going to www.happysmarts.com/book/scales/satisfaction_with _life/second-measurement. Once you have responded to all five items, total up your rating for each item to come up with your overall Satisfaction with Life score.

	STRONGLY DISAGREE				STRONGLY AGREE		
In most ways, my life is close to my ideal.	1	2	3	4	5	6	7
I am satisfied with my life.	1	2	3	4	5	6	7
The conditions of my life are excellent.	1	2	3	4	5	6	7
So far, I have gotten the important things I want in life.	1	2	3	4	5	6	7
If I could live my life over, I would change almost nothing.	1	2	3	4	5	6	7

Chapter 4A

THE FOURTH DEADLY HAPPINESS "SIN": BEING OVERLY CONTROLLING

├────────────────────────────────────┤

A t around seven o'clock on the morning of February 21, 2013, my good friend Jack was driving to his office in Amarillo, Texas. It was an unusually cold and frosty morning and the roads were covered with slick ice, so Jack was driving cautiously. As he got to the top of a bridge on I-40, Jack could see in the distance that the exit he would normally take was swarming with police cars. The cars appeared to have surrounded a pileup involving several vehicles. Believing that he would be unable to take that exit, or that he would find the going terribly slow if he did, Jack decided to take the exit closer to him. Jack was going slowly enough at 20 miles an hour to feel confident that he would be able to change lanes to make it to the exit. But as soon as he turned the wheel, the car started skidding and continued to skid until it came to a stop, now facing the *opposite* direction, on the exit ramp.

Thankfully, there were no cars behind Jack as they would likely have slammed into him, but Jack realized that he would need to quickly move the car out of harm's way. After inching the car over to the shoulder, Jack put the hazard lights on. He then did what any sensible person would: he called a towing company to get his car (and himself) dropped off at his office. To kill the twenty or so minutes that the towing company said it would take for them to arrive, Jack called his mother to catch up with her. He hadn't talked to her in a while. Jack remembers noticing the time on the dashboard when he made the call: 7:14 a.m. That's when things went horribly wrong.

Jack has a rather blurry recollection of what happened next, as is often the case with accidents. His last reliable memory is that of looking through his windshield at a car swerving on the highway. He recalls thinking that the car was going too fast, which it was. (The police would later note that the car was traveling at 63 mph—the speed at which the car's speedometer was stuck.) Perhaps because of its speed, the car did not skid to a halt as Jack's car had; instead, it rammed head-on into his car. The driver of that car was a teenager, who would later report that he had lost control while attempting to take the very exit that Jack had tried to take a little earlier. In one of many ironies of the day, the teenager would state that his only goal, after realizing that he had lost control of his car, had been to avoid running into Jack's car, and that he tried to do so by turning his wheel away from it. In the two or three seconds between noticing the teenager's car bearing down on him and the collision, Jack remembers thinking that these could be his last moments on earth. He also remembers feeling grateful that he was chatting with the person who mattered most to him in life: his mother.

Jack's car, which was totaled, was eventually found some forty feet from where he had parked it on the shoulder. It took Jack several months to get paid by the insurance company for a replacement car, and the medical and other costs associated with the accident would make a major dent in his pocket. That said, it could have been far worse. Although Jack sustained multiple injuries to various parts of his body, none were so debilitating that he needed to be hospitalized for more than a couple of days. Jack considers it a miracle that he escaped with nothing more than severe injuries. Still, he's not sure that he would call himself *lucky*—given all that he had done to avoid being in an accident. He had driven cautiously in the first place. Then once the car had skidded to a halt, he had called a towing company rather than continue to drive. He had also moved his car over to the shoulder when he could have easily tried to drive it to a nearby parking lot. And yet, in retrospect, he might have been better off making any of those decisions than the ones he did.

When I spoke to Jack shortly after the accident, the first thing he said to me was, *"If life wants to screw you over, man, it will find a way to!"*

How Do We Deal with Uncertainty?

In the grand scheme of things, what happened to Jack wasn't anywhere near as horrendous as a death in the family, the loss of a job, or being diagnosed with a fatal disease. But Jack's story captures, as well as any story can, a truth that many of us consider to be an essential fact of life: *you can't take life for granted*. Everything may be going swimmingly one moment and take a 180-degree turn the next. And because we recognize that randomness and unpredictability are a central part of life, we all learn to deal with uncertainty.

But exactly how do we deal with uncertainty?

To address this question, it will be useful to look at how we deal with the mother of all uncertainties: death. As the saying goes, only two things are certain in life: death and taxes. However, unlike taxes, about which we know a lot (or, if you are like me, know someone who knows a lot), we know very little about death. We do not know when or how we will die. Further, we don't know what will happen to us—or indeed, if anything of "us" will remain—after death. And as if this weren't enough, the days and months, and in some cases, years, leading up to death are often accompanied by pain, suffering, and blows to one's dignity. It's hardly surprising, therefore, that the fear of death is among our most intense and prevalent ones, second only to the fear of public speaking (go figure!). How we handle the fear of death can thus offer us insights into how we handle other kinds of uncertainties in life. And as luck would have it, we know quite a bit about how we deal with the fear of death, thanks to research in an area called terror management theory (TMT for short).

Aversion to Uncertainty

In brief, findings from TMT reveal that, when asked to contemplate death, people become even more deeply attached to their previously held values, ideals, and worldviews. Consider one of the earliest studies in the area. Participants in the study were municipal court judges from Tucson, Arizona. The most prominent ideal for judges, one would hope, is that of upholding the law. Consequently, the experimenters hypothesized that the judges would become even more attached to this ideal when reminded of death, and would therefore become more punitive toward lawbreakers. To test this hypothesis, half the judges were given a questionnaire that asked them to contemplate their own death, while the other half were not asked to do this. Then both sets of judges were asked to pass a verdict on a hypothetical case involving a prostitute soliciting customers. Specifically, the judges were asked to indicate the amount of bond money they would demand from the prostitute for her misdemeanor. Findings revealed that judges who had been reminded of death were quite harsh: they levied a bond fee of $455. In comparison, judges who had not been reminded of death were more lenient and levied a much smaller fee: only $50. (If you have just committed a misdemeanor, you'd better hope that you get a judge who hasn't been recently contemplating death!)

In another study, Christian students were asked to fill out a questionnaire that either reminded them of their own death or did not. These students were then presented with verbal descriptions of two fictitious figures. These verbal descriptions made it clear that while both figures shared similar personality traits (e.g., both were equally affable), they differed in terms of religious affiliation: one was a Christian while the other was a Jew. Participants were asked to form evaluative impressions of the two fictitious figures. Findings showed that, among participants who were not reminded of death, the two fictitious figures were rated equally positively. However, among participants reminded of death, the figure who shared their religious identity (the Christian) was rated more positively than the one with a different identity (the Jew).

Could the fear of death cause people not just to hold negative attitudes, but to actually *harm* others? To find out, participants in yet another study were either reminded of their death or not, and then asked, as part of "an unrelated food study," to pour out a quantity of extremely (painfully) hot sauce for another participant to sample. The "other participant" was described as someone who either shared their own political leanings or not. Hot sauce, it turns out, is a popular weapon of choice. People have used it to revolt against the police. Hot sauce has also been used by parents to punish their kids. (You don't want to imagine how.) It is precisely because of its prior use in harming others that the experimenters decided to use hot sauce in their study. (Of course, the experimenters could have used something more potent than hot sauce in their study but, understandably, they didn't want to cause serious harm to the participants.) Findings revealed that participants poured out about *twice* the amount of the hot sauce when the "other participant" had a different political leaning from their own.

What these studies show is that being reminded of death doesn't just make people harbor negative attitudes toward those who are different; it can provoke them to take negative action.

The Need for Control

Why does being reminded of death make people more hostile to those who are different? There are several interrelated reasons, but all of them share the following common feature: the fear of death evokes feelings of uncertainty and lack of control, and people feel threatened by this. So they gravitate toward those things (values, ideals, people, etc.) that make them feel more in control. In other words, the way we deal with the uncertainty of death is to try to wrest back control. And that's precisely how we deal with other types of uncertainty as well: by seeking to make things more certain.

Given that life is full of uncertainties—some glorious and others not— one would imagine that our lives would be one long sequence of multiple attempts at trying to stay in control of things. And that's more or less what findings show. For instance, as we will see next, there are at least half a dozen ways by which we seek to gain or retain control.

The Many Manifestations of the Need for External Control

When our daughter turned six months old, my wife and I wanted to send her to the same day care to which we were sending our son. However, at the time, that day care didn't have space for her. So we put her on the waiting list and, in the meantime, decided to send her to another day care. We didn't know much about this new day care, so we were naturally quite nervous. As it turned out, we needn't have worried. Our daughter adjusted well to this day care—after, of course, the first few heart-wrenching days. You would think that my wife and I would have been delighted at this turn of events. But we weren't. Why? Because we knew that, at some point in the near future, we'd have to decide whether to keep her at that new day care or move her to the one to which we had originally wanted to send her. The uncertainty about what to do was disturbing to us. So disturbing, in fact, that for the next few weeks, my wife and I would analyze, on a daily basis, the pros and cons of keeping her at her present day care versus moving her to the other one. We eventually did move her to the day care our son was going to, and as it turned out, it was an easy decision to make when the time came. (So all our agonizing was really unnecessary.)

One way in which the need for control manifests itself, then, is through the desire for clarity about decisions we are about to make. We want to know that our decisions will be the right ones—ones that will maximize our benefits and gains. A related way in which the need for control manifests itself is through the desire for clarity on the *reasons* for our decisions. Imagine that you have just taken an important exam for which you worked your backside off. You are now nervously awaiting the results, and will know whether you passed in a month. Meanwhile, your friend suggests going on vacation with her to Hawaii after the results of the exam are known. She wants to make arrangements for the vacation and wants you to commit right away. What would you do?

If you are like most people, you can think of several reasons why you'd like to go on vacation if you pass the exam. But what if you fail? Again, if you are like most people, you can think of at least a few good reasons—for example, take your mind off the exam, restore your self-belief, get reenergized to take the exam one more time—to go on vacation even if you fail. So you can think of reasons for going on vacation regardless of the outcome of the exam. And yet, if you are like most people, you can't bring yourself to *commit* to the vacation till you know the exact reasons—to celebrate or recuperate—for going. That is, you are likely to feel uncomfortable saying yes to your friend without having clarity on the reasons underlying your decision.

Yet another way in which we seek to gain control is by exhibiting over-confidence. As findings from numerous studies have revealed, most of us are much more confident about the validity of our opinions, attitudes, and judgments than we ought to be, particularly on difficult and complex topics. Consider a topic we encountered earlier: what happens to us after death. Do we get reincarnated as some of the Eastern religions believe? Or do we go to heaven or hell, as the Judeo-Christians believe? Or do we simply cease to exist, as atheists believe? It's difficult to know for sure. So even if we did subscribe to a particular belief (say, reincarnation), we ought to hold this belief with more doubt than confidence. In other words, we ought to admit that we do not have a good answer to what happens to us after death. But even though we may recognize this at some level (which is why we feel threatened when reminded of death), we appear unwilling to admit it at a more conscious level. Indeed, if anything, most of us come across as being even *more* sure about what happens to us after death than we do about far less complicated questions such as "Does advertising work?" or "What's the weather going to be like tomorrow?"

A final way in which the need for control manifests itself is through the *illusion of control*, which refers to the idea that we believe we wield greater control over outcomes than we actually do. In one study involving a lottery, participants were either given lottery tickets at random or allowed to choose their own. They were then given the opportunity to trade these tickets with other tickets that had a higher chance of winning. Findings showed that participants who had chosen their own tickets were more reluctant to trade their tickets. Why? Because they felt that the act of choosing their own tickets had magically given them the power to beat the objective odds. Illusion of control may be an important reason why most of us are less afraid of driving than we are of flying; when driving, we believe that we are more in control of our destiny than when sitting in an airplane that someone else is piloting—even though the objective odds of getting into an accident are far greater when driving than when flying.

Being in Control Enhances Happiness

If we have such a deep-seated desire for certainty and control, surely it must serve some important purpose? Several studies show it serves at least two important purposes. First, it helps us believe that we can shape outcomes and events to our liking. That is, the more in control we feel, the more efficacious we feel about achieving the outcomes we desire, and this sense of self-efficacy or competence boosts well-being. In other words, an important reason why being in control enhances happiness is because it makes us feel more competent, and this, in turn, evokes a sense that we are progressing toward the important goal of mastery.

Another reason why being in control feels good is because it makes us believe that we aren't under someone else's control. This sense of personal autonomy is, again, a very important goal for us. In an interesting study conducted at an old-age home that documented the importance of autonomy, one set of participants was given control over which plant to grow in their room and which movies to watch over the weekend. Another set of participants was not given control over either decision; rather, they were given a plant to take back to their room and were also told which movies they would get to watch over the weekend. Findings showed that, in the eighteen-month period following this event, only 15 percent of the participants in the former group had died, whereas *double* that proportion (30 percent) in the latter group had died. Before you get too alarmed about these seemingly astronomical rates of death in both groups, let me remind you that the study was done at an old-age home, with participants who were living out their winter years.

In another study, conducted on rats this time, experimenters gave the rats control over when they got to have coke—I am talking about the drug cocaine here, and not the sugary soft drink. One set of rats got to partake of the drug whenever they wanted: they just had to press a lever to get high. The other set did not get to choose when they got the drug; they were given the drug whenever the first set of rats chose to have it. Findings showed that the health of both sets of rats suffered; on average, these rats died earlier than a third set of rats that were not given the drug. But that wasn't the interesting finding. The interesting finding was that the first set of rats— those that had control over when they got to partake of the drug—had a lower mortality rate than the second set. What this tells you is that, if you intend to do drugs, you'd better have control over when you get to do it!

Being Overly Controlling, and Assessing Your Control-Seeking Tendency

Given that being in control serves the goals of both competence and autonomy, and given that it has all these beneficial effects on health and happiness, it wouldn't surprise anyone to know that we seek control. But the question is this: What is the impact of seeking control on happiness? Is the desire for control a good thing or a bad thing?

The answer, it turns out, is: it depends. Specifically, seeking control is a good thing—but only up to a point. Studies show that those with a higher need for control generally set loftier goals and also tend to achieve more. So to the extent that being successful is good for happiness, the desire for control could be a good thing. But what's also been found is that being *too* control-seeking—for example, constantly seeking to make things better, or obsessing about achieving outcomes—isn't a good thing. In other words, there seems to be a tipping point of control-seeking beyond which it lowers happiness levels. Or, put another way, being "overly control-seeking" is not good for happiness, which is why it is a deadly happiness sin.

There are several interesting reasons why being overly control-seeking lowers happiness. But before we get to these reasons, you may be curious about your control-seeking levels. At the end of this chapter there are two scales that will help you answer this question. The first is the "desirability of control" scale, developed by Professor Jerry Burger. The second is the "maximizer-satisficer" scale, developed by Professor Barry Schwartz and his colleagues. (You can find both scales on www.happysmarts.com/book/scales.) If you are unsure about where you stand in terms of control-seeking, you may choose to fill out these scales before continuing with this chapter.

Why Being Overly Controlling of Others Lowers Happiness

To understand the first reason why being overly controlling of others lowers happiness levels, ask yourself this question: how would it feel if you were under someone else's control? Imagine being married to someone overly controlling. Or worse yet, imagine being someone's slave. Being under someone else's control is no fun. This is partly because of our need for autonomy—the desire to be in charge of our own decisions. When someone controls us, they impinge on our autonomy. This desire for autonomy, it turns out, is particularly pronounced among two-year-olds and teenagers. But that's not to say that the rest of us are slouches at it: everyone, regardless of their age, dislikes being controlled. This is partly why our desire to do something goes up when we are restricted from doing it. Studies have shown, for example, that we are likely to buy a larger quantity of a product when there is a restriction on how much of it we can buy than when there is no such limit.

Psychological reactance, which is the term psychologists use to refer to the desire to do the things that are proscribed, explains why being overly controlling of others is not a good idea. When you seek to control others, they exhibit psychological reactance. For example, your attempt to control your spouse's diet may be met with an increased consumption of unhealthy food—just to spite you. Likewise, your attempt to control your kids to finish their homework may be met with grumpiness or other exhibitions of revolt. This is why, in relationships, you can either have control over others, or you can have their love—not both. (Except, of course, if you are Christian Grey, the protagonist in the best-selling novel *Fifty Shades of Grey*.) And because love is such a fundamental need for us, as we saw in chapter 3A, being overly controlling isn't good for happiness.

A related reason why being overly controlling of others lowers happiness is that it results in what the well-known motivational psychologist David McClelland calls "power stress," which is the tendency to get angry and frustrated when others don't behave the way you want them to. In one study, participants high and low in need for control were asked to deliver an extemporaneous speech to an audience consisting of two confederates. These confederates were planted by the experimenters to behave a certain way. For one set of participants, the confederates reacted in a supportive and pleasant manner, but to the other set, they reacted in a negative manner. Here's what the results showed: when the confederates were positive and supportive, both those high and low in need for control felt quite happy. This is not surprising, of course. When the confederates behaved negatively, however, a more interesting result emerged: those high in need for control found it to be far more disturbing, and ended up feeling significantly more negative, than those low in need for control. What this suggests is that, when you seek control over others, you set yourself up for negative feelings—anger, frustration, and disappointment—when they don't behave the way you want them to.

In addition to crowding out others' love and feeling frustrated, there's yet another reason being overly controlling of others lowers happiness. This reason has to do with the quality of decisions we make. It turns out that we make our best decisions when we are exposed to a diverse set of views and inputs. This is why it is important to surround oneself with people from a variety of backgrounds. This means that when we're overly controlling of others, our decision making suffers—because we drive away those who disagree with us and thus surround ourselves with only those who don't mind being controlled: the "yea-sayers."

Why Being Overly Controlling of Outcomes Lowers Happiness

Seeking to control others is one way of exercising control; the other way is seeking control over the external environment—the outcomes and events in one's life. Being overly controlling of outcomes, like being overly controlling of others, also lowers happiness levels for a variety of reasons. Before I get to these reasons, it's important to note that being overly controlling of outcomes is not the same as being keen on achieving the results one desires. Being really keen to achieve desirable outcomes, like getting into a good school or wanting to be in a great relationship, is a good thing. Findings show that having goals boosts happiness. You cross the line into being overly control-seeking when you become *obsessed* with achieving the desired outcomes. That is, you are overly controlling when the desire to achieve outcomes controls you, rather than you being in control of the desire to achieve outcomes.

Professor Robert Vallerand of the Université du Québec à Montréal uses the term "obsessive passion" to refer to being overly eager to achieve the desired outcomes. One reason why being obsessive about achieving outcomes lowers happiness is because, as we saw earlier, life is uncertain. As a result, being overly controlling of outcomes is tantamount to setting oneself up for disappointment. Findings from several studies confirm this. One study showed that being in an overcrowded room dampened the mood of participants higher in need for control to a greater extent because these high need-for-control participants felt that the room wasn't to their liking. Another study found that salespeople were more dissatisfied and performed worse when their level of control in interactions with the customer was lower than desired. Yet another study found that when people are put in situations in which they have lower control than they desire, their blood pressure shoots up. These findings indicate that when life doesn't go according to plan, which happens quite regularly of course, those high in need for control suffer more.

Another reason why being overly controlling of outcomes lowers happiness levels has to do with the quality of decisions we make. Findings show that those high in need for control are more likely to take risks and are also likely to become more superstitious in stressful situations than those low in need for control. For example, those high in desire for control express a higher willingness to drive more rashly than those low in desire for control. They are also more likely to fall prey to the illusion of control—which, you may remember, is to believe that one has more control over a situation than one actually does—and therefore, are likely to lose more money in gambling contexts involving real stakes. Yet another study showed that those high in desire for control are more likely to believe in superstitions (e.g., knocking on wood wards off bad luck) when put under stress.

A final reason why being overly controlling of outcomes lowers happiness is because when you want to control something so badly (say, get a particular job) that you are obsessed with that outcome, you are likely to sacrifice other things that make you happy. Confirming this, findings by Vallerand and his colleagues show that being obsessed about something has a negative impact not just on one's own physical and emotional health, but also on the health of one's relationships.

Can Being Out of Control Be Enjoyable?

Because being overly controlling lowers happiness, it would clearly be useful to figure out ways to, well, control one's control-seeking tendencies. One way to mitigate the desire for control is to learn to appreciate, rather than avoid, uncertainty. As we saw earlier, a big reason why we seek control is because we find uncertainty threatening.

But how could one possibly appreciate uncertainty? A good start is to recognize the importance of uncertainty for spicing up life. We all know, at some level, that uncertainty is important, which is why we avoid reading "spoiler alerts" before going to a movie and wouldn't watch the end of a recorded sporting event before watching the rest of it. And yet, although we instinctively recognize the positive role that uncertainty plays, we also feel threatened by it and believe that it dampens happiness. Consider findings from one study in which participants were told that they would soon be receiving a free dollar. One set of participants was asked to imagine that they would learn why they received the free dollar soon after getting it, while the other set was asked to imagine that they wouldn't learn the reason. Both sets were then asked to indicate how happy they would feel upon receiving the dollar. Findings showed that the first set—those who expected to know the reason for receiving the free dollar—anticipated feeling happier than the second. However, in fact, it was the reverse: those who didn't learn the reason for the free dollar were happier. Summarizing these findings, Todd Kashdan, author of the excellent book *Curious?*, notes that "what we think brings us pleasure"—in this case certainty and control—"is often *the exact opposite* of what does."

If uncertainty is important for happiness, why are we generally averse to it? One reason is that, although uncertainty is a good thing for positive events, it isn't for negative ones. Just as uncertainty can intensify positive feelings when things turn out well, it can intensify negative feelings when they turn out badly. Another reason, I suspect, has to do with how much in control we are of our life. As you may have discovered from personal experience, we can't appreciate uncertainty if we feel that our life is not in control. It's only when life is under control, at least with regard to important things like health, relationships, and financial security, that we are capable of appreciating uncertainty. It follows, therefore, that one way to get yourself to be in a position where you can appreciate uncertainty is to get your life under control first. A big part of this may involve not biting off more than you can chew. In particular, believing that you have enough time on your hands, it turns out, is super important. Most of us lead such fast-paced, frenetic lives that we are constantly under a time crunch. Findings show that the perception of time scarcity (as opposed to "time affluence") is a major happiness killer. Ironically, the more successful we are in life, the more time scarcity we feel. Findings from a recent study help shed light on why this is the case. Participants in this study were asked to play the role of consultants. While one set of students was paid 15 cents per minute for their time, the other half was paid $1.50. Later, once the project was over, these students were asked how stressed they had felt for time, and findings revealed that those who were paid the higher rate reported feeling more stressed. In other words, making more money made the students feel more stressed and squeezed for time.

This suggests that one way to feel less time scarce is to deemphasize the amount of money you make at work. Or at least desist from calculating your hourly wage rate. Another way to feel less time scarce, somewhat counterintuitively, is to engage in social service; findings show that those who engage in social work tend to feel more time abundant—something that you hopefully experienced through the third happiness exercise (creative altruism). Yet another way of mitigating perceptions of time scarcity is through the experience of awe. Findings show that exposure to awe-inducing images—whales, waterfalls, and the like—slows down perception of time, leading to time affluence.

All of these ways of inculcating time affluence should, at least in theory, enhance one's appreciation for uncertainty and thus help mitigate the desire for control. But of all the ways of mitigating the desire for control, the one that perhaps has the best potential is to take what one might call "internal control." Taking internal control means retaining the keys to one's happiness in one's own hands. It means never blaming anyone else for one's unhappiness.

How does one develop internal control and why does it mitigate the desire for external control? You'll have to read the next chapter to find out.

SCALE 1: DESIRABILITY OF CONTROL SCALE

├─────────────────────────────────┤

This scale has twenty items. (You can also fill out the scale on the book's website by going to www.happysmarts.com/book/scales/Desirability_of _control.) For each item, pick a number from 1 through 7, where:

1 = The statement does not apply to me at all.
2 = The statement usually does not apply to me.
3 = Most often, the statement does not apply.
4 = I am unsure about whether or not the statement applies to me, or it applies to me about half the time.
5 = The statement applies more often than not.
6 = The statement usually applies to me.
7 = The statement always applies to me.

Then total up your score, using the scoring scheme that follows the last item on the scale.

You can find the interpretation of your score on page 131.

1. I prefer a job where I have a lot of control over what I do and when I do it.
2. I enjoy political participation because I want to have as much of a say in running government as possible.
3. I try to avoid situations where someone else tells me what to do.
4. I would prefer to be a leader than a follower.
5. I enjoy being able to influence the actions of others.
6. I am careful to check everything on an automobile before I leave for a long trip.
7. Others usually know what is best for me.
8. I enjoy making my own decisions.
9. I enjoy having control over my own destiny.
10. I would rather someone else take over the leadership role when I'm involved in a group project.
11. I consider myself to be generally more capable of handling situations than others are.
12. I'd rather run my own business and make my own mistakes than listen to someone else's orders.
13. I like to get a good idea of what a job is all about before I begin.
14. When I see a problem, I prefer to do something about it rather than sit by and let it continue.
15. When it comes to orders, I would rather give them than receive them.
16. I wish I could push many of life's daily decisions off on someone else.
17. When driving, I try to avoid putting myself in a situation where I could be hurt by another person's mistake.
18. I prefer to avoid situations where someone else has to tell me what it is I should be doing.
19. There are many situations in which I would prefer only one choice rather than having to make a decision.
20. I like to wait and see if someone else is going to solve a problem so that I don't have to be bothered with it.

Scoring Scheme

1. Reverse answer values for items 7, 10, 16, 19, and 20, that is, 1 = 7, 2 = 6, etc.
2. Add all twenty answer values together.

INTERPRETING YOUR DESIRABILITY-OF-CONTROL SCORE

THE MEAN SCORE IS AROUND 100, WITH A STANDARD DEVIATION OF 10

A score of 80 or less	You are less control-seeking than 95% of people
A score of 90 or less	You are less control-seeking than 70% of people
A score between 90 and 110	Your control-seeking tendency is in the average (normal) range
A score of 110 or more	You are more control-seeking than 70% of people
A score of 120 or more	You are more control-seeking than 95% of people

SCALE 2: MAXIMIZER-SATISFICER SCALE

This scale has ten items. (You can also fill out the scale on the book's website by going to www.happysmarts.com/book/scales/Maximizer_satisficer.) For each item, give yourself a score from 1 to 7. 1 means you "completely disagree"; 2 means you "disagree," and so on. The highest number, 7, means you "completely agree."

Then total up your score, using the scoring scheme that follows the last item on the scale.

You can find the interpretation of your maximizer-satisficer score on the following page. (You will also find information on how to jointly interpret your scores on both the desirability of control scale and the maximizer-satisficer scale on that page.)

1. I often fantasize about living in ways that are quite different from my actual life.
2. No matter how satisfied I am with my job, it's only right for me to be on the lookout for better opportunities.
3. When I am in the car listening to the radio, I often check other stations to see if something better is playing, even if I am relatively satisfied with what I'm listening to.
4. When I watch TV, I channel-surf, even while attempting to watch one program.
5. I often find it difficult to shop for a gift for a friend.
6. When shopping, I have a hard time finding clothing that I really love.
7. Renting videos is really difficult. I'm always struggling to pick out the best one.
8. I treat relationships like clothing: I expect to try a lot on before finding the perfect fit.
9. No matter what I do, I have the highest standards for myself.
10. I never settle for second best.

Scoring Scheme

Simply total up your score across all ten items.

Interpreting Your Maximizer-Satisficer Score

A score above 35 implies a maximizer tendency. This means that you have the tendency to constantly look for ways to improve a situation or make a better choice. This is naturally going to lead you to be a little more control-seeking than perhaps you should be. A score above 50 means that you are an *extreme* maximizer. At this level, chances are that others around you have noticed your control-seeking tendencies

A score below 35 means that you have satisficer tendencies; that is, you are generally happy to go with the flow. As it turns out, satisficers tend to be happier than maximizers.

Jointly Interpreting Both the Desirability of Control and Maximizer-Satisficer Scores

The table below provides information on how to jointly interpret the scores across both the desirability of control and maximizer-satisficer scales:

YOUR SCORE ON DESIRABILITY OF CONTROL SCALE	YOUR SCORE ON MAXIMIZER-SATISFICER SCALE	YOUR TENDENCIES
Over 120	Over 50	Definitely Overly Controlling
Over 120 and	Over 35	Most Likely Overly Controlling
Over 110 and	Over 50	Most Likely Overly Controlling
Over 110	Over 35	Probably Overly Controlling
Less than 80	Less than 25	Low Control-Seeking Tendencies

You are definitely overly controlling if your score on the desirability of control is over 120 and your score on the maximizer-satisficer scale is over 50. You are most likely overly controlling if your score on the desirability of control is over 120 and your score on the maximizer-satisficer scale is over 35 or if your score on the desirability of control is over 110 and your score on the maximizer-satisficer scale is over 50. Finally, I would say that you are probably overly controlling if your score on the desirability of control scale is over 110 and your score on the maximizer-satisficer scale is over 35.

On the flip side, you are likely to be below the ideal point of control-seeking if your score on the desirability of control scale is less than 80, particularly if you also score below 25 on the maximizer-satisficer scale. Your low control-seeking tendencies are likely to be a problem particularly in situations in which you are forced to take control or you have a high perceived level of control.

If you didn't fall into any of these categories, you are neither overly controlling, nor are you too low on desire for control—which would be a good thing.

Chapter 4B

THE FOURTH HABIT OF THE HIGHLY HAPPY: GAINING INTERNAL CONTROL

B etween the late 1960s, when I was born, and the mid-1980s, when I left home for college, my mom, my sister, and I would travel for the summer holidays to my grandparents' home in Trichy, India. My uncles and aunts too would descend on Trichy with their own broods. The buildup to the holidays would start a good two months before each trip, and I would sometimes feel so excited by imagining all the fun I would have that I wouldn't be able to fall asleep till the wee hours of the morning. This is not to say that my summers in Trichy were idyllic in every imaginable way; they weren't. For one thing, I would get into a terrible fight with at least one of my cousins on each trip. (It was never my fault, of course.) Further, my cousins and I would often be prevented from doing the things we wanted to do, like watching a Bollywood blockbuster or playing cards, because they were deemed "adult activities" by our wise elders. And then there was the heat; the dog days of summers in Trichy were nothing to be scoffed at.

So overall, it's safe to say that my *imagined* enjoyment of the summer vacations was always far greater than my *actual* enjoyment of them. But what's really curious about all this is that, over the fifteen or so summers I spent in Trichy, I *consistently* overpredicted my enjoyment of them. And it wasn't just me who did this; everyone, including my mother, sister, cousins, uncles, and aunts, were just as guilty of overpredicting enjoyment from the summers in Trichy.

Now, lest you conclude that my family is cuckoo, let me point out that the tendency to overpredict enjoyment from vacations is nearly universal. So the question is not why my family is prone to overpredicting enjoyment from vacations, but rather, why everyone does it. One reason is that we remember past vacations as having been more enjoyable than they actually were. As a result, we expect future vacations to be more enjoyable than they will be. And the reason we remember past vacations as having been more enjoyable than they were is because, once a vacation is over, we selectively reminisce about the positive events.

Interestingly, it's not just with vacations that we overpredict enjoyment; we do it for almost any event. For example, we expect weekends to be more enjoyable than they will turn out to be—which is why the popular restaurant chain is called TGI Fridays and not TGI Sundays. Fortunately, or perhaps unfortunately, we overpredict for negative events as well. This is why heart attacks are more common on Monday mornings, before the workweek has really begun, than at any other time of the week.

The Influence of Thoughts on Feelings

Why do our imaginations wield such a powerful influence over our feelings? One reason is because, when we imagine events, we tend to think of them in undiluted terms. When we dream of a vacation in Cancún, we imagine lying on a flawless stretch of sand, watching a stunning sunset while sipping an ice-cold Corona. We don't imagine that it's raining and that we are stuck in a hotel room with nothing to do—even though that may be just as likely. Another reason is that our brain can't fully tell the difference between reality and imagination. If this weren't the case (that is, if our brain *could* tell the difference between reality and imagination), we wouldn't be emotionally moved by movies and novels, and hence much of the entertainment industry wouldn't exist.

Researchers have long known that our thoughts and imaginations have a powerful influence over our feelings. What researchers also know is that certain kinds of thoughts tend to evoke certain types of emotions. In one study, participants were asked to recollect and write about a past event that evoked a particular type of feeling. Some participants were asked to recall an event that had made them feel sad, while others were asked to recall an event that had made them feel angry, and still others were asked to recall an event that had made them feel proud, and so on. Researchers then analyzed the content of the participants' reports to see if any patterns emerged. They found that, across participants, the set of thoughts that preceded a particular emotion (say, anxiety) showed a remarkable consistency. Further, the pattern preceding one emotion (say, anxiety) was predictably different from that preceding another emotion (say, sadness). Anxiety was almost always preceded by thoughts of uncertainty or lack of control. Sadness, by contrast, was preceded by thoughts about the loss of something valuable, while anger was preceded by thoughts about someone blocking one's progress toward a cherished goal. The thoughts that preceded different types of positive emotions, too, were different from one another in predictable ways. Pride, for example, was preceded by the attribution of positive outcomes to one's own actions. Gratitude, by contrast, was preceded by attribution of positive outcomes to someone else's actions.

When Internal Control Could Be Useful

Consider what these findings suggest. They suggest that, *by merely changing the content of our thoughts, we could control our feelings.* So for example, rather than feel angry at your boss for not giving you a raise, you could, instead, feel gratitude toward him if you focused on the fact that he hasn't fired you. Likewise, rather than feeling sad that your girlfriend is leaving town after spending a week with you, you could feel happy if you focused on all the fun you had during her visit. Extending this logic, it would seem that all one needs to do in order to feel happy (in whichever way one defines happiness) is to interpret events in a way that evokes that feeling.

I don't mean to suggest, of course, that one should always feel happy. Sometimes, one may want to feel sad. For instance, if a good friend is going through a rough patch, you may *want* to feel sad. Likewise, you may *want* to feel contrite for failing to fulfill an important obligation. However, if you are like me, you often wish you could feel happier than you currently are. Imagine that you have an important client meeting coming up tomorrow. If the meeting goes well, your company stands to make a huge profit. If the meeting doesn't go well, your company stands to take a loss. You realize that you give yourself the best shot at nabbing the deal by getting a good night's sleep. But you can't fall asleep because you feel anxious and you are unable to stop thinking of all the ways in which the meeting could go badly. Imagine another situation. You are in an unfamiliar city with just two hours to catch a flight back home, and the bus for which you have been waiting for more than thirty minutes hasn't shown up and there don't seem to be any taxis in the vicinity. In such situations—situations in which you feel frazzled—it would clearly be useful to control your thoughts and feelings so that you can make cool, calm, and collected decisions.

The focus of this chapter is on developing the ability to control one's own thoughts and feelings—an ability that may be called "internal control." Developing internal control, as we'll soon see, is a very important tool in anyone's happiness tool kit.

Taking Personal Responsibility for Your Happiness

Everyone, at one level or another, is familiar with the idea of taking internal control; even children as young as two years old practice it at some level. Nevertheless, very few of us make it a formal objective to develop internal control. In this chapter, I want to take the idea of taking internal control to another level. I want to introduce to you the notion of *taking personal responsibility for your own happiness*. Taking personal responsibility means never blaming someone else or the circumstances for how you feel. It means figuring out ways to be happy despite others' actions and despite the external circumstances.

For the reasons I mentioned earlier, namely, that our thoughts and imaginations have a significant influence on our feelings, it's *theoretically* possible to control one's feelings. That is, if one has complete mastery over one's thoughts, then one would have total control over one's feelings.

How appealing to you is the idea of having total internal control?

If you're like most people, you find the idea appealing overall, but you still have two important concerns with it. One concern is that it will make you delusional. If you can be happy regardless of others' behaviors and regardless of the external circumstances, wouldn't you lose touch with reality?

This concern might seem valid at first blush, but it is based on a mistaken assumption: having control over your thoughts and feelings means being forced to exercise it at all times. In reality, having internal control doesn't mean having to use it, any more than being physically strong means having to use your strength at all times. In other words, if you believe that changing your thoughts and feelings would be delusional in a particular situation, you don't need to exercise internal control.

Another concern is that others would take advantage of you. Here's how one student put it: "If I can be happy regardless of how others behave, wouldn't my colleagues start dumping unpalatable work on me because they know that I won't be pissed off at them for it? Wouldn't my girlfriend be unrepentant even after screwing up because nothing seems to disturb my equanimity?" This concern, too, is based on a faulty assumption—the assumption that taking personal responsibility for your happiness means not holding others accountable for the negative consequences that their actions trigger. In reality, you can simultaneously not blame others for how you feel *and* hold them responsible for the consequences of their actions. Here's an example that illustrates this. Imagine that, due to an administrator's carelessness, you end up missing an important meeting. Further, imagine that missing the meeting has made you angry. Now, in this scenario, if you were someone in full control of your thoughts and feelings, you could easily change the anger into something else. But let's imagine that you choose not to. By choosing not to change your feelings, you would have taken ownership of your feelings and thereby absolved the administrator of being responsible for them. Now imagine that you do choose to change your feelings. Again, by doing so, you would have absolved the administrator of being responsible for your feelings. And yet, the fact that you have absolved him of responsibility for your feelings doesn't in any way restrain you from holding him responsible for the *outcome* (the missed meeting) that his carelessness triggered. So even as you desist from blaming him for how you feel, you could ensure that he resolves the problem that his actions triggered—in much the same way that you would if you did hold him responsible for your anger. Except that because you are now in control of your feelings—rather than the external circumstances being in control of them—the *quality* of your interaction with the administrator would have a very different (a more positive) flavor. As a result, the outcome of your interaction with him would likely yield more positive results, because you would interact with him in a more mature and productive fashion.

Here's another way to appreciate the difference between someone who has taken personal responsibility for his or her own happiness and someone who hasn't. In the scenario that I just described, the internal dialogue of someone who has taken personal responsibility would be along the lines of: "Although your actions have made me feel angry, I am not going to hold you responsible for how I feel—because I can alter my feelings if I so wish. But that doesn't mean that I am going to let you get away with the consequences that your actions have triggered." By contrast, the internal dialogue of someone who hasn't taken personal responsibility would be along the lines of: "Your carelessness has triggered a negative consequence for me, and has also made me feel angry. I am going to hold you responsible both for how I feel and for the negative consequences, and *you better fix them both!*"

The difference between these two perspectives may seem subtle, but is actually profound. One perspective—the perspective of taking personal responsibility—involves acknowledging that, although the external circumstances have control over one's *external* state (the outcomes that one experiences), they do not have control over one's *internal* state (one's feelings). This perspective enables retaining the keys to one's happiness in one's own hands. By contrast, the other perspective—that of not taking personal responsibility—involves conceding that the external circumstances control not only one's external state but also one's internal state. Such a perspective, as you can tell, involves giving up the keys to one's happiness to the external circumstances.

Difference Between Internal and External Control

Developing internal control is clearly crucial if you're serious about happiness. But, as I am sure you have discovered, although it's simple in concept, it's not easy in practice. What might it take to develop internal control?

Before I get to this question, note that while internal control may seem like the same thing as external control (except that it's turned inward), they are, in fact, poles apart. Indeed, in a sense, they are the *opposite* of each other. Specifically, it is when we lack internal control—that is, we lack the ability to regulate our thoughts and feelings—that we seek external control. Or, put differently, the desire for external control arises to compensate for the lack of internal control.

Findings from several studies are consistent with the idea that internal and external control are compensatory forces. In a study that I conducted a while back, I asked participants to list the things that they would like to do when they are feeling "anxious, nervous, or stressed." I found that the more people lacked internal control (control over their feelings), the more their desire for external control—for example, by getting the space around them organized, trying to get to the root of the problem that's making them feel anxious, seeking a calm environment in which they can think better—went up. Other scholars have found similar results. One marketing study found that people like to shop when they feel bad because it helps them compensate for lack of control over their feelings.

The reverse has been shown too: people are more likely to seek internal control when they feel that they don't have a sufficiently high degree of external control. This is one reason why being spiritual or religious helps. Melvin Pollner, for example, found that religious people are happier than nonreligious people because belief in God gives them vicarious control over external events. Along similar lines, findings show that people are more likely to subscribe to superstitions when they lack external control. So superstitions serve as a means to take internal control (control over feelings) when external control is lacking.

The idea that internal control compensates for external control explains how the fourth habit of the highly happy (taking internal control) can help mitigate the fourth deadly happiness sin (being overly controlling). Basically, when one gains sufficient internal control, one doesn't feel the need to control others or the external circumstances as much.

Taking Internal Control: Two Things You Shouldn't Do

Back to the question of what it might take to develop internal control, there are two important "don'ts" to keep in mind. First, don't do things that undermine your confidence in developing internal control. A common way in which people undermine their confidence is by asking themselves whether they can control their thoughts and feelings if something terrible—like breaking a limb or losing a job—was to happen, and then conclude that, because they can't imagine having internal control in these situations, there's no point attempting to seek internal control. As research on goal pursuit shows, self-confidence is key, particularly in the early stages, for achieving goals. So asking yourself whether you can have internal control if something terrible were to happen is the wrong question to ask, as it undermines self-confidence. The *right* question to ask is whether you could have internal control *given the types of commonplace situations that you routinely encounter.* Could you, for example, be happy despite the fact that it's raining outside when you're on vacation? Could you be happy despite the fact that your kid is bawling his head off in public? Could you be happy even if your boss has treated you unfairly?

In this regard, developing internal control is similar to building muscle. Just as you are more likely to build muscle when you exercise using appropriate weights—weights that are neither too light nor too heavy—you are more likely to develop internal control by taking on challenges that are commensurate with your current abilities.* If you find it challenging to maintain your composure in response to everyday events, then that's where you need to start. Once you become adept at regulating your thoughts and feelings in response to such events, you can move on to bigger challenges.

The second "don't" has to do with the *types of thoughts* that you entertain to make yourself feel better. Most of us engage in what are called self-serving biases to make ourselves feel better. Self-serving biases involve taking credit for positive outcomes and blaming others (or luck) for negative ones. Here's an illustration. Imagine that you and a randomly assigned partner participate in a quiz and are given *bogus* feedback on your performance— you are told that your team did either really well or really poorly. To what causes would you attribute your success and failure? If your inclination is to take credit for the success (e.g., "We did well because *I* answered more questions") and blame your partner (e.g., "We did badly because my partner screwed up") for your failure, you are prone to exhibiting self-serving bias. As it turns out, the self-serving bias is very prevalent—particularly among those with higher desire for control.

The good thing about the self-serving bias is that it can make you feel good, particularly in the short run; in the long run, it is likely to backfire. Those who engage in self-serving bias tend to have inflated opinions of their capabilities, and so tend to bite off more than they can chew. In the context of negotiations, for example, those who exhibit higher levels of self-serving

---

* The idea that the challenges one takes on need to be commensurate with one's current skill levels is, of course, consistent with the idea, discussed in chapter 2B, that flow states are most likely when "available ability" matches "required ability."

bias are often overconfident about their ability to get a good deal when, in fact, they perform worse. Likewise, in project planning, those who exhibit self-serving bias are often overly optimistic, leading to failures. Another disadvantage of the self-serving bias is that it's not conducive to building healthy relationships. Those who puff themselves up and put others down, as you can imagine, aren't pleasant to hang out with and unsurprisingly, have a harder time getting along with others, which lowers happiness in the long run.

Taking Internal Control by Practicing Simple Emotion Regulation Tactics

In addition to the two "don'ts" for taking internal control, there are two "dos." The first is learning about and exercising some simple emotion regulation tactics. One such tactic is "situation selection," which involves avoiding situations that one knows (from past experience) evoke unwanted emotions. This is, as you can tell, more of a prevention than a cure tactic, and the simple logic underlying it is that if you don't get to experience an unwanted feeling, you won't need to regulate it. So for example, if you know that watching a horror movie on the eve of an important exam will make you nervous and spoil your sleep, don't watch the horror movie. Likewise, if you know that interacting with a particular person before making a sales pitch is likely to dampen your mood, don't interact with this person. It's really that simple.

Another tactic is "emotion labeling." This tactic literally involves coming up with a label to describe what you are feeling; for example, telling yourself "I am feeling angry" when you experience anger. Findings show that merely labeling your feelings lowers their intensity. If you find this surprising, you are not alone; most people predict that labeling their feelings will intensify them. This may be because we confuse labeling emotions with *ruminating* about them when in fact they are different. Labeling literally means making a note of what you are feeling and moving on. For example, if you are stuck in traffic and are getting increasingly frustrated, you simply tell yourself, "this is frustrating." It does not mean thinking about how much worse the traffic has gotten over the years or bringing to mind all the other things that cause you frustration. In other words, labeling negative emotions means identifying what you are feeling without overanalyzing them, and doing so, findings show, lowers the intensity of the feelings.

Yet another tactic is "attention deployment," which involves directing attention away from the things that trigger negative feelings and toward things that trigger positive ones. This strategy is similar to situation selection, except that you employ it *after* the unwanted feeling has been triggered rather than before. Most of us are, of course, familiar with attention deployment. But what many of us may not know is that the most common way in which we deploy attention—by engaging in the *self-serving bias*—comes with its own negative baggage, as I discussed earlier. The trick is to figure out a way to deploy attention without engaging in the self-serving bias. One way to do this is to define happiness in less egocentric (and more self-transcendental) terms. If you define happiness as hubristic pride, you will naturally gravitate toward puffing yourself up or putting down others in order to feel good. By contrast, if you define it as authentic pride or as love/connection, you will think of other ways (e.g., recalling a past successful attempt, being grateful for being part of a loving family) to feel good.

The final tactic is cognitive reappraisal. This strategy involves reinterpreting the negative situation so as to feel better about it. Say you are feeling stressed out about an impending meeting. In this situation, you could tell yourself that, far from feeling anxious, you should feel *blessed* that your work doesn't involve meaningless menial labor, and that the "problem" you are currently facing is really a "first world problem" that you should be *privileged* to have. Cognitive reappraisal, as you can tell, involves putting things in perspective.

In executing the four emotional regulation tactics (situation selection, labeling emotions, attention deployment, and cognitive reappraisal), it's important to avoid engaging in self-serving bias. What's also important to avoid is *suppressing* negative feelings, because findings show that, contrary to what many of us believe, it doesn't mitigate feelings. This is because the parts of the brain that are activated when we feel negative continue to remain activated even if we suppress the feelings. Further, suppressing emotions takes brain capacity, and this means less leftover capacity to focus on the task at hand. Finally, when we suppress our feelings, others can usually sense it and this increases *their* stress levels and lowers how much they like us. For these reasons, it may not be a good idea to suppress emotions. That doesn't mean, of course, that one should always wear one's feelings on one's sleeve. But it does mean that one shouldn't bank on suppressing emotions as an emotion regulation strategy. It also means that one should actively develop the other strategies—situation selection, labeling emotions, attention deployment, and cognitive reappraisal—to gain internal control.

Taking Internal Control by Leading a Healthier Lifestyle

Emotion regulation tactics offer a powerful way to take internal control. But an arguably more powerful way to take internal control is to lead a healthier lifestyle. A healthy lifestyle involves three main components: eating right, moving more, and sleeping better.* There is overwhelming evidence that each of these components has a big positive effect on both physical and mental health. Thus, leading a healthy lifestyle makes you feel good from the inside out. Further, it improves your ability to handle life's stressors. Many of us, particularly the smart and successful among us, lead exceedingly frenetic lives. As a result, we routinely experience what Dr. Edward Hallowell calls "attention deficit trait" (or ADT). ADT is the feeling that your life is totally out of control—that your plate is too full and that you can't handle the challenges and obligations you have taken on. As Dr. Hallowell puts it, "Sleep, a good diet, and exercise are critical for staving off ADT." So leading a healthy lifestyle—by eating right, moving more, and sleeping better— makes us feel more in control of our lives. And by doing so, it mitigates the desire for external control because, as we saw in the previous chapter, a big reason why we seek external control is because we don't feel sufficiently in control of our lives. By making us feel more in control over our lives and over our internal environment, leading a healthy lifestyle helps mitigate the fourth deadly happiness "sin": being overly controlling.

What Constitutes Eating Right, Moving More, and Sleeping Better?

Eating right—the first component of a healthy lifestyle—may seem simple in concept, but as we all know, there are as many opinions about what constitutes a healthy diet as there are dietitians. That means there isn't much

---

* I've borrowed these terms from Tom Rath's excellent book, *Eat, Move, Sleep.*

agreement on what eating right means. The good news, though, is that almost everyone agrees on what eating *badly* means. It means:

- Eating a lot of processed food—food that comes in cans and packages.
- Eating things that are easily processed by your body, like sugar and simple carbohydrates.
- Not eating enough veggies and fruits.
- Eating a lot of bad fats—basically, trans fat and saturated fat.

Studies show that eating lots of processed food leads to weight gain, diabetes, and inflammation, all of which affect mental health. Studies also show that a diet high in trans fat and saturated fat leads to depression. Trans fat also induces aggression; one study found that those who consume a lot of bad fat are more likely to get into a fight with their spouse. So eating right means avoiding processed foods (particularly sugar) and foods with high saturated or trans fats.

Moving more constitutes a nonsedentary lifestyle. Findings show that sitting for more than six hours a day is one of the worst things you could do to yourself, as it greatly increases the chances of early death. According to a number of studies, sitting is just as bad as smoking when it comes to the risk of heart disease. Another study found, along similar lines, that inactivity kills more people worldwide than does smoking. Yet another study found that, even if you exercise a lot—one hour of vigorous exercise a day, or seven hours of exercise every week—it may still not be enough to counteract the bad effects of sitting. One study found that even among those who exercise a lot, those who spent most of their time sitting had a 50 percent greater risk of death. What this means is that you can't sit all day and exercise for one hour and think you're safe—you need to move more regularly throughout the day.

As for sleeping better, it constitutes getting at least seven hours of good quality sleep per night. If you believe that seven hours per night is way more sleep than you need, consider results from a study in which participants were put behind closed doors with no access to clocks, sunlight, people, and other external factors that affect the amount of sleep we get. The idea was to assess the amount of sleep that people naturally need when they aren't pressured by external factors. Findings showed that 95 percent of people needed between seven and nine hours of sleep per night to feel well rested. Only 2.5 percent of the participants felt well rested with less than seven hours of sleep. So if you feel that you can perform perfectly well with six hours or less of sleep, you may not be aware how much better you could be if you got more sleep.

Several findings confirm that we make worse decisions when sleep deprived. For instance, getting just ninety minutes less sleep than you need lowers your daytime alertness by a third! You are also less likely to make unhealthy food choices if you have slept well. Sleep also affects mood, as I am sure you have realized. One reason for this is that sleep takes the edge off bad memories by assigning meaning to them; if you don't get enough sleep, you are more likely to be anxious and irritable.

The Fourth Happiness Exercise: Schedule Partner Project

Most people recognize the importance of leading a healthier lifestyle, but are equally terrible at translating this recognition into action. That's where the fourth exercise of the highly happy—something I call the "schedule partner project"—comes in. The exercise (detailed instructions are available on the book's website, www.happysmarts.com/book/exercises/schedule _partner_project, and the abridged instructions for which are available in the appendix for this chapter) consists of two main steps. The first step involves connecting with another reader of this book who is also interested in adopting a healthier lifestyle, and setting up a mutually convenient time to chat and motivate each other on a daily basis for an agreed-upon period (say, a month). For example, you may agree to chat at six p.m. each day via Skype or WhatsApp. This step of the exercise is based on an interesting finding from research on goal pursuit: you are much more likely to achieve a goal when you are jointly pursuing it alongside someone else rather than all by yourself. The second step in the exercise involves formulating a plan for leading a healthier lifestyle. On the book's website (www.happysmarts .com/book/exercises/schedule_partner_project), you'll find several useful tips for eating right (e.g., start your meals with healthy items, carry healthy snacks with you), moving more (e.g., set an automated reminder to get out of your chair every twenty minutes or so, exercise in the mornings), and sleeping better (e.g., cool your bedroom by two to four degrees, avoid gadgets that emit blue light in the bedroom). Your task in the second step is to adhere to at least three of these suggestions for the period of the exercise. The third step involves e-mailing this plan to your schedule partner so that he or she has a good understanding of it and can follow up with you on it. The fourth and final step involves executing the plan and motivating your partner to execute his or hers.

I hope that you take advantage of the opportunity to participate in the schedule partner project and that, like many of my students, you too will discover that adopting a healthier lifestyle makes it easier to gain internal control and therefore mitigates the tendency to be overly controlling. What I also hope you discover is that gaining internal control enhances happiness levels not just by helping you retain the keys to happiness in your own hands and by mitigating your desire for external control, but also by giving you a sense of progress toward "personal mastery"—mastery over your own mind.

Chapter 5A

THE FIFTH DEADLY HAPPINESS "SIN": DISTRUSTING OTHERS

W hat makes some countries happy and other countries miserable? Why, for example, are people from Iceland and Switzerland
among the happiest in the world, while those from Moldova
and Qatar are among the least happy? The reason, you may
think, has to do with things like economic prosperity and political climate.
And to be sure, those things matter. In general, the more prosperous a
country, the happier its citizens. Likewise, people who live in stable democracies are happier than those who live in violent autocracies. However,
something else matters more than economic prosperity or political ideology. That something is trust.

John Helliwell, an economist at University of British Columbia, has
been exploring the relationship between trust and happiness for several
years. His findings suggest that trust may be one of *the* most important
determinants of the happiness of countries. Findings from one study
showed, for example, that the more the citizens of a country responded to
the question "Generally speaking, would you say that most people can be
trusted or that you need to be very careful in dealing with people?" with
"most people can be trusted" rather than with "need to be very careful," the
happier the citizens were. In Denmark and Norway—two of the happiest
countries in the world—close to 65 percent of the citizens believe that most
people in their country can be trusted, whereas in Greece and Russia—two

relatively unhappy countries—the proportion is less than 10 percent. (The proportions for some of the world's largest English-speaking countries, namely, the United States, India, Great Britain, and Australia, are 41.2, 34.6, 36.9, and 44.6 percent, respectively.)

In another study that explored the impact of trust on happiness, researchers "accidentally" left twelve wallets containing the equivalent of about $50 in sixteen cities around the world. The wallet also contained the address of its purported owner. After leaving the wallets around, the experimenters sat back and counted the number of wallets that got returned to the "owner." They used the proportion of wallets that were returned as a proxy for the trustworthiness of the country. Once again, trust turned out to be a major determinant of happiness: the greater the proportion of wallets returned, the happier the country.

It's easy to see why trust is so important for happiness. If you did not trust your fellow citizens, particularly those with whom you have routine interactions, life would be difficult. Imagine that you couldn't trust your friends to divvy up a restaurant bill equitably. Or imagine that you couldn't trust any of your colleagues to keep a secret. When you can't trust others, you can't relax, and when you can't relax, you can't be happy. At the same time, however, it's also easy to see how distrusting others can be prudent. Being wary of others can help minimize the chance of being cheated. It can also help generate strategies for neutralizing Machiavellian competitors. So the question is: how can you enhance the chances of being in trustworthy relationships so that happiness is maximized, while minimizing the chances of being cheated?

Figuring out the answer to this question, as we will see, isn't all that simple. And to get to this answer, allow me to share with you the results from a rather interesting set of studies—the so-called trust game studies.

Trust Begets Trustworthiness

Imagine that you have signed up for a study in which you are paired up with someone else. You and your partner are kept in separate rooms, and you are told that you will never get to meet each other. The experimenter gives you both $10 and tells you that you get to act first. You must decide whether to send your money over to your partner or not. If you choose *not* to send the money, the game is over, and both you and your partner walk away with

$10. If you choose to send your money, however, the experimenter will quadruple the amount for your partner, so that he will now have $50 (the original $10, plus $10 × 4). Your partner can now either keep all the money, which means that he walks away with $50, leaving you with nothing, or he can send half the money back to you, which means that each of you would end up with $25.

Imagine that you are given all this information before you are asked to make a decision. You must now decide whether to send $10 to your partner or not. What would you do?

Your decision would depend, of course, on how much you trust your partner. If you send him the money and he doesn't reciprocate, you would go home empty-handed. But by sending him the money, both you and your partner stand a chance of making $15 more than you otherwise would.

In this situation, it is easy to take the cynical point of view—that you *shouldn't* send the money. This view is based on the logic that, once your partner receives your money and makes $50, he would have little incentive to split the money with you. But is this logic valid? Do people who receive $10 from their partner walk away without sharing the money?

As it turns out, a vast majority (over 95 percent) of participants *don't* walk away. Rather, as the Swiss researchers who conducted a study along these lines found, when you trust them, they end up behaving in a trustworthy fashion. In other words, people who are trusted, it turns out, generally reciprocate the trust. One reason for this may be that being trusted releases a hormone called oxytocin, called the "trust molecule" by some. What this suggests is that if we could somehow proactively trust others—that is, trust them before we know for sure that they are trustworthy—we would build mutual trust.

An event from my own childhood underscored this point. I was about ten at that time, and like most kids in India my age, an avid stamp collector. I would spend hours upon hours every week poring over my collection, dreaming of having an even bigger one. Naturally, I was very protective of my stamps and would rarely let them go out of sight, particularly if other stamp collectors were in the vicinity. One day, a kid who had recently moved into our neighborhood invited me to his house to view his stamp collection. His collection was far superior to mine. He had stamps from several exotic locations, like Malta and Zanzibar, and some of his stamps (like the ones from Bhutan) even had 3D images. Although it wasn't unusual for someone to have a better stamp collection than mine, what happened next *was* unusual: the kid offered me a pick of any one of his stamps—*for free!* That is, he told me that I could choose any stamp from his awesome collection, and he would just give it to me, with nothing expected in return. And guess what happened next? Like the participants in the Swiss studies, I repaid his trust. I cycled back home as fast as I could to bring over my *own* stamp collection to make a reciprocal offer.

Suffice it to say that the halo from this experience lasted several days, and the kid and I became BBFs. In our own childlike way, we had discovered how wonderfully uplifting mutual trust can be.

It's not just at the individual level that trusting others begets trustworthiness; the same is true at the organizational level as well. Karma Kitchen, a restaurant founded in Berkeley, California, operates on the basis of trust. At the end of every meal, customers discover that they owe the restaurant precisely $0! Why? Because, they are told, a *previous* customer has paid for their meal. So customers could walk out of Karma Kitchen with the money in their wallets intact. And yet, that's not what most customers do; most are so moved by the experience that they end up paying for a *future* customer's meal. The unbroken, "pay it forward" chain has continued for more than thirty thousand meals over the past eight years. So successful is Karma Kitchen's "business model"—if one could call it that—that branches of the restaurant have opened up in several other locations, including Ahmedabad, Chicago, Washington, D.C., and Tokyo.

Grameen Bank provides another illustration of how people have a propensity to reciprocate trust with trustworthiness. As you might know, the bank (a brainchild of Muhammad Yunus, who won the Nobel Prize for Peace) makes microloans to desperately poor people on trust. Most people think that trusting the desperately poor is a recipe for setting the world record for going out of business. And yet, the payback rate at Grameen is an incredible 98 percent—significantly higher than the 88 percent that is the average for a traditional small-business loan. Another company that serves as an example of trust begetting trustworthiness is Zappos. As Tony Hsieh,

CEO of Zappos, notes in his book *Delivering Happiness*, "We don't have scripts (for our customer service employees) because we trust our employees to use their best judgment when dealing with each and every customer." As a result of such trust, Hsieh goes on to note, "escalations to a supervisor" (whereby customers wish to speak to someone higher up at Zappos) were very rare in the company. Trusting customers was also a core element of the Zappos business model. Customers could, after ordering shoes from the store, try them on and return them without spending a single penny. And—get this—the return period at Zappos was (and continues to be) a *full year.* What did Zappos get in return for trusting employees and customers? Financial success, for one. Zappos was one of the few bright stars in an otherwise bleak landscape after the 2007 financial crisis that sent the world economy into recession. Zappos was eventually bought out by Amazon for an incredible $1.2 billion in 2009. To this day, Zappos continues to be one of the best companies to work for, ranking eighty-sixth in *Fortune*'s 2014 list. According to Hsieh, Zappos achieved remarkable success not despite trusting its employees and customers, but because of it.

Default Distrust

Most of us can understand the idea that trusting others will build mutual trust. And yet, we also feel uncomfortable taking the first step to trust others. In a survey I gave to my students on the first day of class, I found that less than 25 percent were willing to trust another student enough to reveal one of their "insecurities" to them. The willingness to trust others in professional settings is, if anything, likely to be even lower, which is why organizations like Karma Kitchen and Zappos are so remarkable and refreshing.

The reason we are reluctant to proactively trust others has to do with something we discussed in a previous chapter—our hardwired tendency to focus on negative things because they are more diagnostic for our survival. That is, we distrust others by default because, evolutionarily speaking, those who spontaneously distrust others are likely to survive longer than those who do the reverse. So even though people are actually quite trustworthy—particularly if they have been trusted (as we saw from the Swiss studies)—many of us can't bring ourselves to trust others because of our hardwired cynicism. And yet, if everyone (or at least a critical mass) could overcome this predisposition, we would all benefit. Specifically, by proactively trusting others, we would build mutual trust, and this in turn would enhance everyone's happiness.

So the million-dollar question, a question that should be on everyone's lips, is this: how do we get people to become more proactively trusting?

That was the question on my mind as I lay lounging on a beach chair in Goa one winter. The weather was warm, I had had a good night's rest, and I was feeling on top of the world. The only thing missing from my life was an ice-cold bottle of beer. As I lay there on the beach, too lazy to walk to a shack to get a beer and too thirsty to not think of doing it, a vendor carrying beer appeared seemingly out of nowhere and uttered the sweetest words I had heard in a while.

"Care for a beer, Sahib?" he said.

I nearly fell off my chair in surprised delight and mumbled a grateful, "Yes, please!"

"Very good, Sahib," said the vendor. "That will be 120 rupees for the bottle."

I fished around my wallet for the money and discovered that I had only two 100-rupee notes and nothing smaller. So I handed him the two notes, expecting to get 80 rupees back. But the vendor said, "Sorry, Sahib, I don't have change. Give me the money and I will come back with your change in ten minutes."

Put yourself in my shoes. What would you have done? Give him your money and risk never seeing him again? Or ask him to get the change first, before you were willing to buy the beer?

In this situation, you would probably do what I did: give him the money and risk losing the 80 rupees. But you can easily imagine other scenarios in which it wouldn't be so easy to trust others. Imagine, for example, that a colleague wants to use some presentation slides that you painstakingly put together. Or imagine revealing a deep-seated insecurity to your date on the very first outing. It's far more difficult to be proactively trusting in these situations.

David DeSteno, author of the book *The Truth About Trust*, notes that an important feature common to all situations involving trust is a risk-reward trade-off. In the beer-vendor scenario, giving the vendor the 200 rupees would lead to an important reward: a nice little beer buzz. It could also lead to another reward, the reward of having your trust reciprocated.

But on the flip side, trusting the vendor carries two risks: the risk that he may never return with your change, and the risk that you would feel like an idiot if he cheated you. One way to reduce these risks, of course, is not to trust the vendor. But then, by doing so, you wouldn't get to experience the rewards.

How does one resolve this type of risk-reward trade-off?

One way to resolve it is to consider *all* the rewards—and not just the obvious ones that I mentioned above—that you stand to gain from trusting others. To see what I mean by this, let's revisit the beer vendor in Goa.

The Hidden Rewards of Proactive Trust

Imagine that you decide to trust the beer vendor and that, much to your delight, he returns with your change. If this happens, not only would you derive the obvious benefit of having your thirst quenched, you would gain something far more valuable: *the discovery of a trustworthy beer vendor!* Knowing someone you can trust is, for obvious reasons, very valuable. Imagine being embedded in a community of trustworthy relationships. Imagine, for example, that everyone who takes care of things for you—from your lawn mower and your maid to your dry cleaner and your car mechanic (okay, maybe that's pushing it)—are all super trustworthy. Wouldn't it be wonderful to inhabit such a world? It would, and you give yourself a better chance of doing so by being proactively trusting. Or conversely, if you never trusted others proactively, you would lower your chances of inhabiting such a world. Most of us don't typically recognize this—somewhat hidden— benefit of exhibiting proactive trust.

Another hidden benefit of exhibiting proactive trust is that we get to play a critical role in building a culture of trust. As we saw earlier, from the trust game studies, when you proactively trust others, they tend to recipro- cate the trust. This reciprocity of trust, in turn, is likely to lead to a virtuous buildup of mutual trust in society. Thus, by proactively trusting others, we would be doing our part to help build a culture of trust—much like how, by paying taxes, we contribute to society's uplift.

These hidden benefits of exhibiting proactive trust are, of course, coun- tered by the risks associated with it. If you trusted the beer vendor and he didn't return with the change, not only would you be poorer by 80 rupees, you would feel like an idiot. And on top of that, you would also feel quite hurt. As a number of studies have shown, being cheated is very painful. Here's an example that illustrates just how painful being cheated can feel. Imagine that you are looking to buy a car. After negotiating with the dealer, you manage to buy the car for $500 less than a previous customer did. How happy would you feel? Now imagine an alternative scenario. After bargaining with the dealer, you buy the car for a price that the dealer assures you is "the lowest price for which I have *ever* sold the car." You trust him, only to later discover that you paid $500 more than a previous customer did. How angry would you feel? For most people—and I can vouch for this from personal experience—the negativity from being cheated out of a certain amount of money is far greater than the positivity from saving the same amount of money. And it is not just in the context of money that we hate being cheated; we hate being cheated in *any* context, which is why trust is so crucial for the health of relationships. John Gottman, one of the best-known researchers in the area of relationships, finds that it takes as many as *five* trustworthy behaviors to overcome the negative feelings generated by just one untrustworthy behavior!

The Trust Scale

This is why it is important to be smart about when, with whom, and how much to trust others. On the one hand, we wouldn't want to distrust everyone all the time. Doing so would get in the way of reaping some important benefits, including feeling happy. On the other hand, we wouldn't want to trust everyone all the time. So somewhere between extreme trust and extreme distrust trust lies the "sweet spot" of trust: the level at which we get to maximize our happiness. Where exactly does this sweet spot lie?

This is a difficult question to answer. The sweet spot can vary from person to person—depending, for example, on how much it hurts to feel cheated. The sweet spot can also vary from situation to situation. For instance, it makes sense to trust taxi drivers in certain countries more than it does in others. So figuring out the sweet spot of trust can be tricky. But that doesn't mean that it isn't worth an attempt. Part of the answer to figuring out the sweet spot of trust lies in assessing one's default trust levels. If one tends to trust others less than one "should," it follows that the sweet spot lies in the direction of being more trusting, and vice versa.

At the end of the chapter, you'll find a trust scale that can help you assess your default trust levels. By filling out the scale, you will most likely discover what a student of mine—Eunjoo (EJ) Han—and I found in a set of studies we recently ran: that people are, in general, more distrusting of others than they should be.

Social Cynicism

Imagine that, as you are driving down the highway, a driver from another lane abruptly cuts into your lane, forcing you to brake. Which of the following causes, in your opinion, is the most likely explanation for the driver's behavior?

1. The driver is a rude person.
2. The driver must not have noticed you.
3. The driver must be in a rush (e.g., maybe en route to a hospital for an emergency).

Now imagine an alternative scenario: as you are driving on the highway and wish to change lanes, a driver in another lane brakes to allow you to enter his lane ahead of him. Which of the following causes is the most likely explanation for the driver's behavior?

1. The driver is a nice person.
2. The driver is letting you into his lane so that he can get into your lane.
3. The driver must have noticed that you were in a rush.

Across a series of studies, EJ and I asked participants to imagine themselves in this and other scenarios like it. All of the scenarios had a "positive" version, in which participants read that someone behaved in a positive fashion, and a "negative" version, in which other participants read that the same person behaved in a symmetrically negative fashion. For example, in one scenario, participants read that an employee at a firm had just returned from a work-related trip to another city. Participants were then put in one of two conditions. Those in the negative condition read that the employee claimed, as reimbursement, $60 more than he had actually spent on the trip. Those in the positive condition read that the employee claimed $60 less than he had actually spent. Participants were asked to pick one of the following three options as the most likely cause of the employee's actions:

Negative Condition:

1. The employee must be dishonest.
2. The employee was careless and must have made a mistake.
3. The employee was trying to make up for some extra work-related expenses that he incurred on a previous trip.

Positive Condition:

1. The employee must be honest.
2. The employee was careless and must have made a mistake.
3. The employee was trying to pay the company back for some extra reimbursement that he claimed on a previous trip.

Notice something interesting about the three explanations for the employee's behavior. The first explanation—"the employee must be dishonest" and "the employee must be honest"—attributes the behavior to an *internal* cause. By contrast, the third explanation—wherein the employee is trying to correct for a past mistake—attributes his behavior to an *external* cause. (The middle explanation doesn't attribute the cause to either an internal or an external cause.) In providing participants with both an internal and an external explanation for the employee's behavior, EJ and I were trying to assess the extent to which people are cynical—versus trusting—about others.

Imagine, for a moment, that a greater proportion of participants attribute the employee's negative behavior to internal causes (i.e., his dishonesty), and his positive behavior to external causes. Such a finding would suggest that people are more suspicious than trusting of others, because it would indicate that people believe that others' negative behaviors are rooted in internal causes, whereas their positive behaviors are rooted in external ones. The opposite pattern of results—namely, that people attribute others' negative behaviors to external causes and their positive behaviors to internal causes—would indicate that people are more trusting than suspicious of others.

So what did we find? Before I get to the results, I should point out that, apart from how cynical or trusting people are, a separate factor—the prevalence of a behavior—can also affect the type of attributions that people make for others' behaviors. The more prevalent a behavior is—for example, the more commonplace it is for drivers to cut into others' lanes—the more likely that it will be attributed to an external cause (e.g., the "driving culture") than to an internal cause (e.g., "rudeness"). Likewise, the less prevalent a behavior is—for example, the less commonplace it is for employees to underclaim reimbursement—the more likely it is to be attributed to an internal cause (e.g., "honesty") than to an external one (e.g., "company culture"). This makes sense, of course. If a behavior is prevalent, it must mean that the behavior is tolerated by everyone; otherwise, few people would exhibit it. If a behavior is rare, by contrast, the person exhibiting the behavior is going against the grain, which must mean that he or she is inherently motivated to exhibit it. So we controlled for the prevalence of the behavior in our analysis. After doing so, what we found is that people are more suspicious than trusting of others. That is, controlling for the prevalence with which various behaviors occur, we found that negative behaviors are more likely to be attributed to internal causes, while positive behaviors are, relatively speaking, more likely to be attributed to external ones.

This means that when people behave badly, we think it's because they are "mean," "rude," and "unethical." When people behave well, on the other hand, we think it's because their hands were tied by the situation. The crux, in other words, is this: people are, by default, more cynical about others than they are trusting—a finding that is consistent with the idea that people are hardwired to be distrusting.

Where does all of this leave us? The discussion thus far may be summarized as follows:

- Trust is critical for happiness; when we feel we can trust others, we are happier.
- Further, people in general reciprocate trust with trustworthy behavior.
- And yet, our default tendency is to be distrusting, rather than trusting, of others.

What this suggests is that, if we could somehow overcome our tendency to distrust others, we might stand to reap significant gains not just in our own happiness, but also in the happiness of others. What we need, then, is a strategy for becoming more proactively trusting than we currently are—without, of course, becoming gullible.

In the next chapter, I outline precisely such a strategy.

INTERPERSONAL TRUST SCALE (ITS)

Instructions

The following five statements, which form the interpersonal trust scale and can be accessed on the book's website at www.happysmarts.com/its_scale, concern how trusting you are of others. Indicate the degree to which you agree or disagree with each statement by the following scale:

1 = strongly disagree
2 = mildly disagree
3 = agree and disagree equally
4 = mildly agree
5 = strongly agree

Then total up your score, using the scoring scheme that follows the last item on the scale. You can find the interpretation of your score on page 164.

1. In dealing with strangers, one is better off to be cautious until they have provided evidence that they are trustworthy.
2. It is safe to believe that in spite of what people say, most people are primarily interested in their own welfare.
3. In these competitive times one has to be alert or someone is likely to take advantage of you.
4. Most people can't be counted on to do what they say they will do.
5. Most idealists are not sincere and usually do not practice what they preach.

Scoring Scheme

Simply add your score across all five items.

Interpreting Your Trust Score

If your score was 15 or above, you are more distrusting than trusting of others. If, on the other hand, your score was less than 15, you are more trusting than distrusting of others.

An alternative—although untested—scale to the ITS is the set of statements developed by Stephen M. R. Covey and Greg Link in their 2012 book, *Smart Trust.* Here are the items that relate to two ends of the trust spectrum—"blind trust" and "distrust." To see where you fall on the continuum, consider the statements in each of the two columns in the table below and assess the extent to which they reflect your opinions and attitudes:

FIGURING OUT WHETHER DEFAULT TRUST LEVELS ARE TOO HIGH OR TOO LOW	
BLIND TRUST	**DISTRUST**
I trust people too easily and believe whatever they say. As a result, I often get burned.	I am inherently suspicious of people and question whatever they tell me.
I never check up on people or what they tell me; I just always assume the best.	I always feel I have to investigate people's credibility and validate what they say.
I openly and freely share information about anything and everything.	I believe information is power. I hold it close to my chest and give it out only sparingly.
I accept everyone as trustworthy and feel comfortable with the thought of working openly with anyone.	People have to earn my trust before I am willing to work with them.
I trust people to do what they say they will do, and see no reason to question otherwise.	I tightly supervise my direct reports (or my children and others) and thoroughly and frequently check up on their work.

Chapter 5B

THE FIFTH HABIT OF THE HIGHLY HAPPY: EXERCISING "SMART TRUST"

D uring a recent visit to Accra, Ghana, I hired a taxi to take me from my hotel to a radio station where I was to be interviewed. Before getting into the taxi, I asked the concierge how much the ride would cost. I thought he said "fifteen cedis" (the Ghanaian currency) when, in fact, he had said "fifty cedis." The taxi ride seemed really long for just 15 cedis (about $4), but I didn't think much about it, as taxi rides are relatively inexpensive in many developing economies. When I finally got off, the driver asked me for 40 cedis. I gave him the money, but only after giving him a good talking to in which I made multiple references to the research on the importance of trust for happiness, and on how his untrustworthy behavior was ruining it for the rest of us. My chiding had no apparent effect on him—he kept smiling through it—which I took as evidence of his insolence.

It was only after I got back to my hotel and told the concierge what had transpired that I realized my mistake. Far from cheating me, the taxi driver had been quite generous. I naturally felt contrite, but the experience also made me feel good, because it restored my faith in humanity. Later that day, I searched for the taxi driver to apologize, but I couldn't find him; he had left for the day. As I was leaving town the next morning, I handed the concierge a note of apology to be delivered to the driver, which I hope he got.

This experience reminded me of what John Helliwell considers one of the most important themes to emerge from research on trust—a theme that I touched on in the last chapter: *people are far more trustworthy than we give them credit for.* Or, put differently, the average person is far more distrustful of others than he should be. One reason for our high levels of distrust is, of course, that we are hardwired for distrust. Another reason is that we are surrounded by negative news that further reinforces our hardwired cynicism.

But despite the fact that we are genetically and socially conditioned to be distrustful, I still find it surprising that we don't learn to trust others more over time. As rational decision agents, why don't we recognize that it is in our own interest to trust others more? After all, doing so would not only make us more accurately calibrated, it would also enhance our happiness and the happiness of others around us.

Why Don't We Think of Being More Proactively Trusting?

As I mulled over this issue on the flight back home, I realized that there are two main reasons why *I* hadn't adjusted my trust level upward over the years. First, until recently, I hadn't been familiar with the research on trust. For instance, I didn't know that people are more trustworthy than we give them credit for. In particular, before Professor Helliwell told me about it when I interviewed him for my Coursera course, I had never heard of the wallet drop study conducted by the *Toronto Star.* Taking a leaf out of a *Reader's Digest* study, the newspaper had dropped 20 wallets, each containing $200, at various spots in Toronto and then asked random denizens of the city to guess how many of these wallets would be returned. On average, people guessed that 2.3 of the wallets (or about 10 percent) would be returned when, in fact, *16* wallets (80 percent) were returned. So in this case, the difference between people's actual trustworthiness and how trustworthy they were perceived to be was a whopping 70 percent!

Once I got to know about this and other such studies (including the trust game studies that I reviewed in the previous chapter) I started conducting a few of my own little studies to assess the difference between actual and perceived trustworthiness. In one, I described the trust game setup to students in my happiness class and asked them to predict the proportion of participants who would return the money if trusted with $10. On average, the students predicted that only 63 percent would share the money, when in fact (as you may recall), 95 percent do. The studies I conducted with EJ were also inspired by the question of whether people are more cynical about others than they should be. As you will remember, we found that people are more cynical than trusting of others.

In addition to not being familiar with the research on trust, there was another reason I hadn't adjusted my trust levels upward over the years. Like most others, I seem to have better memory for instances in which I had been cheated than for instances when my trust had been validated. For example, being cheated out of $500 by the car dealer all those years back still rankled me, whereas I had all but forgotten about the good Samaritan in Thailand who had returned my misplaced backpack that contained not just my passport but also $2,000 cash! As a result of my selective memory, I realized that I had pretty much conditioned myself to believe that people are, in general, more dishonest than honest.

I realized, therefore, that if I was to steer myself toward becoming more proactively trusting, I would need to do a few things. First, I would need to explicitly remind myself that people, like the taxi driver in Accra, are generally more trustworthy than I give them credit for. Second, I would need to remind myself of *all* the benefits, including the hidden ones, of proactively trusting others. One way to do this is to remind myself that proactively trusting others is an *investment* I am making to embed myself in trustworthy relationships, rather than a risk I am taking. Third, in the instances in which I did get cheated, I would need to figure out ways to minimize the psychological pain, and maximize the positivity from the instances in which my trust was validated. This would be important if I wished to avoid going back to being distrustful of others—or worse, become even more distrustful of others than I had previously been.

And finally, I would need to figure out a way to elicit trustworthy behavior from others. I arrived at this last insight on the basis of something quite well known in social psychology, namely, that people's propensities (attitudes, behaviors, etc.) aren't necessarily set in stone; rather, they are more fluid. As an example, few people are unqualified saints or unequivocal devils; rather, depending on the situation, most of us are capable of exhibiting both saintliness and devilishness. The factor that holds most sway in which propensity—saintliness or devilishness—we exhibit in any given moment is the *context* in which we find ourselves. If we find ourselves in a context (e.g., in church) in which saintliness is expected of everyone, and everyone around us is, in fact, behaving in a saintly fashion, then we are likely to do the same. If, however, we find ourselves in a context in which "devilishness" is not just permitted but actively encouraged (certain areas of Las Vegas spring to mind here), we are more likely to tread on the devilish end of the spectrum. In other words, the extent to which people exhibit trustworthiness is not set in stone; few people are always trustworthy or untrustworthy. Findings show, for example, that only around 5 percent are entirely untrustworthy. (Paul Zak, a researcher who works in this area, uses the technical term *bastards* to refer to such people.) The rest of us fall somewhere in the trustworthy-untrustworthy continuum and, depending on context, can exhibit either propensity.

What this suggested to me is that, if I was to increase my odds of enjoying trustworthy behavior from others, I would need to figure out ways to elicit such behavior from them.

The Four Components of Exercising "Smart Trust"

Over the past few years, I have put in place a set of strategies that have helped me practice each of the following four components of exercising what I call "smart trust"*:

- Remind myself that people are more trustworthy than I give them credit for.
- Remind myself of the benefits—including hidden ones—of proactive trust.
- Minimize pain from being cheated, and maximize positivity from having my trust validated.
- Elicit more trustworthy behavior from others.

I call these components of exercising smart trust because they steer me toward being more trusting of others while at the same time preventing me from becoming overly trusting. In other words, they help me hover around the "sweet spot" of trust that I talked about in the previous chapter.

The first and second components do not need elaboration, as we have

---

* Covey et al. use the same term to refer to a similar concept in their book, *Smart Trust*.

already discussed them at length. The one thing I will add here is that you might find it useful, as I have, to explicitly make a note of the proportion of occasions in which your trust is validated versus not. (Your journal would be a good place to do this.) To this day, I am somewhat surprised to find that my trust is validated far more often than it is not, somewhere on the order of 10:1. Here's an example. Just the other day, I hired a transportation company to move my stuff from one city in India to another. They demanded that I pay the full price up front. Because they also had possession of my stuff, I really would have been in serious trouble if they had failed to deliver it, particularly as I wasn't going to be in India for a while. However, the stuff arrived right on time, just as the company had promised. Earlier—before I embarked on the quest to exercise smart trust—I wouldn't have registered this as evidence of people's trustworthiness, but nowadays, I do. And that helps me to be more trusting of people.

Keeping a record of the number of times your trust is validated has another advantage: it is a good way to maximize the positivity from having your trust validated, which is part of the third component of smart trust. Another part of this component is minimizing the pain from being cheated. As we've already seen, being cheated hurts a lot, which makes it all the more important to figure out ways to minimize the pain; otherwise, we run the risk of going back to being distrusting by default.

What can you do to minimize the pain of being cheated?

Strategies for Minimizing the Pain of Having Your Trust Violated

Perhaps the most important thing you can do is practice forgiveness. But before I discuss what forgiveness is and how to practice it, allow me to share with you two other simple strategies that have worked for me. The first strategy involves perspective taking. Most of the time, the consequences of being cheated are not very high. In particular, assuming that you are materially much better off than most people in the world, the material impact that being cheated has on you is likely to be far less significant than it would be for most other people. So what if a taxi driver in Ghana takes you for a ride (literally and metaphorically)? So what if a beer vendor in Goa vanishes with my 80 rupees? Being cheated of 200 rupees here or $50 there is not going to make a huge dent in your wallet. Another way to look at it is this:

if people like you and me—who are so much better off than most others—can't bring ourselves to do our bit to enhance trust levels in society, we really can't expect those who are worse off to do it. (This is particularly the case the smarter and more successful you are; as DeSteno discusses in *The Truth About Trust*, the S-and-S are more prone to being distrusting.) Taking this perspective helps assuage the pain of being cheated. As it turns out, there is reason to believe, based on some recent findings, that the poor are more worthy of trust than the rich; there appears to be something about being wealthy that corrupts our moral uprightness.

The second strategy involves making an explicit resolution to hold those who violate your trust accountable for their actions. Here's how I practice this. Before trusting someone, I decide that I am not going to let them go scot-free if they cheat me; I tell myself that I am going to chase them down and give them a piece of my mind if they do. Of course, the purpose of chasing them down is not to take *revenge*; rather, it is to try to understand what led them to violate my trust. Whether I actually follow up on this resolution or not, I've discovered that making it allows me to be more trusting of others. The reason for this may have to do with the clarity I gain on what I would do if I was cheated. This clarity not only helps me be more trusting of others, it also helps assess when, whom, and how much I should trust. For instance, in situations where I couldn't possibly track the person I trusted, I'm less prone to proactively trusting others. Likewise, I am less likely to be proactively trusting if the stakes are so high that I couldn't help but feel vengeful if I was cheated.

The third strategy—forgiveness—holds a special place for me because of a personal experience. Soon after getting my MBA in 1992, I joined as a management trainee a well-known advertising firm in India called Lintas. One of my first projects at Lintas was to develop a short video for a company called Sterling Tree Magnum. I was told that the video needed to be ready in two days flat, so I went to work immediately. I shot the footage for a day and a half and then got to editing it in a private studio. (Lintas outsourced shooting and editing to third parties.) If you have ever done any editing, you know that it takes far longer than you initially anticipate. In this case, a job for which I had originally budgeted six hours took me three times as much. When I finally got the job done, it was in the nick of time: it was eight a.m.—I had pulled an all-nighter—and the meeting at which the video was required was a mere two hours away. I still needed to get the video transferred from the master to VHS, get back home for a quick shower and bite, and then ride my bike to Lintas for the ten a.m. meeting. But just as I got ready to leave the studio, its proprietor told me that I'd have to pay Lintas's past dues before I could leave!

Imagine my plight. I was famished, smelly, and irritable. Further, I was too junior to know anything about Lintas's past dues—so I felt it didn't really concern me. On top of it, I was too frazzled from having worked all night to think straight. I tried calling Lintas, but no one was in the office yet. (Work in India starts fashionably late.) So I did something totally stupid. I tried to run away with the videotape. Or to be more precise, I tried to nonchalantly stroll out with the videotape tucked under my arm. The ploy didn't work, of course. The proprietor sent some goons after me and they pried the videotape out of me. I was so angry that I turned back and threw a four-letter expletive at the proprietor. He didn't take it too kindly, as you might expect, but what he did next stunned me: he slammed the videotape on the ground and stomped on it till it was smashed to smithereens. Although I was a boy and boys supposedly don't cry, tears welled up in my eyes. I was aghast that all my effort had come to nothing in a matter of seconds. (In my frazzled state, I had forgotten that the original master tape was still intact and that a duplicate could easily be made.) I was seething with anger as I rode my bike back to Lintas. (My original plan of going home, taking a shower, etc., had to be abandoned, of course.)

To cut a long story short, everything turned out well as far as the videotape was concerned. The accountant at Lintas settled the past dues, and a new copy of my video got sent to our office just in time for the meeting. But although the meeting went well (the CEO sent me a handwritten note congratulating me on the job), that wasn't enough to quell my rage at the studio's proprietor. All through the meeting, I was fixated on taking revenge.

It would have been relatively easy for me to take revenge too. All I needed to do was call the studio, act as if I were calling from another advertising agency, and book studio time for a whole day and never show up. (These were pre-caller-ID days and it was possible to make studio reservations over the phone.) Or better yet, ask the studio to send camera and crew to a remote location for a shoot that would never happen. The studio would incur significant costs that they couldn't recoup from anyone. Thankfully, though, I never acted on the plan for revenge. I say "thankfully" because it is by overcoming my desire for revenge that I avoided propagating a cycle of negativity. It feels good to take revenge, of course—which is why so many movies and novels revolve around this theme—but what's also undeniable is that revenge seeking is a cause, perhaps the leading cause, of much misery in the world. I was glad that, in this instance at least, I didn't cause further misery.

There is another reason why I am thankful that I didn't act on my desire for revenge. It's because I learned a very important lesson as a result: *forgiveness is more for the self than for the other.* To understand how I arrived at this insight, it will be useful to walk you through why I decided against taking revenge. It was because of a chat that I had with an older gentleman, who also worked at Lintas. After he heard me rant about what had happened at the studio, he took me aside. During our conversation, he told me that he knew the proprietor of the studio personally and was thus aware of what was going on in his life. His teenage son had recently been killed in a car accident and, further, one of the movies he had recently produced had bombed at the box office. Plus, Lintas had indeed not paid the studio a significant amount of past dues. "It's just unfortunate that you were caught in the crossfire," he continued, "and I think his behavior was childish, but I think this little background should help you understand why he behaved as he did."

The chat not only doused my fiery rage. It also made me realize the truth in the saying: *knowing is understanding, and understanding is forgiving.* By understanding what the proprietor was going through, I found it easier to forgive him. And by forgiving him, I realized that I was the one to benefit the most from it. The rage and anger that had originally been eating me away from the inside was gone, and it felt good to get rid of it.

Practicing Forgiveness: The Fifth Happiness Exercise

Think of someone you dislike—not someone you hate with all your guts (hopefully, you don't know anyone like that), but someone you merely dislike. Let's call this person "X." Now, imagine that you were born with X's genetic material. That is, you had X's looks, body odor, inherent tastes, intelligence, aptitudes, and so on. Further, imagine that you had X's upbringing and experiences as well: you were born into the family in which X was born. So imagine that you had X's parents, grew up in the same neighborhood and city, went to the same school, had the same set of friends, etc.

Do you think you would behave any differently from how X behaves?

Most people realize, perhaps after a moment of startled pause, that the answer to the question is no. In other words, the "person X" thought experiment helps one realize that people act in pretty much the only way they know how. And once this realization sinks in, one is naturally more likely to get past the knee-jerk tendency to judge others' behaviors as "good" and "bad," and go to the next step: of trying to understand *why* people behave the way they do. One may, for example, wonder about the type of upbringing or parental support they might have had, or about the set of stressors they might be facing. This understanding, in turn, would lead one to experience what Sonja Lyubomirsky in *The How of Happiness* calls a "shift in thinking," such that one's desire to harm others is replaced by the desire to do them good.

And this shift in thinking, if you consider it, has more of a beneficial effect on *oneself* than on others. Harboring vengeful thoughts, studies show, has a significant negative effect on both your mental and physical health. Of course, if you act out such thoughts, it might hurt others as well. But doing so is also likely to propagate a cycle of negativity that comes back to hurt you. So whichever way you look at it—whether you merely harbor grudges or act on them—you suffer. Or, conversely, you benefit (both mentally and physically) by shedding thoughts of revenge.

Several studies confirm this. In one study, conducted with women older than sixty-five who had been hurt by a negative interpersonal experience, participants were assigned to either a "forgiveness" condition or a "control" condition. Participants in both conditions met for eight weeks, one day a week. Those in the forgiveness condition were given training on how to forgive; those in the control condition, by contrast, weren't. Results showed that anxiety levels dropped and self-esteem levels increased significantly in the former condition. In another study, people who had experienced romantic infidelity from their partners were given forgiveness training or not, and findings showed that those who had received the training carried far less emotional burden than those who hadn't.

If you can see how forgiving others can be beneficial for well-being, but at the same time are reluctant to be forgiving because it seems unfair to do so, allow me to point out two things. First, it's not necessary to forgive everyone all the time. You can pick and choose when, whom, and for what you want to forgive. Sometimes not forgiving someone else for doing something wrong is the right thing to do—as Dan Ariely argues in *The Upside of Irrationality*. Second, forgiving is not the same as trying to reconcile with someone who violated your trust—much less condoning the act. It is merely an attempt at mitigating the vengeful feelings you harbor so that you can get on with your life. As the popular saying goes, "Holding on to a grudge is like allowing someone else to stay in your head rent free." Why allow that to happen?

I hope this understanding of what forgiveness is—and what it isn't— makes it easier to consider practicing it. You can check out the detailed instructions for it on the book's website: www.happysmarts.com/book/ exercises/forgiveness, and the abridged instructions for it in the appendix for this chapter.

Eliciting Trustworthiness from Others

Learning how to forgive, as an impressively large number of findings have shown, is one of the most powerful ways of boosting happiness levels. But as I have found from the experience of my students, it is as difficult to practice as it is effective. This is mainly because, by forgiving someone, you feel like you are letting someone who has wronged you get away scot-free. One way to get over this obstacle is to remind yourself that forgiveness is something you do for *yourself* rather than for another. Another way is to make it less likely that others cheat you. Forgiveness, I have discovered, is much easier when you exercise it sparingly, rather than regularly.

This brings us to the fourth and final component of exercising smart trust: figuring out ways to elicit trustworthy behavior from others. As I mentioned earlier, most people are capable of both trustworthy and untrustworthy behavior, and the factor that plays a big role in how they behave is the context. In contexts in which trustworthy behavior is expected, most people are likely to exhibit trustworthiness, and vice versa. This means that the extent to which you trust others has to be informed by context. This in turn means being aware of the norms of the context in which you are operating. If you are in a context—such as getting a taxi in Istanbul or an auto rickshaw in Chennai, my hometown—in which untrustworthiness is rife, you'd obviously want to be less trusting.

But across all contexts, there are a number of things you could do to increase the odds of eliciting trustworthy behavior from others. The first and perhaps most important thing is to be better liked. It turns out that the more people like you, the less they will cheat you. One way to be better liked is to emphasize the common features between yourself and the other person. Remember the study that Kim Corfman and I conducted—the one in which we asked participants to view TV ads that they either liked or disliked? As you may recall, we found that participants enjoyed the experience of watching the ads more when they were in the company of those who shared their opinions. This is partly because these participants liked being in the company of those who shared their opinions. Numerous other studies have also found that perceived similarity between oneself and another is a very important determinant of liking. This means that if you're in a taxi in Istanbul, for example, and discover that you and the taxi driver are both fans of the same football team, you'd want to emphasize that similarity. Not only will you have a much more engaging conversation, you will also reduce the chance of being cheated by the taxi driver.

Apart from emphasizing self-other commonalities, there are a number of other ways of being better liked, including showing warmth and friendliness—as opposed to competence and professionalism. Amy Cuddy, a researcher who works on leadership, finds that most leaders make the mistake of wanting to come across as competent, rather than as warm. Competent leaders, she finds, are more feared. Warm leaders, by contrast, are better liked—and therefore, more trusted. Another way to be better liked is to act in a trustworthy fashion yourself. Of course, when you are interacting with someone for the first time, you may not get an opportunity to exhibit your trustworthiness, but if you do get the chance, grab it with both hands. You can also signal your trustworthiness by throwing in a story or two that highlights it. (You want to be careful not to appear boastful or too square, of course.) Yet another way to be better liked is to apologize if and when you screw up. Findings show that firms that screw up and apologize are better liked than those that don't.

Besides doing things to be better liked, another way to elicit trustworthiness from others is to quickly build a history of mutually trustworthy behavior. Findings show that the greater the amount of mutually trust-worthy behavior between two parties, the lower the likelihood of either party defecting. One way to establish such a history is to take a few small initial risks and proactively trust others first. For example, pay for a new colleague's meal first, trusting that he will reciprocate for the next meal. Or divulge some small insecurity you harbor about yourself first, trusting that your colleague will be forthcoming about her own insecurity. A rule of thumb I use in this context is that I will trust someone else three times in small ways. With people from whom reciprocal trustworthiness is not forthcoming, I am reluctant to increase the stakes.

Putting the four components of "smart trust" into practice has yielded significant rewards—both material and psychological—for me, and I hope that your experience, too, will be similar.

Chapter 6A

THE SIXTH DEADLY HAPPINESS "SIN": PASSIONATE/INDIFFERENT PURSUIT OF PASSION

├──────────────────────────────────┤

Although I started my PhD at a large state school in the southwest, I finished it at a large private school in the northeast: the Stern School of Business at New York University. There's a story behind how this happened. Soon after I joined the state school in the southwest, the department there broke up. Several of the professors left to join other schools. Those who stayed urged me to continue at the school, while those who left advised me to transfer to another school. It was a very confusing time for me. I wasn't sure what to do. On the one hand, I would have liked to continue at the state school. I had forged some great friendships in the area. I also liked my mentor and had a fantastic working relationship with her. Further, transferring schools would have meant losing a year, which wasn't appealing to me; like most students, I wanted to finish my education as soon as possible so that I could start seeing some real money. On the other hand, the fact that several professors were leaving the school meant that my training would suffer. And the exodus of professors would, I felt, have a negative effect on the reputation of the school and hence on my chances of getting a good job. So I felt that it might be a good idea to leave.

In the end, everything worked out well. I did transfer, and joined the Stern School of Business in 1995. Although it took me longer to get my PhD as a result, the extra time was well worth it. I ended up doing a dissertation on a topic that was very close to my heart: on the influence of moods and emotions on judgments and decisions. Had I stayed on at the other school, it's likely that I would have done my dissertation on a different topic, one that was less close to my passion.

So if someone were to ask me today whether it was a good thing or a bad thing that the department at the state school broke up, I'd probably say "good thing." In other words, what seemed like a bad thing at the time turned out to be a good thing in retrospect.

My Friend's Story

The same year that I studied at the state school (1994), a close friend of mine also left India for the United States. He came from a relatively poor background and his educational qualifications too were quite mediocre. However, he overcame these obstacles by dint of his efforts and managed to become a very good computer programmer. (He learned to program, of all places, at a public computer at the British embassy in Chennai, India.) He became such a good programmer, in fact, that some talent scouts spotted him and got him a fabulous job at a top U.S. firm. Within a month of landing in the United States, my friend had impressed his employers and was starting to make some serious money. When I visited him in the summer of 1995, just before I entered Stern, he was flying high. He had acquired a fancy new car and was living in a posh apartment in the Bay Area. Soon, however—by early 1996—his life took a turn for the worse. He would call me frequently, about thrice a week, to seek advice on how to deal with his "toxic" boss. Shortly thereafter, he was having problems with everyone: his landlord, girlfriend, and neighbors. And to cope with these problems, he started to drink.

Within three years of coming to the United States, my friend was forced to go back to India because he got fired from literally every job he took up. Going back to India was a major blow for him because he much preferred the work culture in the United States and had also gotten used to the creature comforts of the West. But because he had burned bridges with every employer, he wasn't able to get anyone to even write him a reference letter, let alone hire him back.

His despondence at not being able to get back to the United States, and his growing dependence on alcohol to cope with it, were starting to take a toll on him. When I saw him in July 2007—by then, he had been back in India for ten years—he had become a pale shadow of his former self.

Then, in October of that year, I got the news that I dreaded: my friend had passed away. His hostel-mates (he was at that time living in a hostel room alone) had noticed that he had not emerged from his room for a couple of days. After knocking on his door and failing to elicit a response, they had peered into his room through the ventilator and had found him sprawled, lifeless, on the bed.

When I spoke to my friend's relative later that week, he told me this: "Most people think that he was supremely lucky to get that job in the U.S. I, however, think that he was *unlucky* to get that job. He was emotionally immature when he left for the U.S. He was overly dependent on his mother and his friends for support. Going to the U.S. cut him off completely from this support network. Of course, you tried to help him as much as you could, but he needed someone near him—someone to meet him on a daily basis—which you couldn't do. So he became increasingly lonely over time. And to cope with his loneliness, he started to drink. After that, it all went downhill."

My friend's relative paused for a second and then continued, "I often wonder how things might have turned out had he not left for the U.S. when he did. If he had stayed back in India for even a couple of more years, I feel things would have turned out very differently. For one, he would have had more time to develop some much-needed people skills. Further, because the IT industry in India was just starting to take off right around that time, he would have been able to develop some project management skills too. Eventually, like most of his peers in the IT sector, he too would have gone to the U.S., but it would have happened after he had had time to mature and develop."

"Good Thing, Bad Thing, Who Knows?"

There are two main themes that emerge from the stories I've just recounted. First, the outcomes that we experience are often completely outside our control. Who would have thought that the department at the state school would break up and that I would change schools as a result? Similarly, who could have predicted that my friend—someone with a questionable educational background and zero contacts—would land a dream job in the United States?

I don't mean to suggest, of course, that *all* our outcomes are outside our control. Many "simple" outcomes—outcomes that occur in the immediate future and those whose achievement depends only on our own actions—are within our control. For example, if you wished to scratch your nose right now or to stifle a yawn (go ahead, do it!), there's no doubt you could achieve those things. However, when the outcomes become even a little more complex, our control over them drops exponentially. There's not much you could do to ensure that the five-course meal you intend to prepare for this weekend's get-together will turn out exactly as you want it to, and even less to ensure that your guests will enjoy it as much as you hope. And when it comes to even more complex outcomes—such as finding your ideal life partner or landing a dream job—you wield even less control.

The second theme that emerges from the stories is, to me, an even more intriguing one: people hold far stronger opinions about the "goodness" and "badness" of outcomes than they ought to. When the department at the state school broke up, I was *convinced* that it was a bad outcome. Likewise, when my friend got the dream job in the United States, he was *convinced* that it was a good outcome. But boy, were we both wrong.

At some level, we all know—or *should* know—that we don't have the ability to figure out all the downstream consequences that an outcome will trigger. When I started my PhD, there's certainly no way I could have figured out what my life would be like if the department broke up. Likewise, my friend could not have known how his life would turn out if he moved to the United States. And because we lack the ability to figure out the downstream consequences of outcomes, we also lack the knowledge to calculate the overall impact that the outcome will have on our life. In other words, expressed in business-speak, we lack the knowledge to calculate the "net present value" (NPV) of any outcome. An outcome that currently seems positive (e.g., getting married to a sweetheart) may well turn out later—as it often does—to be negative. And likewise, an outcome (e.g., divorce) that currently seems negative may later turn out to be the best thing that happened. That's just how life is—unpredictable and whimsical. As such, we shouldn't hold strong views about the goodness and badness of outcomes we experience.

This idea is best captured in a story often told in Indian circles. Here's how it goes:*

There was once a farmer who owned a horse and had a son.

One day, his horse ran away. The neighbors came to express their concern: "Oh, that's too bad. How are you going to work the fields now?" The farmer replied: "Good thing, bad thing, who knows?"

In a few days, his horse came back and brought another horse with her. Now the neighbors were glad: "Oh, how lucky! Now you can do twice as much work as before!" The farmer replied: "Good thing, bad thing, who knows?"

The next day, the farmer's son fell off the new horse and broke his leg. The neighbors were concerned again: "Now that he is incapacitated, he can't help you around the farm, that's too bad." The farmer replied: "Good thing, bad thing, who knows?"

Soon, the news came that a war had broken out, and all the young men were required to join the army. The villagers were sad because they knew that many of the young men would not come back. But the farmer's son could not be drafted because of his broken leg. His neighbors were envious: "How lucky! You get to keep your only son—he doesn't have to go to war." The farmer replied: "Good thing, bad thing, who knows?"

Unlike the farmer in the story, most of us find it difficult to reserve our judgments about outcomes. Imagine, though, that like the farmer, you *could* reserve your judgments about outcomes. That is, imagine that you too could say—and mean it when you say it—"Good thing, bad thing, who knows?" after every outcome.

Does that way of living sound appealing to you?

If you are like the students in my class, you are not so sure. Although you can see how not judging outcomes, especially negative ones, can be a good thing, you also have some reservations about being like the old man in the "good thing, bad thing, who knows?"—let's call it the GTBTWK—

---

* For my Coursera course on happiness, I got Professor Srikumar Rao—whom we encountered in the Introduction—to recite this story. You can catch his version of the story (which is slightly different from the one presented here) at https://www.coursera.org/learn/happiness/lecture/PMte2/week-5-video-7-the-6th-deadly-happiness-sin-distrusting-life.

story. In particular, most of my students have two big concerns. First, by being like the old man, they fear they would run the risk of never feeling happy again. As one of my students put it, "If I didn't feel happy upon getting a good job or getting married to my sweetheart, why would I feel happy about anything at all?" Another concern is that they wouldn't find *any* goals worthy of pursuit. Imagine that whenever you considered a goal—say, that of finishing this book—you said to yourself, "Good thing, bad thing, who knows?" Clearly, you would be far less motivated to read the book than you would be if you thought of this goal as a positive and desirable one.

But are these concerns really valid?

To assess the validity of the first concern—that if you delinked your happiness from outcomes, you would never get to experience happiness again—allow me to engage you in a thought experiment.

The Need to Be Busy

Imagine that you are in an unfamiliar city for some work. After finishing up work, you get into your rental car to drive back to your hotel. Your trusty GPS tells you that you can take one of two routes. Taking the shorter route, let's call this Route A, will get you to your hotel in thirty minutes. Taking this route, however, will involve idling for about ten minutes at a construction site; for these ten minutes, you will have no option but to sit in your car doing nothing. Taking the longer route, let's call it Route B, will not involve any idling. However, it will involve driving for a longer duration—40 minutes in all—to reach your hotel. So your two options are:

Route A, which involves a thirty-minute drive, including ten minutes of idling time, or

Route B, which involves a forty-minute drive with no idling time.

Which route would you prefer?

From a purely "economic" perspective—that is, in terms of time and effort involved—Route A clearly dominates Route B. However, from a more "psychological" perspective, it's not clear which route is better. If you are averse to spending time idling—doing nothing—then Route B may be more appealing even though it is longer.

Recently, I posed this scenario to students in one of my classes, and it turned out that most (78 percent) preferred Route B. To these students, "doing nothing" for ten minutes was disagreeable enough to make the longer and more time-consuming route more attractive.

Chris Hsee and his colleagues at the University of Chicago refer to people's aversion to doing nothing as "the need to be busy." In one study, participants were asked to fill out a survey. After completing the survey, participants were told that they would need to drop it off at another location. Participants were given the option of dropping the survey at either a nearby location (a two- to three-minute round-trip) or a faraway one (a twelve- to fifteen-minute round-trip). Participants were further told that, after dropping off the survey, they would have to return to the experimental room to wait out the remainder of the time. That is, participants understood that, if they chose the nearby location, they would spend more time doing nothing after they returned; if they chose the faraway location, they would spend less time doing nothing, but would have to expend extra time and effort walking to and from the drop-off location. For reasons that will become clear shortly, participants were also told that, as a token of appreciation for completing the survey, they would be given a piece of candy at the drop-off location. One set of participants (those in the "same candy" condition) was told that they would get the same candy (either dark chocolate or light chocolate) regardless of the drop-off location they chose. Another set of participants (those in the "different candy" condition), by contrast, was told that they would get one type of candy at the nearby location (either light chocolate or dark chocolate) and another type of candy at the faraway location (the other type of chocolate). Thus, participants in the "different candy" condition had some justification for choosing the faraway location; walking the longer distance would give them the opportunity to consume a different type of candy.

Hsee and his colleagues were interested in participants' preference of location: would they choose the nearby location or the faraway one? Findings revealed that participants' preference depended on whether they had justification for walking to the faraway location. Specifically, among participants in the "same candy" condition, only 32 percent chose the faraway location. By contrast, among participants in the "different candy" condition, 59 percent chose the faraway location. Thus, participants who had some reason, even if it was only a trivial one, for walking to the faraway location preferred "being busy" to "being idle." Results from a follow-up study showed the same results. In this study, participants were first asked to complete a survey and then *forced* to drop it off at either the nearby location or the faraway one. After dropping off the survey, participants waited out the rest of the time in the experimental room. (Those who dropped the survey at the nearby location waited for a longer duration than those who dropped it off at the faraway location.) Then, once this waiting period was over, participants were asked to report their happiness levels by responding to the question "How happy did you feel in the last fifteen minutes?" Findings showed that participants who were forced into busyness—by being told to drop the survey off at the faraway location—were happier than those who were forced into idleness.

When Does Being Busy Make Us Happier?

What these findings suggest is that people are far happier being busy than being idle. Of course, people may not always prefer busyness over idleness. People who feel overworked, for example, may prefer doing nothing to doing something. (Doing nothing sounds quite attractive to me right now!) Further, people may not be happy if they are kept busy for busyness's sake— as we just saw, people need a reason to be busy. However, so long as these relatively simple qualifications are met, it appears that people would prefer doing something to doing nothing.

And if people don't just have a reason to be busy but find what they are doing to be *meaningful*, then there's an even greater chance that they'd be happy. I say this on the basis of a clever set of studies that Dan Ariely—the behavioral economist whom we encountered in chapter 2—and his colleagues conducted. In one of these studies, Dan and his colleagues asked participants to assemble pieces of a Lego set that eventually took the shape of a Bionicle.* Each time the participants assembled a Bionicle, they were paid money for it, but the amount they were paid got progressively smaller over time: for the first Bionicle, they were paid $2, for the second, they were paid $1.89, for the third, $1.78, and so on. Some of the participants were told that the Bionicles they had assembled would be given away as toys to children.

---

* BIONICLE is a line of construction toys created by the LEGO Group and marketed primarily to five-to-sixteen-year-olds.

These participants thus felt that assembling the Bionicle was a meaningful activity—it would make some kids happy. Other participants, by contrast, were told that the Bionicles they had assembled would be disassembled soon afterward so that future participants could assemble them. These participants felt that the task was a relatively meaningless one. Dan and his colleagues were interested in whether being meaningfully busy would make a difference in the number of Bionicles that the participants assembled. And it did! On average, those in the "meaningful" condition assembled 2.5 more Bionicles than those in the "meaningless" condition.

Most of us can, of course, readily relate to the idea that being meaningfully busy is better than being meaninglessly busy. This is because we know, from personal experience, that we are happier doing something meaningful than doing something meaningless. The findings on flow (discussed in chapter 2B), for example, are entirely consistent with the idea that being meaningfully busy makes us happy.

Implications of the Need to Be Busy: Process (vs. Outcome) as a Source of Happiness

The fact that we are happier when we are busy than when not, and the fact that we are even happier when doing something meaningful—rather than meaningless—has a very important implication. It suggests that we don't need to depend on outcomes for happiness—*we could derive all our happiness from the process of working toward outcomes*. We could, for example, derive happiness from *preparing* for an exam or from *planning* for a vacation. That is, even if we don't eventually pass the exam or go on the vacation, we could still derive significant happiness from working toward these outcomes. Of course, the *type* of emotions we experience if we delink happiness from outcomes would change. We'd perhaps rarely feel hubristic or authentic pride, because those are outcome-based, and not *process-based*, emotions. However, in the bargain, we'd rarely feel the outcome-based negative emotions, such as dejection or shame. We'd perhaps also feel much more absorbed and at peace with our lives, because those emotions are more likely when we focus on deriving happiness from process (as opposed to outcomes).

Overall, this wouldn't be such a bad bargain.

The Second Concern

To summarize, then, it seems that delinking happiness from outcomes will not lead to never feeling happy again. This is because outcomes are only one source of happiness, the other source being the process of working toward outcomes. That takes care of the first concern with delinking happiness from outcomes, but what about the second concern—that delinking happiness from outcomes would kill the motivation to pursue goals? This concern is based on the logic that, if all outcomes become equally attractive (good thing, bad thing, who knows?), we wouldn't know which outcome to pursue.

Here's a colorful illustration of this concern. Imagine that you are a handsome boy—even if you're neither handsome nor a boy—and imagine that a beautiful girl has just proposed to you. If you manage to successfully delink happiness from outcomes, wouldn't you be indifferent to whether you married this person or not, because getting married to her wouldn't make you any happier than not getting married to her? And extending this logic, wouldn't you be indifferent to all the other outcomes in your life? If so, delinking happiness from outcomes would lead you to become passive and indifferent to life, right? No, wrong!

The reason that delinking happiness from outcomes doesn't mean you would become indifferent to life (and not know which goal to pursue) has to do with a seemingly subtle, but actually very important, difference: delinking happiness from outcomes refers to judging outcomes only *after* they have occurred, and not *before* they have occurred. That is, before an outcome has occurred, you *would* have a preference for some outcomes over others. However, once an outcome has occurred, you wouldn't judge it as "good" or "bad." In other words, you would have what might be called "preoccurrence preference," but you wouldn't have what might be called "postoccurrence judgmentalism."

If these terms sound too technical, don't worry; the concept itself is really simple. In the example where a girl has just proposed to you, delinking happiness from outcomes would mean that you *would* have a preference for whether you wished to marry her or not. And that preference would, ideally, be based on your goals and values. You might believe that getting married to her will promote your chances of pursuing flow, or of being a kind and compassionate person. If so, you'd say "Yes, absolutely, my dear!" If, on the other hand, you think that getting married to her will make it more difficult for you—or her—to lead a meaningful life, you'd say "No" and perhaps add, "It's because of me—not you!" But once the outcome has occurred—imagine that you are now married to her—you wouldn't take this outcome for granted and believe that, from now on, your life is going to be a bed of roses. You would recognize that what appears to be a desirable outcome may lead to downstream consequences that aren't necessarily desirable, so you would do two things. First, you would work toward avoiding those undesirable outcomes to the best of your ability. Second, you would focus on deriving happiness from the *processes* you put in place: for example, being involved in activities that both you and your partner find meaningful, rather than taking the partnership—or your partner—for granted. And by relying on processes for your happiness, rather than on the past outcome of being married, you'd avoid a trap that many married people fall into: the trap of believing that, by simply being married to a particular person, life is going be a fairy tale: "they lived happily ever after."

Three Broad Approaches to Goal Pursuit

One way to think about what I have just discussed is this: there are three broad approaches you can take to goals. The first approach, which is the one most of us take, might be called the "obsessive pursuit of passion." This approach involves having a strong preference for certain outcomes over others both before and after they have occurred. If the old man in the GTBTWK story had had this approach toward goals, he would have agreed with the villagers when they came to him and said, "Oh, you poor man, your son can never get married now," or when they said, "Oh, you lucky man, your son doesn't have to go to war."

The second broad approach you can take is what might be called "indifferent pursuit of passion." This approach involves being indifferent to outcomes both before *and* after they occur. This would lead to a lifeless pursuit of goals. Such a person would be devoid of curiosity or interest—which are, as we saw in chapter 1, important ways of defining happiness. This is the approach you would take if you misunderstood what delinking happiness from outcomes really means and concluded that it means not having a preference for outcomes even before they occur. I see many people falling into this trap and have to confess that I myself fell into it when I was in my early twenties. I was desperately in search of happiness then (some things never change) and believed that the way to happiness was to welcome any and all outcomes that occurred in my life. The idea of welcoming—or accepting—all outcomes is an important one, and one that we will explore in greater depth in chapters 7A and 7B, but this welcoming attitude should happen *after* an outcome has unfolded and not before.

There are two problems with being welcoming of any and all outcomes even before they have occurred. The first is that it's not possible to be this way. That is, whether you like it or not and whether you know it or not, you are going to have desires—to eat, to scratch an itch, to take a breath, etc. So you would only be deluding yourself by thinking that you are equally welcoming of whether you get to eat or not, whether you get to scratch an itch or not, or whether you get to breathe or not. At the visceral level, you *always* have a preference for certain outcomes over other outcomes. Of course, you could deny that you have these preferences, but if you did, it would lead to the second problem, which is this: your life would be devoid of, well, life. You might think that you are being "cool" and "easygoing" by pretending that you don't have any preferences, but in reality, as studies show, indifference to outcomes doesn't just make other people like you less, it is also a sign of helplessness and depression.

This leads me to the third approach, which I believe is the optimal one from the standpoint of maximizing happiness. This approach, which is the sixth habit of the highly happy, is what I call "the dispassionate pursuit of passion." It involves having a preference for certain outcomes over others *before* they have occurred, but being nonjudgmental about them *after* they have occurred. The dispassionate pursuit of passion might seem like a very difficult thing to pull off—and it is. That's because it is much easier to hold a consistent view of things. We all have a need for consistency, as Bill Swann, one of my colleagues from the University of Texas at Austin, has shown in many studies. So holding one view of an outcome before it occurs, and then changing that view after it has occurred, is tough. But it's not impossible to pull off, and it is well worth the effort because, for reasons we will see in the next chapter, it not only enhances happiness levels, it also enhances the chances of success.

Chapter 6B

THE SIXTH HABIT OF THE HIGHLY HAPPY: DISPASSIONATE PURSUIT OF PASSION

S mart person that you are, I'm sure you've caught on to one of the main ways in which I test my "happiness hypotheses": in-class experiments in which I use my students as guinea pigs. Of course, my intention in conducting these experiments is always noble, even if I say so myself. I want to help my students, and by extension, others, lead happier, more fulfilling lives. So I often use the in-class experiments to refine the most important aspect of my course and this book: the happiness exercises. As I often tell my students, although the concepts in this book (like *flow* or *attachment theory* or *maximizer mind-set*) are interesting, they aren't all that useful for improving happiness levels; it's the happiness exercises that serve this purpose. Indeed, I would go so far as to say that you could ignore the concepts in this book and still see a huge improvement in happiness levels just by doing the happiness exercises, but the reverse isn't possible.

Now, although my students understand the importance of partaking in the happiness exercises, they aren't equally enthusiastic about all of them; they find some of the exercises to be more appealing than others. Why? Because some, like "defining and incorporating happiness" and "creative altruism," make them feel good from the get-go. Some others, by contrast, like "journal keeping" and "healthy lifestyle," have little effect on their emotional well-being at first; these exercises take time to take effect, which makes them less appealing. And then there's the rest, like "mental chatter" and "expressing gratitude," which actually make the students feel *worse* at first, before delivering a salubrious result. This makes these exercises quite unappealing; most students shun them like toddlers shun broccoli.

The exercise that I have in mind for this chapter—called "3 good things with a twist"—is one of those that evokes negative feelings at first. And because I know this means that my students are likely to shun it, I have devised a clever way of getting them to do it: I impose the exercise on them without warning during class (after first locking the door so they can't escape, of course).

The reason I am telling you all this is that I am about to do something very similar with you: I am going to have you do a short exercise that will likely make you feel a little bad at first. But you have my word that it will improve your happiness levels in the long run.

Ready? Here's what I want you to do. Think of a relatively intense negative event, such as a breakup with a "soul mate" or being slammed with a DWI (driving while intoxicated) charge, that happened to you a while—say, two or more years—back. Then, open your laptop and type up what happened in some detail. (Or, if you are old-fashioned, take out a notepad and write about it.) Done?

Now, using a seven-point scale, where 1 = "not at all" and 7 = "intensely," come up with a number in response to each of the following two questions:

1. How negative did you feel at the time that the event occurred?
2. How negative do you now feel about the event?

Once you have come up with these responses, answer one more question: How *meaningful* do you now consider the negative event to be? That is, do you feel that you have learned something useful from it—lessons that you wouldn't have learned had the event not occurred? That is, did the event help you grow and evolve in any meaningful way? Answer this question using a seven-point scale, where 1 = "not at all meaningful," and 7 = "extremely meaningful."

The "Reminisce and Reflect" Exercise

If you are like most of my students, you discovered two things from this exercise. First, you discovered that you feel far less negative about the event now than you felt when it occurred. Second, despite its negativity, you now consider the event to be meaningful. Why? Because you learned something useful from it—lessons you would not have learned had the event not occurred. As a result, you may have even discovered—as a nontrivial proportion of my students do—that not only do you feel less negative about the event, you actually feel *positive* about it now!

When I conduct my exercise—which I call the "reminisce and reflect exercise"—in class, I don't ask all of my students to recall a negative event from way back: I ask only a quarter of them to do so. I ask another quarter to recall a more recent negative event—something that happened in the past month. I ask the rest of the students, roughly half the class, to recall a positive, rather than a negative, event. And of these students, I ask about half to recall an event from the distant past, while I ask the rest to recall an event from the recent past.

So in the end, I have four groups of students: those who have recalled a negative event from way back (Group 1) or from the recent past (Group 2), and those who have recalled a positive event from way back (Group 3) or from the recent past (Group 4). I ask all four groups to do the things I asked you to do: 1) provide two sets of ratings for the event: how positive or negative they felt about it when it occurred, and how they feel about it now, and 2) provide an evaluation of how meaningful they now consider the event to be.

As the figure below shows, my students' judgments of both positive and negative events change with time. Specifically, both become less intense over time. This is not surprising, of course. We know from personal experience that our feelings toward both negative and positive events generally become less intense with time. What *is* interesting, however, is that this change is more pronounced for negative—versus positive—events. This suggests that negative events lose their sting more rapidly than positive ones lose their glow, which is cool. For instance, we will likely continue to savor the positive feelings from our first kiss and from our last vacation long after they are over, but not harbor negative feelings about losing money

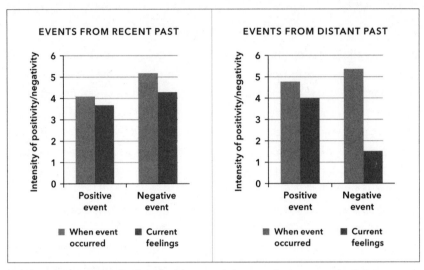

Our feelings toward past events change with time, with past negative events showing the most (positive) change—particularly for distant (vs. recent) events

in a scam or failing an exam for as long. What's also interesting is that the decay in intensity of feelings is most pronounced for events that took place in the distant (versus near) past. This suggests that, although we eventually get around to changing our feelings toward negative events, it doesn't happen immediately; it takes time.

None of these results is, however, as interesting as the next one I am about to share with you. This result has to do with how *meaningful* people find past events to be. It turns out that people find past negative events to be significantly more meaningful than they do past positive events. The reason for this is that negative events provide far greater opportunity for growth and learning than do the positive ones. Of course, some water needs to have flowed under the bridge since the negative event occurred for this to happen. That is, we can't as easily see the meaning in negative events that have recently transpired. However, the fact that once a sufficient amount of time has passed, it is negative (rather than positive) events that are seen as more meaningful is striking. What's even more striking—and to me, *the* most interesting finding of all—is that the past events that we find the most meaningful are often *the ones that we were the most intensely negative about when they occurred!*

Think, for a minute, about what this means. This means that *the very events that you currently consider to be the most negative will likely be the ones that you later come to cherish.* Thus, it is events like loss of a job, separation from a partner, or onset of a serious ailment that we later come to appreciate more than the more mundane events such as being reprimanded by the boss, getting a speeding ticket, or getting into a fight with a friend. This insight is consistent with something that Sonja Lyubomirsky, whom we encountered in chapter 2B, notes in her book *The Myths of Happiness*:

> We may think we know whether a particular turning point should make us laugh or cry, but the truth is that positive and negative events are often entwined, rendering predictions about consequences—which may cascade in unexpected ways—exceedingly complex. [When] we consider the single best thing that has happened to us during past years—and the single worst thing—we may be surprised to learn that they are often one and the same.

The Role of "Trust in Life"

The fact that people's feelings about past events change, often quite drastically, is quite consistent with findings from an area of research called "affective misforecasting." These findings show that we consistently overestimate both the duration and intensity of our feelings toward current events. For example, we expect the heartache from a breakup to last far longer and to be far worse than it turns out to be. Likewise, we expect the euphoria from winning a lottery to last far longer and be far more intense than it proves to be.

As it turns out, there are many reasons why our feelings toward past negative events change with time, including something I mentioned earlier: negative events make us learn and grow in ways we wouldn't have if they hadn't occurred. For instance, we are likely to be more compassionate and kind—and therefore practice the need to love and give—if we have experienced pain and suffering than if we haven't. Negative events can also make us wiser—more capable of dealing with the "curveballs" that life often throws at us. Another reason why we come to see past negative events in a brighter light with time is because of the "bragging rights" they afford. Although you may not have enjoyed the grueling hike up Kilimanjaro or relished the hideous dish that you were persuaded to eat on a "cultural tour" of a strange new land (think fried worms—disgustingly delicious!) *while* they happened, they likely served a useful purpose on your first date or at dull office parties. Finally, negative events can also make us feel better about ourselves. We feel stronger and more resilient when we reminisce about negative events and realize that we have lived through them. This may be why an incredibly high proportion of people—somewhere between 70 and 80 percent—who've lost a loved one report finding something positive about that experience. Likewise, two thirds of cancer survivors attest that their lives have changed for the better after developing (and subsequently being cured of) the disease.

The fact that our feelings toward past negative events turn more positive with time suggests one way we could nurture the sixth habit of the highly happy, the dispassionate pursuit of passion. The dispassionate pursuit of passion, as you may recall, involves having a preference for certain outcomes over others *before* they occur, but being nonjudgmental about them *after* they occur. The first part—having preferences for certain outcomes over others—is the easy part. (As I mentioned in the previous chapter, we almost always have preferences for certain outcomes over others.) It is the second part—being nonjudgmental about outcomes after they occur—that's tough. One way to practice this part, however, is by consciously reminding ourselves that, if we are bound to revise our feelings about past negative events anyway, we might as well consider doing the same with *current* negative events. This recognition, in turn, can help us become less judgmental about outcomes we are currently experiencing. Imagine, for example, that you've fallen sick and as a result have to miss the year-end office party. (Assume that you were excited about attending the year-end party, however unrealistic that may seem.) By recalling a previous occasion of falling sick, and by reflecting on the reasons why you no longer consider the occasion to be negative (perhaps you fell in love with the nurse who brought you back to health? Perhaps you got to lie in bed and watch your favorite TV reruns?), you can bring yourself to view the current negative event with less negativity.

How effective is the "reminisce and reflect" exercise for withholding judgments of outcomes? Can merely reminiscing about past negative events actually help you cultivate "postoccurrence nonjudgmentalism"?

The short answer is yes. I know this both from personal experience and from the experience of my students. But there's a catch—the exercise won't work as effectively if it isn't accompanied by an implicit *trust in life*. By implicit trust in life, I mean the belief that good things are going to happen to you and that life, by nature, is more benign than malign or indifferent. The reason such trust is important is because it paves the way for you to be more open, looking for the positive consequences that negative outcomes trigger. As you can imagine, if you do not register the positive consequences that negative events trigger, you will likely wallow in their negativity. For example, if after a flight you *had* to get on is canceled, you aren't open to looking for the positive consequences that the event has triggered, you'll be less likely to notice a new massage parlor that's opened up at the airport. You may also be less likely to chat with the person sitting next to you on the later flight who proves to be a useful contact. An implicit trust in life is, in other words, invaluable for moving on quickly past disappointing events to welcome exciting new ones. The question, of course, is: how does one inculcate such implicit trust in life?

Before I get to this question, I have to tell you that one of the biggest fears many of my students have in taking my course is that conversation is going to turn, sooner or later, to "woo woo" topics—like God or spirituality. If you harbored a similar fear in starting this book, you'll be happy (or should I say *un*happy?) to know that that time has come now. The topic of trust in life, as you'll see, is inextricably woven with that of spirituality.

Placebo Effects: When Subjective Beliefs Shape Objective Reality

A person who believes that "life is benign," in contrast to one who believes that "life is malign," will naturally trust that good things will happen to him. Everyone recognizes this intuitively. What many of us don't immediately realize, however, is that it is impossible *not* to have an opinion about whether life is good, bad, or indifferent. Even those who do not hold an explicit belief about whether and how much life can be trusted will reflect their beliefs in the implicit attitudes they harbor toward life—in, for example, how optimistic they are, or in how resilient they are after a setback.

What's even more difficult for many to comprehend—and this may be particularly true for the S-and-S—is that there is no "scientifically valid" belief about how much life can be trusted. Or, put differently, the belief that "life can be trusted" and the associated belief that "everything happens for the best" isn't any less scientifically valid than are the competing beliefs, that "life is indifferent" or that "life is malign and can't be trusted."

That's the reason I seldom get into an argument with anyone on whether life is good, bad, or indifferent. Such arguments are generally pointless; at best, everyone walks away even more firmly entrenched in their original belief, and at worst, there is bad blood. So I am not going to persuade you to adopt the attitude that "life can be trusted" and that "everything happens for the best." But given your scientific bent, I believe you would be curious to know why the view that "life can be trusted" is no less scientific—and no more delusional, I might add—than the view that "life is indifferent" or that "life is malign."

This reason, in short, has to do with placebo effects, which refers to the idea that, at least in some contexts, our subjective beliefs about the truth shape the objective truth. Consider one study conducted by Don Price, a researcher at the University of Florida at Gainesville, and his colleagues. In the study, patients with IBS (irritable bowel syndrome, a painful stomach condition) were divided into three groups. In all three groups, a balloon was inflated in the patients' rectums. After that, they were asked to rate how painful this experience was. Before the balloon was blown, patients in one group were given an anesthetic (lidocaine) that mutes feelings. The pain experienced by this group, represented by the dark dashed line in the graph,

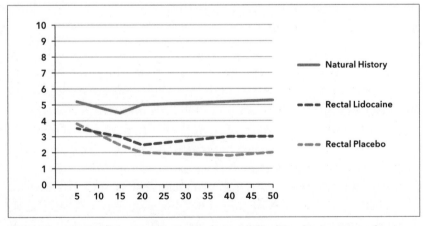

The reported pain of those given a placebo painkiller (Vaseline) was even lower than that of those given a real painkiller!

was significantly lower than that experienced by the second group of patients—represented by the solid line—that wasn't given any anesthetic.

The interesting group, however, was the third one, who were given a placebo—specifically Vaseline—and told that they had been given something known to "powerfully reduce pain in most people." As you can see from the light dashed line in the graph, this set of patients experienced the *least* amount of pain—even lower than that experienced by the group that got the anesthetic!

To those who are familiar with placebo effects, these results won't come as a surprise. Placebo effects are so prevalent in medical contexts that any test of the effectiveness of a new drug involves comparing it with a control condition in which a placebo drug, like a sugar pill, is given to patients. What these placebo effects tell us is that our beliefs can shape our reality. If you think that a pill is going to cure a disease, there seems to be an objectively greater chance that it *will* cure the disease than if you think that it won't.

As it turns out—and here's where it gets really interesting—placebo effects are not restricted to medical contexts; they occur in other contexts as well. In marketing, findings show that if you believe imbibing a particular drink will improve your cognitive skills, it will. In the context of learning, the findings of Carol Dweck and her coauthors show that those who believe that intelligence levels can be altered are more likely to get smarter over time than those who believe that intelligence levels are fixed at birth. Henry Ford, who once said, "whether you think you can, or you think you can't—you're right," seems to have had an intuitive grasp of the power of "placebo beliefs."

What all of these findings share in common is that, in many contexts, our subjective beliefs can shape the objective reality. I don't mean to suggest, of course, that every subjective belief shapes objective reality. For example, no matter how firmly you believe that the Earth has two moons, it's not going to change the objective reality. However, what's also equally true is that, in some contexts, there's no denying that our subjective beliefs do shape objective reality.

And not acknowledging this fact is a grossly unscientific thing to do.

Given that background on placebo effects, let me get to a question of great relevance to our topic: What's the most rational belief to have about whether life can be trusted or not? Is it that life is benign? Or is it that life is malign? Or perhaps it is that life is indifferent?

The answer, it turns out is: all of the above. This is because one's belief about life falls firmly in the domain of placebo effects. To a person who believes that "life is benign" and that "life can be trusted," life does turn out to be benign and trustworthy. To a person who believes the opposite, life's experiences offer ample evidence in support of the view that life is malign. And likewise, a person who's in the middle will find convincing evidence in support of the view that life is indifferent.

So there's no way to scientifically prove that any of the three hypotheses— that life is benign, or malign, or indifferent—is more accurate than the others. However, what can be proven is that from a *utilitarian* perspective—that is, from the perspective of maximizing happiness—it is better to believe that life is benign than it is to believe otherwise. Findings from a variety of disparate streams provide support for this notion. For instance, findings from the area of religion and spirituality show that those who hold a spiritual attitude toward life lead happier lives than those who don't.* Likewise, findings show that optimists and those who hold a more positive outlook toward life are happier than their more pessimistic counterparts.

Of course, it's one thing to recognize that it's more useful to trust life and entirely another thing to adopt that belief. What can one do to develop greater trust in life? One practice that has great potential is gratitude. As I mentioned earlier, in chapter 2B, Sonja Lyubomirsky considers gratitude a meta strategy, in part because it improves one's outlook toward life and therefore instills an implicit faith in the trustworthiness of life.† In chapter 2A, I discussed how being grateful after successes happen can mitigate the need for superiority. Obviously, it's easier to be grateful when something positive happens. But as the Catholic Benedictine monk David Steindl-Rast noted in his popular TED talk, we could be grateful even when negative things happen—not for the negative things that happened, but for the

---

* For my Coursera course, I had the pleasure of interviewing Professor Kenneth Pargament of Bowling Green University on the definition of spirituality and on why a spiritual outlook improves well-being. You can watch excerpts from this interview at https://www.coursera.org/learn/happiness/lecture/jisbD/week-5-video-11-going-spiritual.

† As mentioned earlier (in chapter 2B), I queried Professor Lyubomirsky on why she considers gratitude to be a meta strategy. You can see her response to this question at https://www.coursera.org/learn/happiness/lecture/Tx8Zm/week-2-video-13-summary-of-week-2.

opportunities that arose because of those events. And when you actively look to be grateful for the opportunities that negative events trigger, you are naturally going to be less judgmental about "negativity" of outcomes—because you recognize that these positive opportunities would not have come about if the event hadn't occurred.

This brings me to the sixth happiness exercise, which is adapted from the "reminisce and reflect" exercise that I had you participate in earlier. I call this exercise "3 good things with a twist." In short, the exercise involves keeping a journal in which you note three "bad" things that happened to you during the day that later turned out to be good. The idea is to practice the ability to "connect the dots" for small, everyday "negative" events in your life so that it becomes second nature to be nonjudgmental of negative outcomes.

You can find the detailed instructions for this exercise in the website for the book: www.happysmarts.com/book/exercises/3_good_things_with _a_twist, and the abridged instructions in the appendix for this chapter. And because I have already made you do a version of this exercise (namely, the "reminisce and reflect" exercise), I hope you won't let the initial negativity that this exercise induces stop you from completing it!

Chapter 7A

THE SEVENTH DEADLY HAPPINESS "SIN": MIND ADDICTION

A ll you single ladies out there, here's a thought experiment for you. Imagine that you've just signed up for a speed-dating event. Speed dating, as you may know, involves "dating" several people in quick succession for very short periods of time. In a typical speed-dating event, around twenty men and twenty women meet one another for about five minutes each. Once everyone has finished meeting all potential partners, each person decides on the people with whom he or she would like to go out on a *real* date. If there's a match—say, Lady L is interested in Gentleman G and there is reciprocal interest from him—they would go out. If Lady L is also interested in Gentleman M, but alas, there's no interest on his side, then Lady L would be out of luck—at least as far as Gentleman M is concerned.

Imagine that, just before going out on a speed date, you make a list of traits you wish to see in your partner. Being the smart person that you are, you decide that the most important trait for you is "smartness and wittiness." "Being romantic" comes next, because after all, who doesn't like being swept off her feet? Other attributes, like "culinary skills" and "strong hands" (important for getting good massages, you know), figure next on your list, but let's ignore these for now.

Imagine that, at the speed-dating event, you meet the two gentlemen featured below. Gentleman X, it turns out, is the smartest, wittiest person

GENTLEMAN X

GENTLEMAN Y

Smart and Witty; Not Romantic

Not Smart or Witty; Very Romantic

in town, while Gentleman Y is—how do I put it politely?—not the sharpest knife in the drawer. However, Gentleman Y has something else going for him: he knows how to turn up the romance. Gentleman X, by contrast, is more like Don Quixote than Don Juan when it comes to the fine art of romancing.

Imagine, finally, that you have time to date only one of these two characters because, like all the other S-and-S out there, you lead a super busy life doing super cool things.

Who would you choose: Gentleman X or Gentleman Y? (Be honest now; you don't get extra points for being politically correct!)

If you are like most ladies in the experiments that my collaborator Szu-chi Huang, a professor of marketing at Stanford University, and I have conducted, you would prefer Gentleman Y—the handsome dude. Why? Because although he isn't the smarter and wittier of the two, you can't help but be bowled over by his killer looks. (And, let's face it, looks *are* important.)

Now, here's the crux of what I am trying to get at, so pay careful attention. Having chosen Gentleman Y, would you feel compelled to revise the importance of "being romantic" upward and that of "smartness and wittiness" downward so that you could more easily justify your choice?

Most people, it turns out, do end up adjusting the importance of "being romantic" and "smartness and wittiness" after choosing Gentleman Y.

Before I get to why this is significant, allow me to point out that you don't *have* to adjust the importance of these attributes in order to justify choosing Gentleman Y; you could just as easily justify your choice by pointing to his superior looks. For example, if a friend asks whether your choice of Gentleman Y means that you now think "being romantic" is more important than "smartness and wittiness," you could say, "No, I continue to think that 'smartness and wittiness' is more important than 'being romantic,' but what's *also* important to me—and I must admit that I *just* now realized this—is physical attractiveness." You might even add, if you were in the mood to be totally honest, "Come to think of it, 'physical attractiveness' may be *the* most important attribute in a date for me!"

But chances are, you wouldn't say any of this—either because you wouldn't even be aware that your preference for Gentleman Y was influenced by his looks or because, even if you were aware of this, you wouldn't feel comfortable admitting that your choice was based on looks. Either way, in trying to justify your choice of Gentleman Y, you would feel compelled to revise the importance of "being romantic" and "smartness and wittiness."

Szu-chi and I have documented the tendency to revise attribute-importance ratings across a variety of contexts: from choice of dates and job candidates to choice of e-book readers, food items, hotels, and college courses.

The Desire for "Rationality" and Its Link to the Seventh Deadly Happiness Sin: Mind Addiction

The idea that many of our decisions are based on emotions is, of course, not newsworthy; most of us are aware that emotions play a huge role in influencing decisions. What's also not news is that we often feel compelled to justify our emotional decisions on the basis of "rational" reasons, which is why we have the term *post hoc rationalization*. What *is* newsworthy, however, is that we feel uneasy admitting that our decisions are driven by feelings. The reason we feel uneasy about admitting the influence of feelings is because of an implicit assumption we harbor: that our feelings serve to hinder, rather than enhance, the quality of our judgments and decisions. It is this assumption that underlies our tendency to feel uncomfortable about admitting that our decisions are influenced by feelings, and more generally, by gut instincts.

Chris Hsee—the professor from the University of Chicago whom we encountered in chapter 6B—and his colleagues use the term *lay rationalism* to refer to our desire to appear uninfluenced by feelings. Professor Hsee and his colleagues have conducted several studies to document just how far we will go to avoid being seen as susceptible to emotional influences. In one study, participants were given a choice between two chocolates, one that was four times the size of the other. To most people, the "rational" thing to do in this situation is to choose the bigger chocolate. However, the catch was that the bigger chocolate looked disgusting: it looked like a bug. The smaller chocolate, which was shaped like a typical chocolate, by contrast, looked more appealing. Thus the experimenters cleverly pitted the desire to choose the rationally more appealing option (the bigger chocolate) against the emotionally more appealing one (the better-looking chocolate).

Which chocolate should a participant choose? There is no universally correct answer of course, but to the extent that one finds the idea of eating something shaped like a bug to be revolting, one should choose the smaller, but better-looking, chocolate. However, to the extent that one has bought into the idea of lay rationalism—that is, the more one believes that it isn't rational to base one's choice on such trivial attributes as looks—one would feel compelled to choose the bigger chocolate. And that's exactly what happened: 68 percent of the participants in the experiment chose the chocolate that looked like a bug.

Needless to say, they didn't enjoy the chocolate much.

The fact that people seek to underplay the importance of feelings and gut instincts over thoughts and thoughtful deliberations in making their decisions may, at first blush, seem like a good thing. After all, feelings and gut instincts often lead us astray. Who among us can deny falling prey to the allure of gut instincts and feelings? There is a reason why sayings like "never judge a book by its cover," "act in haste, repent at leisure," and "look before you leap" are popular, and why the story of Ulysses and the Sirens is recounted to this day.

But just as relying too heavily on feelings and gut instincts can be a mistake, so can its opposite: underestimating the importance of gut instincts and feelings. I use the term "mind addiction" to refer to the tendency to ignore or underestimate the importance of gut instincts and feelings. Mind addiction stems from two interrelated beliefs: (1) that the most reliable way to solve any problem is through thoughtful deliberation, and (2) that feelings and gut instincts serve more to detract from, rather than enhance, the quality of judgments and decisions. For reasons we are about to see, mind addiction is a significant reason why many of us—particularly the S-and-S among us—aren't as happy as we could be, which is why it is the seventh deadly happiness sin.

Mind Addiction and Devaluing Happiness

The first and most obvious reason why mind addiction lowers happiness is that it leads to devaluing happiness. I've already touched on one study—the chocolate study—that provides evidence for this; choosing the bug-shaped chocolate despite realizing that it's not the happiness-maximizing thing to do is clearly an example of devaluing happiness. Several other studies have similarly documented how mind addiction leads to devaluing happiness. In one study, freshmen at the University of Virginia were offered a choice among five different posters. Participants were told that they would be given a print of their chosen poster to take back home. Before being asked to indicate their choice, one set of participants was asked to think about and then articulate the reasons for their choice. The other set was not compelled to think of reasons for their choice. Both sets of participants were then granted their choice. As it turned out, thinking about the reasons for their choice had a significant effect on the choice: participants in the first group chose a different type of poster from the ones in the second. A few weeks later, both sets of participants were asked to indicate how satisfied they were with their choices. Findings showed that the second set of participants— those who *hadn't* been asked to think long and hard about reasons for their choice—were more satisfied with their choice than the first set. Similar results have been obtained across other choice contexts—like choice of jams and college courses.

What do these findings indicate? They indicate that to make happiness-maximizing choices, it may sometimes be better to base our decisions on feelings and gut instincts than on thoughts and thoughtful deliberations. This does not mean, of course, that it's *always* better to rely on feelings and gut instincts; sometimes—for example, in deciding which stock options to buy—it may be better to rely on thoughtful deliberations. Toward the end of the chapter, I will discuss when it may be better to rely on feelings and gut instincts and when not. For now, let me turn to why mind addiction can sometimes lead to devaluing happiness, for such an understanding can help us uncover some other ways mind addiction gets in the way of happiness.

The Intelligence in Feelings and Gut Instincts

One reason "thinking too much" gets in the way of making happiness-maximizing choices is because thoughts distract us from the intelligence in our feelings and gut instincts. As findings from several studies suggest, our gut instincts and feelings aren't random and arbitrary; rather, they are the repository of a lot of useful information that served us well in our adaptive past. In one particularly startling demonstration of this idea, researchers exposed participants, who were students at Harvard University, to very short—three seconds or less—video clips of several professors. The audio portion in these clips was muted such that participants could not hear the professors speak; they could only see them. After viewing each clip, participants were asked to rate each professor on a number of personality dimensions, including "warmth," "enthusiasm," and "professionalism." The researchers then assessed whether these "thin slice judgments"—so called because they were made on the basis of minimal exposure—could predict the professors' *end-of-semester* teaching ratings. And incredibly, they did!

Many of my students find this result so surprising they can scarcely believe it. Needless to say, the result has been replicated several times over. In one replication, Rebecca Naylor—a professor of marketing at Ohio State University—and I assessed whether judgments made of car salesmen on the basis of their *photographs* could predict their long-term success at selling cars. We went to a local car dealership that agreed to participate in the study and asked for both the photographs and sales records of its salesmen. We then asked our undergraduate students to predict—based on the photographs of the salesmen—how good they would be at selling cars. And guess what? The undergraduates' predictions were significantly positively correlated with the salesmen's actual sales records!

Think for a minute about what these findings indicate. They indicate that our "snap" judgments—judgments we make of others within seconds of meeting them or on the basis of just their photographs—can be very accurate. In yet another study that revealed just how accurate judgments based on feelings and gut instincts can be, the neural activity of participants watching the popular show *American Idol* was measured as the contestants competed onstage. The neural activity gave the experimenters a good idea of the participants' gut-level liking for the various contestants. Later—a full two years after the show was over—researchers examined the correlation between the participants' gut-level likings of various contestants and these contestants' eventual commercial success as artists. And once again, the correlations turned out to be significant and positive: the more the participants liked a contestant at the level of gut instincts and feelings, the more commercially successful the contestants turned out to be.

If our feelings and gut instincts are as accurate as these findings suggest, why do we ignore or underestimate their importance?

How We Learn Overreliance on Thoughts and Thoughtful Deliberation

I suspect that there are several reasons why we underestimate the importance of feelings and gut instincts. One reason has to do with our educational system, which typically emphasizes thoughtful deliberation as the only means to analyze and arrive at solutions to all our problems and challenges. If there is one theme that pervades almost everything we learn in schools, it is that it is better to rely on our mind than on our heart to solve problems. In fact, we learn that the more thought we expend on solving a problem, the better the solution we arrive at will likely be. And because we are products of this system, we learn to view our feelings and gut instincts with suspicion.

Another reason we underestimate the importance of feelings and gut instincts, I believe, has to do with the types of goals we seek. Most goals we seek tend to be *quantitative* in nature—goals such as losing a certain number of pounds by the end of the year, or amassing a certain amount of wealth by retirement. We seek quantifiable goals because they are more concrete and, as we saw in chapter 1A, we find concrete goals more appealing than abstract ones. As it turns out, when it comes to achieving quantitative goals, we may in fact be better off basing our decisions on thoughtful deliberation than on feelings and gut instincts. For example, we are more likely to achieve a weight-loss goal if our food choices are based on caloric value rather than on the foods' looks. Likewise, we are more likely to achieve our target for retirement savings if we make investment decisions based on thoughtful deliberation rather than on gut feel. So an important reason for our overreliance on thoughts and thoughtful deliberation may be that a majority of the goals we seek tend to be quantitative. Or, put differently, if we were to pursue a different set of goals—goals that are more qualitative, such as "maximizing enjoyment" or "enhancing trust"—mind addiction might be less prevalent.

Yet another reason we underestimate the importance of feelings and gut instincts may have to do with the need for connectivity with others. As we saw in chapter 4A, the desire to forge and maintain bonds is as primal as it gets, and as it turns out, those who rely on thoughtful deliberation to make decisions may have a better chance of connecting with others. This is partly because we consider decisions based on thoughtful deliberations to be less subjective or self-centered. As a result, compared with those who make decisions based on feelings and gut instincts, we think of those who base their decisions on thoughtful deliberation to be more objective and less prone to favoritism, whims, or self-serving biases. Along similar lines, another reason we prefer to forge bonds with people who make decisions based on thoughtful deliberation is because of our educational system, as a result of which we come to think of those who rely on thoughtful deliberation to be more "reasonable" and "sensible."

So there are several reasons why we learn to ignore or underestimate the importance of feelings and gut instincts. As a result of these reasons, many of us come to subscribe to the notion that we come up with our best ideas by relying on thoughtful deliberation rather than on feelings and gut instincts. But what if, in fact, the opposite was true? What if our best ideas were produced by our feelings and gut instincts?

Feelings and Gut Instincts as the Real Source of Creativity and Inspiration

You may not have heard of August Kekulé, but how he came up with the idea for the molecular structure for benzene is a fascinating illustration of the role that our feelings and gut instincts—or more generally, our subconscious—play in generating ideas. If you still remember your high-school chemistry, you'll recall that molecules are made of two or more elements. You may also remember that all the elements have a certain valence. A dumbed-down way to understand valence is this: if an element that has a valence of 1 (hydrogen) is combined with an element that has a valence of 2 (oxygen), then two parts of the first element are needed to combine with one part of the second element to produce a molecule. This is why water (H_2O) consists of two parts hydrogen and one part oxygen, and is represented pictorially as follows:

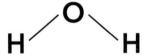

So far, so good? Now, let's look at some other exciting molecules and their molecular structures. It turns out that carbon has a valence of 4. As such, if carbon and hydrogen were to combine, the most natural molecule to emerge would be methane (CH_4), a noxious gas. The molecular structure for methane—you guessed it—is:

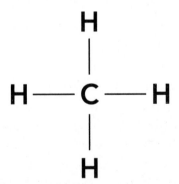

However, that's not the only molecule that a combination of carbon and hydrogen can produce. It turns out that benzene—which has 6 carbon atoms—is also made up of carbon and hydrogen. Now, if you knew that benzene is made up of 6 carbon atoms, how many atoms of hydrogen would you expect it to contain? If you guessed 24, your guess would be correct, but your answer would be wrong! It turns out that benzene has only 6 atoms of hydrogen! How could that be? That's the question that dogged many a mid-nineteenth-century chemist living in Europe.

You think your life sucks? Well, spare a thought for these chemists, who were running around in circles trying to figure out the molecular structure of benzene. No matter how hard they tried, however, they were unable to crack this puzzle. (If you have time to spare, you may want to work on this problem. To help you get started, let me propose a structure that is incorrect, but can nevertheless give you an idea of how to go about solving the puzzle.)

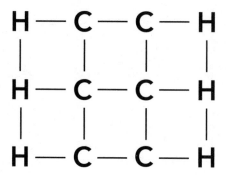

Enter August Kekulé, who had been working on the problem of benzene's structure for several years, but to no avail. Then one fine day (evening, to be precise), he had a daydream.

In his daydream . . .

black balls of carbon turned into black imps with forked tails that began racing around the room and would soon be upsetting the apparatus of the laboratory. He was ready to run the rascals out. Then, almost suddenly, the confusion died away as each imp grabbed the tail of the one ahead of him, the six waved to him as the group whirled by.

Kekulé awoke with a start, realizing that the imps were acting out the formula for benzene. As his hand grabbed the sketching pencil, the imps went back to being black balls of carbon. How simple the arrangement turned out to be: *the carbon atoms of benzene form a ring!*

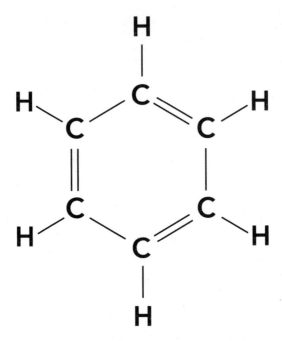

From where did Kekulé get the idea of the benzene ring? Not from thoughtful deliberation for sure. The idea came from his subconscious. Kekulé's experience was by no means an outlier. Almost every creative idea that anyone has ever had is generated by the subconscious. As a recent—and more lighthearted—example, Harry Potter's story came to J. K. Rowling seemingly from out of nowhere.

This is not to say, of course, that thoughtful deliberation has no role to play in generating creative ideas; indeed, it plays a critical role. Findings show that it is only those who have thought long and hard about a problem who make themselves "available" to the ideas generated by the subconscious. Kekulé, for instance, had worked not just in the area of molecular structures, but in the specific area of the structure of molecules containing *carbon atoms* for a long time—more than ten years. Rowling, too, had been writing stories since she was a child. However, thoughtful deliberation can only go so far in generating ideas, particularly inspiring ones. Our most inspiring ideas are almost always the product of the subconscious. Or, put differently, without the cooperation of feelings and gut instincts, thoughtful deliberation would be severely handicapped. This is because, ultimately, the source of all of our ideas—and not just our most creative and inspiring ones—is our subconscious. Hence, far from helping the process of idea generation, thoughtful deliberations distract us from being able to tap into the subconscious, therefore hindering the idea generation process. This is why our best ideas come to us when we are not actively thinking of the problem we are trying to solve, but rather are thinking of something else altogether.

Tapping into the Creativity of Feelings and Gut Instincts

Thomas Edison, who once said that "ideas come from outer space" (indicating that it's difficult to pinpoint the source of ideas), recognized this, and therefore devised a clever way of circumventing thoughts to tap into the creative potential of his subconscious feelings and instincts. Like many others, he too had noticed that his best ideas came to him when he wasn't actively thinking about the solution to a problem; rather, they came to him in that twilight zone between being awake and asleep. So he would often take a catnap on his favorite armchair, holding a steel ball in each hand. On the two sides of the armchair were metal pans, placed strategically on the floor below both his hands so that, just at the point when he fell asleep, the balls would roll out of his hands and into the metal pans. The sound from the clanging balls would wake him up—just in time to record any insights he might have had!

Unlike Edison, however, most of us—and this might be particularly true for the S-and-S among us—fail to recognize the role of our feelings and gut instincts in generating our most inspiring ideas and therefore fail to take advantage of the most potent source of creativity in us.

Mind Addiction and Delusionary Lack of Self-awareness

So far, I've discussed two problems that arise from mind addiction—devaluing happiness and denying ourselves the opportunity to tap into the source of our creative potential. Both problems arise from underestimating the intelligence in feelings and gut instincts. The next set of problems associated with mind addiction is rooted in a different phenomenon: *lack of self-awareness.*

As we saw earlier, mind addiction stems at least partly from our desire for "rationality." It is this desire that leads us to pretend—as Szu-chi Huang and I found—that our judgments and decisions are not influenced by feelings and gut instincts when in fact they are. While such pretense may make us feel good in the moment—by making us believe that we have acted "rationally"—it exacerbates another problem that many mindfulness researchers consider to be one of the most significant causes of our unhappiness: the problem of lack of self-awareness.

For my Coursera course on happiness, I interviewed many scholars, including Professor Richie Davidson of the University of Wisconsin at Madison.* Professor Davidson is best known for pioneering the use of neuroimaging technology for documenting the effects of mindfulness practice on the brain. He was the first to show, for example, that "expert" meditators (those who have practiced mindfulness for ten thousand hours or more) have a thicker left prefrontal cortex—the part of the brain that's associated with being happy—than do novices. According to Davidson, lack of self-awareness is one of the biggest happiness killers. Why? One reason is because, without a certain level of self-awareness, one is unlikely to recognize the ways in which one might be sabotaging one's own happiness. Here's a simple example that illustrates this idea. Imagine, just for kicks, that although you are someone who places a great deal of emphasis on being superior to others, you also want to appear as if you couldn't care less about superiority. That is, imagine that although you are actually very status conscious, you wish to believe that you couldn't care two hoots about your standing relative to others. Imagine also (again, just for kicks) that although you are deeply insecure and needy in relationships, you believe that you are the epitome of secure attachment. Now, the less self-aware you are, the more easily you could pull off this self-delusion; that is, the more easily you could convince yourself that you aren't status conscious or insecure when in fact you are. Such self-delusion may, at first blush, seem like a good thing, as it permits you to harbor a positive, if inaccurate, self-image. However, in the long run, the self-delusion is almost certain to get in the way of your happiness for the many reasons we reviewed in earlier chapters: you *can't* sustain your happiness levels if you chase superiority or are desperate for love. No matter how cleverly you may brush these "sins" under the carpet,

---

* You can watch excerpts from this interview, in which Professor Davidson talks about a common misconception about mindfulness and also offers tips on how to overcome obstacles to practicing mindfulness at https://www.coursera.org/learn/happiness/lecture/ADpWa/week-6-video-9-some-other-obstacles-to-mindfulness-including-logistical-ones.

sooner or later, you'll be "found out." So from the perspective of maximizing happiness, the more sensible thing to do would be to stop deluding yourself and become more honest so that you can get to the bottom of the ways in which you may be sabotaging your own happiness.

In addition to fostering self-honesty, there's another reason why self-awareness is important for happiness: it is essential for exhibiting the required level of *flexibility* in dealing with life's challenges. To understand what I mean, consider something I just mentioned—that self-honesty is critical for leading a happier life. While this statement is generally true, what's also true is that self-honesty is not always a good idea. As I am sure you know from personal experience, being brutally honest about one's frailties and foibles can sometimes be counterproductive; just as there's a time and place for being candid with others, there's a time and place for self-honesty as well. Specifically, self-honesty is only productive if one's self-esteem—or, alternatively, one's capacity for self-compassion—is high enough. In situations in which one's self-esteem or capacity for self-compassion is found wanting, it would be better not to be completely honest with oneself because doing so could deliver a hard enough blow to one's self-worth that one never recovers from it.

A story involving the Buddha epitomizes this idea quite nicely. In the story, the Buddha is walking toward a forest with his disciples. The disciples are afraid to enter the forest—because who knows what terrifying things it might be hiding? And yet, having trudged through the forest a number of times, the Buddha knows that he can guide his disciples safely through it. So what does the Buddha do? Although he's obviously a strong proponent of mindfulness (which, as we will discover in the next chapter, is all about self-honesty), he doesn't force his disciples to face their fears head-on. Rather, he downplays their fears to make them feel good. He does this because, in his assessment, the disciples are not ready to face their fears at this point; their fears are too high for them to be fully mindful of it. So the need of the hour is confidence building, rather than self-honesty.

The central idea that this story emphasizes is flexibility. Specifically, it highlights that, although it may be generally preferable not to indulge in self-serving delusions, indulging in them on occasion—such as when one is already reeling from a series of blows to one's self-esteem—may be the prudent thing to do. A similar flexibility is, of course, called for in many other contexts as well, including that of choosing between any of the happiness "sins" and "habits" we have discussed thus far. That is, although it would be best to avoid committing the sins in general, there could be occasions in which doing so is more judicious. For instance, in contexts in which one's survival is at stake, it may be better to chase superiority than to pursue flow. Likewise, in contexts in which one hasn't received much love or nurturance for a long time, it may be better to exhibit neediness in the company of someone who's willing to indulge it than not, and so on. If flexibility in dealing with life's challenges is crucial, then self-awareness becomes critical, because flexibility comes more easily to those who are more self-aware. This is because it takes self-awareness to determine whether shining the light of self-honesty on oneself will serve to disinfect or scald one.

The flexibility that self-awareness allows can also help in figuring out when to rely on feelings and gut instincts and when to do the reverse—that is, rely on thoughtful deliberation—in tackling problems and challenges. The decision of whether to go with gut feel or thoughtful deliberation may ultimately be more of an art than a science. However, certain broad generalizations can be made. First, it seems that our gut instincts are a lot more intelligent when it comes to stimuli with which our ancestors were familiar than with those our ancestors would not have seen. Findings from some remarkable studies showed that it is easier to teach human infants, and even rats and monkeys, to be scared of dangerous stimuli that our ancestors would have encountered, such as snakes, than to teach them to be afraid of stimuli unfamiliar to our ancestors (such as geometric shapes or electricity outlets). For instance, even cage-reared rats that have never encountered cats were found to exhibit instinctive fear when exposed to cat fur.

One reason we are so good at judging people may be precisely because, being the social animals we are, our ancestors would have had a lot of experience in dealing with people. Second, our gut instincts are likely to be very handy when it comes to domains in which we *personally* have a lot of experience. Thus, for instance, an experienced museum curator's gut feel about the authenticity of a piece of art is likely to be more accurate than the judgments to which he arrives on the basis of thoughtful deliberation. Likewise, an experienced doctor's gut feel about the disease ailing a patient can be more accurate than the diagnosis she arrives at after thoughtful deliberation. On the flip side, our gut feel is unlikely to come in handy when we personally do not have much experience in a field. For example, a novice's intuition about the authenticity of a piece of art or of the disease ailing a patient is unlikely to be accurate. Thus in fields in which one has little experience, it would be prudent not to make decisions based on gut feel but instead to make them based on thoughtful deliberation.

Another context in which we may be better off making decisions based on gut feel is when the outcome we seek is an emotional or "hedonic" one. We have already seen evidence in favor of this idea in the experiment with posters: participants who chose posters based on gut feel were happier than those who chose it based on thoughtful deliberation. On the flip side, therefore, we may be better off basing our decision on thoughtful deliberation when the outcome we seek is a functional one. In looking to buy an apartment or a piece of land as an investment, or when deciding whether to ask for a "hit" or not in blackjack, we would be better off basing our decision on thoughtful deliberation than on gut feel. Yet another context in which it may be better to go with gut feel is when we are looking to make a satisfactory choice—and not necessarily the "best" choice—and we have limited time on our hands. In this situation, studies show that our long-term satisfaction with our decision is likely to be higher when we do not engage in thoughtful deliberation, but rather make a decision based on gut feel.

A final context in which it may be better to go with thoughtful deliberation is when making a decision on behalf of a group, particularly if the outcome you're looking for is a functional one (e.g., recruiting someone for an open position in your organization) rather than a hedonic one (e.g., choosing a venue for the end-of-year party). This is because, as I mentioned earlier, people like those who make decisions based on thoughtful deliberation more than those who make them based on feelings and gut instincts.

In sum, there are a number of variables that can have a bearing on whether to make a decision based on feelings and gut instincts or thoughtful deliberation. And a more self-aware person—for example, someone who is conscious of whether she is seeking a hedonic or a functional goal—is more likely to be aware of the relevance of these variables and therefore to be more capable of making the right call. Self-awareness, in other words, can help one exhibit the required flexibility in going either with feelings and gut instincts or with thoughtful deliberation, depending on context.

Given how central self-awareness is for happiness, I've included a self-awareness scale at the end of this chapter, in case you are curious to assess your own levels of self-awareness.

Mind Addiction and the Problem of Ignoring the "Source Within"

Self-awareness, as we have seen, is crucial for making intelligent, happiness-enhancing decisions in a variety of contexts. A final way in which self-awareness is critical is that it helps in recognizing the ways in which the mind gets in the way of happiness. In particular, it helps one recognize that there's a seemingly mysterious thing that happens when one attempts to observe the goings-on—both within, and outside of, oneself—without commenting, judging, categorizing, or ruminating about them: *one feels less stressed and more happy*. That is, self-awareness helps one realize that there's a source of happiness *within* us—a source that can potentially be accessed at all times, if only one knew how.

I'll explain what I mean by this in the next chapter.

SELF-AWARENESS SCALE

The self-assessment of self-awareness has two parts. The first part is a ten-item scale, and can be accessed and completed on the book's website, at www.happysmarts.com/book/scales/self-awareness, as well. The second part is described after the ten-item scale, and to complete that part, you'll need a partner.

Instructions for Part 1

To get a sense of your self-awareness levels, answer either "True" or "False" to each of the following statements. If you are tempted to think long and hard about a statement, or if you feel that there are too many nuances and exceptions, resist. The most accurate results come from making a snap judgment about whether a question is true or false about you.

1. Often, when someone asks me why I am so angry or sad, I respond (or think to myself), "But I'm not!"
2. When those closest to me ask why I treated someone brusquely or meanly, I often disagree that I did any such thing.
3. I frequently—more than a couple of times a month—find that my heart is racing or my pulse is pounding, and I have no idea why.
4. When I observe someone in pain, I feel the pain myself both emotionally and physically.

5. I am usually sure enough about how I am feeling that I can put my emotions into words.

6. I sometimes notice aches and pains and have no idea where they came from.

7. I like to spend time being quiet and relaxed, just feeling what is going on inside me.

8. I believe I very much inhabit my body and feel at home and comfortable with my body.

9. I am strongly oriented to the external world and rarely take note of what's happening inside my body.

10. When I exercise, I am very sensitive to the changes it produces in my body.

Scoring Scheme for Part 1 and Interpreting Your Score

Give yourself one point for each True response to questions 4, 5, 7, 8, and 10; score one point for each False response to questions 1, 2, 3, 6, and 9. Score zero for each False response to 4, 5, 7, 8, and 10, and for each True response to 1, 2, 3, 6, and 9. A score of eight or higher means you are self-aware; a score of 3 or below means you are "self-opaque."

Instructions for Part 2

For this part, have a partner take your pulse for thirty seconds while you direct your attention internally and try to detect your own heartbeat. Focus your awareness on your internal bodily sensations, and do your best (without touching your wrist or anyplace else to feel a pulse) to sense your heartbeat and count the number of beats. Do this three more times—that is, four thirty-second trials. Compare your counts with those of your partner. The closer the match, the more self-aware you are.

Chapter 7B

THE SEVENTH HABIT OF THE HIGHLY HAPPY: MINDFULNESS

magine that you're given the opportunity to be a fly on the wall for any event. Which event would you choose? Would it be for a surreptitious meeting between JFK and Marilyn Monroe? Or would it be for the meeting between Mahatma Gandhi and Lord Mountbatten on the night that India achieved freedom from Great Britain?

Whatever event you choose, the idea of being a fly on the wall is that you are a disinterested observer. Not an *uninterested* observer, mind you, but a *disinterested* one. *Uninterested* means being bored and not interested. *Disinterested*, by contrast, means being unbiased, neutral. So one could be disinterestedly interested in something, which is what you would want to be if you were a fly on the wall for a momentous event. That is, you would want to merely observe the goings-on without adding to or taking away anything from it. You wouldn't want to attract attention to yourself or change what was happening. In fact, even if you wished to change something—say, for example, you would have liked for JFK to sing "Happy Birthday" to Marilyn Monroe instead of what actually happened (not that I know for sure), or you would have liked Lord Mountbatten to be dressed like Gandhi when they met—you would know that, as a fly on the wall, you don't have the power to change things. You'd simply have to accept whatever was going on and be thankful for the opportunity to watch the momentous event unfolding.

Now imagine that, instead of being a fly on the wall for an external momentous event, you're a fly *in* the wall—in the wall of your head, to be precise—for an *internal* momentous event. For which internal momentous event, you ask? For the *current* internal momentous event, of course!

Like the fly *on* the wall, as a fly *in* the wall, you wouldn't want to attract attention to yourself, or change anything that was happening. The one difference would be that you *could* change things in your head if you wished. For example, if you had the thought, "I am a despicable slob for polishing off a whole tub of ice cream in ten minutes flat," you could change the thought to "What do you expect? I'm going through a rough patch; anyone in my shoes would've done the same!" But imagine, for a moment, that you are able to control the urge to change things and were thus capable of merely observing what was going on.

In a nutshell, that's what mindfulness is all about; it is the metaphorical equivalent of being the fly in the wall of your head. That is, mindfulness involves observing whatever is going on in your head with great interest and curiosity, but in a nonclingy sort of way. You could, of course, be mindful of something that's going on outside of you as well—like a sunset or a movie. But typically, the practice involves observing an aspect of one's internal environment, such as one's own thoughts or breath.

Stepping Out of the GATE of the Mind

To get a more concrete idea of what mindfulness involves, allow me to introduce you to another metaphor I often use—something I call the "GATE model." Imagine that as you are reading this book, the following thought suddenly pops into your head: "Oh my God, it's six p.m. already. I'm going to be late picking up my son from day care!" Typically, when we have such a thought, it triggers another thought ("I always slip up and never finish things on time! I should get more on top of things."). This thought, in turn, might trigger an emotion (e.g., shame), which might trigger an action (e.g., slamming the book shut and rushing to the car) or a goal (appeasing your son for being late by getting him a snack).

In this example, the original thought ("I'm late") has triggered a web of consequences involving other thoughts, emotions, actions, and goals. If you stopped to think about it, you'd realize that it's not just this thought, but almost every thought that evokes other thoughts, emotions, actions, and goals. One way to characterize what constitutes our ordinary, day-to-day experience, then, is that we are immersed in a web of GATEs—Goals, Actions (or Action-tendencies), Thoughts, and Emotions. Or, put differently, our life involves being caught in a web of consequences that life's experiences, interacting with the GATEs of our mind, weave for us. For instance, if we get shouted at by our boss, we may experience anger that, in turn, triggers thoughts of revenge that trigger certain actions which trigger other feelings that trigger another set of thoughts or goals that trigger new actions, and so on.

This is, of course, "normal," in the sense that we operate this way most of the time. Now, if the web in which we are caught happens to be a good one—for example, when the boss shouts at us, we react in a healthy fashion—then it's not so bad. But what if our propensity is to weave a GATE web that's not healthy? Imagine, for example, that our default response to being criticized by someone is to engage in denial or retribution, rather than, say, to attempt to assess the validity of the criticism in an objective fashion. Unfortunately, as findings from research on "overthinking" and "rumination" show, many of us are caught in precisely such unhealthy GATE webs. This is particularly true when we are confronted with a negative stimulus like, say, news of a terrorist attack. One way to break an unhealthy GATE web is to replace the "deadly happiness sins" with the "habits of the highly happy." Doing so makes it more likely that the web triggered by an event is more positive than negative.

There is, however, another way to break a negative GATE web. This way, of course, is to step outside the GATE of your head, to merely observe what's going on—to be a fly in the wall of your head.

The First Paradox of Mindfulness: Being Distant and Yet Intimate with the Object of Observation

The idea of "being a fly in the wall of your head" or of "stepping out of the GATE of your mind" makes it appear that mindfulness involves distancing yourself from the object of your observation. But although mindfulness does involve observing things as if they were happening to someone else, the somewhat paradoxical outcome of such an attempt is that you get in more intimate touch with the object of your observation.

To understand why this is so, it will be useful to consider the difference between what some researchers call "bare attention" and something that might be called "mind attention." Mind attention involves understanding the object of one's observations through the filter of the mind by commenting, judging, categorizing, or ruminating about it. The seventh deadly happiness sin, mind addiction—which is the tendency to overrely on thoughtful deliberation—is a product of mind awareness. Bare attention, by contrast, involves merely observing whatever is going on without commenting, judging, categorizing, or ruminating about it. Bare attention is, for most of us, difficult to sustain for any length of time—particularly in the early stages of practicing mindfulness. But conceptually at least, it's fairly easy to grasp what bare attention involves: going back to merely observing without any accompanying mental activity. For example, if, in the process of trying to merely observe your thoughts ("I'm late to pick up my son!"), you have another thought ("I'm so sloppy") or feeling (shame), bare attention would involve observing, without any accompanying commentary, these thoughts and feelings too.

An important consequence of observing something with bare attention is that the *pace* at which the mind races from one aspect of the GATE web (say, a thought) to another (a feeling) abates. As a result, the whole GATE web calms down, and in the process, one gets in more intimate touch with the object of one's observation. Or, put differently, once the mental activity that typically distracts us from the object of our observation becomes less pronounced, we get closer to the object of our observation. When listening to a piece of music, we become more capable of registering the subtler sounds, and likewise, when observing the bodily changes associated with an emotional state, we become more capable of noticing the subtler sensations associated with that state.

So, although taking the perspective of bare attention does involve observing things as if they were happening to someone else, if one manages to do it right—that is, if one manages to keep one's mind out of it—one would end up getting closer to the object of observation. Indeed, if one managed to keep the mind entirely out of the way, one would get to experience what the English mystic Douglas Harding called "headless-ness"—the feeling that the observer in you and the object of your observation have merged and become one.

The Second Paradox of Mindfulness: How Being in Intimate Touch with Negativity Mitigates It

If mindfulness involves getting in intimate touch with the object of one's observation, it might seem that being mindful of negative feelings would intensify them. But in fact, mindfulness mitigates negative feelings, which is another paradox associated with mindfulness. One way to resolve this paradox is to think of negative feelings as clouds. From a distance, clouds can seem opaque and substantial, as you might have noticed on a climb up a mountain. And yet once you enter them, you realize that they are actually quite transparent and insubstantial. In much the same way, from a distance—that is, from the perspective of the mind—feelings can seem solid and substantial (and therefore scary, if they are negative). But if you manage to overcome the desire to change or avoid them and are capable of merely observing the bodily sensations associated with them, they become far less substantial.

The reason is because, from the vantage point of bare attention, negative feelings reduce to a mere set of sensations. What the mind labels "anxiety," for example, reduces to sensations like clamminess in the palms and feet, a slightly faster heart rate, undulations (or "butterflies") in the stomach—nothing, in other words, that is inherently scary or even unpleasant. But the same sensations, when judged, categorized, and ruminated or commented upon, not only take on an ominous flavor, but also tend to persist because the mental activity keeps the GATE web alive. By merely observing a negative feeling, in other words, you allow the GATE web to slow and calm down and therefore allow the negative feelings to die more quickly.

The Third Paradox of Mindfulness: Mitigating Negativity and Intensifying Positivity

The fact that being mindful of negative feelings—or, more precisely, observing the bodily sensations associated with negative feelings more closely—mitigates these feelings might lead one to conclude that being mindful of positive feelings too would mitigate these feelings. But in fact, the *reverse* happens, which is yet another paradox of mindfulness. That is, seemingly incredibly, being mindful intensifies positive feelings even as it mitigates negative ones!

Findings from a megastudy involving more than sixteen thousand participants helped document this rather intriguing phenomenon. The researchers who conducted it—Matt Killingsworth and Dan Gilbert—were interested in examining what happens to people's happiness levels when they are mind-wandering versus not. Think of "mind-wandering" as roughly the opposite of being mindful. When mind-wandering, your mind is all over the place, and isn't focused on any one thing. A *New Yorker* cartoon* captured the idea of mind-wandering better than perhaps any I know: it shows three panels, with the same guy featured in all. In the first panel, the man is at work, but thinking about playing golf; in the second, he's playing golf and thinking about having sex; while in the third, he's having sex and thinking about work!

To figure out the effects of mind-wandering on happiness levels, Killingsworth and Gilbert asked participants to download an app onto their smart phones. The app was programmed to contact the participants at random times of the day for the duration of the study. Whenever contacted, participants were instructed to answer three questions. One question asked participants to indicate the activity in which they were engaged at the time their apps contacted them. They could select any one of twenty-two different activities—like eating, working, exercising, being stuck in traffic, having sex—that differed in terms of pleasantness. Another question asked them to indicate whether they were mind-wandering or not, that is, whether their mind was focused on what they were doing or—like the man in the cartoon—was elsewhere. Finally, they were asked to indicate how happy or unhappy they were.

Here's what the findings showed: regardless of whether the activity was pleasant or not, participants were less happy when they were mind-wandering versus not. Or, put differently, people were happiest, even when doing something unpleasant, when their mind was in the here and now than when it wasn't. This means that you are *always* better off—in terms of enhancing happiness levels—being mindful than not.

---

* The cartoon can be accessed at www.condenaststore.com/-sp/Man-at-work-thinking -about-golf-golfing-thinking-about-sex-having-sex-t-New-Yorker-Cartoon-Prints _i8545392_.htm.

Happiness Is Our Nature

How could it be that mindfulness mitigates negativity even as it enhances positivity?

There appear to be several reasons for this. One reason has to do with something I call the BAA phenomenon, which is short for Behavior Affects Attitude. We all know that our attitudes affect our behavior. For instance, we can all see how a person who believes that "life is a zero-sum game"—that one can only win if someone else loses—is more likely to seek superiority than one who believes that "life's pie can be grown." Likewise, we can also see how a person who trusts others by default is more likely to be willing to sign off a deal on a handshake than one who distrusts others by default. What many of us don't realize, however, is that our behaviors can affect our attitudes too. For example, someone who regularly practices gratitude will likely become less prone to chasing superiority. Similarly, practicing kindness and compassion will likely mitigate neediness and avoidance. One reason behavior affects attitude is because of something called self-perception: when we observe that we have behaved a certain way (e.g., compassionately), we search for explanations for that behavior and conclude that it must be because our attitude is consistent with that behavior. In other words, behaving as if we are compassionate, even if we don't really feel so compassionate, eventually leads us into thinking and feeling like a compassionate person. (The happiness exercises work on the BAA principle, of course, which is why they are worth trying out even if you don't believe they will work for you.)

The BAA principle offers one explanation for why mindfulness makes us happy: when we are mindful, we behave *as if* we are happy. To understand what I mean, consider how a happy person behaves. Consider, in particular, that happy people are in the moment, as findings on flow reveal. Specifically, a prominent feature of flow is being in the moment and, as we saw in chapter 2B, flow enhances enjoyment. Now consider that a prominent feature of mindfulness, too, is being in the moment. So it follows—from BAA—that being mindful would make you happy.*

---

* Indeed, one could argue that mindfulness is an even more powerful determinant of happiness than flow because, unlike flow, which is dependent on the cooperation of external

Yet another reason mindfulness enhances happiness is that it literally changes the structure of the brain to make it a "happier brain." Specifically, as I mentioned briefly in the previous chapter, the practice of mindfulness thickens the left prefrontal cortex, which is a part of the brain associated with higher levels of happiness. Practicing mindfulness also lowers the activation of the amygdala, which is associated with worrying and stress. In other words, mindfulness boosts happiness levels by simultaneously thickening parts of the brain associated with positivity and deactivating parts of the brain associated with stress and worrying.

Of course, it's not entirely clear *why* our brain changes in response to mindfulness. After all, all you're trying to do when being mindful is merely observe whatever is going on in a nonjudgmental way. That is, at its core, mindfulness is really all about letting reality play itself out without intervening or controlling it in any way. Why should this boost positivity? Consider that the exact opposite could just as easily have happened. That is, the attempt to merely observe reality without intervening or controlling it could have thinned out parts of the brain associated with well-being and activated the parts associated with anxiety and depression. The fact that the attempt to connect with reality has a salubrious, rather than a detrimental, effect on our brain leads me to the third, and rather intriguing, reason mindfulness enhances happiness: *happiness is our fundamental nature.*

This idea—that, at our core, our nature is to be joyful and blissful—is a prevalent theme in some of the world's oldest religions, such as Hinduism and Buddhism. So in that sense, the idea is not new. What's new, however, is that evidence from neuroscience backs this claim. As a result, at least some scientists are of the view that the old wisdom traditions might be on to something. For example, Alan Wallace, a world-renowned expert on mindfulness and author of several books, including *Minding Closely* and

---

circumstances (specifically, a match between available and required abilities), mindfulness is less dependent on external circumstances. That is, you could be mindful of an activity (e.g., breathing) for which available ability overwhelms required ability. From the perspective of flow, such situations should evoke boredom, and normally they do. However, if you can train your mind to be capable of paying attention to subtle and nuanced features of the object of your observation, then it's possible to experience states of absorption just as deep as those evoked in high flow. This means that mindfulness is a skill that can be employed across a wider variety of situations than can flow, which makes it more powerful.

Balancing the Mind, believes that *happiness is the default state of the mind.* Likewise, Shauna Shapiro, a professor at Santa Clara University and a researcher who works on mindfulness, in a conversation with me acknowledged that "we are of Buddha nature," meaning that our fundamental nature is one of positivity.*

Helping us connect with our inner source of happiness may be the most powerful reason mindfulness makes us happier, but it is certainly not the only one. I have already touched on a number of ways in which mindfulness boosts positivity, including that it helps us get more immersed in the moment—to experience a flowlike state. As a result, even the most mundane of events assume a certain "specialness"—perhaps even extraordinariness. For instance, as those who have practiced mindfulness at some length can vouch, even something as seemingly mundane as observing the breath can be so interesting as to hold one's attention for several hours at a stretch. Here's how the world-famous atheist, neuroscientist, and philosopher Sam Harris sums up this idea in his book *Waking Up*:

> One of the first things one learns in practicing meditation is that nothing is intrinsically boring—indeed, boredom is simply a lack of attention. Pay sufficient attention, and the mere experience of breathing can reward months and years of steady vigilance.

Mindfulness, Self-awareness, and the Mitigation of Mind Addiction

In addition to these relatively direct ways, there is a set of more indirect ways in which mindfulness boosts positivity. The first of these indirect ways has to do with *self-awareness,* which, for reasons I discussed in the previous chapter, is critical for happiness. To understand how mindfulness boosts self-awareness, imagine participating in a study in which you are shown a string of numbers or letters in quick succession on a computer screen. Now imagine that this string has a lot of letters (like A, D, Z, X, etc.),

---

* You can catch an excerpt of this interview on my Coursera course at https://www.coursera.org/learn/happiness/lecture/tVwu3/week-6-video-6-the-benefits-of-mindfulness-ii.

but once in a while, a number (e.g., 3) comes up. And whenever a number comes up, imagine that your task is to press a particular key (say, the space bar) on your keyboard.

Now, what's been found is that, when you're scanning the environment for something, you get excited when you find it. The excitement may not be intense enough for you to notice at a conscious level, but studies show that it is intense enough to disrupt your ability to notice the second incidence of the same stimulus. For example, if you are looking for a number in an alphanumeric string and a number comes up, your chances of noticing a second number in the string would be significantly impaired if this second number shows up quickly after the first. Needless to say, the more excited you are upon seeing the first number, the less likely you are to notice the second. This is called "attentional blink deficit" because your attention "blinks" (and therefore misses) the second incidence of the stimulus you are looking for.

Interestingly, it turns out that most people fail to register the second number in an alphanumeric string if it comes within half a second of the first. So half a second is the duration for which attentional blink typically lasts. However, what's even more interesting is that this duration can be reduced through mindfulness practice. In one study, researchers tested the ability to detect the second stimulus in an alphanumeric string for seventeen participants who had undergone rigorous mindfulness training. They compared the results from this group with that from a second group of twenty-three participants who had undergone a much less rigorous mindfulness training. Findings showed that, while *every one* of the participants in the first group improved in their ability to detect the second stimulus, only sixteen of the twenty-three participants in the second group did. (Sixteen out of twenty-three may seem like a lot, but remember that this group got some mindfulness training too.) What these results suggest is that it's possible to reduce attentional blink through practicing mindfulness.

Why does mindfulness help mitigate attentional blink? Because it increases self-awareness: it helps you notice the onset of the excitement that would otherwise blind you from seeing the stimuli you are looking for, and by doing so, allows you to control it. Or, put differently, the practice of mindfulness helps you be more capable of noticing the subtle, yet influential, bodily sensations that you are experiencing, including ones associated with your feelings and gut instincts. This self-awareness, in turn, allows you not just to practice greater self-honesty, but also to be more flexible in how you respond to situations—both of which, for reasons I discussed in the previous chapter, are critical for happiness in many ways, including overcoming the seventh deadly happiness sin: mind addiction.

Physiological Benefits of Mindfulness

Another indirect way in which mindfulness enhances psychological well-being is by improving physical health. As already mentioned, mindfulness results in the thickening of the left prefrontal cortex, as a consequence of which we feel happier. There's another, equally important positive consequence from cortical thickening: it slows down the aging of the brain, which in turn promotes one's mental acuity. Another beneficial physiological change from mindfulness is the reduced expression of genes that produce inflammations in the body. As a result of this, we can handle stress far better. Findings from one study showed that those who practiced mindfulness were far less prone to stress when told to give a speech and perform mental calculations in front of an audience.

Yet another physiological benefit of mindfulness is that it improves heart health. Studies have shown that, among those who practice mindfulness, something known as "vagal tone" improves. Things like blood pressure and arrhythmia (irregular heartbeat) and other symptoms of poor heart health are all affected by the vagal tone. So mindfulness directly affects heart health. Vagal tone improves psychological health too—by making you a more compassionate person. A final physiological benefit of mindfulness is that it has been shown to prevent the shortening of telomeres, which offer protection to the ends of chromosomes in the cells of our body and thus help prevent the onset of diseases like cancer and also slow down aging.

Given all these physiological benefits of mindfulness, you wouldn't be surprised to learn that it can help cure other physical ailments too—like skin disease. One study involving patients with psoriasis revealed that, compared with a control group who received no mindfulness training, those who received mindfulness training were cured much faster.

Mindfulness Boosts Chances of Success

In addition to enhancing well-being in both direct and indirect ways, mindfulness also improves one's chances of success in the workplace by boosting something called "response flexibility"—the ability to pause before acting or reacting. That is, mindfulness enhances one's chances of career success by fostering the ability to react to situations in a more conscious manner. So rather than reacting to situations in an instinctive, preprogrammed manner, one develops the capacity to respond in a more considered way. Say you've just received an angry e-mail from a client. Or imagine that you've been unfairly accused by your neighbor of mistreating his pet. In such situations, one's instinctive response may be to react in an equally provocative fashion, increasing the chances that an unproductive altercation ensues. With the practice of mindfulness, however, one acquires the ability to step back and choose one's response. As you can easily imagine, response flexibility can come in very handy in interpersonal situations, particularly ones that involve tricky exchanges.

Motivational Obstacles to Taking Up Mindfulness Practice

As we have just seen, there are a slew of both physiological and psychological benefits from practicing mindfulness. And yet most of us—particularly, perhaps, the smart-and-the-successful—aren't well versed in this practice. Why is this?

One reason is that, as Dan Harris notes in his humorous book *10% Happier*, many of us can't shake off the belief that mindfulness is "woo woo" or unscientific. However, as we have seen, mindfulness is merely an attempt to perceive reality, whether it is the reality inside our head or the reality outside, *as it is*—without judging, commenting, or clinging to it. Specifically, as I mentioned earlier, mindfulness is the attempt to observe reality (or a slice of reality on which one chooses to focus) in a disinterestedly interested way. What's "woo woo" or unscientific about that?

The only person who would find mindfulness unscientific is one who's convinced that he already has an accurate view of reality and sees things exactly as they are. Such a person clearly hasn't really had a rich enough set of life experiences to realize that the mind can be deceptive. Perhaps the starkest example of the mind's power to deceive is the blind spot. Although we literally can't see what's in our blind spot—the spot in our visual field where some nerves connect to the retina—we wouldn't know this from our experiences. The blind spot is, of course, quite a literal example of how our mind deceives us—and in this case, in a beneficial way—but the literature on judgment and decision making is littered with unproductive ways in which our mind deceives us. For instance, we are programmed to see patterns even if they don't actually exist, leading us to infer meaning in totally random events. As a somewhat quirky example, many people saw a "devil" in the smoke of the 9/11 attacks on the World Trade Center. Similarly, many of us are convinced that basketball players (as well as other athletes) go through "hot hands" and "cold hands" even when the players' performance is merely going through random sequences. Tom Gilovich, a psychologist at Cornell University, has devoted an entire book titled *How We Know What Isn't So* to this phenomenon. To assume that whatever our mind tells us is the "truth and nothing but the truth" is, thus, to be unaware that our mind can be as much a source of delusion as it can be a source of clarification. As such, the practice of mindfulness, which gets us to become more familiar with both our mind and our feelings and instincts, can help us better discern when our mind is deluding us and when it is guiding us.

Another objection to mindfulness many people have is that it will make them soft and weak. "One moment," people imagine telling themselves after considering taking up mindfulness practice, "I was an effective— if somewhat hard-nosed—leader, and the next moment, I was spouting inane things like, 'make love, not war,' and following the likes of Oprah and Chopra!" There is, as we saw earlier, some truth to the idea that mindfulness kindles compassion. However, that doesn't mean it will make you soft and weak—unless you equate being compassionate with being soft and weak, which, unfortunately, many of us do. This is why, as my coauthors and I documented in a series of studies, many consumers believe ethical products (for example, tires made out of biodegradable materials) can't be as durable. But the truth is, it is possible to be both compassionate and strong; in fact, some of the world's most well-respected leaders, like Mahatma Gandhi, Mandela, Mother Teresa, and Martin Luther King, were the epitome of both strength and compassion. Of course, one can more readily think of leaders (like Steve Jobs or Jack Welch) who had the reputation of being uncaring. However, the theme that emerges from a larger number of data points, as we saw in chapter 3B, is that it is the leaders who are kind and compassionate (specifically, the "givers") who are more likely to rise to the top of their organizations.

And if that still doesn't convince you, consider this: Novak Djokovic, at the time of this writing the world's number-one men's singles tennis player, uses mindfulness to overcome the psychological negativity from the significantly greater crowd support that two of his competitors, Roger Federer and Rafael Nadal, get. Consider also that the U.S. Marine Corps is exploring how mindfulness can benefit its soldiers—something it wouldn't dare do if it feared that it would make them soft and weak.

In addition to believing that mindfulness is "woo woo" and that it might lead to weakness and softness, there are at least two other obstacles that prevent many people from taking it up. First, many of us believe that we are incapable of being mindful. This is because of a prevalent misconception about mindfulness: that it involves not thinking. A funny *New Yorker* cartoon, which shows two monks in a meditative pose and one of them saying to the other, "Are you not thinking what I'm not thinking?," captures this idea well.*

In reality, mindfulness is not about not thinking. Rather, it's about "changing one's relationship with thoughts," as Richie Davidson noted in a conversation I had with him.† Specifically, as discussed earlier, mindfulness has to do with merely observing thoughts without judging, commenting, or otherwise getting entangled in them.

A related obstacle that many people harbor is that it will take too long to reap the benefits from practicing mindfulness. I have to confess that I myself harbored this belief for a very long time, which is why I decided to put myself through a rather grueling ten-day silent Vipassana meditation retreat. I felt that it was only by taking such a drastic step that I would get to realize some of the benefits of the practice. I don't regret going on the retreat and, in fact, cherish it as one of the most memorable experiences I've

---

* The cartoon can be accessed at www.condenaststore.com/-sp/Are-you-not-thinking-what-I-m-not-thinking-New-Yorker-Cartoon-Prints_i8543907_.htm.

† You can watch excerpts from my interview with Professor Davidson at https://www.coursera.org/learn/happiness/lecture/ADpWa/week-6-video-9-some-other-obstacles-to-mindfulness-including-logistical-ones.

had. However, what I know now is that it is not necessary to put oneself through such a grueling experience to derive the benefits of mindfulness. Findings from one paper showed that even twelve minutes of mindfulness practice a day can work wonders. Indeed, even just five minutes a day for five weeks may be enough to increase left-side baseline activity in the frontal cortex—a pattern that, as I discussed earlier, has been associated with positive emotions.

Obstacles to Sustaining the Mindfulness Practice

As many obstacles as there are that keep us from taking up mindfulness practice, there are just as many that prevent us from sustaining it once we have taken it up. One such obstacle has to do with logistics: finding the time, space, and energy to practice mindfulness regularly. Many of us lead such frenetic lives that we don't find enough time to have a relaxed lunch or play with our kids, so spending twenty minutes or even half that time every day on practicing mindfulness is simply out of the question.

When I spoke to Richie Davidson, I asked him for advice on overcoming this logistical problem. His suggestion was to start with very short sessions—on the order of a one- or two-minute session a day! His point was that, surely, everyone can spare one or two minutes, right? And it's not just that everyone can spare one or two minutes, there's something else about starting out with super-short sessions that's important: one is much less likely to be frustrated and therefore, much less likely to give it up. If you start with twenty-minute sessions instead, and end up fidgeting most of the time, there's a good chance you'll feel frustrated and give up the practice. By contrast, if you spend only two minutes on it, there's little chance of being defeated by frustration.

And speaking of frustration, the frustration of setting high expectations and not being able to achieve them is perhaps the biggest obstacle to sustaining a mindfulness practice. In some ways, getting to know all the benefits of mindfulness is a curse because such knowledge can set up sky-high expectations against which our actual experiences pale in comparison. So, much like how comparing our current levels of happiness with our ideal levels of happiness can be pernicious, as we saw in chapter 1B, comparing the actual experience of trying to be mindful with what one would ideally like the experience to be can be very frustrating.

The good thing about getting conversant with the benefits of mindfulness is that it can motivate you to start the practice. The bad news, however, is that it can set expectations unrealistically high, which can get in the way of being mindful. I've devised three strategies to overcome the burden of having high expectations before I start a mindfulness session. First, I remind myself quite explicitly before each session that no session is like any other. So I tell myself that my only aim is to see how reality is going to turn out to be this time—for the next ten or fifteen minutes, or for however long I plan to practice mindfulness. I also tell myself that I am going to accept whatever happens completely and unconditionally, even if what happens is that I never manage to step out of the GATE of my mind. Second, I set the intention of being as dedicated to the goal of being a "fly in the wall" as I can. I tell myself that's the one and only goal I am going to have for the entire session. That is, I tell myself that I am not going to let any other goal—such as the goal of getting into flow or of feeling compassionate—get in the way of being a fly in the wall. And finally, I tell myself that the instant I find myself distracted from the goal of being the fly in the wall—which invariably happens multiple times in every session!—I am going to use a combination of self-compassion and dispassionate pursuit of passion to get back to that goal.

As you may recall, self-compassion mainly involves being kind and compassionate to oneself. In the context of a mindfulness practice, this means not being harsh on myself for failing to adhere to the goal of being the fly in the wall. The dispassionate pursuit of passion involves pursuing an outcome—in this case, of being a fly in the wall—to the best of one's ability, but then fully accepting whatever outcome unfolds without judging it. What happens in any given moment—that is, regardless of whether I discover that I have succeeded or failed to adhere to the goal of being a fly in the wall—I strive to go back to being a fly in the wall in the present moment.

To summarize, I tell myself the following three things just before, and during, each mindfulness session:

• Each session is new and so don't have any expectations.
• The only goal is to be a fly in the wall, and no other goal matters.

- When I deviate from this goal, use a combination of self-compassion and dispassionate pursuit of passion to course-correct.

These three things, I have discovered, help me adopt the right attitude before and during the mindfulness session. Once the mindfulness session is over, I tell myself one more thing to motivate myself for the next session. I tell myself that "there's no such thing as a bad mindfulness session." This is not just wishful thinking. Several studies have shown that what's most important about mindfulness practice is regularity. So long as you have tried sincerely to be the fly in the wall, you will have taken at least a small step toward becoming better at being mindful in any situation.

The Presence Practice

In the previous few sections, I have discussed several obstacles that keep us from checking out mindfulness and from sustaining the practice. I hope that by busting some of these myths about mindfulness and also by shedding light on what it is and what it isn't, I've helped you become more open to trying it. Further, I hope that the discussion of some of the logistical obstacles and how to overcome them has given you some insights into how to sustain the practice. This leads me to the seventh—and final—happiness exercise: the "presence practice," which is a type of mindfulness practice.

Earlier, I used the analogy of "the fly in the wall" to explain mindfulness. Specifically, I equated mindfulness to being a fly in the wall of your head—observing your GATEs (thoughts, emotions, etc.) without commenting or judging them. Now, it turns out that observing the goings-on in the mind is very difficult for most people. Most people find it easier to observe a *bodily sensation* rather than what's going on in the mind. In particular, it seems that observing the breath is perhaps the easiest way to practice mindfulness. There are many reasons why the breath is a good thing to observe. It is constantly changing—you are always breathing in or breathing out or holding your breath—so it's a little more interesting to observe than, say, the sensations in your hands. At the same time, it's not so much in flux—like your thoughts—that it's difficult to observe. It is also something that's gross enough to observe—unlike, say, your heartbeat, which is usually much more subtle. But at the same time, the breath is also capable of becoming very subtle. Finally, the breath is right on the edge of being voluntary and under your control and involuntary and out of your control, which allows you to practice being a mere observer without trying to change things.

If you choose to observe your breath as a mindfulness practice, you would simply become aware of the sensations you feel on a particular part of your body as you breathe. You could, for example, focus on the sensations on the walls of your nostrils as you breathe in and breathe out. As you do this, you may notice that both breathing in and breathing out put some pressure on the walls of your nostrils. Or you may start to notice that the incoming breath is just a little bit cooler than the outgoing one. Or that the breathing happens mainly through one—the left or the right—nostril for a period of time and then it switches. If you continue to pay attention to the sensations that breathing causes on and around your nostrils, you may start to notice even more subtle things—like the hairs inside your nasal passage moving with your inhalations or exhalations, or that your inhalations cool your palate. In the process of being aware of all this, your breath is likely to become calmer and quieter—more subtle—and also more drawn out.

Of course, all of these things will happen only if you aren't distracted by thoughts. And that's where your ability to merely observe your thoughts and let them pass—as if you were a fly in the wall—comes in. In being a fly in the wall, it's best not to judge yourself for negative thoughts like "Man, I can't even focus on my breath for five seconds at a stretch." Just forget what happened in the past and come back to becoming aware of the sensations caused by the act of breathing.

This is what you would do if your mindfulness practice involved observing your breath. Now, although, as I mentioned just a little while back, observing your breath is easier than observing the mind, even that isn't easy for most of us. This is where the "presence practice" comes in. It's a technique that one of my good friends, Vijay Bhat, developed specifically for busy people—people who have too much on their plate and don't already have a mindfulness practice going. Of course, you may already have a regular mindfulness practice that you are happy with. If so, you can simply participate in the presence practice with open-minded curiosity; I am sure you will enjoy it. But if you don't have a mindfulness practice and you find that the "presence practice" makes you experience some of the benefits of being mindful, you can use it for as long as you want. The main objective of this video is to let you get a glimpse into a particular type of mindfulness practice and then leave it up to you to decide if you find it useful or not.

You can find the detailed instructions for presence practice on www .happysmarts.com/book/exercises/presence_practice, and the abridged instructions in the appendix for this chapter.

Chapter 8
THE ROAD AHEAD

├────────────────────────────────────┤

The point of philosophy is to start with something so simple as not to seem worth stating, and to end with something so paradoxical that no one will believe it.

Bertrand Russell

Now that you have almost completed the book, if someone was to pose the Genie Question to you again, would happiness figure on your wish list?

I hope it does! As we saw earlier, the most common reasons people say they wouldn't wish for happiness aren't really valid. For example, as I discussed in chapter 1B, the belief that happiness is too abstract isn't valid; happiness can be defined in concrete terms—as authentic pride, love, abundance, or harmony. Likewise, the belief that happiness will make one lazy or selfish, as well as the belief that it is fleeting, isn't necessarily valid. But maybe you didn't put happiness on your Genie wish list because you have other concerns about asking the Genie for happiness. You may believe that happiness should be earned, and not be granted for free. Or you may fear that putting happiness on your wish list would be tantamount to handing over the keys to your life to the Genie—who knows what it may have to do to keep you happy?

Whether happiness does or doesn't figure on your wish list, what's clear is that the Genie Question is really hypothetical because, as far as we know at least, the Genie doesn't exist. But here's something that's *not* hypothetical: being your own Genie. Being your own Genie means two things. First, it means figuring out what to put on your wish list; I hope that reading this book has persuaded you to prioritize—but not pursue—a life of happiness and fulfillment. Second, it means knowing how to achieve the things on your wish list. So if happiness is on your wish list, being your own Genie means knowing the answer to this question: *what are the determinants of a happy and fulfilling life?*

Happiness Is an MBA!

A bird's-eye view of this book's content would suggest that, once our basic necessities are met, we need three main things to be happy. The first thing we need is to feel that we are good at something—dancing, painting, teaching, etc. Let's call this the need for "Mastery." We discussed this need in several contexts, including how one of the reasons we seek superiority is so that we can assess our progress toward Mastery. We also discussed it in the context of flow—how flow enhances happiness by enabling progress toward Mastery. Yet another context in which we discussed Mastery is "taking personal responsibility for happiness." A big reason why taking personal responsibility—or "internal control"—enhances happiness is because it fosters *personal* Mastery—Mastery over one's own thoughts and feelings.

The second thing we need is to feel a sense of intimacy or connection with at least one other person. Let's call this the need to "Belong." We discussed this need in many contexts as well, including "the need to be loved" and "the need to love (and give)." It is the need to Belong that, among those who didn't get sufficient or the right kind of love and nurturance, makes some of us needy and the others among us avoidant. It is the same need that is at least partly responsible for why we feel happy when we exhibit kindness and generosity, and why we like it when others reciprocate trust with trustworthiness.

The third thing we need is to feel a sense of freedom—to feel that we, rather than others—are the authors of our own judgments and decisions. Let's call this the need for "Autonomy." We discussed this need in many contexts, including how higher status fulfills it, and how it provokes psychological reactance among those who feel controlled by others. The need for Autonomy also figured in the discussion of internal control—specifically, how gaining internal control enhances happiness by granting us Autonomy over our own thoughts and feelings—and also in the context of mindfulness.

In short, the three things we need in order to be happy (once our basic needs are met) are: Mastery, Belonging, and Autonomy—in short, an "MBA"! That's right, what you need to be happy is an MBA, and I would strongly recommend getting it at either the McCombs School of Business or the Indian School of Business!

The "Two Approaches to an MBA" Framework

Jokes apart, to those who are familiar with *self-determination theory*, the idea that Mastery, Belonging, and Autonomy are critical for happiness wouldn't come as a surprise. The importance of all three needs has been

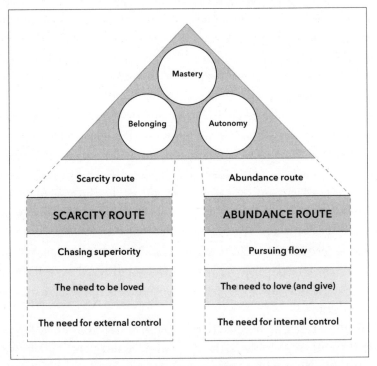

The two routes to MBA: why the approach one takes toward Mastery, Belonging, and Autonomy matters for happiness

well documented across several findings. What would be news, however—and I consider this to be the main contribution of this book—is that the fulfillment of Mastery, Belonging, and Autonomy, while necessary, isn't sufficient. What's also critical is *using the right approach or route in seeking fulfillment of these needs.*

There are two routes to Mastery: pursuing superiority and pursuing flow. Likewise, there are two routes to Belonging: desperation for love and the need to love (and give). In the case of Autonomy, the two routes are the need for external control and the need for internal control. As you can see from the figure above, I've labeled the first set of routes the "scarcity" route and the second set the "abundance" route.

The word "scarcity" captures an important element common to all three of the first set of routes. A person who seeks superiority over others is someone who believes that life is a zero-sum game. This person thinks that the things (wealth, power, fame, etc.) she needs to be happy are scarce, which is why she ends up seeking superiority over others. If she didn't perceive these things to be scarce, but believed they were in fact abundant, she wouldn't be as motivated to seek superiority over others. Likewise, a person who is desperate for the love of others believes that his cup of love is not full—or not full enough—which is why he feels incomplete and needs someone else to "complete" him. He may also feel that he has nothing of value to offer to others, which may, in turn, trigger neediness or avoidance. These types of self-perceptions—"I'm not worthy enough," "I'm not complete," and the like—have a strong scarcity-related theme to them. Being overly controlling of others and of outcomes, too, stems from scarcity orientation. Specifically, being overly controlling stems from the perception that one doesn't have enough of another person's respect, love, or trust, or that one hasn't experienced enough "desirable" outcomes. That is, the tendency to be overly controlling stems from the perception that, unless one imposes oneself on others or on situations, the outcomes that one desires aren't likely to occur, and in that sense, stems from perceived scarcity of desirable outcomes. Thus the "deadly sins"—of chasing superiority, being needy or avoidant, and being overly controlling—all stem from a scarcity orientation.

By contrast, the three alternative routes to MBA stem from an abundance orientation. It is when one feels adequately taken care of that one is more likely to pursue something purely for the enjoyment that one derives from it (flow), rather than for extrinsic rewards. Likewise, it is when one feels abundant—like a king or a queen—that one feels truly capable of generosity. Similarly, it is when one feels abundant in terms of confidence to handle whatever life throws at one that one feels comfortable to let go of external control and seek internal control instead.

So as I mentioned briefly at the end of chapter 1B, the recipe for leading a life of happiness and fulfillment ultimately boils down to weaning oneself away from scarcity orientation and toward abundance orientation. This is why, as you may have noticed, all happiness exercises are, in one way or another, aimed at mitigating the scarcity orientation and instead, nurturing the abundance orientation.

The Win-Win-Win Solution

The "two approaches to MBA" framework reiterates the "win-win-win" aspect of the happiness recipe that I briefly touched upon in the Introduction. Specifically, the framework suggests that the abundance orientation, which underlies the habits of the highly happy, promotes not only altruism, but also chances of success by fostering both creativity and maturity in interactions with others. That's not to say, of course, that the happiness habits will always enhance success—or even happiness. As we saw in chapter 3B, while being kind and compassionate is a good thing, being indiscriminately giving may not improve happiness or success. Likewise, as we saw in chapter 5A, there's an ideal point beyond which proactively trusting others hurts, rather than helps, chances of success and happiness. More generally, in settings where our survival is at stake—such as in war zones or under conditions of poverty—the happiness habits may, far from enhancing happiness and success, jeopardize both. So the recipe outlined in this book is not a *general* recipe—in the sense that it does not apply to everyone under all conditions. Rather, it's a recipe that is relevant particularly for the S-and-S. Specifically, it's a recipe that is tailored to those whose basic necessities have been met, and who are involved in creative or intellectual endeavors.

Most people buy the idea that the recipe outlined in this book offers a win-win-win solution. But at the same time, many also harbor an important concern—the concern that, if a critical mass of people were to adopt this recipe, we would collectively suffer. Specifically, the concern is that societal-level progress and productivity would fall off a cliff if a critical mass of people were to adopt the happiness habits. This concern stems from the assumption that a scarcity orientation is necessary to keep those doing menial but critical tasks—like flipping burgers and cleaning toilets— motivated to do their jobs.

How valid is this assumption? Would societal-level progress and pro- ductivity in fact fall off a cliff if a critical mass of people were to adopt the happiness habits?

One way to address the concern is through a thought experiment. Imagine that everyone in the world decided, one fine day, to take up only flow-inducing jobs—jobs that are engaging and meaningful. So for example, imagine that, starting today, no one was willing to flip burgers or clean toi- lets. Such a turn of events is, of course, extremely unlikely, because a signif- icant proportion of the world's population is caught up in the struggle to meet basic needs and will therefore take up *any* job that pays the bills. But let's ignore this fact for now. If few people were willing to take up menial-but- critical jobs, then the most likely consequence—which follows from a simple supply-demand logic—would be this: those willing to take up the menial- but-critical jobs would command higher wages. This wouldn't be such a bad thing for at least two reasons. First, higher wages for the working poor would improve the lot of those at the "bottom of the pyramid." Second, assuming the operation of free-market forces, opportunistic entrepreneurs would step in to figure out alternative ways to meet the demand for menial-but-critical jobs. Specifically, after perhaps a brief period of chaos, machines and robots would take the place of humans currently doing these jobs. Such a turn of events would, again, be welcome, as it would not only improve the average levels of employee satisfaction, but would also help the economy evolve in new and exciting directions.

But what if the desire to find meaningful and engaging jobs makes our workforce lazy and unproductive?

Such a question arises from an implicit assumption that many of us make—the assumption that people are, by nature, lazy, and that the only way to motivate them is by incentivizing them through extrinsic rewards like money. I suspect that an important reason we subscribe to this as- sumption is because we do not find our current jobs to be engaging or meaningful. As a result, because we ourselves wouldn't work a minute longer if we weren't paid extra to do so, we assume that everyone else must be in the same boat. However, as several studies on intrinsic motivation have repeatedly shown, not only would people work harder, they would also work *smarter* if they enjoyed what they did than if they were merely motivated to pursue extrinsic rewards. This means that the belief—that seeking meaning and engagement at work would lead to laziness and unproductivity—is misplaced.

This is not to say that those who pursue meaning and engagement at work would be willing to work hard on *any* job, of course; by definition, they wouldn't work hard on jobs they find meaningless. As such, those who seek meaning and engagement at work may be less willing to do certain things—like work for a cigarette company or for a fast-food chain—that they believe cause more harm than good for the world. They may also be less willing to be part of a system that pollutes our rivers or endangers animals. This, in turn, may lower the productivity of certain types of industries. But that wouldn't be such a bad thing. As a great number of social scientists have observed, the gravest dangers that we collectively face today—from climate change and species decimation to wealth inequality and water scarcity—are unlikely to be resolved by continuing on the "business as usual" path of pernicious hyperproductivity. We give ourselves a better shot of averting, and perhaps even resolving, these dangers if we scale back those endeavors that create more harm than good.

So in other words, if a critical mass of us were to adopt the recipe outlined in this book, societies would likely evolve in a different, and arguably *better*, direction. We may produce fewer widgets, so to speak. For example, fast food chains may sprout a little less frequently, and the next iPad may take more time to arrive. But the widgets that we do produce will be more meaningful, and will be produced in a more sustainable fashion. As a result, our economic activity would serve not just a few stakeholders—such as the manufacturers, the retailers, and the customers—but also those who are external to the market: the animals, the indigent, and future generations.

A Win-Win-Win-*Win* Solution

To summarize, it appears that the recipe for a happy and fulfilling life is, in fact, not just a "win-win-win" solution, but a "win-win-win-*win*" solution. Specifically, apart from boosting happiness levels, chances of success, and altruism at the personal level, it is likely to boost *meaningful productivity* at the societal level.

Those who believe that "life's a zero-sum game" and "people are lazy by nature" will find it difficult to come to terms with the idea that there's seemingly no catch in the recipe for happiness. "If," they may ask, "the recipe for happiness offers a win-win-win-win solution, how come no one seems to know this? Why hasn't the recipe caught on? Why do people continue to feverishly pursue material wealth, power, and fame? Why don't we see more evidence of altruism and generosity?"

This is a valid question and one with which I, too, have grappled for years. Over time, I have developed a three-part response to it. The first part is this: Although the question of what makes us happy and fulfilled is nearly as old as humanity itself, it was only recently that we began a concerted effort at taking a systematic, scientific approach to answer this question. As a result, we previously didn't have much scientific backing for the idea that the recipe for happiness offers a win-win-win-win solution. Or, put differently, until recently, if someone had discovered from personal experience that the things that make one happy also promote success, altruism, and meaningful productivity, he would have had a very difficult time convincing others of it. But thanks to the sheer weight of emerging scientific evidence, it's much easier now to see how and why the determinants of happiness lead to other benefits as well. In other words, adoption of happiness "habits" has been slow until now because we had little scientific evidence of its "win-win-win-win." With the emergence of the new "science of happiness"—positive psychology—however, this is all set to change.

The second part of my answer has to do with perhaps the most important megatrend that has characterized the evolution of human beings in the past few decades. Perhaps due to the convergence of a number of factors—including unprecedented levels of peace, incredible technological advancements, and increasing access to information—the average person living in developed nations enjoys a far better standard of living than that which even the kings and queens of yore enjoyed. As Sonja Lyubomirsky notes in *The How of Happiness*, "a compelling case can be made that the level of material comfort you are experiencing today is equivalent to how the top 5 percent lived a mere half a century ago!" As a result, with each passing year, an ever increasing number of people in the world know, *from personal ex-*

perience—rather than as an abstract concept—that greater wealth does not automatically translate into greater happiness. A natural consequence of this trend is an increase in genuine interest in learning about the determinants of happiness and fulfillment. As a result, I expect future generations to be less scarcity-minded and more abundance-minded.

The third part of my answer also has to do with a megatrend, but one that is taking place at the level of the firm, rather than at the level of the individual. This megatrend has to do with the evolution toward, as John Mackey and Raj Sisodia put it in their best seller *Conscious Capitalism*, "conscious" business practices. Until just a few decades back, the typical business enterprise operated more on the basis of the "life's a zero-sum game" ideology than on the basis of "there's room for everyone to grow." As a result, firms exhibited the types of behaviors—hypercompetition, lack of trust, Machiavellianism—that are associated with a scarcity orientation. While the firms that exhibited these types of scarcity-oriented behaviors may have been more likely to survive in the old economy, it appears that firms that exhibit a different—more abundance-oriented—type of behavior are likely to *thrive* in the emerging new economy. Sisodia and his coauthors find, for example, that in the period between 1992 and 2012, firms that exhibited conscious business practices—such as taking a "multiple-stakeholder" view that improves everyone's well-being and not just the company's profits— made a whopping 110 percent more profits than those that did not exhibit these practices!

Why are firms becoming more conscious? There are multiple reasons for it, including an increasing demand for more meaningful work, a growing recognition that unconscious business practices are self-destructive, and the emergence of something that Jeremy Rifkin—a professor of management at Wharton—calls *biosphere consciousness*, which stems from the recognition that we are all deeply interconnected and interdependent. Whatever the reasons for it, what's clear is that there is a shift in business culture toward greater consciousness, and that this shift should make increasing numbers of people more receptive to the recommendations in this book.

The "win-win-win-win" nature of the happiness recipe is one of its most important features, and the sooner we recognize it, the better off we will all be. Or conversely, the longer we continue to be skeptical about the recipe's beneficial impact on success, altruism, and meaningful productivity, the longer we will take to adopt it. And the longer that we—the S-and-S—take to adopt it, the longer it will take for the rest of humanity to do so. Put another way, if we—with everything going for us—can't bring ourselves to accord greater priority to happiness and fulfillment, it's unlikely that the less fortunate among us can. In this sense then, I believe that the S-and-S have an *obligation* to prioritize happiness and fulfillment so that the rest of humanity can follow suit.

But even if one feels motivated to accord greater priority to leading a life of happiness and fulfillment, replacing the happiness "sins" with the happiness "habits" will not be easy. This is because, although the recipe may seem simple in theory, it's not easy in practice. There is a straightforward reason why the recipe is simple in theory: it has a ring of *familiarity*, which makes it instinctively appealing. The recipe is familiar because most cultures and traditions espouse values that are consistent with it. For instance, growing up, most of us would likely have been encouraged by caretakers to be generous and kind. Likewise, we are likely to have been told about the importance of pursuing our passion. Most of us will likely have been exposed, in one form or another, to even the more esoteric happiness habits, including the dispassionate pursuit of passion and mindfulness.

While the recipe's familiarity makes it instinctively appealing, it's difficult to put into practice mainly because we are surrounded by people who act in ways that are antithetical to it. In private-sector corporations in particular, we see blatant violations of the abundance orientation; self-interest and greed are, for instance, rampant. We also see obsessive, rather than dispassionate, pursuit of passion. Further, corporate culture is characterized more by distrust than by trust. Thus, even as we recognize the merits of happiness habits at one level, the fact that we are surrounded by people who think and act in ways that are at odds with it shakes our confidence in it, and we wonder, "Is this really a practical recipe?"

Why are people, particularly those in the business world, prone to greed and cynicism? More generally, why do people act in ways that not only vitiate the culture for everyone else, *but lower their own happiness levels*?

There are several reasons for this. Perhaps the most important one is this: for much of our evolution as a species, we have been concerned more about surviving than about thriving or flourishing. And because our chances of survival are greater when we operate from a scarcity orientation, we are more prone to exhibiting greed and cynicism in contexts that evoke a scarcity orientation. That is, we are more likely to exhibit greed and distrust in corporate settings because most businesses used to—and to a large extent, continue to—operate from a scarcity orientation. In other words, *cultural inertia* is a big reason why people think and act in ways that are antithetical to leading a happy and fulfilling life.

Another reason people act in ways that lower their own happiness levels is because of the evaluability of goals, which refers to the idea that people accord greater importance to goals that are easier to measure, *even if they are less important*. Because the goals that are easier to measure—such as making more money—happen to encourage interpersonal comparison and competition, we see more exhibitions of greed and cynicism. This suggests that the better we become at quantifying and measuring things like "employee well-being" and "sustainability"—and initiatives are already under way to do so—the more people will think and act in ways that are consistent with the abundance orientation.

A final reason we "see" people acting in ways that undermine their own happiness is because of our tendency to pay greater attention to others' negative behaviors over positive ones—a topic we discussed in chapter 5B. That is, because we selectively pay greater attention to others' negativity, we believe that others operate in a more scarcity-oriented fashion than they actually do, and this in turn prompts us to act in scarcity-minded ways too.

But despite the fact that replacing the happiness "sins" with the happiness "habits" may be difficult, it's worth attempting, because it is the most reliable way of boosting one's own happiness levels.

The Three Strategies for Sustaining Higher Happiness Levels

Soon I will have you fill out the now-familiar Satisfaction with Life Scale one last time. I fully expect your happiness levels to have improved because, if you have gotten this far, you have obviously been both open-minded and diligent. But just because your happiness levels have improved doesn't mean that you will find it easy to maintain them; it's going to take quite a bit of conscious effort—and smarts. The reason for this is that, as several scholars like Jonathan Haidt in *The Happiness Hypothesis* and Chip and Dan Heath in *Switch* have noted, old habits die hard. Our old habits—the cause of our lower happiness levels—have been conditioned into us for years, if not decades. For example, at work you are probably surrounded by messages that reinforce the need for superiority and, more generally, the scarcity orientation. Likewise, on TV and other media, you are probably bombarded with negative stories that instill distrust of others and of life. During the course of reading this book, you may have managed to keep some of these negative influences at bay, but now that you are done with the book, those old conditionings will likely reassert themselves.

What can you do to break—or at least mitigate—your old counterproductive habits and reinforce the new and productive ones?

I posed this question to several thought leaders, including Marshall Goldsmith, author of several best sellers including *What Got You Here Won't Get You There,* and Art Markman, professor of social psychology at UT Austin and author, again, of several best sellers such as *Smart Thinking* and *Smart Change.* Using their input, I have developed three strategies that I know, based on the experience of my students, to be effective in sustaining higher happiness levels.

The first strategy hinges on something Goldsmith discovered after interviewing several thousand employees across hundreds of organizations. He discovered that one of the main reasons we find it difficult to sustain higher levels of happiness is that we lose touch with the happiness habits and exercises. We tell ourselves that we will (re)start the exercises in a few weeks—once the current "crazily busy period" is over. This is a dangerous "dream" (as Marshall puts it) because it can sound very reasonable to tell yourself that you'll start something in a few weeks or months. But before you know it, the weeks and months turn into years and decades, and soon you are, as Pink Floyd sang, "shorter of breath and one day closer to death."

So it's very important to make a strong commitment to do, *on a daily basis starting today*, the things that mitigate the happiness "sins" and reinforce the "habits." This leads me to the first strategy for sustaining happiness, which is to "respond to daily questions" posed by what Goldsmith calls a "peer coach." A peer coach is someone who will ask you a series of questions on an everyday basis to make sure that you are on track to mitigating the happiness sins and reinforcing the happiness habits. There are a number of questions that the peer coach could pose to you, but for the purposes of this book, I've identified fourteen questions that will help you replace the happiness sins with the habits. You can find these questions at www.happysmarts.com/book/exercises/daily_questions.

The second and third strategies are based on Markman's distillation of why we find it difficult to replace old, unproductive habits with new and more productive ones. One reason for this is that we underestimate the power of "context"—the people with whom we surround ourselves, and the environments in which we put ourselves. For instance, most of us don't realize how pernicious the influence of scarcity-minded people and environments can be on our thoughts and actions. On the flip side, most of us don't realize how salubrious exposure to nature can be for both mental and physical health. The second strategy for enhancing happiness levels thus involves choosing the contexts to which you expose yourself more judiciously. For example, make it easier to eat right by giving yourself greater access to healthy (as opposed to unhealthy) snacks. Likewise, if you know someone who makes you feel scarcity minded, avoid his or her company—at least until such time as you are immune to their negativity. Similarly, if you discover that being out in nature reinforces an abundance orientation, make the effort to go hiking or camping on a regular basis. In the "Resources" section of the book's website (www.happysmarts.com/book/resources), you will find books, movies, videos, and articles that help mitigate the scarcity orientation and reinforce the abundance orientation. Take advantage of this list and, while you are about it, share your own set of resources with us!

One of the most critical aspects of our environment is, of course, the people with whom we surround ourselves. This is because, as we saw in chapters 3A and 3B, we are an exceedingly—perhaps excruciatingly—social species. What the others around us say and do matters so much to us that, as Markman put it, "the goals that other people pursue are literally contagious." What Markman means is that if you find yourself in the company of people who are pursuing certain goals, you, too, find these goals attractive. This suggests that if you join hands with other seekers of happiness and fulfillment, you will make greater progress toward this goal.

As it turns out, finding fellow seekers of happiness and fulfillment has never been easier. As I mentioned in the Introduction, my online Coursera course on happiness has, as of this writing, attracted more than 100,000 students from literally every country in the world. Many incredible things have happened since the course was launched, one of them being this: two sets of learners started Facebook groups for the course that, at last count, had more than 2,000 members. Several of these members routinely contribute stories, news items, and perspectives that serve to reinforce the happiness habits. I would encourage you to join this community. Or you could choose to join my own Facebook page (search for "happy smarts" on your Facebook page). You can also sign up to receive free daily e-mails from www.dailygood.org. This is a website that Nipun Mehta (the cofounder of Karma Kitchen) and his friends started after recognizing that few media outlets disseminate good news—of people behaving in kind, trusting, and forgiving ways.* I find that reading an e-mail from DailyGood helps reinforce the abundance orientation.

Of course, in addition to being part of these virtual communities, it would be important to have face-to-face meetings with like-minded people, say, once a week. Perhaps you could start such a group in your own city! As part of these face-to-face meetings, you could consider serving as a mentor to someone, to help them figure out how to lead a happier and more fulfilling life. Markman finds that mentoring someone else helps you stay motivated in the "squishy middle stage" of goal pursuit: when the excitement of starting to adopt a new habit has worn off, and you are still quite far from reaching your goal. A word of caution about serving as a mentor, though: most people don't like to get happiness advice. This may be because we all have our own pet theories about happiness that we don't like challenged. So pick and choose your mentees carefully. Close friends and family are okay, but think twice before advising neighbors and colleagues.

The third and final strategy is to tell yourself the story that you are open-minded and aren't closed to evolving in new ways, even if doing so involves questioning your most deeply held worldviews. As I mentioned in the Introduction, open-mindedness is hugely important for happiness. It's easy to get wedded to the idea that "I'm an introvert, so I can't do the 'ex-

---

* You can catch an excerpt of my interview with Nipun—whom I find to be among the most inspiring people—here: https://www.coursera.org/learn/happiness/lecture/pDBVu/week-3 -video-12-interview-with-nipun-mehta-optional.

pressing gratitude' exercise" or that "I am a flow person, so I can't hang out with status seekers." Although some of these types of identities (a flow person) are better than others (a status seeker), all identities ultimately are constraining. So the more you believe that you don't have a set identity, and that you can change into whoever you need to become in order to lead a happier life—that is, the more you give yourself the freedom to evolve—the more easily you will be able to adopt new happiness habits.

One of the best ways to become more open-minded, I have found, is to practice mindfulness. This is because, as we saw in chapter 7B, mindfulness involves being open to, and accepting of, whatever emerges. Therefore, the practice of mindfulness naturally instills open-mindedness. The problem with mindfulness, of course, is that it is difficult to sustain the practice—until, that is, it becomes a habit. For this reason, I have made available a six-week (forty-two-day) "mindfulness camp" for those interested in cultivating it. You can learn more about the camp at www.happysmarts.com/book/exercises/mindfulness_camp.

I hope that by implementing the three strategies for sustaining happiness, you will find it easier to lead a life of greater happiness and fulfillment. Doing so would, of course, be the smart thing to do because, *if you aren't happy, how smart are you really?*

And with those words, allow me to bid you good-bye . . . for now. I started the book by noting how, because of the advent of social media, it's so much easier to get back in touch with old friends. The same could be said for staying in touch with new friends.

THE THIRD HAPPINESS MEASUREMENT

├─────────────────────┤

For each of the five items below, circle a number from 1 through 7, where 1 = "strongly disagree" and 7 = "strongly agree." You can also fill out the scale online by going to www.happysmarts.com/book/scales/satisfaction_with _life/third_measurement. Once you have responded to all five items, total up your rating for each item to come up with your overall satisfaction with life score.

	STRONGLY DISAGREE				STRONGLY AGREE		
In most ways, my life is close to my ideal.	1	2	3	4	5	6	7
I am satisfied with my life.	1	2	3	4	5	6	7
The conditions of my life are excellent.	1	2	3	4	5	6	7
So far, I have the important things I want in life.	1	2	3	4	5	6	7
If I could live my life over, I would change almost nothing.	1	2	3	4	5	6	7

ACKNOWLEDGMENTS

When people learn that I am a business-school professor teaching a course on happiness, they are surprised—and I don't blame them. After all, so much of business is focused on making money that it is often seen as the opposite of happiness. And yet, here I am. Not only have I been teaching a "classroom" course on happiness for five years running, I even have an online course on the topic (see www.coursera.org/course/happiness). And now this: a book on happiness.

For reasons I will get to in a minute, much of this journey has been immensely gratifying. However, I'd be lying if I claimed that it has been easy. When I first put pen to paper for this book in the summer of 2010, I thought it would take me a year—maybe two, tops—to finish it. Boy, was I mistaken! By the time the book is launched, it will have taken me *six years* to finish it. In these six long years, I have spent more time thinking about, and working on, this book than would be considered judicious from the point of view of advancing my academic career. (Tenure-track faculty at research universities are expected to publish journal articles—not books.)

But in the end, as the saying goes, "the juice has been worth the squeeze." For allowing me the freedom to do what I felt was right, I thank Eli Cox, the then chair of my department, and Tom Gilligan, the then dean of McCombs, for approving my course on happiness. I should also thank my colleagues in the marketing department at McCombs and, more generally, the marketing academic community, for fostering a culture of open-mindedness that permits researchers to pursue their passion.

Next on my list come my friends—in particular, Andrew Gershoff, Ashesh Mukherjee, Frenkel ter Hofstede, Prem Khatri, Rohit Deo, and last but not least, Neelesh Marik—all of whom played to perfection the delicate balancing act of providing me with the right blend of emotional and intellectual support. I should also thank my collaborators on various projects— Aaron Rochlen, Alok Kumar, Ashesh Mukherjee, Bin Gu, Chip Heath, Christopher Blazina, Eunjoo Han, Hyunkyu Jang, Jae Hong, Jeff Loewenstein, Julie Irwin, Kaavya Bector, Kim Corfman, Mark Alpert, Michael Luchs, Michel Pham, Michelle Chen, Prabhudev Konana, Ravi Chitturi, Rebecca Reczek, Sridhar Balasubramanian, Sunaina Chugani, Suresh Ramanathan, Vijay Mahajan, Wayne Hoyer, and Yaacov Trope—for helping me arrive at the "seven sins/habits/exercises" framework that formed the backbone of this book. A huge shout-out also goes to the social scientists from a variety of disciplines, including behavioral economics, neuroscience, organizational behavior, consumer behavior and, of course, positive psychology, for generating the set of insights on which I have leaned heavily. In particular, I'd like to thank the following for sharing their ideas with me through informal chats: Art Markman, Barbara Fredrickson, Dan Ariely, Ed Diener, Jamie Pennebaker, Jerry Burger, Ken Pargament, Kristin Neff, Kristina Durante, Marshall Goldsmith, Melanie Rudd, Mike Norton, Mihaly Csikszentmihalyi, Nipun Mehta, Phillip Shaver, Reb Rebele, Richie Davidson, Sonja Lyubomirsky, Shauna Shapiro, Srikumar Rao, Steven Tomlinson, Sunaina Chugani, Swati Desai, Tom Gilovich, and Vijay Bhat.

This brings me to the 1,000-plus students from my "classroom" course on happiness at McCombs and at ISB. I thank you for your courage and open-mindedness in taking my class, for pushing me to think more clearly about the topic, and for providing me with feedback on previous versions of the chapters from this book. Without your input, this book would obviously have remained just a concept. I would also like to thank the more than 100,000 Coursera students who have taken, or are currently enrolled in, my online course. In particular, I'd like to thank the 654 students who read sample chapters from this book and helped me refine them through their feedback. The chapters also benefited from feedback from several scholars, including Andrew Gershoff, Luis Martins, Prabhudev Konana,

Steven Fearing, Linda Golden and the students in her class, Susan Broni-arczyk (and the participants in her lab, particularly Neetika Bhargava), and my philosopher and guide for life, Michel Pham. Special thanks go to Carol Atwood, Dragos Moldovan, Pham Ho, Ritesh Prasad, Robert Lalor, Roshni Kanchan, Sankar Vyakaranam, and to my dear wife for going through the galley pages with a fine-tooth comb to identify and correct typos.

When Eric Nelson, currently at Portfolio, contacted me in the spring of 2012 to see if I'd be interested in writing a book on happiness, I was agent-less. Thanks, Eric, for serving as my agent until January 2015, and then as my editor since; I am indebted to you for the faith you've placed in me. Thanks also for putting me in touch with Susan Rabiner (who took over as my agent in 2015); Susan, you've done an awesome job of shepherding me through the publishing process. Thanks also go out to Kaushik Viswana-than and Vivian Roberson at Portfolio, for guiding me through the final steps.

Confirming the experience of many other authors, I, too, found that writing a book is more challenging than one initially expects it will be. I am indebted to my parents, in-laws, children, and, in particular, my sweet wife, for being a constant and unstinting source of support. Now that the book is done, I promise to be home earlier, and to do whatever you guys want me to—including playing board games!

Last, I'd like to thank two megatrends for making the environment favorable for me to pursue my life's passion. The first megatrend concerns the emergence of the field of positive psychology, because of which, I be-lieve, we have advanced our understanding of happiness more in the last two decades than in all previous years put together. The second megatrend concerns the growth in the number of smart-and-successful people who have realized, as a matter of personally experienced truth, rather than as an abstract concept, that more wealth, power, fame, control, and beauty do not add up to a happier life. It is these people who, I believe, will eventually turn the cultural tide away from a scarcity orientation and toward an abundance orientation, and in the process, cocreate a world in which everyone wins.

Raj Raghunathan
January 1, 2016
Austin, Texas

APPENDIX

The instructions for the happiness exercises are adapted from the original instructions that are available on the book's website: www.happysmarts.com/book/exercises/. I recommend doing the exercise on the website, if at all possible, since the online instructions are designed to provide a richer and more immersive experience—which means that the exercises will likely have a bigger impact on your happiness. If you are unable to complete the exercise online, however, you may follow these instructions.

INSTRUCTIONS FOR THE FIRST HAPPINESS EXERCISE: DEFINING AND INCORPORATING HAPPINESS*

Background

To prioritize (but not pursue) happiness, it is clearly important to gain clarity on what happiness means to you, and also important to figure out what things (stimuli, activities) make you happy in the way you define it.

Objective

This exercise will help you: (1) gain a sharper, more concrete understanding of what happiness means to you, and (2) identify the things (stimuli, activities) that lead you to experience the state you equate with happiness.

---

* The instructions for this exercise have been adapted, in part, from the "positivity portfolio" exercise discussed by Professor Barbara Fredrickson in her book, *Positivity*.

Steps

There are two steps in this exercise:

1. The first step is to define happiness; that is, figure out the types of emotional experiences with which you associate the term "happiness." As we saw earlier, happiness could be defined as:
   - Love/connection
   - Joy
   - Authentic pride
   - Hubristic pride
   - Harmony
   - Abundance

   ### Happiness could also be defined as*

   - Gratitude: the feeling when we acknowledge some benefit we have received from someone or something.
   - Serenity: the feeling when things are going just right; usually accompanied by peacefulness and tranquility.
   - Inspiration: the feeling that comes from experiencing something moving and emotionally uplifting.
   - Awe: the feeling of wonder or reverence toward something extremely powerful and admired.
   - Hope: the feeling that things will turn out for the best.
   - Amusement/laughter: the feeling when experiencing something fun, funny, or playful.
   - Interest: the feeling when you are curious or engaged in something.

Consider these definitions and ask yourself which one—or ones—you are most drawn to. Then, write (or type) out your own definition of happiness, remembering that it could be a combination of two or more emotional experiences, or an entirely different type of feeling.

Note: It's quite likely that you are going to revise and refine your definition of happiness over the course of the next few months. I started out with my definition as "feeling lighthearted and energetic," and later changed it to "being in love with whatever I am doing in the current moment." A few years later, my definition was "being joyful, but not at the cost of compassion or rationality." My current definition is "being

---

* Along with love, pride, and joy, these seven emotions round up Professor Barbara Fredrickson's list of "ten positive emotions."

fully accepting of whatever is going on, even if it is aversive, with an attitude of compassion (toward oneself and others) and self-awareness."*

2. The second step involves thinking of three or four things that lead you to feel happy in the way that you have defined it.

The four things that lead me to experience a sense of compassion (for oneself and others) and self-awareness are:

- Reminding myself that everyone has problems and that, for the most part, people have the *intention* to be kind
- Watching elevating movies like *Zindagi Na Milegi Dobara* [play a clip of the song "Señorita" for eight to ten seconds] or *Before Sunrise*
- Going for a run (or exercising in general)
- Hanging out with my family

Try to think of three to four things—more, if you can—that reliably help you experience the feeling with which you equate "happiness". Then, write these things on a piece of paper and, if you're up for it, stick it someplace you can see it frequently—like the mirror in your bathroom or the wall of your closet.

That's it—you're done with the exercise. If you are open to it, share your definition of happiness and the list of things that make you happy with us at www.happysmarts .com/exercises/defining_incorporating_happiness.

INSTRUCTIONS FOR THE SECOND HAPPINESS EXERCISE: EXPRESSING GRATITUDE†

Background
As I discussed, gratitude boosts happiness for a variety of reasons—which is why Professor Sonja Lyubomirsky calls it a "meta strategy." This exercise involves expressing gratitude to a person who has had a positive influence in your life.

Objective
To help you assess (and hopefully, see for yourself) the impact of expressing gratitude on happiness levels.

---

* See my discussion of self-awareness in chapter 7B.

† The instructions for this exercise are adapted from M. E. Seligman, T. A. Steen, N. Park, and C. Peterson, "Positive Psychology Progress: Empirical Validation of Interventions," *American Psychologist* 60 (5) (2005), 410–21. An adaptation of these instructions with actual participants can be seen on the following video by SoulPancake: https://www.youtube .com/watch?v=oHv6vTKD6lg (the video can also be accessed by searching for "Gratitude the science of happiness" on www.youtube.com.

Steps

This exercise involves writing a letter of gratitude by following these four steps:

1. Think of someone who had a positive influence on your life. This person can be someone from your past (e.g., teacher, mentor) or present (e.g., friend, spouse). It's ideal if you can think of someone who is still alive. If you prefer to write your gratitude letter to someone who's passed on, that's fine, too, but note that you will then need to read the letter to someone who knew this person. For example, if the person to whom you want to write your letter is your late uncle, you could choose your uncle's sister, wife, son, or daughter as the recipient of the letter.
2. Think of all the reasons why this person had a positive influence in your life and then write down your thoughts. Make this a relatively longish note, but not too long. You should aim to write three or four paragraphs.

Note: It's best to avoid saying anything that has a chance of being construed as negative. That is, you may want to avoid statements like "Even though you aren't a great-looking person, you never let that get you down." So scan your letter to see if it contains something that could be interpreted negatively, and if it does, consider removing or revising it. If in doubt about something you want to say, check with someone else who knows the person to whom you are writing your letter.

3. If the person to whom you wrote the letter is still alive, read your letter out loud to him or her. You could either call the person over the telephone or—better yet—pay a visit and read the letter face-to-face. You may want to print your note before reading it. If you are unable to call or visit the recipient of your letter, e-mail it.

If the person is no longer alive, or is not in a position to receive your letter (e.g., he or she is in critical condition in the hospital), read or e-mail your letter to the person you identified earlier—someone who knows the person to whom you wrote your letter. Again, it's best to read the letter face-to-face or over the telephone.

4. The final step involves reflecting on the following questions: What did you feel at various stages of this project—when writing the letter, when conveying the information to him or her (or to the person who knew him or her), and when waiting for the response? And how did you feel after receiving a response?

This exercise is one of my favorites since, although it may be difficult to do (many people feel awkward expressing gratitude), it invariably brings warmth and cheer to all concerned parties—including me! So, please do consider sharing your experience with everyone at www.happysmarts.com/book/exercises/expressing_gratitude.

INSTRUCTIONS FOR THE THIRD HAPPINESS EXERCISE: CREATIVE ALTRUISM

Background

Remember the pranks we used to play as kids—like letting the air out of someone's bicycle or throwing toilet paper over a neighbor's house? In this exercise, too, you'll be asked to play a prank—except that it won't be just you who's having all the fun; the "victim" of your prank will too.

Objective

The objective is to assess for yourself whether being kind and generous ("the need to love and give") is as reliable a source of happiness as it has been found to be across several studies.

Steps

This exercise involves the following four steps:

1. The first step involves coming up with the idea for your "altruistic prank." Your idea could be: leave a box of dark chocolate outside your favorite neighbor's door. Or it could be to dress up like Mickey Mouse, stand on a busy street corner, and give everyone who passes you a bear hug.

Note: If you need help with coming up with ideas, visit the website for this exercise (www.happysmarts.com/book/exercises/creative_altruism).

Once you have your idea, write (or type) it out. Seeing and reading it will give you clarity on how to execute it.

2. The second step involves coming up with a plan for executing your idea. Exactly when and how are you going to carry out your plan? If your plan is to leave a box of dark chocolate outside your neighbor's door, you need to think about: When are you going to buy the chocolate and from where? What size? When (at what time) will you leave the bag outside your neighbor's door? Will the box be gift-wrapped and if so, who'll do it? Writing (or typing) your plan will give you greater clarity on the obstacles you are likely to face in executing the plan.

3. Step 3 is the most important one, and involves executing your idea. In executing the idea, keep in mind the "three rules for giving":

   • **Contain your cost of giving.** Make sure you don't overwhelm yourself—or your resources.

- **Make it fun for both parties.** Do something that's fun not just for others, but for yourself as well.
- **Register the impact**. Make sure that you are there to see the impact of your act on the recipient (even if the recipient can't see you). So, for example, if you leave a box of chocolates for your neighbor, be sure to watch her reactions when she sees the box.

Note: If you feel that your plan doesn't adhere to the "rules for giving" or if you are not happy with the plan for any reason, this is the time to revise it.

4. The final step involves answering the following four questions about your experience with this exercise:
   - What was your idea and how did you plan on executing it?
   - How did you execute your plan? Did you stick to the three rules for giving? If not, why not?
   - How did the recipient feel? In answering this question, recollect what the recipient said and did.

How did the exercise make you feel at various points (during planning, execution, etc.)? Although this exercise is one of the most elaborate and time-consuming ones, you'll have a lot of fun doing it. Please consider sharing your experience with us at www .happysmarts.com/book/exercises/creative_altruism.

INSTRUCTIONS FOR THE FOURTH HAPPINESS EXERCISE: SCHEDULE PARTNER PROJECT*

Background
Outside of having a great social life, leading a healthy lifestyle is perhaps the single biggest thing you could do to boost your happiness levels. Leading a healthier lifestyle will give you greater internal control and therefore allow you the flexibility to exercise optimal levels of external control.

Objective
The exercise is designed to help you lead a healthier lifestyle than you currently do, specifically, "eat right," "move more," and "sleep better."†

---

* The online instructions involve partnering someone else in this project; the instructions in this book do not.

† These are the terms that Tom Rath uses in his excellent book *Eat Move Sleep*.

Steps

The exercise involves the following three steps:

1. The first step involves coming up with a healthy lifestyle plan. Consider the following changes that you could make to lead a healthier lifestyle and select at least three items from each of the three categories (eating right, moving more, and sleeping better).

Eating right

- Put unhealthy items (e.g., potato chips) in hard-to-reach places and healthy items (e.g., carrot sticks) in easier-to-reach places.
- Replace larger plates or bowls with smaller ones (if you are overweight).
- Replace white plates/bowls with plates of a different color.
- If you often eat out, carry a bag of healthy snacks with you (fruits or nuts) to tide you over in case you get hungry.
- Start your meals with healthy items (e.g., fresh, raw veggies instead of rice, chips, or fries).
- Eat a healthy breakfast (e.g., eggs, oatmeal, or steamed items, such as idlis—steamed rice cakes—rather than fried items, such as hash browns, or simple carbs, such as sugary cereal or white bread and jam).
- Reduce sugar intake (from, say, ten spoons a day—across all your drinks—to six).
- Reduce consumption of items (e.g., a trail mix bar) that have more than ten grams of sugar from, say, five items a day to three or fewer).
- Take longer (ideally, twenty minutes) to finish a meal that you typically rush through.
- Eat at least one meal (ideally, dinner) with friends or family.
- Eliminate snacking after dinner.

Note: If you are already doing all of the above things—or you aren't interested in them—you could choose to make any other three changes (e.g., not eating anything after 8 p.m., or consuming, on average, fewer than two alcoholic drinks per day) that constitute "eating right."

Moving more

- Get a pedometer and maintain a record of how much you have walked each day.
- Put in reminders—on Outlook or another computer program—to remind you to take a break every twenty to thirty minutes.
- Get a treadmill or elliptical machine for home (and use it every day for at least a few minutes)!
- Exercise (doesn't need to be intense) for twenty minutes to start the day off.

- Form a neighborhood exercise group and take a morning or evening walk/jog/ bike ride (or something else) together.
- Engage in short bursts of intense activity (to a level where you find it difficult to speak).
- Reduce the amount of time spent sitting (e.g., on bus rides, choose to stand).
- Reduce the amount of time spent sitting while watching TV (e.g., watch it while walking on a treadmill instead).
- Make it a rule to walk if you are going somewhere less than X miles away (you get to choose "X").

Note: If you are already doing all of the above activities—or you aren't interested in them—you could choose to make any other three changes (e.g., joining a yoga class, volunteer to walk your neighbor's dog) that constitute "moving more."

Sleeping better

- Minimize sources of artificial light (e.g., TV, iPad) in bedroom.
- Get white noise machine for the bedroom.
- Follow regular sleep schedule (e.g., go to bed at 10 p.m. every night and wake up no earlier than 6 a.m.)
- Prevent stress from spoiling sleep (e.g., never check e-mail after 7 p.m.; don't argue with spouse on which TV channel to watch).
- Take a warm shower thirty minutes before sleep.
- Eat early dinner (no food an hour and a half before going to sleep).
- Make bedroom two or three degrees cooler than the rest of the house (if this is not energy inefficient); use thick blankets if needed.
- Exercise sometime during the day (exercise improves quality of sleep).

Note: If you are already doing all of the above—or you aren't interested in them—you could choose to make any other three changes (e.g., no checking e-mail after 9 p.m.; no arguments with spouse after 8 p.m.!) that constitute "sleeping better."

2. The second step involves putting in place reminders to do the things in your plan on a consistent—everyday—basis for the coming two weeks. You could, for example, type in the reminders in Outlook (or other program). Or you could pencil in, ahead of time, reminders in your journal.
3. The third and final step involves typing (or writing) your response to the following three questions:
   - What three "healthy lifestyle" changes did you make in each of the three (eating right, moving more, sleeping better) categories?
   - How well were you able to stick to your plan? Why or why not?
   - Was the exercise useful to you? Why or why not?

As always, please consider sharing your responses to these questions with us at www
.happysmarts.com/book/exercises/schedule_partner_project.

INSTRUCTIONS FOR THE FIFTH HAPPINESS EXERCISE: FORGIVENESS*

Background
As the Buddha once said, holding on to anger is like grasping a hot coal with the intent
of throwing it at someone else; you are the one who gets burned. So, if it helps, think of
this exercise as a purely selfish one—one that will help you feel better and move on—
rather than as something that you are doing for the sake of the person who wronged
you.

Objective
The objective is to write—but not send—a letter of forgiveness to someone who has
hurt you.

It may help you to note that this is one of the more difficult exercises since most
of us can't bring ourselves to let go of the anger we feel at someone who's treated us
unfairly. And yet, as numerous findings show, holding on to anger and resentment
hurts us more than it hurts the others. So it will be worth your while to complete the
exercise even if you don't feel up to it.

Steps
The exercise involves the following three steps:

1. First, recall the incident that caused you harm or pain, and write about it. Don't
spend too much time wallowing in the negative emotions that the incident
evokes in you. In as matter-of-fact a manner as you can, write down (or type
out) details of the events that transpired, how it made you feel, and why. If the
event continues to hurt you, mention why and state what you wish the person
had done instead.

2. The second step is to write a letter in which you first reflect on what you wrote
in Step 1, and then elaborate on the factors that may have pressured the person
who wronged you to act in the way that he or she did. For example, perhaps the
person wronged you because he was facing tremendous financial constraints. Or
perhaps he was misinformed by someone else. Do your best to come up with any
and all factors that might have propelled the person to behave in the manner
that he or she did. Your objective is to come up with a set of explanations (on

---

* The instructions for this exercise are based on a similar exercise described by Sonja
Lyubomirsky described in her book, *The How of Happiness*.

behalf of the wrongdoer) to allow you to end your letter with: "I realize now that what you did was the best you could at that time, and I forgive you." Once you have written out your letter, read it carefully and make any necessary revisions.

Important note: Writing a letter of forgiveness can make you feel overwhelmed. If this happens, put aside this exercise for now and revisit it in a few days or weeks. Alternatively, try doing the exercise for an "easier" event—something about which you don't feel quite as strongly.

3. The third and final step involves achieving something known as "psychological closure"—a sort of mental marker that symbolizes that the event is closed. Achieving closure will make it easier for you to move on. Perhaps the best way to achieve the psychological closure is to seal your letter in an envelope and then either burn it or drop it in the trash. And as you are doing this, tell yourself, "With this act, I consider this incident closed." As tacky as this might seem, findings show that achieving psychological closure helps lower the tendency to dwell on past hurtful events.*

As with the other exercises, please consider sharing your experience of this exercise with us at www.happysmarts.com/book/exercises/forgiveness. We'd love to hear from you!

INSTRUCTIONS FOR THE SIXTH HAPPINESS EXERCISE: 3 GOOD THINGS (WITH A TWIST)†

Background
There's a very powerful happiness-enhancing exercise called "three good things" that Professor Martin Seligman of the University of Pennsylvania—considered by many as the "father of positive psychology"—is credited with inventing. That exercise involves making a note in your journal of three good things that happened to you each day for a period of time (say, fifteen days). Professor Seligman found that 94 percent of those who had kept a record of three good things for a mere fifteen days showed a significant improvement in happiness levels. The exercise even lifted some of them out of severe depression!

---

* X. Li, L. Wei, and D. Soman, "Sealing the Emotions Genie: The Effects of Physical Enclosure on Psychological Closure," *Psychological Science* 21(8) (2010): 1047–50.

† The instructions for this exercise have been adapted from an exercise called "three good things," developed by Martin Seligman of the University of Pennsylvania. The exercise is discussed in his book, *Authentic Happiness*.

Objective

Like "three good things," this exercise involves making a note in your journal of three good things that happened to you each day for some time (in this case, one week). However, there is a twist: I want you to make a note of those things that started out *badly*—but eventually turned good.

This can be a little tricky to understand, so let me give you some examples. Perhaps you were stuck in heavy traffic on the way to work (negative event). But because of this, maybe you got to hear a string of your favorite songs on the radio—songs you hadn't heard in a while (positive consequence). Or, during lunch, maybe you found that the meal that you ordered wasn't tasty, which forced you to have a late-afternoon snack (negative event). But that may have led to your bumping into an old friend whom you hadn't seen in a while (positive consequence). In both these examples, what seemed like a bad event at first led, later, to a positive outcome. The idea is to "connect the dots"—in hindsight—so as to recognize that almost every event that starts out negative paves the way for a positive consequence. Such recognition, in turn, will help mitigate the tendency to exhibit "post-occurrence judgmentalism" and thereby, help nurture the dispassionate pursuit of passion.

Note 1: It's important that you don't pick major negative events for this exercise. For example, don't pick "getting fired from work," or "kid falling violently ill." Although, as we saw from the "reminisce and reflect" exercise that even intensely negative events could in the long run lead to positive outcomes, it's naturally difficult to look past the negativity of intensely negative events. In addition, the positive outcomes from such negative events usually take some time to unfold. For these reasons, for the purpose of this exercise, focus only on mildly negative events for this exercise—like misplacing a dollar, failing to find your favorite brand of cereal in the grocery store, or having to fill up gas when you are already late for work.

Note 2: At first, you'll likely find it very difficult to think of anything positive to come out of negative events. This is because when we think of something negative, our mind immediately thinks of other negative things—something that I touch upon in chapter 7B. These negative thoughts will blind you from seeing the positive outcome(s) triggered by the negative event(s). But if you persevere, you will see that almost every negative event triggers at least one positive event. The way to persevere is to ignore the negative thoughts triggered by the negative event and focus instead on replaying in your mind's eye the consequences triggered by the negative event. In doing so, you are bound to identify at least one positive thing that came out of it. This positive consequence may not fully compensate for the negative event, but it will at least lower the intensity of the negativity associated with the event.

Steps

The exercise involves the following four steps:

1. Step 1 is to think of at least one and up to three mildly negative events that happened to you and describe what occurred in a sentence or two in your journal.
2. The second step involves identifying at least one and up to three positive consequences that occurred as a result of each negative event. If it helps, close your eyes and replay each negative event, one at a time, and trace the set of events that they triggered. This will make it easier to identify the positive consequences that unfolded as a result of the negative events. Once you have identified something positive triggered by a negative event, make a note of it. Then, move on to the next negative event and do the same. Once you have identified at least one positive event for each of the negative events that happened, go to the next step.
3. Step 3 involves connecting the dots—writing about the chain of events, starting from the original negative occurrence, that led to the eventual positive outcome(s). Do this for each of the original negative events for a whole week (seven days).
4. The fourth and final step involves reviewing your notes for the previous seven days and answering the following questions:
   - Overall, how easy or difficult was this exercise for you? Why?
   - Do you feel more confident now that most events are not "purely" positive or negative? Why (or why not)?
   - Typically, those who do this exercise for a week tend to spontaneously look for positive consequences that are triggered by seemingly negative events. Did you feel that this happened to you? (If yes, provide examples. If no, tell us why this may not have happened to you.)

That's it for the exercise. It's really simple in theory, but as you will probably experience, it's not that easy in practice—mostly because many of us are strongly wedded to judging outcomes as good or bad and can't adopt the "good thing, bad thing, who knows?" attitude easily. But with practice, as many of my students have discovered, you *will* make progress toward being a little less judgmental of outcome. That should, in turn, make it easier to practice dispassionate pursuit of passion. As with the other exercises, please share your experience with us at www.happysmarts.com/book/exercises/3_good _things_with_twist.

INSTRUCTIONS FOR THE SEVENTH HAPPINESS EXERCISE: PRESENCE PRACTICE*

Background
The presence practice is a type of mindfulness practice that was developed by Vijay Bhat specifically for business executives—the smart-and-successful people with very little time on their hands.

Objective
The presence practice nurtures a variety of interrelated qualities, including bare attention, self-awareness, self-compassion, and belonging.

Steps
The presence practice involves the following seven steps:

1. After sitting in a comfortable position (either on the ground or on a chair), with the spine erect, scan your body with the recognition that a **relaxed body** is the foundation of a state of presence. Begin with the top of your head, and scan all the way down to the tips of your toes . . . and then back up. Consciously let go of any tightness or stiffness you come across, paying particular attention to your neck and shoulders, the small of your back, and your knees—areas where many of us carry tension. As your body settles, your attention will automatically go to your breath.

2. The second step is to observe your breath. An **even breath** is the first signal of presence. Simply observe your breath as you inhale (your abdomen will rise) and exhale (your abdomen will fall). You don't need to regulate your breath in any way . . . just notice your normal, steady, rhythmic breath.

3. The third step is to observe your mind. A **clear, calm, quiet mind** is the second signal of presence. Bring your attention to the screen of your mind and notice what thoughts and scripts are running there. Our monkey minds usually flit from one thought to another, unbidden. Just like you would do on your computer screen, shut down all the open windows and applications of the mind, gently and firmly. When your mind becomes clear and quiet, it can focus fully and you can bring all its resources to bear on one thing at a time.

4. The fourth step is to bring your attention to your physical heart. An **open heart** is the third signal of presence. Feel the warmth in your chest area. Now become aware of your emotional heart: the place from which you relate, connect, and

---

* The instructions for this exercise are reproduced with the permission of Vijay Bhat of Roots and Wings (a management consulting company based in Mumbai, India).

engage with others. Try to open your emotional heart, first a crack, and then wider and wider so you can receive the true feelings, emotions, and even vulnerabilities of others and, equally, to reveal your true feelings, emotions, and vulnerabilities to others. Remember, you are in a safe space.

5. The fifth step is to notice subtle, fleeting, nuanced sensations around you. A **"sensitive sonar"** is the fourth signal of presence. Allow your anxious self-orientation to fall away and send out your antennae to pick up the subtlest of signals from the external environment. Notice all the sounds, textures, aromas, and energies swirling around you, which you otherwise may overlook. When you are fully aware of the context, you can respond appropriately.

6. The sixth step is to achieve something called **"energetic induction,"** which is the fifth signal of presence. When the first four qualities are in place, energetic induction happens effortlessly. Your sense of presence will radiate outward and make you feel comfortable about including yourself in others' lives and concerns and allowing them to be included in your life and concerns. Focus on cultivating this inclusive attitude, inviting/welcoming others into your life in the present moment.

7. The seventh and final step involves noticing how your internal state has changed (if it has), and then saying these affirmations out loud:

> *The reality of this moment . . . is that . . . I have nothing to defend*
> *The reality of this moment . . . is that . . . I have nothing to promote*
> *The reality of this moment . . . is that . . . I have nothing to fear*
> *The only reality of this moment . . . is that . . . I AM HERE NOW.*

As with the other exercises, we'd love to hear from you about your experience with this one. So, share it with us at www.happysmarts.com/book/exercises/presence_practice.

NOTES

├──────────┤

Introduction

2 **we . . . cope better . . . than we expect to:** see T. D. Wilson, et al., "Focalism: A Source of Durability Bias in Affective Forecasting," *Journal of Personality and Social Psychology* 78(5) (2000): 821; and D. T. Gilbert et al., "Immune Neglect: A Source of Durability Bias in Affective Forecasting," *Journal of Personality and Social Psychology* 75(3) (1998): 617. For misforecasting in consumer contexts, see V. M. Patrick, D. J. MacInnis, and C. W. Park, "Not as Happy as I Thought I'd Be? Affective Misforecasting and Product Evaluations," *Journal of Consumer Research* 33(4) (2007): 479–89. For a more reader-friendly version, see https://en.wikipedia.org/wiki/Affective_forecasting.

2 **we . . . give . . . negative events from . . . past a positive spin:** See A. Keinan and R. Kivetz, "Productivity Orientation and the Consumption of Collectable Experiences," *Journal of Consumer Research* 37(6) (2011): 935–50.

2 **It is precisely because:** For findings on how women are less willing to have another child during childbirth, but change their mind later, see J. J. Christensen-Szalanski, "Discount Functions and the Measurement of Patients' Values: Women's Decisions During Childbirth," *Medical Decision Making* 4(1) (1983): 47–58. For findings on "empathy gaps" in decisions regarding sexual acts (and how people are more willing to engage in risky sexual behavior in the "heat of the moment"), see D. Ariely, and G. Loewenstein, "The Heat of the Moment: The Effect of Sexual Arousal on Sexual Decision Making," *Journal of Behavioral Decision Making* 19(2) (2006): 87. For a review of the literature on "empathy gap," see L. Van Boven, et al., "Changing Places: A Dual Judgment Model of Empathy Gaps in Emotional Perspective Taking," *Advances in Experimental Social Psychology* 47 (2013): 117–71.

2 **as the graph . . . suggests:** Source of the graph: R. W. Robins, et al., "Global Self-esteem Across the Life Span," *Psychology and Aging* 17(3) (2002): 423. For a perspective on how and why happiness levels improve after the "midlife crisis," see L. L. Carstensen, et al., "Emotional Experience in Everyday Life Across the Adult Life Span," *Journal of*

Personality and Social Psychology 79(4) (2000): 644. For a more reader-friendly version, see www.economist.com/node/17722567.

2 **our most miserable days:** Happiness levels seem to improve after the "midlife crisis," however; see Carstensen, et al., "Emotional Experience in Everyday Life Across the Adult Life Span." For a more reader-friendly version, see www.economist.com/node/17722567.

4 **don't automatically translate into happiness:** See G. E. Vaillant, *Triumphs of Experience* (Cambridge, MA: Harvard University Press, 2012).

4 **the primary purpose of education:** The University of Texas's core purpose, "To Transform Lives for the Benefit of Society," is aligned with what I believe ought to be the primary purpose of education.

4 **life's most important questions:** Among the other "life's important questions" that interest me are: 1) Why is there anything (the Universe, life, etc.) at all, as opposed to nothing?, and 2) How did consciousness emerge from seemingly nonconscious matter? For an excellent discussion of each topic, see, respectively, J. Holt, *Why Does the World Exist?: An Existential Detective Story* (New York: W. W. Norton, 2012), and J. M. Schwartz, and S. Begley, *The Mind and the Brain* (New York: Springer Science and Business Media, 2009).

5 **100,000 students on January 1, 2016:** Projection based on expected growth in number of enrolled learners in the course.

5 **the world's most popular MOOC:** Coursera is an initiative of Stanford University to democratize education. You can learn more about it by going to: https://en.wikipedia.org/wiki/Coursera.

5 **top-ten list of Coursera courses:** In terms of number of "active learners" (which refers to the number of students who have watched at least one lecture).

5 **class-central.com:** See https://www.class-central.com/provider/coursera?sort=rating-up. As of October 27, 2015, the course ranked #4 of all Coursera courses offered up until that point.

5 **I regularly get e-mails from students:** You can read many of the reviews for the course by going to www.class-central.com/mooc/2860/coursera-a-life-of-happiness-and-fulfillment#course-all-reviews.

5 **the field of positive psychology:** For more on the origins and objectives of positive psychology, see M. E. Seligman, T. A. Steen, N. Park, and C. Peterson, "Positive Psychology Progress: Empirical Validation of Interventions," *American Psychologist* 60(5) (2005): 410–21, and S. L. Gable and J. Haidt, "What (and Why) Is Positive Psychology?" *Review of General Psychology* 9(2) (2005): 103–10. For a more user-friendly version, see https://en.wikipedia.org/wiki/Positive_psychology.

6 **the tendency to find closure or meaning:** Work by Pennebaker and others suggests that the attempt to find meaning and closure for events, even negative ones, helps improve happiness levels. See J. W. Pennebaker, "Putting Stress into Words: Health, Linguistic, and Therapeutic Implications," *Behaviour Research and Therapy* 31(6) (1993): 539–48. For related research, see J. W. Pennebaker, "Writing About Emotional Experiences as a Therapeutic Process," *Psychological Science* 8(3) (1997): 162–66, and J. W. Pennebaker, T. J. Mayne, and M. E. Francis, "Linguistic Predictors of Adaptive Bereavement," *Journal of Personality and Social Psychology* 72(4) (1997): 863. For a nice summary of the research on how writing about emotional experiences can be therapeutic, see J. W. Pennebaker, *Opening Up: The Healing Power of Emotional Expression* (New York: Guilford, 1997).

6 **they are rooted in deep-seated goals, desires, and values:** The idea that motivations, cognitions, and emotions are intertwined is well accepted in psychology. As an example of the interlinkages among these three aspects, see R. S. Lazarus, "Cognition

and Motivation in Emotion," *American Psychologist* 46(4) (1991): 352. See also, for a compatible view, N. H. Frijda, P. Kuipers, and E. Ter Schure, "Relations Among Emotion, Appraisal, and Emotional Action Readiness," *Journal of Personality and Social Psychology* 57(2) (1989): 212.

6 **akin to popping peppermints to smother bad breath:** I thank my friend Neelesh Marik for suggesting this analogy.

6 **if one aspires . . . to enhance:** Work from a variety of fields, including cognitive behavioral therapy (CBT), group dynamics, and PTSD, reveals that it is better to confront problems head-on than to "brush them under the carpet." For example, for patients with PTSD, prolonged exposure therapy, which involves telling, revisiting the trauma-causing event multiple times—rather than avoiding it—has been found to eventually alleviate the condition. For example, one study showed that among rape victims PTSD was alleviated to a greater extent for those who underwent prolonged exposure therapy than for those who were asked to pay "minimal attention" to the traumatic incident. See, for a review of the literature, E. Foa, E. Hembree, and B. O. Rothbaum, *Prolonged Exposure Therapy for PTSD: Emotional Processing of Traumatic Experiences Therapist Guide* (New York: Oxford University Press, 2007).

7 **I naturally wanted others to be just as miserable:** Work by Abraham Tesser and his colleagues suggests that our self-view depends on how we perceive ourselves to stack up to others, particularly those whom we consider closest to us (our colleagues, siblings, etc.); see A. Tesser and J. Campbell, "Self-evaluation Maintenance and the Perception of Friends and Strangers," *Journal of Personality* 50(3) (1982): 261–79, and J. D. Campbell and A. Tesser, "Self-evaluation Maintenance Processes in Relationships," in *Understanding Personal Relationships: An Interdisciplinary Approach*, eds. S. Duck and D. Perlman (Thousand Oaks, CA: Sage Publications): 107–35. This tendency is prevalent even among children: A. Tesser, J. Campbell, and M. Smith, "Friendship Choice and Performance: Self-evaluation Maintenance in Children," *Journal of Personality and Social Psychology* 46(3) (1984): 561. For a review of the literature, see A. Tesser, "Toward a Self-evaluation Maintenance Model of Social Behavior," *Advances in Experimental Social Psychology* 21 (1988): 181–228.

7 **the more educated . . . the less happy:** See Michalos (2008), who probably conducted the most comprehensive study on the topic. He refers to his finding that higher levels of education lower satisfaction levels as the "connoisseur effect" (363); see also Frey and Stutzer (2002), who suggest that education has only an indirect effect on happiness—through increasing income. Sources: B. S. Frey and A. Stutzer, "What Can Economists Learn from Happiness Research?," *Journal of Economic Literature* (2002): 402–35; A. C. Michalos, "Education, Happiness and Wellbeing," *Social Indicators Research* 87(3) (2008): 347–66.

7 **intelligence is virtually unrelated to happiness:** See R. G. Watten, J. L. Syversen, and T. Myhrer, "Quality of Life, Intelligence, and Mood," *Social Indicators Research* 36 (1995): 287–99. The specific quote (on p. 296) is "Intelligence is virtually unrelated to QOL [Quality of Life]. Thus, we find IQ to be a variable of minor interest for future QOL studies."

8 **one might expect it to be:** The relationship between money and happiness is quite complicated and has emerged as a relatively controversial topic. What almost all researchers agree with, however, is that money isn't as powerful a source of happiness as most people naively believe. For perhaps the most comprehensive treatment of the topic, see ch. 6, "Can Money Buy Happiness?," of E. Diener and R. Biswas-Diener, *Happiness: Unlocking the Mysteries of Psychological Health* (Malden, MA: Blackwell Publishing, 2008).

8 **Fame too has little effect:** C. P. Niemiec, R. M. Ryan, and E. L. Deci, "The Path Taken:

Consequences of Attaining Intrinsic and Extrinsic Aspirations in Post-College Life," *Journal of Research in Personality* 43(3) (2009): 291–306. For a more reader-friendly summary of this paper, see abcnews.go.com/Health/Healthday/story?id=7658253. One reason that fame lowers happiness is that it appears to induce self-consciousness; see M. Schaller, "The Psychological Consequences of Fame: Three Tests of the Self-consciousness Hypothesis," *Journal of Personality* 65 (1997): 291–310.

8 **My colleagues Hyunkyu Jang:** R. Raghunathan, H. Jang, and R. Soster, "Negativity Dominance: The Paradoxical Co-existence of Positive Self-views and Negative 'Mental Chatter,'" working paper, University of Texas at Austin.

8 **Thoughts related to inferiority:** The idea that one's self-assessment (e.g., how positive one feels about oneself) is dependent on how one stacks up to others has a long tradition of research in psychology, starting with Festinger's (1954) theory of social comparisons. More recent research suggests that such social comparisons, which are often spurred by the desire to feel good about oneself and therefore rooted in the desire to be superior to others, typically deflate, rather than enhance happiness levels; e.g., see S. Lyubomirsky and L. Ross, "Hedonic Consequences of Social Comparison: A Contrast of Happy and Unhappy People," *Journal of Personality and Social Psychology* 73(6) (1997): 1141. For a perspective on how social comparisons in consumption contexts affect self-worth, see also M. L. Richins, "Social Comparison, Advertising, and Consumer Discontent," *American Behavioral Scientist* 38(4) (1995): 593–607. For a more general review of the literature on "keeping up with the Joneses" and how it influences judgments and decisions, see R. H. Frank, *Luxury Fever: Why Money Fails to Satisfy in an Era of Excess* (New York: The Free Press, 1999). In chapter 2A of this book, I discuss the various reasons why "chasing superiority" lowers happiness levels.

8 **Thoughts about lack of love and connectivity:** The idea that thoughts related to lack of love and connectivity are rooted in insecurities about relationships is perhaps the most important theme of an area of research called "attachment theory." I review much of this literature in chapter 3A.

8 **Thoughts about lack of control:** I discuss the relationship between desire for control and, among other things, the "maximizer mind-set" in chapter 4A.

9 **less happy version of my former self:** You can read a full-blown account of my negativity in an article titled "When the Bottom Fell Out," available on the book's website: www.happysmarts.com/about_Raj.

9 **Many of us believe:** Among my students, a vast majority (typically more than 75 percent of the class) believe that "the desire to be better than others" is an important determinant of success.

9 **the ability to be an "island":** Many of us seem to believe that kind and compassionate people aren't effective leaders and vice versa; see S. T. Fiske, A. J. Cuddy, and P. Glick, "Universal Dimensions of Social Cognition: Warmth and Competence," *Trends in Cognitive Sciences* 11(2) (2007): 77–83, and J. Aaker, K. D. Vohs, and C. Mogilner, "Nonprofits Are Seen as Warm and For-profits as Competent: Firm Stereotypes Matter," *Journal of Consumer Research*, 37(2) (2010): 224–37. As part of this belief system, many of us also seem to subscribe to the notion that being a good leader calls for a certain level of "cold-heartedness" and perhaps even the propensity to act in unethical ways. My colleagues Michael Luchs, Rebecca Naylor (now Reczek), and Julie Irwin examined the perceived negative correlation between ethicality and efficacy in the context of evaluating products; see M. G. Luchs et al., "The Sustainability Liability: Potential Negative Effects of Ethicality on Product Preference," *Journal of Marketing* 74(5) (2010): 18–31.

9 **although the need for superiority:** I discuss how the need for superiority gets in the way of success in chapters 2A and 2B.

9 **the world's best leaders:** I discuss how leaders who are "loving and giving" are more likely to succeed in chapter 3B.

9 **The need for control:** The relationship between need for control and success is discussed in chapters 4A and 4B.

11 **"happiness strategy fit":** S. Lyubomirsky, *The How of Happiness: A Scientific Approach to Getting the Life You Want* (New York: Penguin, 2008), 70–73.

12 **"Satisfaction with Life Scale":** E. D. Diener et al., "The Satisfaction with Life Scale," *Journal of Personality Assessment* 49(1) (1985): 71–75.

12 **happiness this scale measures:** E. Diener, R. Inglehart, and L. Tay, "Theory and Validity of Life Satisfaction Scales," *Social Indicators Research* 112(3) (2013): 497–527. An online version of this article can be accessed at: http://stat.psych.uiuc.edu/~ediener/Documents/Diener-Inglehart-Tay_Validity%20of%20ls%20measures.pdf; see also E. Diener (ed.), *Assessing Well-being: The Collected Works of Ed Diener* (vol. 39) (New York: Springer Science and Business Media, 2009). See also W. Pavot and E. Diener, "Review of the Satisfaction with Life Scale," *Psychological Assessment* 5(2) (1993): 164–72, and E. Sandvik, E. Diener, and L. Seidlitz, "Subjective Well-being: The Convergence and Stability of Self-report and Non-self-report Measures," *Journal of Personality* 61(3) (1993): 317–42. For a general review of various scales that measure subjective well-being (or happiness), see Diener (ed.), *Assessing Subjective Well-being: The Collected Works of Ed Diener.*

15 **Interpreting your satisfaction with life score:** Based on interview with Ed Diener.

Chapter 1A: The First Deadly Happiness "Sin": Devaluing Happiness

18 **Most psychologists:** Several scholars, including Mihaly Csikszentmihalyi, Dan Gilbert, Jonathan Haidt, and Sonja Lyubomirsky, have all stated, in one way or another, that happiness is our most important goal. See M. Csikszentmihalyi, "If We Are So Rich, Why Aren't We Happy?," *American Psychologist* 54(10) (1999): 821; and M. Csikszentmihalyi, *Flow: The Psychology of Optimal Experience* (New York: Harper & Row, 1990); D. Gilbert, *Stumbling on Happiness* (Toronto: Vintage Canada, 2009); J. Haidt, *The Happiness Hypothesis: Finding Modern Truth in Ancient Wisdom* (New York: Basic Books, 2006); Lyubomirsky, *The How of Happiness: A Scientific Approach to Getting the Life You Want* (New York: Penguin, 2008). See also E. Diener, "Subjective Well-being: The Science of Happiness and a Proposal for a National Index," *American Psychological Association* 55(1) (2000): 34; and E. Diener, and S. Oishi, "The Desirability of Happiness Across Cultures," unpublished manuscript, University of Illinois, Urbana-Champaign, 2006.

18 **even many economists:** See R. Layard, *Happiness: Lessons from a New Science* (London: Allen Lane, 2005). See also J. E. Stiglitz, A. Sen, and J. P. Fitoussi, Report by the Commission on the Measurement of Economic Performance and Social Progress (Paris: Commission on the Measurement of Economic Performance and Social Progress, 2010).

18 **the Declaration of Independence:** The relevant passage is: "All men are created equal, that they are endowed by their Creator with certain unalienable Rights, that among these are Life, Liberty and the pursuit of Happiness."

19 **Along with my two trusty colleagues:** R. Raghunathan, S. Chugani, and A. Mukherjee, "The Fundamental Happiness Paradox," working paper, University of Texas at Austin, 2014.

19 **happiness *is* a very important goal:** Several other studies have confirmed that happiness is people's number-one goal, not just in the United States, but worldwide. See Diener, "Subjective Well-being." See also Diener and Oishi, "The Desirability of Happiness Across Cultures." They found, in a survey of more than ten thousand respondents

from forty-eight nations, that the average importance rating of happiness was the highest of the twelve possible attributes, with a mean of 8.03 on a 1–9 scale (compared with 7.54 for "success," 7.39 for "intelligence/knowledge," and 6.84 for "material wealth").

21 **The paradox refers to the idea:** See Raghunathan, Chugani, and Mukherjee, "The Fundamental Happiness Paradox."

25 **the *projective technique*:** The projective technique has a long and rich history of use in the social sciences, including consumer research; see D. Rapaport, "Principles Underlying Projective Techniques," *Journal of Personality* 10(3) (1942): 213–19. For examples of use of the projective technique in consumer research, see S. Donoghue, "Projective Techniques in Consumer Research," *Journal of Family Ecology and Consumer Sciences/Tydskrif vir Gesinsekologie en Verbruikerswetenskappe* 28(1) (2000); M. G. Luchs et al., "The Sustainability Liability: Potential Negative Effects of Ethicality on Product Preference," *Journal of Marketing* 74(5) (2010): 18–31; M. Haire, "Projective Techniques in Marketing Research," *Journal of Marketing* (1950): 649–56, and M. Hussey and N. Duncombe, "Projecting the Right Image: Using Projective Techniques to Measure Brand Image," *Qualitative Market Research* 2(1) (1999): 22–30.

26 **in our next study:** R. Raghunathan, S. Chugani, and A. Mukherjee (2015, study 2), "The Fundamental Happiness Paradox."

27 **Our final study:** R. Raghunathan, S. Chugani, and A. Mukherjee (2015, study 3) "The Fundamental Happiness Paradox."

Chapter 1B: The First Habit of the Highly Happy: Prioritizing–but Not Pursuing–Happiness

31 **Because the original pair was:** Technically, I felt like I was losing $25, because it was "half off" the second pair.

32 **otherwise difficult to understand:** R. Reber, N. Schwarz, and P. Winkielman, "Processing Fluency and Aesthetic Pleasure: Is Beauty in the Perceiver's Processing Experience?," *Personality and Social Psychology Review* 8(4) (2004): 364–82; see also N. Novemsky et al., "Preference Fluency in Choice," *Journal of Marketing Research* 44(3) (2007): 347–56. For related research, see C. K. Hsee, "The Evaluability Hypothesis: An Explanation for Preference Reversals Between Joint and Separate Evaluations of Alternatives," *Organizational Behavior and Human Decision Processes* 67(3) (1996): 247–57.

32 **would otherwise be:** This is similar to how harboring negative beliefs about healthy food (e.g., believing that healthy food is less tasty) makes such food less appealing; see R. Raghunathan, R. W. Naylor, and W. D. Hoyer, "The Unhealthy = Tasty Intuition and Its Effects on Taste Inferences, Enjoyment, and Choice of Food Products," *Journal of Marketing* 70(4) (2006): 170–84.

32 **Here's a sampling:** For a review of the various ways in which positivity has been found to be "functional," that is, have a positive effect on consequences that matter (e.g., health, intimacy, etc.), see S. Lyubomirsky, L. King, and E. Diener, "The Benefits of Frequent Positive Affect: Does Happiness Lead to Success?," *Psychological Bulletin* 131(6) (2005): 803–55, and J. DeNeve et al., "The Objective Benefits of Subjective Well-being," in J. Helliwell, R. Layard, and J. Sachs, eds., *World Happiness Report 2013* (New York: UN Sustainable Development Solutions Network, 2013). For a nontechnical review of the literature, see S. Achor, *The Happiness Advantage: The Seven Principles of Positive Psychology That Fuel Success and Performance at Work* (New York: Random House, 2011). If you are interested in the impact of a "happy" business culture on firm productivity and performance, see T. Hsieh, *Delivering Happiness: A Path to Profits, Passion, and Purpose* (New York: Grand Central Publishing, 2010).

33 **Happy employees . . . perform objectively better:** B. M. Staw and S. G. Barsade,

"Affect and Managerial Performance: A Test of the Sadder-but-Wiser vs. Happier-and-Smarter Hypotheses," *Administrative Science Quarterly* (1993): 304–31. For findings on how happy employees are more likely to elicit more favorable evaluations from supervisors and others, see B. M. Staw, R. I. Sutton, and L. H. Pelled, "Employee Positive Emotion and Favorable Outcomes at the Workplace," *Organization Science* 5(1) (1994): 51–71.

33 **Happy employees earn more:** See E. Diener and R. Biswas-Diener, "Will Money Increase Subjective Well-being?," *Social Indicators Research* 57(2) (2002): 119–69; see also M. Pinquart and S. Sörensen, "Influences of Socioeconomic Status, Social Network, and Competence on Subjective Well-being in Later Life: A Meta-analysis," *Psychology and Aging* 15(2) (2000): 187.

33 **Happier (optimistic) CEOs:** J. B. Foster et al., "Setting the Tone for Organizational Success: The Impact of CEO Affect on Organizational Climate and Firm-Level Outcomes," *17th Annual Meeting of the Society for Industrial and Organizational Psychology*, Toronto, Ontario, Canada, 2004.

33 **Happier CEOs receive higher performance ratings:** M. A. Pritzker, "The Relationship Among CEO Dispositional Attributes, Transformational Leadership Behaviors and Performance Effectiveness" (doctoral dissertation, ProQuest Information & Learning, 2002).

33 **Happier batsmen in cricket:** P. Totterdell, "Catching Moods and Hitting Runs: Mood Linkage and Subjective Performance in Professional Sport Teams," *Journal of Applied Psychology* 85(6) (2000): 848.

33 **Happy people volunteer more:** R. F. Krueger, B. M. Hicks, and M. McGue, "Altruism and Antisocial Behavior: Independent Tendencies, Unique Personality Correlates, Distinct Etiologies," *Psychological Science* 12(5) (2001): 397–402; see also P. A. Thoits and L. N. Hewitt, "Volunteer Work and Well-being," *Journal of Health and Social Behavior* (2001): 115–31.

33 **Happy people . . . judge others favorably:** R. A. Baron, "Interviewer's Moods and Reactions to Job Applicants: The Influence of Affective States on Applied Social Judgments," *Journal of Applied Social Psychology* 17 (1987): 911–26, and R. A. Baron, "Interviewers' Moods and Evaluations of Job Applicants: The Role of Applicant Qualifications," *Journal of Applied Social Psychology* 23 (1993): 253–71; see also W. B. Griffitt, "Environmental Effects of Interpersonal Affective Behavior: Ambient Effective Temperature and Attraction," *Journal of Personality and Social Psychology* 15 (1970): 240–44.

33 **share their good fortune:** Aderman, "Elation, Depression, and Helping Behavior," *Journal of Personality and Social Psychology* 24 (1972): 91–101.

33 **contribute more money to charity:** M. R. Cunningham, J. Steinberg, and R. Grev, "Wanting to and Having to Help: Separate Motivations for Positive Mood and Guilt-Induced Helping," *Journal of Personality and Social Psychology* 38 (1980): 181–92; and A. M. Isen, "Success, Failure, Attention and Reaction to Others: The Warm Glow of Success," *Journal of Personality and Social Psychology* 15 (1970): 294–301.

33 **are also more likely to donate blood:** M. N. O'Malley and L. Andrews, "The Effect of Mood and Incentives on Helping: Are There Some Things Money Can't Buy?," *Motivation and Emotion* 7 (1983): 179–89.

33 **are more likely to volunteer for an extra experiment:** Aderman, "Elation, Depression, and Helping Behavior"; R. A. Baron and M. I. Bronfen, "A Whiff of Reality: Empirical Evidence Concerning the Effects of Pleasant Fragrances on Work-Related Behavior," *Journal of Applied Social Psychology* 24 (1994): 1179–1203; R. A. Baron, M. S. Rea, and S. G. Daniels, "Effects of Indoor Lighting (Illuminance and Spectral Distribution) on the Performance of Cognitive Tasks and Interpersonal Behaviors: The Potential Mediating

Role of Positive Affect," *Motivation and Emotion* 16 (1992): 1–33; L. Berkowitz, "Mood, Self-awareness, and Willingness to Help," *Journal of Personality and Social Psychology* 52 (1987): 721–29; and A. M. Isen and P. F. Levin, "Effect of Feeling Good on Helping: Cookies and Kindness," *Journal of Personality and Social Psychology* 21 (1972): 384–88.

33 **positive feelings tend not to last long:** Barbara Fredrickson discusses this point in several places, including in her Coursera course "Positive Psychology," as well as in her book *Positivity* (New York: Three Rivers Press, 2009).

35 **Prioritizing—but Not Pursuing—Happiness:** This exercise is adapted from a similar exercise (involving building a "positivity portfolio") that Professor Barbara Fredrickson describes in *Positivity*.

36 **To find out:** K. Goldsmith, D. Gal, R. Raghunathan, and L. Cheatham, "Happiness in the Workplace: Employees Who Focus on Maximizing Happiness Become Happier," working paper, Northwestern University. The actual study was a little more complex than this and included a third condition, which I have left out here for the sake of simplicity.

36 **as several studies have found:** See I. B. Mauss et al., "Can Seeking Happiness Make People Unhappy? Paradoxical Effects of Valuing Happiness," *Emotion* 11(4) (2011): 807; and J. W. Schooler, D. Ariely, and G. Loewenstein, "The Pursuit and Assessment of Happiness Can Be Self-defeating," *The Psychology of Economic Decisions* 1 (2003): 41–70.

37 **as Daniel Kahneman . . . has noted:** See D. Kahneman and A. Tversky, "Experienced Utility and Objective Happiness: A Moment-Based Approach," *The Psychology of Economic Decisions* 1 (2003): 187–208. See also D. Kahneman and J. Riis, "Living, and Thinking About It: Two Perspectives on Life," *The Science of Well-being* (2005): 285–304. See Kahneman's TED talk on the same topic (which he calls the "riddle of experience vs. memory") at www.ted.com/talks/daniel_kahneman_the_rid dle_of_experience_vs_memory. For related work, see J. F. Helliwell and S. Wang, "Weekends and Subjective Well-being," *Social Indicators Research* 116(2) (2014): 389–407, who show that although life satisfaction ratings remain stable across weekdays and weekends, there is significantly greater happiness, laughter, and enjoyment on weekends.

37 **people differ in what makes them happy:** This reason was mentioned to me by Ed Diener—known as "Dr. Happiness"—during an interview I did with him for my Coursera course, "A Life of Happiness and Fulfillment." The Coursera course is free and can be accessed at www.coursera.org/course/happiness.

38 **In one survey;** Results of the survey can be obtained by writing to me at raj.raghuna than@mccombs.utexas.edu.

38 **how these emotions may be defined:** R. Raghunathan, S. Chugani, and K. Bector, "Happiness vs. Happiness: Happiness Defined Through Content Analysis of Retrospectively Recounted Incidents," working paper, University of Texas at Austin, 2014.

38 **Hubristic pride is the feeling that:** For a discussion of the differences between "authentic" and "hubristic" pride, see J. L. Tracy and R. W. Robins, "The Psychological Structure of Pride: A Tale of Two Facets," *Journal of Personality and Social Psychology* 92(3) (2007): 506–25; and J. L. Tracy et al., "Authentic and Hubristic Pride: The Affective Core of Self-esteem and Narcissism," *Self and Identity* 8(2–3) (2009): 196–213; for further discussion on how these two types of pride may not be as different from each other as originally conceptualized, see C. Holbrook, J. Piazza, and D. M. Fessler, "Conceptual and Empirical Challenges to the 'Authentic' Versus 'Hubristic' Model of Pride," *Emotion* 14(1) (2014): 17–32. For a more reader-friendly version of Tracy and Robins's perspective on pride, see www.sciencedaily.com/releases/2007/06/070615214643.htm,

and H. Wray, "Two Faces of Pride," accessed at www.psychologicalscience.org/only human/2007/06/two-face-of-pride.cfm.

38 **Barbara Fredrickson . . . and her colleagues:** In *Positivity*, Fredrickson mentions at least seven other positive feelings that could be associated with the term "happiness."

40 **Although both harmony and abundance:** Both harmony and abundance (in the way I have defined them here) share common features with a state of positivity that Dambrun and his colleagues call "authentic-durable" happiness; see M. Dambrun et al., "Measuring Happiness: From Fluctuating Happiness to Authentic–Durable Happiness," *Frontiers in Psychology* 3 (16) (2012): 1–11.

40 **recent research by Michaël Dambrun:** See ibid. Dambrun et al. do not use the terms "harmony" or "abundance," but the characteristics they associate with what they call "authentic-durable happiness" share significant overlap with harmony and abundance as I have defined them. The paper can be accessed at www.ncbi.nlm.nih.gov/pubmed/22347202.

40 *deal with whatever comes:* See www.ncbi.nlm.nih.gov/pubmed/22347202.

Chapter 2A: The Second Deadly Happiness "Sin": Chasing Superiority

44 **gets my goat?:** Turns out I am not alone in finding repeating something that I have already done aversive. See D. Ariely, E. Kamenica, and D. Prelec, "Man's Search for Meaning: The Case of Legos," *Journal of Economic Behavior & Organization* 67(3) (2008): 671–77.

44 **a well-known song:** The song in question was the psychedelic masterpiece "Row, Row, Row Your Boat."

45 **the most important kid in class:** The way my son and the other children responded to the teacher is consistent with what's known as the Pygmalion effect. The Pygmalion effect—sometimes referred to as the Rosenthal effect—refers to the phenomenon whereby the greater the expectation placed upon one, the better one performs. The effect is named after the Greek myth of Pygmalion, a sculptor who fell in love with a statue he had carved. See T. R. Mitchell and D. Daniels, "Motivation," in *Handbook of Psychology: Industrial and Organizational Psychology*, vol. 12, edited by W. C. Borman et al. (Hoboken, NJ: John Wiley & Sons, 2003), 225–54. For findings on the Pygmalion effect in the context of teacher-student relationships, see R. Rosenthal and L. Jacobson, "Pygmalion in the Classroom," *The Urban Review* 3(1) (1968): 16–20; and J. E. Brophy and T. L. Good, *Teacher-Student Relationships: Causes and Consequences* (New York: Holt, Rinehart & Winston, 1974).

45 **self-esteem is at its lowest among high school kids:** See R. W. Robins et al., "Global Self-esteem Across the Life Span," *Psychology and Aging* 17(3) (2002): 423, who find that self-esteem is lowest during teenage years.

45 **And is it any surprise, too, that middle age:** Ibid.

46 **"Superior" people . . . more likely to survive:** The idea that "superior" people—people higher in status, wealth, etc.—have a longer life span is well accepted among evolutionary biologists. Evidence consistent with this theory has been found across several studies, including the famous "Whitehall" studies; see M. Marmot and R. Wilkinson (eds.), *Social Determinants of Health* (Oxford, UK: Oxford University Press, 2005); and M. G. Marmot et al., "Health Inequalities Among British Civil Servants: The Whitehall II Study," *The Lancet* 337(8754) (1991): 1387–93. See M. G. Marmot, *The Status Syndrome: How Social Standing Affects Our Health and Longevity* (New York: Times Books, 2004), for a review of how status affects our health.

46 **valedictorians get better scholarships:** The allocation of resources to talented people has arguably taken a more extreme turn in the past few decades, characterized by a development that the economist Robert Frank, author of *Luxury Fever*, calls "Winner

Take All." R. Frank, *Luxury Fever: Why Money Fails to Satisfy in an Era of Excess* (New York: Simon & Schuster, 2001).

46 **we internalize the need for superiority:** The idea that social comparisons (which often take place with the intention of boosting one's self-esteem) happen relatively automatically was proposed quite early by Festinger and has since been backed by several other researchers. See M. D. Alicke and O. Govorun, "The Better-than-Average Effect," in *The Self in Social Judgment* 1 (New York: Psychology Press, 2005), 85–106; L. Festinger, "A Theory of Social Comparison Processes," *Human Relations* 7(2) (1954): 117–40. See J. V. Wood, "Theory and Research Concerning Social Comparisons of Personal Attributes," *Psychological Bulletin* 106(2) (1989): 231, for a review.

46 **to measure up to our *own* standards:** As early as 1902, Cooley observed that our self-worth stems from what he called the "looking glass self"—our views of how we appear in the eyes of others. See C. H. Cooley, *Human Nature and the Social Order* (New York: Scribner, 1902).

47 **that of *mastery*:** The two other important goals, according to self-determination theory, are relatedness (or belonging—a desire for connection with others) and autonomy—the perception that one has the freedom to act and think in the ways one wants. See R. M. Ryan and E. L. Deci, "Self-determination Theory and the Facilitation of Intrinsic Motivation, Social Development, and Well-being," *American Psychologist* 55(1) (2000): 68.

47 **we must be regressing or stagnating:** Festinger, "A Theory of Social Comparison Processes."

47 **feel the pressure to be more accommodating:** See S. T. Fiske, "Controlling Other People: The Impact of Power on Stereotyping," *American Psychologist* 48(6) (1993): 621, who argues that the lower one's status, the greater the pressure to be accommodating.

47 **selectively upload . . . most flattering images:** Chou and Edge (2012) showed that those who spend more time on Facebook are more likely to believe that other people are leading better lives. H. T. G. Chou and N. Edge, "'They Are Happier and Having Better Lives than I Am': The Impact of Using Facebook on Perceptions of Others' Lives," *Cyberpsychology, Behavior, and Social Networking* 15(2) (2012): 117–21.

47 **Facebook triggers more negative feelings:** C. Huang, "Internet Use and Psychological Well-being: A Meta-analysis," *Cyberpsychology, Behavior, and Social Networking* 13(3) (2010): 241–49. For a more reader-friendly review of the literature on the impact of exposure to social media on well-being, see www.newyorker.com/tech/elements/how-facebook-makes-us-unhappy. That said, however, social media may also have a positive impact on people's moods. Findings from one of the largest-ever studies of Facebook—involving over a billion updates on the website—found that positive emotions spread faster than do negative ones. See L. Coviello et al., "Detecting Emotional Contagion in Massive Social Networks," *PLOS ONE* 9(3) (2014): e90315. For a more reader-friendly version of the article, see http://www.spring.org.uk/2014/03/happiness-is-contagious-and-powerful-on-social-media.php.

48 **propensity . . . to wear their university's jersey:** R. B. Cialdini et al., "Basking in Reflected Glory: Three (Football) Field Studies," *Journal of Personality and Social Psychology*, 34(3) (1976): 366. For more related findings, see R. B. Cialdini and K. D. Richardson, "Two Indirect Tactics of Image Management: Basking and Blasting," *Journal of Personality and Social Psychology* 39(3) (1980): 406–15.

48 **Consider results from one study:** A. Tesser, M. Millar, and J. Moore, "Some Affective Consequences of Social Comparison and Reflection Processes: The Pain and Pleasure of Being Close," *Journal of Personality and Social Psychology* 54(1) (1988): 49. I am referring here to Study 3 in the paper.

48 **Happy people are generally more successful:** This is a theme I discussed at some

length in chapter 1B; for perhaps the most comprehensive reviews of the impact of happiness on success (defined in multiple ways), see S. Lyubomirsky, L. King, and E. Diener, "The Benefits of Frequent Positive Affect: Does Happiness Lead to Success?," *Psychological Bulletin* 131(6) (2005): 803, and DeNeve et al., "The Objective Benefits of Subjective Well-being," in J. Helliwell, R. Layard, and J. Sachs, eds., *World Happiness Report 2013* (New York: UN Sustainable Development Solutions Network, 2013).

48 **The famous "Whitehall" studies:** For an excellent review of the findings from the Whitehall studies, see Marmot, *The Status Syndrome.* The link between status, or more precisely, self-esteem, and happiness has been explored by a number of other studies as well and, in general, there is a positive relationship between the two. For a review, see T. Pyszczynski et al., "Why Do People Need Self-esteem? A Theoretical and Empirical Review," *Psychological Bulletin* 130(3) (2004): 435.

49 **known as the Whitehall studies:** They were named after the government building in which these employees worked.

49 **higher in status enjoy better self-esteem:** See K. O'Donnell, et al., "Self-esteem Levels and Cardiovascular and Inflammatory Responses to Acute Stress," *Brain, Behavior, and Immunity* 22(8) (2008): 1241–47, who find that those low in self-esteem exhibited greater heart rate variability and higher heart rates in general (both established coronary heart disease risk factors) while performing stressful tasks. So to the extent that those lower in status are also lower in self-esteem, we can expect them to suffer worse heart health, leading to lower levels of happiness.

49 **greater autonomy . . . makes them happier:** H. Kuper and M. Marmot, "Job Strain, Job Demands, Decision Latitude, and Risk of Coronary Heart Disease Within the Whitehall II Study," *Journal of Epidemiology and Community Health* 57(2) (2003): 147–53.

51 **the "better-than-average" effect:** Alicke and Govorun, "The Better-than-Average Effect."

51 **must therefore be deluding themselves:** Although "better-than-average" might, at first blush, seem to contradict "negativity dominance"—the tendency to engage in negative "mental chatter"—it doesn't. Findings from studies that my coauthors (Sean Jang and Robin Soster) and I have conducted suggest that people think they are better than average in terms of positive traits (like kindness) while, at the same time, harboring negative thoughts and feelings (such as anxiety and stress) about the ability to deal and cope with everyday problems and challenges.

52 **proxy measures for . . . wealth, power, and fame:** The idea that consumption behavior could be used to signal status has been around for a while and was perhaps first systematically studied by Thorstein Veblen. More recently, Robert Frank, the economist from Cornell, and others (e.g., Berger and Ward) have also explored the phenomenon. Sources: J. Berger and M. Ward, "Subtle Signals of Inconspicuous Consumption," *Journal of Consumer Research* 37(4) (2010): 555–69; Frank, *Luxury Fever*; T. Veblen, *The Theory of the Leisure Class* (Oxford, UK: Oxford University Press, 2007).

52 **materialistic focus . . . is one of the biggest happiness killers:** There are numerous studies showing the negative effect that materialism has on happiness, including T. Kasser et al., "Changes in Materialism, Changes in Psychological Well-being: Evidence from Three Longitudinal Studies and an Intervention Experiment," *Motivation and Emotion* 38(1) (2014): 1–22; M. A. Bauer et al., "Cuing Consumerism Situational Materialism Undermines Personal and Social Well-Being," *Psychological Science* 23(5) (2012): 517–23; and R. Pieters, "Bidirectional Dynamics of Materialism and Loneliness: Not Just a Vicious Cycle," *Journal of Consumer Research* 40(4) (2013): 615–31.

53 **why earning more doesn't enhance happiness levels:** See *Happy Money*—an excellent book that summarizes other important reasons why more money doesn't mean

more happiness. E. Dunn and M. Norton, *Happy Money: The Science of Smarter Spending* (New York: Simon & Schuster, 2013). For a more theoretical discussion of the impact of money on happiness, see ch. 6, "Can Money Buy Happiness?," in Diener and Biswas-Diener, *Happiness: Unlocking the Mysteries of Psychological Health.*

53 **to experience the same psychological boost:** Some of my own work has shown that people adapt to things quickly and need a new boost in the happiness- (or pleasure-) providing stimulus to experience the same level of happiness (or pleasure) again; see R. Raghunathan and J. R. Irwin, "Walking the Hedonic Product Treadmill: Default Contrast and Mood-Based Assimilation in Judgments of Predicted Happiness with a Target Product," *Journal of Consumer Research* 28(3) (2001): 355–68. For a review of this topic (known as "hedonic adaptation") see S. Frederick and G. Loewenstein, "Hedonic Adaptation," in D. Kahneman, E. Diener, and N. Schwarz (eds.), *Well-being: The Foundations of Hedonic Psychology* (New York: Russell Sage Foundation, 1999).

53 **lottery winners are no happier than nonwinners:** An early paper to document this phenomenon has, as you may know, become a classic. P. Brickman, D. Coates, and R. Janoff-Bulman, "Lottery Winners and Accident Victims: Is Happiness Relative?," *Journal of Personality and Social Psychology* 36(8) (1978): 917.

53 **reason for the discontent of materialistic people:** See M. L. Richins, "Social Comparison, Advertising, and Consumer Discontent," *American Behavioral Scientist* 38(4) (1995): 593–607.

54 **promotes self-centeredness and lowers compassion:** Paul Piff and his colleagues have documented across a number of studies that wealthier people, on average, are less generous and compassionate than their not-so-wealthy counterparts; see P. K. Piff, et al., "Having Less, Giving More: The Influence of Social Class on Prosocial Behavior," *Journal of Personality and Social Psychology* 99(5) (2010): 771. You can see Paul Piff's TED talk on the topic at: https://www.youtube.com/watch?v=bJ8Kq1wucsk. For a great example of how the need to be wealthy can lead to unethical behaviors, see A. Raghavan, *The Billionaire's Apprentice: The Rise of the Indian-American Elite and the Fall of the Galleon Hedge Fund* (London: Hachette UK, 2013). See also Daniel Pink, who reviews studies that show materialistic people are less ethical. D. H. Pink, *Drive: The Surprising Truth About What Motivates Us* (New York: Penguin, 2011).

54 **in favor of money, power, and fame:** K. M. Sheldon and T. Kasser, "Pursuing Personal Goals: Skills Enable Progress, but Not All Progress Is Beneficial," *Personality and Social Psychology Bulletin* 24(12) (1998): 1319–31.

54 **were far less happy with their lives:** C. Nickerson et al., "Zeroing In on the Dark Side of the American Dream: A Closer Look at the Negative Consequences of the Goal for Financial Success," *Psychological Science* 14(6) (2003): 531–36.

54 **suffer from mental disorders:** P. Cohen and J. Cohen, *Life Values and Adolescent Mental Health* (New York: Psychology Press, 1996).

54 **more vulnerable to depression:** M. H. Kernis, "Measuring Self-esteem in Context: The Importance of Stability of Self-esteem in Psychological Functioning," *Journal of Personality* 73(6) (2005): 1569–1605.

54 **foundations . . . of superiority shaky and unstable:** S. Harter, *The Construction of the Self: A Developmental Perspective* (New York: Guilford Press, 1999).

54 **blind to one's foibles and failings:** See Kristin Neff (p. 2), where she states, "such [self-positivity] biases can obscure needed areas of improvement." K. D. Neff, "Self-compassion, Self-esteem, and Well-being," *Social and Personality Psychology Compass* 5(1) (2011): 1–12.

54 **sacrificing long-term learning and growth:** For an exploration of how high need for superiority—or self-esteem—can lower performance in certain contexts, see R. F. Baumeister et al., "When Ego Threats Lead to Self-regulation Failure: Negative Conse-

quences of High Self-esteem," *Journal of Personality and Social Psychology* 64(1) (1993): 141; and C. Sedikides, "Assessment, Enhancement, and Verification Determinants of the Self-evaluation Process," *Journal of Personality and Social Psychology* 65 (1993): 317–38; for a review of the positive and negative effects of self-esteem (and the need for it) on performance and productivity, see R. F. Baumeister et al., "Does High Self-esteem Cause Better Performance, Interpersonal Success, Happiness, or Healthier Lifestyles?," *Psychological Science in the Public Interest* 4(1) (2003): 1–44.

54 ***Give and Take:*** A. Grant, *Give and Take: A Revolutionary Approach to Success* (London: Hachette UK, 2013).

54 **In one study:** See A. M. Grant, S. Parker, and C. Collins, "Getting Credit for Proactive Behavior: Supervisor Reactions Depend on What You Value and How You Feel," *Personnel Psychology* 62(1) (2009): 31–55.

55 **when they don't get the respect . . . they deserve:** R. F. Baumeister, L. Smart, and J. M. Boden, "Relation of Threatened Egotism to Violence and Aggression: The Dark Side of High Self-esteem," *Psychological Review* 103(1) (1996): 5.

55 **takers . . . less happy than givers:** For a review, see J. Crocker and L. E. Park, "The Costly Pursuit of Self-esteem," *Psychological Bulletin* 130(3) (2004): 392.

55 **the more you compare . . . the less happy you will be:** S. Lyubomirsky and L. Ross, "Hedonic Consequences of Social Comparison: A Contrast of Happy and Unhappy People," *Journal of Personality and Social Psychology* 73(6) (1997): 1141.

56 **results from one study:** J. Crocker et al., "Downward Comparison, Prejudice, and Evaluations of Others: Effects of Self-esteem and Threat," *Journal of Personality and Social Psychology* 52(5) (1987): 907.

56 **more pronounced when we feel insecure:** W. K. Campbell and C. Sedikides, "Self-threat Magnifies the Self-serving Bias: A Meta-analytic Integration," *Review of General Psychology* 3(1) (1999): 23.

56 **makes us more self-centered and materialistic:** M. A. Bauer et al., "Cuing Consumerism Situational Materialism Undermines Personal and Social Well-Being," *Psychological Science* 23(5) (2012): 517–23.

57 **over 80 percent in 2014:** For the data from 2014, see p. 44 of findings from The American Freshman Surveys, accessed from www.heri.ucla.edu/monographs/TheAmerican Freshman2014-Expanded.pdf. The statistic from the 1970s is from Dacher Keltner's introductory lecture for the course "The Science of Happiness" on EDx. The course can be accessed at www.edx.org/course/science-happiness-uc-berkeleyx-gg101x-1 or by searching for "The science of happiness" on search engines such as Google. See also *Luxury Fever* by Robert Frank for many examples of how the need for superiority is stoked in the pursuit of materialistic yardsticks of success.

58 **Materialism scale:** M. L. Richins and S. Dawson, "A Consumer Values Orientation for Materialism and Its Measurement: Scale Development and Validation," *Journal of Consumer Research* 19(3) (1992): 303–16.

Chapter 2B: The Second Habit of the Highly Happy: Pursuing Flow

61 **first documented . . . in the 1970s:** See J. W. Getzels and M. Csikszentmihalyi, *The Creative Vision* (New York: Wiley, 1976); see also M. Csikszentmihalyi, *Beyond Boredom and Anxiety* (San Francisco: Jossey-Bass, 2000). For a review of concepts and studies related to flow, see M. Csikszentmihalyi, *Flow: The Psychology of Optimal Experience* (New York: Harper & Row, 1990).

61 **In one of his best-known studies:** M. Csikszentmihalyi and J. LeFevre, "Optimal Experience in Work and Leisure," *Journal of Personality and Social Psychology* 56(5) (1989): 815.

62 **And, if so, what is it?:** This question I have imputed to Professor Csikszentmihalyi is

not explicitly articulated in his publications; nevertheless, one can infer that this was the question he was after. At a conference that I coorganized in San Antonio, Texas, in 2013, Csikszentmihalyi was one of the keynote speakers and I confirmed with him that I wouldn't be off the mark to suggest that he was interested in assessing what was common to the experiences that people from various walks of life find meaningful.

63 **characterized by certain common features:** See J. Nakamura and M. Csikszentmihalyi, "Flow Theory and Research," *Handbook of Positive Psychology*, 2009, 195–206, and J. Nakamura and M. Csikszentmihalyi, "The Concept of Flow," *Handbook of Positive Psychology*, 2002, 89–105, for reviews. Professor Csikszentmihalyi provides a summary of flow's characteristics in his TED talk, which can be accessed here: https://www.youtube.com/watch?v=fXIeFJCqsPs.

64 **to be incredible:** According to a survey of Germans and Americans, only about a third of participants have rarely (or never) experienced flow. Gallup poll (1998) cited in K. Asakawa, "Flow Experience and Autotelic Personality in Japanese College Students: How Do They Experience Challenges in Daily Life?," *Journal of Happiness Studies* 5(2) (2004): 123–54.

65 **matched by the skill levels of your opponent:** G. B. Moneta and M. Csikszentmihalyi, "The Effect of Perceived Challenges and Skills on the Quality of Subjective Experience," *Journal of Personality* 64(2) (1996): 275–310. Professor Csikszentmihalyi also talks about the importance of match between available and required abilities toward the end of his TED talk, which can be accessed here: https://www.youtube.com/watch?v=fXIeFJCqsPs.

65 **playing against someone who is just above your level:** See G. B. Moneta and M. Csikszentmihalyi, "Models of Concentration in Natural Environments: A Comparative Approach Based on Streams of Experiential Data," *Social Behavior and Personality* 27(6) (1999): 603–37. These authors state, on p. 630, that "concentration is optimized when the perceived challenges of the task stretch a bit one's perceived capabilities. This deviation from a strict interpretation of balance is consistent with Deci and Ryan's (1985) definition of 'optimal challenges' as stimuli which simultaneously are (a) congruent enough with the organismic structures to be assimilated, and (b) discrepant enough with the organismic structures to require a change and a new integration of the existing structures." The Deci and Ryan (1985) citation is E. L. Deci and R. M. Ryan, *Intrinsic Motivation and Self-determination in Human Behavior* (New York: Springer Science & Business Media, 1985).

66 **In one study:** T. P. Rogatko, "The Influence of Flow on Positive Affect in College Students," *Journal of Happiness Studies* 10(2) (2009): 133–48.

66 **has to do with mastery:** M. Csikszentmihalyi and I. S. Csikszentmihalyi, *Optimal Experience: Psychological Studies of Flow in Consciousness* (Cambridge, UK: Cambridge University Press, 1992).

66 *have* **to master that domain:** As made popular by Malcolm Gladwell in *Outliers*, researchers agree that, in general, it takes about ten thousand hours (or about ten years) of practice to master a domain; K. A. Ericsson, R. T. Krampe, and C. Tesch-Römer, "The Role of Deliberate Practice in the Acquisition of Expert Performance," *Psychological Review* 100(3) (1993): 363. Note, however, that there are exceptions to this general rule; see B. N. Macnamara, D. Z. Hambrick, and F. L. Oswald, "Deliberate Practice and Performance in Music, Games, Sports, Education, and Professions: A Meta-analysis," *Psychological Science* 25(8) (2014): 1608–18.

67 **flow doesn't . . . come at . . . cost of another's:** This reason was mentioned to me in the interview that I did with Professor Csikszentmihalyi, which can be accessed at https://www.coursera.org/learn/happiness/lecture/hMLNh/week-2-video-7-why-flow-enhances-happiness. See also Moulard et al. (2014), who suggest that people who are

motivated by their true passions as opposed to external motivations such as prestige or profits hold an esteemed place because they are perceived as more authentic and less superficial; J. G. Moulard et al., "Artist Authenticity: How Artists' Passion and Commitment Shape Consumers' Perceptions and Behavioral Intentions Across Genders," *Psychology & Marketing* 31(8) (2014): 576–90.

67 **Often, we embark on . . . a goal:** Van de Ven and coauthors find that feeling envious can spur us to set and achieve goals; however, they differentiate between "benign" and "malicious" envy and find that the former is associated with the desire to pull oneself up, whereas the latter triggers the desire to pull others down. N. Van de Ven, M. Zeelenberg, and R. Pieters, "Leveling Up and Down: The Experiences of Benign and Malicious Envy," *Emotion* 9(3) (2009): 419.

68 **the less capacity . . . to the task at hand:** This reason was mentioned to me both by Dan Ariely and by Mihaly Csikszentmihalyi when I interviewed them for my Coursera course, and is consistent with several findings on how monitoring performance lowers chances of success. The interview with Dan Ariely can be accessed at https://www .coursera.org/learn/happiness/lecture/q2fSM/week-2-video-3-is-need-for-superiority -important-for-success. The interview with Mihaly Csikszentmihalyi can be accessed at https://www.coursera.org/learn/happiness/lecture/hMLNh/week-2-video-7-why-flow -enhances-happiness.. For research on choking under pressure, see R. F. Baumeister, "Choking Under Pressure: Self-consciousness and Paradoxical Effects of Incentives on Skillful Performance," *Journal of Personality and Social Psychology* 46(3) (1984): 610. In the context of sports, it is well established that thinking about how to do something (e.g., get the basketball in the basket)—which is more likely when one compares how well one is doing to someone else—tends to lower performance; e.g., see J. Dandy, N. Brewer, and R. Tottman, "Self-consciousness and Performance Decrements Within a Sporting Context," *The Journal of Social Psychology* 141(1) (2001): 150–52. Comparing oneself with others is likely to be particularly detrimental to performance in creative and intellectual tasks, because the monitoring process takes up brain capacity that could otherwise be used in the task at hand; see K. O. McGraw and J. C. McCullers, "Evidence of a Detrimental Effect of Extrinsic Incentives on Breaking a Mental Set," *Journal of Experimental Social Psychology* 15(3) (1979): 285–94. For a review of the various reasons why monitoring one's performance (which social comparison triggers) is likely to lower performance, see R. F. Baumeister and C. J. Showers, "A Review of Paradoxical Performance Effects: Choking Under Pressure in Sports and Mental Tests," *European Journal of Social Psychology* 16(4) (1986): 361–83.

68 **pay attention . . . to what's happening right now:** See W. T. Gallwey, *The Inner Game of Tennis: The Classic Guide to the Mental Side of Peak Performance* (New York: Random House, 2010).

68 **doing well in almost any domain:** See chapter 1, "Pay More for Less," in D. Ariely, *The Upside of Irrationality: The Unexpected Benefits of Defying Logic at Work and at Home* (New York: Harper, 2010).

68 **In one study:** This study is referred to in ibid. For a related study, see study 2 in D. Ariely et al., "Large Stakes and Big Mistakes," *The Review of Economic Studies* 76(2) (2009): 451–69.

69 **As those studies showed:** See E. L. Deci, R. Koestner, and R. M. Ryan, "A Meta-analytic Review of Experiments Examining the Effects of Extrinsic Rewards on Intrinsic Motivation," *Psychological Bulletin* 125(6) (1999): 627, for a review.

69 **carrots and sticks . . . worsen . . . performance:** See *Drive* by Daniel Pink for an eminently readable review of many interesting studies on the impact of intrinsic and extrinsic rewards on performance. D. H. Pink, *Drive: The Surprising Truth About What Motivates Us* (New York: Penguin, 2011).

69 **twice as many . . . are dissatisfied with their jobs:** See S. Adams, "Unhappy Employees Outnumber Happy Ones by Two to One Worldwide," *Forbes*, Oct. 10, 2013, accessed at www.forbes.com/sites/susanadams/2013/10/10/unhappy-employees-outnumber-happy-ones-by-two-to-one-worldwide/. In the United States, according to a survey conducted by Conference Board—a not-for-profit economic research institute—fewer than half of American workers are satisfied with their jobs. *Miami Herald*, Oct. 20, 2015, accessed at http://www.miamiherald.com/news/business/biz-columns-blogs/cindy-krischer-goodman/article40524411.html.

69 **job satisfaction in the United States was much higher:** State of the American Workplace, Gallup Poll, 2013. According to this poll, over 70 percent of U.S. employees were "disengaged" in 2013 (see http://employeeengagement.com/wp-content/uploads/2013/06/Gallup-2013-State-of-the-American-Workplace-Report.pdf). In the 1970s and 1980s, by contrast, only 40 percent were disengaged.

71 **(85 percent) know where our passion lies:** This figure is mentioned in a talk that Professor Vallerand gave in Montreal, which can be accessed at www.youtube.com/watch?v=kulUtp0KyiQ.

71 **stable life:** M. Csikszentmihalyi, *Evolving Self* (New York: Perennial, 1994). For a summary of Csikszentmihalyi's thoughts on this topic, see the following short (seven-minute) YouTube video: www.youtube.com/watch?v=7dSzKnf5WWg. (The video can be accessed by Googling "Mihaly thinking allowed.") Not only is the myth of "the depressed lonely creative genius" just that—a myth—it turns out that creative people are also more responsible than we typically think they are; see M. Csikszentmihalyi and J. Nakamura, "Creativity and Responsibility," in *The Systems Model of Creativity* (Dordrecht: Springer Netherlands, 2014), 279–92.

71 **calls "grit":** A. L. Duckworth et al., "Deliberate Practice Spells Success: Why Grittier Competitors Triumph at the National Spelling Bee," *Social Psychological and Personality Science* 2(2) (2011): 174–81; A. L. Duckworth et al., "Grit: Perseverance and Passion for Long-Term Goals," *Journal of Personality and Social Psychology* 92(6) (2007): 1087; for related—and very insightful—thoughts, see S. Pressfield, *The War of Art: Break Through the Blocks and Win Your Inner Creative Battles* (New York and Los Angeles: Black Irish Entertainment LLC, 2002). Angela Duckworth's TED talk on grit can be accessed at https://www.youtube.com/watch?v=YMYGaRJNW_8.

72 **intellectual/creative tasks:** For a particularly well-articulated summary of this idea, see Dan Pink's RSAnimate talk at www.youtube.com/watch?v=u6XAPnuFjJc. (The video can be accessed by Googling "Dan Pink RSAnimate.") You may also consider reading my own thoughts on the topic at the following website: www.psychologytoday.com/blog/sapient-nature/201301/the-myopia-farsightedness-0. (The site can be accessed by Googling "Myopia of farsightedness.")

72 ***Working Identity:*** H. Ibarra, *Working Identity: Unconventional Strategies for Reinventing Your Career* (Cambridge, MA: Harvard Business Press, 2003).

74 **enhance your chances of achieving it:** E. Berkman and M. D. Lieberman, "The Neuroscience of Goal-Pursuit: Bridging Gaps Between Theory and Data," in G. Moskowitz and H. Grant (eds.), *The Psychology of Goals* (New York: Guilford Press, 2009), 98–126.

74 **"best possible life" exercise:** I used to call it the "Ideal Life" exercise but decided to change it to "best possible life" because "ideal" seemed too idealistic for many of my students and they therefore felt the exercise to be daunting. By contrast, "best possible" seemed more achievable to them.

75 **we are often our own worst enemies:** This was mentioned to me by Professor Neff when I interviewed her for my Coursera course, which can be accessed at https://www.coursera.org/learn/happiness/lecture/8OmBu/week-2-video-10-a-practice-for-when-

things-are-not-going-well-self-compassion. She also raises this theme in many of her scholarly articles including this review of "self-compassion": K. Neff, "Self-compassion: An Alternative Conceptualization of a Healthy Attitude Toward Oneself, *Self and Identity* 2(2) (2003): 85–101. For a review of her work on self-compassion, see K. Neff, *Self-compassion* (London: Hachette UK, 2011).

75 **motivate us to do better next time:** See K. D. Neff, "Self-compassion, Self-esteem, and Well-being," *Social and Personality Psychology Compass* 5(1) (2011): 1–12.

75 **negative self-talk . . . actually demotivates us:** This was mentioned to me by Professor Neff when I interviewed her for my Coursera course, which can be accessed at https://www.coursera.org/learn/happiness/lecture/8OmBu/week-2-video-10-a-practice -for-when-things-are-not-going-well-self-compassion.

77 **There are several studies:** For a review of the various positive effects of expressing gratitude, see R. A. Emmons, *Thanks!: How the New Science of Gratitude Can Make You Happier* (New York: Houghton Mifflin Harcourt, 2007).

77 **One study showed:** See S. B. Algoe, J. Haidt, and S. L. Gable, "Beyond Reciprocity: Gratitude and Relationships in Everyday Life," *Emotion* 8(3) (2008): 425.

77 **lower levels of envy and depression:** J. J. Froh et al., "Gratitude and the Reduced Costs of Materialism in Adolescents," *Journal of Happiness Studies* 12(2) (2011): 289–302.

77 **gratitude a "meta-strategy":** See S. Lyubomirsky, *The How of Happiness: A Scientific Approach to Getting the Life You Want* (New York: Penguin, 2008).

Chapter 3A: The Third Deadly Happiness "Sin": Desperation for Love

79 **everyone lives happily thereafter:** The movie, in case you are interested in seeing it, is *Kasam Paida Karne Wale Ki*.

79 **Indeed, the behaviorists believed:** See J. B. Watson, *Behaviorism* (New York: W. W. Norton, 1924); and J. Wolpe, "Psychotherapy by Reciprocal Inhibition," *Conditional Reflex: A Pavlovian Journal of Research & Therapy* 3(4) (1968): 234–40. For a brief yet insightful review of this literature, see chapter 6, "Love and Attachments," in J. Haidt, *The Happiness Hypothesis: Finding Modern Truth in Ancient Wisdom* (New York: Basic Books, 2006).

80 **He was out to prove something else:** H. F. Harlow, M. D. Harlow, and S. J. Suomi, "From Thought to Therapy: Lessons from a Primate Laboratory," *American Scientist* 59 (1971): 538–49. For a more elaborate discussion of Harlow's research and its impact, see D. Blum, *Love at Goon Park: Harry Harlow and the Science of Affection* (New York: Basic Books, 2011).

80 **never been done before:** A. J. Blomquist and H. F. Harlow, "The Infant Rhesus Monkey Program at the University of Wisconsin Primate Laboratory," *Proceedings of the Animal Care Panel* 11 (1961):57–64.

80 **soon after they were born:** The baby monkeys were typically separated from their mothers six to twelve hours after their birth; H. F. Harlow, "The Nature of Love," *American Psychologist* 13(12) (1958): 673.

80 **denied the babies the opportunity to be cuddled:** These and several other facts in this section are from *Love at Goon Park* by Deborah Blum.

80 **the lab monkeys grew up to be psychologically damaged:** Ibid.

80 **Harlow's lab were different:** Harlow, Harlow, and Suomi, "From Thought to Therapy."

80 **human infants deprived of love:** R. A. Spitz, "The Psychogenic Diseases in Infancy—An Attempt at their Etiologic Classification," *Psychoanalytic Study of the Child* 6 (1951), 255–75.

81 **In one of their best-known experiments:** For a description of this and other experiments, see Harlow, "The Nature of Love."

82 **Findings proved Harlow right:** See figure 5 (on p. 676) in ibid., which summarizes the results.

82 **In follow-up experiments:** These experiments are described in Blum, *Love at Goon Park*; see also H. F. Harlow, "Love in Infant Monkeys," *Scientific American* 200(6) (1959): 68–74.

83 **monkeys' capacity for love and nurturance:** For similar findings on rats, see T. Y. Zhang and M. J. Meaney, "Epigenetics and the Environmental Regulation of the Genome and Its Function," *Annual Review of Psychology* 61 (2010): 439–66. These researchers found that rat pups that had been licked and groomed by their mothers (or mother figures) grew up into psychologically healthier adults.

83 **René Spitz was one of the pioneers:** R. A. Spitz, *The First Year of Life: A Psychoanalytic Study of Normal and Deviant Development of Object Relations* (New York: International Universities Press, 1965).

83 **Bowlby found that the juveniles:** J. Bowlby, *Attachment and Loss*, vol. 3 (New York: Basic Books, 1980).

84 **we continue to have an intense desire:** C. Hazan and P. Shaver, "Romantic Love Conceptualized as an Attachment Process," *Journal of Personality and Social Psychology* 52(3) (1987): 511. See also R. F. Baumeister and M. R. Leary, "The Need to Belong: Desire for Interpersonal Attachments as a Fundamental Human Motivation," *Psychological Bulletin* 117(3) (1995): 497.

84 **captured in a Greek myth:** J. M. Cooper and D. S. Hutchinson (eds.), *Plato: Complete Works* (Cambridge, MA: Hackett, 1997).

84 **no challenge seems insurmountable:** Part of the lyrics to one of my favorite Hindi movie songs goes something like this: *Without you, I guess I could manage to rise up after a fall; but with you in my arms, my dear, I can twirl the world around as if it were a ball!* (I've taken some poetic license here in translating the lyrics to the song, *"O mere dil ke chain"* by Kishore Kumar from the movie *Mere Jeevan Saathi*.)

84 **Being in love . . . one of our most cherished experiences:** See D. Kahneman et al., "A Survey Method for Characterizing Daily Life Experience: The Day Reconstruction Method," *Science* 306(5702) (2004): 1776–80. Of twenty-five activities that respondents in the study these authors conducted were asked to rate, being in "intimate relationships" emerged as the most positive.

84 **emotional connection with others:** According to Barbara Fredrickson, love can be felt even with those with whom we interact temporarily. See B. Fredrickson, *Love 2.0: Creating Happiness and Health in Moments of Connection* (New York: Plume, 2014).

84 **early study by . . . Asch:** The experiment is nicely summarized in S. E. Asch, "Opinions and Social Pressure," *Readings About the Social Animal* 193 (1955): 17–26.

85 **replicated in several other experiments:** See, for review, R. Bond and P. B. Smith, "Culture and Conformity: A Meta-analysis of Studies Using Asch's (1952b, 1956) Line Judgment Task," *Psychological Bulletin* 119(1) (1996): 111.

85 **desire to form and maintain bonds:** M. Deutsch and H. B. Gerard, "A Study of Normative and Informational Social Influences upon Individual Judgment," *Journal of Abnormal and Social Psychology* 51(3) (1955): 629.

85 **In a set of experiments that:** R. Raghunathan and K. Corfman, "Is Happiness Shared Doubled and Sadness Shared Halved? Social Influence on Enjoyment of Hedonic Experiences," *Journal of Marketing Research* 43(3) (2006): 386–94.

86 **A host of psychological and physiological illnesses:** J. T. Cacioppo and W. Patrick, *Loneliness: Human Nature and the Need for Social Connection* (New York: W. W. Norton & Company, 2008).

87 **One study explored:** E. Diener and M. E. Seligman, "Very Happy People," *Psychological Science* 13(1) (2002): 81–84. For similar results on how connection with others is

perhaps the single most important determinant of well-being, see also J. F. Helliwell, "Well-Being, Social Capital and Public Policy: What's New?," *The Economic Journal* 116(510) (2006): C34–C45, in which the author writes: "respondents who have frequent contacts with family, friends and neighbors have SWB almost a full point higher, on the 10-point SWB scale, than those with no such contacts." (SWB is short for "Subjective Well-Being," a term that researchers use to refer to happiness.) See also Cacioppo and Patrick, *Loneliness*, where the authors state (on p. 5), "When people are asked what pleasures contribute most to happiness, the overwhelming majority rate love, intimacy, and social affiliation above wealth or fame, even above physical health."

87 **strength of social relationships:** G. E. Vaillant, *Triumphs of Experience* (Cambridge, MA: Harvard University Press, 2012).

87 **the *top two* happiest categories:** Kahneman et al., "A Survey Method for Characterizing Daily Life Experience."

87 **Findings from another study:** This study is reported by Shawn Achor on his HBR blog; see https://hbr.org/2011/07/what-giving-gets-you-at-the-of.

88 ***the need to belong:*** R. F. Baumeister and M. R. Leary, "The Need to Belong: Desire for Interpersonal Attachments as a Fundamental Human Motivation," *Psychological Bulletin* 117(3) (1995): 497.

88 **we are often desperate for love and connection:** Ibid.

88 **may be referred to as "neediness":** Researchers prefer the term "anxious attachment" or "anxious attachment style" to "neediness"; however, there is at least one set of researchers who have used the term "neediness." See S. S. Rude and B. L. Burnham, "Connectedness and Neediness: Factors of the DEQ and SAS Dependency Scales," *Cognitive Therapy and Research* 19(3) (1995): 323–40.

88 **rooted in deep-seated insecurities about relationships:** M. D. S. Ainsworth et al., *Patterns of Attachment: A Psychological Study of the Strange Situation* (New York: Psychology Press, 2014); see also M. S. Ainsworth, "Infant–Mother Attachment," *American Psychologist* 34(10) (1979): 932; and Hazan and Shaver, "Romantic Love Conceptualized as an Attachment Process."

89 **two researchers—Cindy Hazan and Phillip Shaver:** Hazan and Shaver, "Romantic Love Conceptualized as an Attachment Process."

89 **neither neediness nor avoidance is good for happiness:** M. Mikulincer and P. R. Shaver, "Adult Attachment and Happiness: Individual Differences in the Experience and Consequences of Positive Emotions," in *The Oxford Handbook of Happiness*, S. David, I. Boniwell, and A. C. Ayers (eds.) (New York: Oxford University Press, 2012), 834–46.

89 **Results from one study:** K. Kafetsios and G. D. Sideridis, "Attachment, Social Support and Well-being in Young and Older Adults," *Journal of Health Psychology* 11(6) (2006): 863–75.

89 **than secure dependents:** W. Eng et al., "Attachment in Individuals with Social Anxiety Disorder: The Relationship Among Adult Attachment Styles, Social Anxiety, and Depression," *Emotion* 1(4) (2001): 365.

89 **devalue things that are easily available:** A. R. Pratkanis and P. H. Farquhar, "A Brief History of Research on Phantom Alternatives: Evidence for Seven Empirical Generalizations About Phantoms," *Basic and Applied Social Psychology* 13(1) (1992): 103–22.

89 **even more desperate for connection:** P. L. Wachtel, *Psychoanalysis and Behavior Therapy: Toward an Integration* (New York: Basic Books, 1977). See also J. T. Cacioppo and L. C. Hawkley, "People Thinking About People: The Vicious Cycle of Being a Social Outcast in One's Own Mind," in *The Social Outcast: Ostracism, Social Exclusion, Rejection, and Bullying*, 2005, 91–108; and S. K. Egan and D. G. Perry, "Does Low Self-regard Invite Victimization?," *Developmental Psychology* 34(2) (1998): 299–309.

90 **not conducive to happiness:** This idea was expressed to me by Prof. Phillip Shaver when I interviewed him for my Coursera course. As of Jan. 1, 2016, however, I hadn't managed to edit this interview into the Coursera course (I conducted my interview too late). But I hope to include an excerpt from the interview in "Version 2.0" of the course. Several studies, including that conducted by Hazan and Shaver (1987)—referred to earlier—provide evidence in support of the thesis that the needy tend to view themselves in a more negative light than do the secure or even the avoidant. For example, see J. Spasojević and L. B. Alloy, "Rumination as a Common Mechanism Relating Depressive Risk Factors to Depression," *Emotion* 1(1) (2001): 25–37, who note that neediness was associated with the tendency to ruminate on negative thoughts about oneself. Similar findings have been documented by S. Nolen-Hoeksema, B. E. Wisco, and S. Lyubomirsky, "Rethinking Rumination," *Perspectives on Psychological Science* 3(5) (2008): 400–24.

90 **spoils the quality of their relationships:** See K. Kafetsios and J. B. Nezlek, "Attachment Styles in Everyday Social Interaction," *European Journal of Social Psychology* 32(5) (2002): 719–35; and J. A. Feeney and P. Noller, "Attachment Style as a Predictor of Adult Romantic Relationships," *Journal of Personality and Social Psychology* 58(2) (1990): 281. See also the following papers, which document similar results: M. B. Levy and K. E. Davis, "Lovestyles and Attachment Styles Compared: Their Relations to Each Other and to Various Relationship Characteristics," *Journal of Social and Personal Relationships* 5(4) (1988): 439–71; J. P. R. Keelan, K. L. Dion, and K. K. Dion, "Attachment Style and Heterosexual Relationships Among Young Adults: A Short-Term Panel Study," *Journal of Social and Personal Relationships* 11(2) (1994): 201–14; and J. A. Simpson, "Influence of Attachment Styles on Romantic Relationships," *Journal of Personality and Social Psychology* 59(5) (1990): 971.

90 **avoidants experience lower job satisfaction:** M. Krausz, A. Bizman, and D. Braslavsky, "Effects of Attachment Style on Preferences for and Satisfaction with Different Employment Contracts: An Exploratory Study," *Journal of Business and Psychology* 16(2) (2001): 299–316.

90 **Avoidants are also prone:** D. L. Vogel and M. Wei, "Adult Attachment and Help-Seeking Intent: The Mediating Roles of Psychological Distress and Perceived Social Support," *Journal of Counseling Psychology* 52(3) (2005): 347.

90 **avoidants aren't very effective as leaders:** R. Davidovitz et al., "Leaders as Attachment Figures: Leaders' Attachment Orientations Predict Leadership-Related Mental Representations and Followers' Performance and Mental Health," *Journal of Personality and Social Psychology* 93(4) (2007): 632. As these authors state, "leaders' attachment-related avoidance was negatively associated with prosocial motives to lead, with the failure to act as a security provider, and with followers' poorer socioemotional functioning and poorer long-range mental health."

90 **Avoidants too feel frustrated:** This idea was mentioned to me by Prof. Phillip Shaver, during an interview I did with him for my Coursera course. As of Jan. 1, 2016, however, I hadn't managed to include the interview in the Coursera course. I hope to include the interview in "Version 2.0" of the course.

91 **temporarily boost feelings of . . . security:** M. Mikulincer and P. R. Shaver, "Attachment Security, Compassion, and Altruism," *Current Directions in Psychological Science* 14(1) (2005): 34–38.

91 **make one feel more secure:** M. Mikulincer et al., "Attachment, Caregiving, and Altruism: Boosting Attachment Security Increases Compassion and Helping," *Journal of Personality and Social Psychology* 89(5) (2005): 817–39.

91 **"find, remind, and bind" emotion:** S. B. Algoe, "Find, Remind, and Bind: The Functions of Gratitude in Everyday Relationships," *Social and Personality Psychology Compass* 6(6) (2012): 455–69.

91 **mitigating neediness and avoidance:** S. L. Shapiro, K. W. Brown, and G. M. Biegel, "Teaching self-care to Caregivers: Effects of Mindfulness-Based Stress Reduction on the Mental Health of Therapists in Training," *Training and Education in Professional Psychology* 1(2) (2007): 105.

92 **the "self-soothing" system:** See P. Gilbert and C. Irons, "Focused Therapies and Compassionate Mind Training for Shame and Self-attacking," in P. Gilbert (ed.), *Compassion: Conceptualisations, Research and Use in Psychotherapy* (London: Routledge), 263–325. The idea that self-compassion can lead one to become more secure in relationships (and thereby improve relationship quality) was also mentioned to me by Prof. Kristin Neff when I interviewed her for my Coursera course. The interview can be accessed at https://www.coursera.org/learn/happiness/lecture/8OmBu/week-2-video-10-a-practice-for-when-things-are-not-going-well-self-compassion.

93 **Loneliness Scale:** D. W. Russell, "UCLA Loneliness Scale (Version 3): Reliability, Validity, and Factor Structure," *Journal of Personality Assessment* 66(1) (1996): 20–40.

96 **ECR Scale and Scoring Scheme:** This scale is from M. Wei et al., "The Experiences in Close Relationship Scale (ECR)—Short Form: Reliability, Validity, and Factor Structure," *Journal of Personality Assessment* 88(2) (2007): 187–204.

98 **Self-Compassion Exercise:** These instructions are from Kristin Neff's website, which can be accessed at www.selfcompassion.org/self_compassion_exercise.pdf. The site has more exercises and other resources, including mp3 (audio) files of instructions for the exercises.

Chapter 3B: The Third Habit of the Highly Happy: The Need to Love (and Give)

100 **In a survey that posed a similar question:** E. W. Dunn, L. B. Aknin, and M. I. Norton, "Spending Money on Others Promotes Happiness," *Science* 319(5870) (2008): 1687–88. These authors found that 69 out of 109 participants (or 63 percent) said they thought spending money on themselves would make them happier.

100 **one study conducted at the University of British Columbia:** Ibid.

102 **seemingly incredible—finding from a survey:** L. B. Aknin et al., "Prosocial Spending and Well-being: Cross-cultural Evidence for a Psychological Universal," *Journal of Personality and Social Psychology* 104(4) (2013): 635.

102 **researchers conducted a study:** Ibid.

102 **per-capita GDP of a mere $657.37:** These figures were accessed on September 16, 2015, from www.indexmundi.com/facts/indicators/NY.GDP.PCAP.CD/rankings.

103 **spending money on others made people happier:** For a reader-friendly and insightful review of the relevant literature on this topic, see ch. 5, "Invest in Others," in E. Dunn, and M. Norton, *Happy Money: The Science of Smarter Spending* (New York: Simon & Schuster, 2013).

103 **The positive effects of altruism on happiness:** Ibid.

103 *cute aggression:* O. R. Aragón et al., "Dimorphous Expressions of Positive Emotion Displays of Both Care and Aggression in Response to Cute Stimuli," *Psychological Science* 26(3) (2015): 259–73.

103 **In one study, twenty toddlers:** L. B. Aknin, J. K. Hamlin, and E. W. Dunn, "Giving Leads to Happiness in Young Children," *PLOS ONE* 7(6) (2012): e39211.

104 **Several other studies have confirmed it too:** F. Warneken and M. Tomasello, "Altruistic Helping in Human Infants and Young Chimpanzees," *Science* 311(5765) (2006): 1301–3; for a reader-friendly summary of this paper, see http://greatergood.berkeley.edu/article/item/what_motivates_kids_to_help_others and http://greatergood.berkeley.edu/article/item/little_helpers/. See also Dunn and Norton, *Happy Money*, for a review of the findings on the impact of altruism on happiness.

105 **Consider findings from one study:** C. E. Schwartz and R. M. Sendor, "Helping Others Helps Oneself: Response Shift Effects in Peer Support," *Social Science & Medicine* 48(11) (1999): 1563–75.

105 **researchers measured how helpful participants:** This study is cited on p. 130 of S. Lyubomirsky, *The How of Happiness: A Scientific Approach to Getting the Life You Want* (New York: Penguin, 2008). Other studies have found support for reciprocity effects of generosity, including the Algoe et al. (2008) study cited in chapter 2B; S. B. Algoe, J. Haidt, and S. L. Gable, "Beyond Reciprocity: Gratitude and Relationships in Everyday Life," *Emotion* 8(3) (2008): 425. For a review of the area, see R. L. Trivers, "The Evolution of Reciprocal Altruism," *Quarterly Review of Biology* (1971): 35–57.

105 **giving and physical health:** E. W. Dunn et al., "On the Costs of Self-interested Economic Behavior: How Does Stinginess Get Under the Skin?," *Journal of Health Psychology* 15(4) (2010): 627–33.

106 **we tell ourselves the story:** G. M. Williamson and M. S. Clark, "Providing Help and Desired Relationship Type as Determinants of Changes in Moods and Self-evaluations," *Journal of Personality and Social Psychology* 56(5) (1989): 722.

106 **small gesture of generosity will do:** Z. Chance and M. I. Norton, "I Give, Therefore I Have: Giving and Subjective Wealth," working paper, Yale University, 2014.

106 **generosity has such a big effect on happiness:** I had the privilege of interviewing Michael Norton—the researcher who has probably done the most work on the effects of prosocial behavior on happiness in recent years—for my Coursera course. Mike summarizes many of the findings I have just reviewed in the interviews, which can be accessed at https://www.coursera.org/learn/happiness/lecture/ABiEE/week-3-video -8-why-the-need-to-love-and-give-enhances-happiness. To read about the effects of generosity on well-being, see J. A. Piliavin, "Doing Well by Doing Good: Benefits for the Benefactor," in C. L. M. Keyes and J. Haidt (eds.), *Flourishing: Positive Psychology and the Life Well-Lived* (Washington, DC: APA, 2003), 227–47.

106 **being compassionate makes us "soft":** See J. Aaker, K. D. Vohs, and C. Mogilner, "Nonprofits Are Seen as Warm and For-profits as Competent: Firm Stereotypes Matter," *Journal of Consumer Research* 37(2) (2010): 224–37. For related research, see M. G. Luchs et al., "The Sustainability Liability: Potential Negative Effects of Ethicality on Product Preference," *Journal of Marketing* 74(5) (2010): 18–31.

106 *Give and Take:* A. Grant, *Give and Take: A Revolutionary Approach to Success* (London: Hachette UK, 2013).

106 **In one study:** This study is cited in ibid. Here's how Adam Grant interprets these findings: Imagine that you and I are both earning $60,000 a year. I give $1,600 to charity; you give $2,500 to charity. Although you gave away $900 more than I did, according to the evidence, you'll be on track to earn $3,375 more than I will in the coming year. Surprising as it seems, people who give more go on to earn more.

107 **"work altruists" or "work isolators":** Details of this study can be obtained on the following website, accessed on September 16, 2015: https://hbr.org/2011/07/what -giving-gets-you-at-the-of.

107 **"giving feels better . . . than getting ever does":** Ibid.

107 **caretakers of Alzheimer's patients:** B. A. Esterling et al., "Chronic Stress, Social Support, and Persistent Alterations in the Natural Killer Cell Response to Cytokines in Older Adults," *Health Psychology* 13(4) (1994): 291.

108 **otherish givers . . . have a bigger . . . impact:** Grant, *Give and Take*. In addition to "otherish" and "selfless" givers, Adam Grant talks of two other categories of people: "takers" (who are, as the term suggests, self-centered and mainly motivated by gaining from others) and "matchers," who are interested in fairness and equity; matchers feel obliged to give if someone gives first and, likewise, feel entitled to get when they give

to someone. I interviewed Reb Rebele, one of Grant's collaborators on projects, for my Coursera course on this topic. The interview can be accessed at https://www.coursera .org/learn/happiness/lecture/LWoDi/week-3-video-9-the-rules-for-giving-when -does-giving-enhance-happiness-and.

108 **two main strategies:** Ibid. Reb Rebele elaborates on these strategies in my Coursera course. You can see excerpts from our interview at https://www.coursera.org/learn/ happiness/lecture/LWoDi/week-3-video-9-the-rules-for-giving-when-does-giving-enhance-happiness-and.

108 **those who . . . witness the impact of . . . generosity:** See chapter 5, "Invest in Others," in Dunn and Norton, *Happy Money.*

108 **$10 Starbucks gift card:** L. B. Aknin et al., "It's the Recipient That Counts: Spending Money on Strong Social Ties Leads to Greater Happiness Than Spending on Weak Social Ties," *PLOS ONE* 6(2) (2011): e17018.

109 **strangers, as more selfish than selfless:** J. P. Mitchell, C. N. Macrae, and M. R. Banaji, "Dissociable Medial Prefrontal Contributions to Judgments of Similar and Dissimilar Others," *Neuron* 50(4) (2006): 655–63.

110 *lot* **of kindness and generosity in the world:** An ad for Coca-Cola (of all things!) captures the prevalence of kindness and generosity quite well—via a security camera. The ad can be accessed here: www.wimp.com/colacameras (or by Googling "coca cola security camera commercial").

110 **negative stories are favored:** According to the following article, "bad news outweighs good news by as much as seventeen negative news reports for every one good news re- port": www.psychologytoday.com/blog/wired-success/201012/why-we-love-bad-news. Media stories continue to be negative (or have become increasingly negative) despite lower rates of crime: http://positivenews.org.uk/2015/culture/media/17119/traditional -media-questioning-focus-negative-news-claims-radio-documentary/. Media focuses more on negative (vs. positive) news in the financial sector: https://reutersinstitute.pol itics.ox.ac.uk/sites/default/files/Media%20Coverage%20of%20Banking%20and%20Fi nancial%20News.pdf. For a good review of how negative coverage in the media shapes our perceptions and fears, see B. Glassner, *The Culture of Fear: Why Americans Are Afraid of the Wrong Things: Crime, Drugs, Minorities, Teen Moms, Killer Kids, Mutant Microbes, Plane Crashes, Road Rage, & So Much More* (New York: Basic Books, 2010).

110 *Happiness Hypothesis:* J. Haidt, *The Happiness Hypothesis: Finding Modern Truth in Ancient Wisdom* (New York: Basic Books, 2006).

110 **"bad is stronger than good":** Baumeister et al. (2001) provide an excellent review of the variety of domains in which "bad" outweighs "good" (in terms of capturing our attention); R. F. Baumeister et al., "Bad Is Stronger than Good," *Review of General Psy- chology* 5(4) (2001): 323.

110 **five positive remarks:** This "five to one" rule is based on a number of findings documented by John Gottman and his colleagues; see, for a review, J. Gottman, and N. Silver, *The Seven Principles for Making Marriage Work: A Practical Guide from the Country's Foremost Relationship Expert* (New York: Harmony, 2015).

111 **three positive experiences:** The 3:1 ratio of positive to negative experiences is referred to as the "Losada ratio" (after one of the authors of the paper in which this ratio was first acknowledged as being important for "flourishing"); B. L. Fredrickson and M. F. Losada, "Positive Affect and the Complex Dynamics of Human Flourishing," *American Psychol- ogist* 60(7) (2005): 678. There is, however, some controversy about this rule; see N. J. Brown, A. D. Sokal, and H. L. Friedman, "The Complex Dynamics of Wishful Thinking: The Critical Positivity Ratio," *American Psychologist* 68(9) (2013): 801–13.

114 **Satisfaction with Life Scale:** E. D. Diener et al., "The Satisfaction with Life Scale," *Jour- nal of Personality Assessment* 49(1) (1985): 71–75.

Chapter 4A: The Fourth Deadly Happiness "Sin": Being Overly Controlling

117 **fear of death:** S. Solomon, J. Greenberg, and T. Pyszczynski, "A Terror Management Theory of Social Behavior: The Psychological Functions of Self-esteem and Cultural Worldviews," *Advances in Experimental Social Psychology* 24(93) (1991): 159.

117 **terror management theory:** See, for review, J. Greenberg, S. Solomon, and T. Pyszczynski, *Terror Management Theory of Self-esteem and Cultural Worldviews: Empirical Assessments and Conceptual Refinements* (San Diego: Academic Press, 1997). For an engaging overview of this literature, see *Flight from Death: The Quest for Immortality*, a documentary based on Ernst Becker's Pulitzer Prize–winning book *Denial of Death* (on which TMT is at least partly based), and on TMT itself. (Sheldon Solomon, one of the researchers involved in the development of TMT, is featured quite extensively in the documentary.) See E. Becker, *The Denial of Death* (New York: Simon & Schuster, 2007), and *Flight from Death: The Quest for Immortality* (2005), producers Greg Bennick and Patrick Shen.

117 **earliest studies in the area:** A. Rosenblatt et al., "Evidence for Terror Management Theory: I. The Effects of Mortality Salience on Reactions to Those Who Violate or Uphold Cultural Values," *Journal of Personality and Social Psychology* 57(4) (1989): 681.

118 **Christian students were asked to:** J. Greenberg et al., "Evidence for Terror Management Theory II: The Effects of Mortality Salience on Reactions to Those Who Threaten or Bolster the Cultural Worldview," *Journal of Personality and Social Psychology* 58(2) (1990): 308.

118 **pour out . . . extremely . . . hot sauce:** H. A. McGregor et al., "Terror Management and Aggression: Evidence That Mortality Salience Motivates Aggression Against Worldview-Threatening Others," *Journal of Personality and Social Psychology* 74(3) (1998): 590.

118 **didn't want to cause serious harm:** For a discussion of this topic, see J. D. Lieberman et al., "A Hot New Way to Measure Aggression: Hot Sauce Allocation," *Aggressive Behavior* 25(5) (1999): 331–48.

119 **a different political leaning:** Had I been a participant in the study, I might have poured out more hot sauce for someone I liked—as I happen to like hot sauce myself and get teary-eyed (with gratitude) when someone makes me an extra spicy meal. But the point of the study is well taken: people reminded of death do not just harbor negative attitudes, but actually *act* in a hostile fashion against those they perceive to be different from themselves.

119 **at least half a dozen ways:** Here are some ways in which we seek to gain or retain control (even if it is only perceived control): (1) Illusion of control: E. J. Langer, "The Illusion of Control," *Journal of Personality and Social Psychology* 32(2) (1975): 311. (2) Overconfidence: D. A. Moore and P. J. Healy, "The Trouble with Overconfidence," *Psychological Review* 115(2) (2008): 502. (3) Psychological closure: A. W. Kruglanski and D. M. Webster, "Motivated Closing of the Mind: 'Seizing' and 'Freezing,'" *Psychological Review* 103(2) (1996): 263. (4) Decision avoidance: C. J. Anderson, "The Psychology of Doing Nothing: Forms of Decision Avoidance Result from Reason and Emotion," *Psychological Bulletin* 129(1) (2003): 139. (5) Cognitive dissonance: L. Festinger, *A Theory of Cognitive Dissonance*, vol. 2 (Palo Alto, CA: Stanford University Press, 1962). And (6) Predecisional distortion: J. E. Russo, M. G. Meloy, and V. H. Medvec, "Predecisional Distortion of Product Information," *Journal of Marketing Research* (1998): 438–52.

120 **clarity on the *reasons* for our decisions:** A. Tversky and E. Shafir, "Choice Under Conflict: The Dynamics of Deferred Decision," *Psychological Science* 3(6) (1992): 358–61.

120 **exhibiting overconfidence:** For a review, see Moore and Healy, "The Trouble with Overconfidence."

120 **particularly on difficult and complex topics:** Ibid.

121 *illusion of control:* Langer, "The Illusion of Control." For a review of illusion of control, see P. K. Presson and V. A. Benassi, "Illusion of Control: A Meta-analytic Review," *Journal of Social Behavior & Personality* 11(3) (1996): 493–510.

121 **involving a lottery:** Langer, "The Illusion of Control."

121 **less afraid of driving than . . . flying:** A. Tversky and D. Kahneman, "Judgment Under Uncertainty: Heuristics and Biases," *Science* 185(4157) (1974): 1124–31.

121 **achieving the outcomes we desire:** A. Bandura, "Self-efficacy: Toward a Unifying Theory of Behavioral Change," *Psychological Review* 84 (1977): 191–215.

121 **self-efficacy . . . boosts well-being:** The idea that self-efficacy and competence boost well-being is one of the main themes of self-determination theory; see, for a review, R. M. Ryan and E. L. Deci, "Self-determination Theory and the Facilitation of Intrinsic Motivation, Social Development, and Well-being," *American Psychologist* 55(1) (2000): 68–78. See also C. Peterson and M. E. Seligman, "Explanatory Style and Illness," *Journal of Personality* 55(2) (1987): 237–65.

121 **aren't under someone else's control:** L. A. Leotti, S. S. Iyengar, and K. N. Ochsner, "Born to Choose: The Origins and Value of the Need for Control," *Trends in Cognitive Sciences* 14(10) (2020): 457–63.

121 **personal autonomy is . . . a very important:** Ryan and Deci, "Self-Determination Theory and the Facilitation of Intrinsic Motivation, Social Development, and Well-being."

121 **study conducted at an old-age home:** J. Rodin and E. J. Langer, "Long-term Effects of a Control-Relevant Intervention with the Institutionalized Aged," *Journal of Personality and Social Psychology* 35(12) (1977): 897.

122 **conducted on rats this time:** S. I. Dworkin, S. Mirkis, and J. E. Smith, "Response-Dependent Versus Response-Independent Presentation of Cocaine: Differences in the Lethal Effects of the Drug," *Psychopharmacology* 117(3) (1995): 262–66.

122 **tend to achieve more:** J. M. Burger, "Desire for Control and Achievement-Related Behaviors," *Journal of Personality and Social Psychology* 48(6) (1985): 1520–33. For related research on the other positive effects of the desire for control, see A. Bandura and R. Wood, "Effect of Perceived Controllability and Performance Standards on Self-regulation of Complex Decision Making," *Journal of Personality and Social Psychology* 56(5) (1989): 805–14; and J. M. Burger, "Effects of Desire for Control on Attributions and Task Performance," *Basic and Applied Social Psychology* 8(4) (1987): 309–20.

123 **being overly control-seeking lowers happiness:** Although Jerry Burger, a professor at Santa Clara University and one of the pioneers in the area of the desire for control, is a huge proponent of the idea that seeking control is a good thing, he acknowledged and agreed (when I interviewed him for my Coursera course) that seeking too much control would lead to the types of negative effects discussed in this chapter. As of Jan. 1, 2016, I hadn't managed to edit my interview with Jerry Burger in the Coursera course (I conducted my interview too late). But I hope to include an excerpt from the interview in "Version 2.0" of the course.

123 **desire to do something:** A. Litt, U. Khan, and B. Shiv, "Lusting While Loathing: Parallel Counterdriving of Wanting and Liking," *Psychological Science* 21(1) (2010): 118–25.

123 **buy a larger quantity:** B. Wansink, R. J. Kent, and S. Hoch, "An Anchoring and Adjustment Model of Purchase Quantity Decisions," *Journal of Marketing Research* (1998): 71–81. For a more general discussion of how "scarcity" increases perceived value (of the scarce item), see ch. 7, "Scarcity," of Robert Cialdini's excellent book *Influence: Science and Practice*, vol. 4 (Boston: Pearson Education, 2009). (The book can be accessed at www.iiit.ac.in/~bipin/files/Dawkins/July/Robert%20Cialdini%20-%20Influence%252C%20 Science%20and%20Practice.pdf.) See also A. R. Pratkanis and P. H. Farquhar, "A Brief

History of Research on Phantom Alternatives: Evidence for Seven Empirical General-izations About Phantoms," *Basic and Applied Social Psychology* 13(1) (1992): 103–22.

123 ***Psychological reactance:*** J. W. Brehm, *A Theory of Psychological Reactance* (Oxford, UK: Academic Press, 1966).

123 **being overly controlling:** Controlling others may lead to anger, which has been shown to lead to the desire for control by Lemay et al. (2012). So trying to control oth-ers may spur reciprocal desire for control by these others; E. P. Lemay Jr., N. C. Overall, and M. S. Clark, "Experiences and Interpersonal Consequences of Hurt Feelings and Anger," *Journal of Personality and Social Psychology* 103(6) (2012): 982.

124 **participants high and low in need for control:** Technically, participants' "need for power" was manipulated in the study, but for all practical purposes, the need for power is the same thing as the need for control. See E. M. Fodor and D. P. Wick, "Need for Power and Affective Response to Negative Audience Reaction to an Extemporaneous Speech," *Journal of Research in Personality* 43(5) (2009): 721–26. For conceptually compatible results, see K. L. Sommer et al., "Sex and Need for Power as Predictors of Reactions to Disobedience," *Social Influence* 7(1) (2012): 1–20.

124 **we make our best decisions:** See work by Charlan Nemeth and colleagues, e.g., C. J. Nemeth, and M. Ormiston, "Create Idea Generation: Harmony Versus Stimulation," *European Journal of Social Psychology*, 37(3) (2007): 524–35, and C. J. Nemeth et al., "The Liberating Role of Conflict in Group Creativity: A Study in Two Countries," *Eu-ropean Journal of Social Psychology* 34(4) (2004): 365–74. For a reader-friendly review of this literature, see www.newyorker.com/magazine/2012/01/30/groupthink. For re-lated findings on how exposure to diverse views improves quality of decisions, see K. W. Phillips, K. A. Liljenquist, and M. A. Neale, "Is the Pain Worth the Gain? The Ad-vantages and Liabilities of Agreeing with Socially Distinct Newcomers," *Personality & Social Psychology Bulletin* 35(3) (2009): 336–50.

125 **desire to achieve outcomes controls you:** Such a desire parallels what Prof. Robert Vallerand of the Université du Québec à Montréal calls "obsessive" (versus harmoni-ous) passion. He discusses the difference between obsessive and harmonious passion and why the latter is preferable in many articles, including this review piece: R. J. Val-lerand et al., "Les Passions de l'Ame: On Obsessive and Harmonious Passion," *Journal of Personality and Social Psychology* 85(4) (2003): 756–67. His perspectives are also summarized in a talk that he gave in 2012, which can be accessed at www.youtube .com/watch?v=kulUtp0KyiQ (the talk can also be accessed by Googling "Robert Valle-rand talk").

125 **being in an overcrowded room:** J. M. Burger, J. A. Oakman, and N. G. Bullard, "De-sire for Control and the Perception of Crowding," *Personality and Social Psychology Bulletin* 9(3) (1983): 475–79.

125 **salespeople were more dissatisfied:** R. R. Mullins et al., "You Don't Always Get What You Want, and You Don't Always Want What You Get: An Examination of Control-Desire for Control Congruence in Transactional Relationships," *The Journal of Applied Psychology* 100(4) (2014): 1073–88.

125 **their blood pressure shoots up:** S. Watanabe, M. Iwanaga, and Y. Ozeki, "Effects of Controllability and Desire for Control on Coping and Stress Responses," *Japanese Journal of Health Psychology* 15(1) (2002): 32–40.

125 **when life doesn't go according to plan:** See A. Brouillard, S. Lapierre, and M. Alain, "Le bonheur et ses relations avec le désir de contrôle et la perception de contrôle," *Re-vue Québécoise de Psychologie* 20(2) (1999): 223–40, and C. Amoura et al., "Desire for Control, Perception of Control: Their Impact on Autonomous Motivation and Psycho-logical Adjustment," *Motivation and Emotion* 38(3) (2014): 323–35.

126 **drive more rashly:** T. B. Hammond and M. S. Horswill, "The Influence of Desire for

Control on Drivers' Risk-Taking Behaviour," *Transportation Research Part F: Traffic Psychology and Behaviour* 4(4) (2001): 271–77.

126 **lose more money in gambling contexts:** J. M. Burger and D. A. Schnerring, "The Effects of Desire for Control and Extrinsic Rewards on the Illusion of Control and Gambling," *Motivation and Emotion* 6(4) (1982): 329–35.

126 **more likely to believe in superstitions:** G. Keinan, "The Effects of Stress and Desire for Control on Superstitious Behavior," *Personality and Social Psychology Bulletin* 28(1) (2002): 102–8. Along similar lines, the famous psychoanalyst Carl Jung has suggested that people undergoing trauma (such as Europeans after the Second World War) may indulge in delusionary beliefs in order to gain perceived control over chaotic life situations. See C. G. Jung, *Flying Saucers: A Modern Myth of Things Seen in the Sky* (Psychology Press, 2014).

126 **being obsessed . . . has a negative impact:** T. Curran et al., "The Psychology of Passion: A Meta-analytical Review of a Decade of Research on Intrapersonal Outcomes," *Motivation and Emotion* (2015): 1–25; R. J. Vallerand, "On Passion for Life Activities: The Dualistic Model of Passion," *Advances in Experimental Social Psychology* 42 (2010): 97–193. For a review of the topic, see Vallerand et al., "Les Passions de l'Ame."

126 **receiving a free dollar:** T. D. Wilson et al., "The Pleasures of Uncertainty: Prolonging Positive Moods in Ways People Do Not Anticipate," *Journal of Personality and Social Psychology* 88(1) (2005): 5–21. For related research, see G. S. Berns et al., "Predictability Modulates Human Brain Response to Reward," *The Journal of Neuroscience* 21(8) (2001): 2793–98; J. Vosgerau, K. Wertenbroch, and Z. Carmon, "Indeterminacy and Live Television," *Journal of Consumer Research* 32(4) (2006): 487–95, and A. Valenzuela, B. Mellers, and J. Strebel, "Pleasurable Surprises: A Cross-cultural Study of Consumer Responses to Unexpected Incentives," *Journal of Consumer Research* 36(5) (2010): 792–805.

127 ***Curious?:*** T. Kashdan, *Curious?* (New York: HarperCollins e-books, 2014).

127 **Can intensify negative feelings:** B. A. Mellers and I. Ritov, "How Beliefs Influence the Relative Magnitude of Pleasure and Pain," *Journal of Behavioral Decision Making* 23(4) (2010): 369–82.

127 **time scarcity . . . is a major happiness killer:** T. Kasser and K. M. Sheldon, "Time Affluence as a Path Toward Personal Happiness and Ethical Business Practice: Empirical Evidence from Four Studies," *Journal of Business Ethics* 84(2) (2009): 243–55. For a reader-friendly summary of how time scarcity lowers happiness and increases stress, see B. Schulte, *Overwhelmed: How to Work, Love, and Play When No One Has the Time* (New York: Macmillan, 2015).

127 **the more successful . . . the more time scarcity:** S. E. DeVoe and J. Pfeffer, "When Time Is Money: The Effect of Hourly Payment on the Evaluation of Time," *Organizational Behavior and Human Decision Processes* 104(1) (2007): 1–13; for related findings, see D. S. Hamermesh and J. Lee, "Stressed Out on Four Continents: Time Crunch or Yuppie Kvetch?," *The Review of Economics and Statistics* 89(2) (2007): 374–83, and W. Ng et al., "Affluence, Feelings of Stress, and Well-being," *Social Indicators Research* 94(2) (2009): 257–71. For a reader-friendly summary of the importance of time abundance for well-being, see www.bostonglobe.com/ideas/2012/09/08/how-make-time-expand/26nkSfyQPEetCXXoFeZEZM/story.html. The article can be accessed by Googling "How to make time expand Boston Globe."

127 **Findings from a recent study:** S. E. DeVoe and J. Pfeffer, "Time Is Tight: How Higher Economic Value of Time Increases Feelings of Time Pressure," *Journal of Applied Psychology* 96(4) (2011): 665–76.

127 **tend to feel more time abundant:** C. Mogilner, Z. Chance, and M. I. Norton, "Giving Time Gives You Time," *Psychological Science* 23(10) (2012): 1233–38.

128 **leading to time affluence:** M. Rudd, K. D. Vohs, and J. Aaker, "Awe Expands People's Perception of Time, Alters Decision Making, and Enhances Well-being," *Psychological Science* 23(10) (2012): 1130–36.

129 **Desirability of Control Scale:** J. M. Burger and H. M. Cooper, "The Desirability of Control," *Motivation and Emotion* 3(4) (1979): 381–93.

132 **Maximizer-Satisficer Scale:** B. Schwartz et al., "Maximizing Versus Satisficing: Happiness Is a Matter of Choice," *Journal of Personality and Social Psychology* 83(5) (2002): 1178–97.

134 **Jointly Interpreting:** I arrived at this "joint interpretation" based on my understanding of these scales, as well as on my conversation with Jerry Burger, after I interviewed him for my Coursera course. As of Jan. 1, 2016, I hadn't managed to edit in my interview with Jerry Burger in the Coursera course (I conducted my interview too late). But I hope to include an excerpt from the interview in "Version 2.0" of the course.

135 **Low control-seeking tendencies:** Being too low on desirability of control is just as detrimental for happiness as being too high on it, particularly in circumstances where perceived control is high. For more on the topic, see G. W. Evans, D. H. Shapiro, and M. A. Lewis, "Specifying Dysfunctional Mismatches Between Different Control Dimensions," *British Journal of Psychology* 84(2) (1993): 255–73.

Chapter 4B: The Fourth Habit of the Highly Happy: Gaining Internal Control

137 **tendency to overpredict enjoyment from vacations:** T. R. Mitchell et al., "Temporal Adjustments in the Evaluation of Events: The 'Rosy View,'" *Journal of Experimental Social Psychology* 33(4) (1997): 421–48. For related findings, see L. Van Boven and L. Ashworth, "Looking Forward, Looking Back: Anticipation Is More Evocative than Retrospection," *Journal of Experimental Psychology: General* 136(2) (2007): 289.

137 **we selectively reminisce about the positive events:** Mitchell et al. (1997) offer this as one of the reasons for the "rosy view" effect; see Mitchell et al., "Temporal Adjustments in the Evaluation of Events."

137 **we expect weekends to be:** R. Raghunathan and A. Mukherjee, "Hope to Enjoy Is More Enjoyed than Hope Enjoyed," unpublished manuscript, University of Texas at Austin, 2011.

137 **heart attacks are more common:** See www.drsinatra.com/heart-attack-risk-factors-rise-on-mondays; see also www.nytimes.com/2006/03/14/health/14real.html?_r=0.

137 **we tend to think of them in undiluted terms:** T. Mitchell and L. Thompson, "A Theory of Temporal Adjustments of the Evaluation of Events: Rosy Prospection and Rosy Retrospection," *Advances in Managerial Cognition and Organizational Information Processing* 5 (1994): 85–114. The idea that we think of both distant (vs. near) future and past events in "undiluted" terms is consistent with something called "Construal Level Theory" (or CLT for short), advanced by Yaacov Trope and Nira Liberman; N. Liberman and Y. Trope, "The Role of Feasibility and Desirability Considerations in Near and Distant Future Decisions: A Test of Temporal Construal Theory," *Journal of Personality and Social Psychology* 75(1) (1998): 5. For a review of CLT, see Y. Trope and N. Liberman, "Construal-Level Theory of Psychological Distance," *Psychological Review* 117(2) (2010): 440.

137 **brain can't fully tell the difference:** It is because our brain can't tell the difference between imagination and reality that visualizing works so well, and is routinely used to improve the skill levels in sports and other fields (e.g., music); see http://drdavidhamilton.com/visualisation-alters-the-brain-body/, and http://newhopeoutreach.wordpress.com/related-articles/recovery-from-abuse/healing-emotional-memories/real-or-imagined-the-brain-doesnt-know/.

137 **thoughts . . . have . . . influence over . . . feelings:** I. J. Roseman, "Appraisal Determi-

nants of Discrete Emotions," *Cognition & Emotion* 5(3) (1991): 161–200; A. Ortony, G. L. Clore, and A. Collins, *The Cognitive Structure of Emotions* (Cambridge, UK: Cambridge University Press, 1990). Some of my own research is based on what is called "cognitive theories of affect," according to which feelings are often the product of thoughts; see R. Raghunathan and M. T. Pham, "All Negative Moods Are Not Equal: Motivational Influences of Anxiety and Sadness on Decision Making," *Organizational Behavior and Human Decision Processes* 79(1) (1999): 56–77, and R. Raghunathan, M. T. Pham, and K. P. Corfman, "Informational Properties of Anxiety and Sadness, and Displaced Coping," *Journal of Consumer Research* 32(4) (2006): 596–601.

137 **In one study:** I. J. Roseman, M. S. Spindel, and P. E. Jose, "Appraisals of Emotion-Eliciting Events: Testing a Theory of Discrete Emotions," *Journal of Personality and Social Psychology* 59(5) (1990): 899–915.

139 **you feel frazzled:** A. F. Arnsten, "Enhanced: The Biology of Being Frazzled," *Science* 280(5370) (1998): 1711–12.

139 **even children as young as two:** T. J. Gaensbauer, "Regulation of Emotional Expression in Infants from Two Contrasting Caretaking Environments," *Journal of the American Academy of Child Psychiatry* 21(2) (1982): 163–70; see also J. J. Campos, R. G. Campos, and K. C. Barrett, "Emergent Themes in the Study of Emotional Development and Emotion Regulation," *Developmental Psychology* 25(3) (1989): 394–402.

140 **more mature and productive fashion:** I arrive at this conclusion based on the logic that the quality of our decisions (including those involving others) is better when our "executive functioning" isn't impaired in any way, and numerous studies show that executive functioning is impaired by stress and negative feelings. See A. F. Arnsten, "Stress Signalling Pathways That Impair Prefrontal Cortex Structure and Function," *Nature Reviews Neuroscience* 10(6) (2009): 410–22. For a more general, and eminently readable overview of this topic, see D. Rock, *Your Brain at Work* (New York: Harper Business, 2009), 120.

141 **retaining the keys to one's happiness:** Aristotle, in articulating what he called the "principle of moderation," was seemingly referring to this very idea of internal control. "Anybody can become angry—that's easy," he said, "but to be angry with the right person and to the right degree and at the right time and for the right purpose, and in the right way . . . that's hard." Source: http://thinkexist.com/quotation/anyone_can _become_angry-that_is_easy-but_to_be/12809.html.

141 **we seek external control:** The idea that internal (or self) control and external control are compensatory is implicit in several scholarly articles, including Astin and Shapiro (1997, 68). In discussing this idea, these authors refer to a quote by a participant in one of their studies. The quote, "I don't think I have enough self-control to let go of (external) control . . . ," suggests that one needs to have sufficient internal control to let go of external control; J. A. Astin and D. H. Shapiro, "Measuring the Psychological Construct of Control: Applications to Transpersonal Psychology," *Journal of Transpersonal Psychology* 29 (1997): 63–72. See also Easterline (1992), who finds that techniques such as meditation, which enable one to gain a greater internal control, help lower the desire for external control; B. Easterline, "Measuring Stress and Control in Meditators Through Trait, State, and In Vivo Experience Sampling," unpublished doctoral dissertation. California Institute of Integral Studies, 1992.

142 **lack of control over their feelings:** J. J. Kacen, "Phenomenological Insights in Mood and Mood-Related Consumer Behaviors," *Advances in Consumer Research* 21 (1994): 519. The article can be accessed at www.acrwebsite.org/search/view-conference-pro ceedings.aspx?Id=7648.

142 **belief in God gives . . . vicarious control:** M. Pollner, "Divine Relations, Social Relations, and Well-being," *Journal of Health and Social Behavior* (1989): 92–104.

142 **subscribe to superstitions:** G. Keinan, "The Effects of Stress and Desire for Control on Superstitious Behavior," *Personality and Social Psychology Bulletin* 28(1) (2002): 102–8.

142 **self-confidence is key:** S. C. Huang, Y. Zhang, and S. M. Broniarczyk, "So Near and Yet So Far: The Mental Representation of Goal Progress," *Journal of Personality and Social Psychology* 103(2) (2012): 225–41.

143 **self-serving biases:** For a review of the self-serving bias, see W. K. Campbell and C. Sedikides, "Self-threat Magnifies the Self-serving Bias: A Meta-analytic Integration," *Review of General Psychology* 3(1) (1999): 23–43.

143 **higher desire for control:** J. M. Burger and L. T. Hemans, "Desire for Control and the Use of Attribution Processes," *Journal of Personality* 56(3) (1988): 531–46.

143 **make you feel good:** S. E. Taylor and J. D. Brown, "Illusion and Well-being: A Social Psychological Perspective on Mental Health," *Psychological Bulletin* 103(2) (1988): 193.

143 **In the context of negotiations:** L. Babcock and G. Loewenstein, "Explaining Bargaining Impasse: The Role of Self-serving Biases," *The Journal of Economic Perspectives* (1997): 109–26. For a related discussion of how the self-serving bias could lead to myopia in the context of organizational decisions, see L. Larwood and W. Whittaker, "Managerial Myopia: Self-serving Biases in Organizational Planning," *Journal of Applied Psychology* 62(2) (1977): 194–98. For a broader review of how overly positive beliefs lead to bad decisions, see B. Ehrenreich, *Bright-Sided: How the Relentless Promotion of Positive Thinking Has Undermined America* (New York: Macmillan, 2009).

144 **in project planning:** Ehrenreich, *Bright-Sided.*

144 **aren't pleasant to hang out with:** C. R. Colvin, J. Block, and D. C. Funder, "Overly Positive Self-evaluations and Personality: Negative Implications for Mental Health," *Journal of Personality and Social Psychology* 68(6) (1995): 1152. For related research, people dislike those who engage in "bragging" (which is presumably associated with the tendency to engage in self-serving bias), see I. Scopelliti, G. Loewenstein, and J. Vosgerau, "You Call It 'Self-exuberance'; I Call It 'Bragging': Miscalibrated Predictions of Emotional Responses to Self-promotion," *Psychological Science* 26(6) (2015): 903–14.

144 **"situation selection":** For a review of various emotion regulation tactics, see K. N. Ochsner and J. J. Gross, "The Cognitive Control of Emotion," *Trends in Cognitive Sciences* 9(5) (2005): 242–49.

144 **lowers their intensity:** M. D. Lieberman et al., "Putting Feelings into Words: Affect Labeling Disrupts Amygdala Activity in Response to Affective Stimuli," *Psychological Science* 18(5) (2007): 421–28

144 **most people predict:** M. D. Lieberman et al., "Subjective Responses to Emotional Stimuli During Labeling, Reappraisal, and Distraction," *Emotion* 11(3) (2011): 468–80.

144 *ruminating* **about them:** Ruminating about—or "overthinking"—negative emotions does intensify them; see S. Nolen-Hoeksema, "The Role of Rumination in Depressive Disorders and Mixed Anxiety/Depressive Symptoms," *Journal of Abnormal Psychology* 109(3) (2000): 504–11.

145 **lowers the intensity of the feelings:** Lieberman et al., "Putting Feelings into Words."

145 **cognitive reappraisal:** Cognitive reappraisals form the foundation of perhaps the most effective approach for treating depressions—Cognitive Behavioral Therapy (or CBT). For findings that support the idea that emotions can be regulated by conscious thought, see A. S. Heller et al., "Reduced Capacity to Sustain Positive Emotion in Major Depression Reflects Diminished Maintenance of Fronto-striatal Brain Activation," *Proceedings of the National Academy of Sciences* 106(52) (2009): 22445–50. For reviews of the field of CBT, see A. C. Butler et al., "The Empirical Status of Cogni-

tive-Behavioral Therapy: A Review of Meta-analyses," *Clinical Psychology Review* 26(1) (2006): 17–31; and K. S. Dobson (ed.), *Handbook of Cognitive-Behavioral Therapies* (New York: Guilford Press, 2009). For a reader-friendly discussion of the basic tenets of CBT and to apply some of the techniques in your own life, see S. C. Hayes and S. Smith, *Get Out of Your Mind and into Your Life: The New Acceptance and Commitment Therapy* (Oakland, CA: New Harbinger Publications, 2005); and M. E. Seligman, *Learned Optimism: How to Change Your Mind and Your Life* (New York: Vintage, 2011).

145 **even if we suppress the feelings:** P. R. Goldin et al., "The Neural Bases of Emotion Regulation: Reappraisal and Suppression of Negative Emotion," *Biological Psychiatry* 63(6) (2008): 577–86.

145 **how much they like us:** A variety of findings show that expressive people are more liked, since it is through expression that we communicate and communication is key to connect with others (which, as we saw in chapter 3A, is a very important goal). For example, less expressive people have fewer social relationships; T. English et al., "Emotion Regulation and Peer-Rated Social Functioning: A 4-Year Longitudinal Study," *Journal of Research in Personality* 46(6) (2012): 780–84; see also I. B. Mauss et al., "Don't Hide Your Happiness! Positive Emotion Dissociation, Social Connectedness, and Psychological Functioning," *Journal of Personality and Social Psychology* 100(4) (2011): 738–48. Suppressing emotions after making a sacrifice also "sours" relationships with romantic partners; E. A. Impett et al., "Suppression Sours Sacrifice: Emotional and Relational Costs of Suppressing Emotions in Romantic Relationships," *Personality and Social Psychology Bulletin* 38(6) (2012): 707–20. Further, those who suppress emotions receive less social support; S. Srivastava et al., "The Social Costs of Emotional Suppression: A Prospective Study of the Transition to College," *Journal of Personality and Social Psychology* 96(4) (2009): 883–97. Those who are expressive, by contrast, elicit greater cooperation from others; R. T. Boone and R. Buck, "Emotional Expressivity and Trustworthiness: The Role of Nonverbal Behavior in the Evolution of Cooperation," *Journal of Nonverbal Behavior* 27(3) (2003): 163–82.

146 **eating right, moving more, and sleeping better:** I've borrowed these terms from Tom Rath's excellent best seller, *Eat Move Sleep*; T. Rath, *Eat Move Sleep: How Small Choices Lead to Big Changes* (Arlington, VA: Missionday, LLC, 2013).

146 **"attention deficit trait" (or ADT):** E. M. Hallowell, "Overloaded Circuits," *Harvard Business Review* (January 2005): 11–15.

146 **as there are dietitians:** Timothy Caulfield discusses some of the causes of this confusion and also provides tips on how to navigate this "complex" environment in his insightful book *The Cure for Everything: Untangling Twisted Messages About Health, Fitness, and Happiness* (Boston: Beacon Press, 2012).

147 **fight with their spouse:** "Does Fatty Food Impact Marital Stress?," *Science Daily*, April 24, 2012, accessed at: www.sciencedaily.com/releases/2012/04/120424095502.htm.

147 **increases the chances of early death:** I. M. Lee et al., "Effect of Physical Inactivity on Major Non-communicable Diseases Worldwide: An Analysis of Burden of Disease and Life Expectancy," *The Lancet* 380(9838) (2012): 219–29.

147 **sitting is just as bad as smoking:** A number of studies have shown this, including P. Katzmarzyk et al., "Sitting Time and Mortality from All Causes, Cardiovascular Disease, and Cancer," *Medicine & Science in Sports & Exerc*ise 41(5) (2009): 998–1005. For popular articles covering this finding, see www.huffingtonpost.com/the-active -times/sitting-is-the-new-smokin_b_5890006.html?ir=India&adsSiteOverride=in; www. dailymail.co.uk/news/article-2001824/Sitting-dangerous-smoking-study-shows.html; www.runnersworld.com/health/sitting-is-the-new-smoking-even-for-runners; and

www.dailymail.co.uk/femail/article-2622916/Work-desk-Then-experts-worrying
-news-Why-sitting-bad-smoking.html.

147 **inactivity kills more people worldwide:** A. A. Thorp et al., "Sedentary Behaviors and Subsequent Health Outcomes in Adults: A Systematic Review of Longitudinal Studies, 1996–2011," *American Journal of Preventive Medicine* 41(2) (2011): 207–15; E. G. Wilmot et al., "Sedentary Time in Adults and the Association with Diabetes, Cardiovascular Disease and Death: Systematic Review and Meta-analysis," *Diabetologia* 55 (2012): 2895–905.

147 **50 percent greater risk of death:** N. Owen, A. Bauman, and W. Brown, "Too Much Sitting: A Novel and Important Predictor of Chronic Disease Risk?," *British Journal of Sports Medicine* 43(2) (2009): 81–83.

147 **getting at least seven hours:** H. P. Van Dongen et al., "The Cumulative Cost of Additional Wakefulness: Dose-Response Effects on Neurobehavioral Functions and Sleep Physiology from Chronic Sleep Restriction and Total Sleep Deprivation," *Sleep* 26(2) (2003): 117–26. The paper can be accessed at: http://www.ncbi.nlm.nih.gov/pubmed/12683469. For a more reader-friendly version of the paper, see http://www.nytimes.com/2011/04/17/magazine/mag-17Sleep-t.html?_r=0.

148 **ninety minutes less sleep than you need:** M. D. Manzar, W. Zannat, and M. E. Hussain, "Sleep and Physiological Systems: A Functional Perspective," *Biological Rhythm Research* 46(2) (2015): 195–206.

148 **unhealthy food choices:** R. K. Golley et al., "Sleep Duration or Bedtime & Quest: Exploring the Association Between Sleep Timing Behaviour, Diet and BMI in Children and Adolescents," *International Journal of Obesity* 37(4) (2013): 546–51.

148 **anxious and irritable:** E. Van der Helm et al., "REM Sleep Depotentiates Amygdala Activity to Previous Emotional Experiences," *Current Biology* 21(23) (2011): 2029–32; L. C. Griffith and M. Rosbash, "Sleep: Hitting the Reset Button," *Nature Neuroscience* 11(2) (2008): 123–24.

Chapter 5A: The Fifth Deadly Happiness "Sin": Distrusting Others

150 **trust and happiness for several years:** See, for reviews, J. F. Helliwell and R. D. Putnam, "The Social Context of Well-being," *Philosophical Transactions—Royal Society of London Series B Biological Sciences* (2004): 1435–46; J. F. Helliwell, "Social Capital, the Economy and Well-Being," in K. Banting, A. Sharpe, and F. St-Hilaire (eds.), *The Review of Economic Performance and Social Progress; The Longest Decade: Canada in the 1990s* (Montreal: Institute for Research on Public Policy, 2001), 43–60; and J. F. Helliwell and S. Wang, *Trust and Well-being* (No. w15911), National Bureau of Economic Research, working paper, 2010. The last paper can be accessed at www.nber.org/papers/w15911. See also R. D. Putnam, *Bowling Alone* (New York: Simon & Schuster, 2001), for an overview of the importance of interpersonal trust for well-being.

150 **the happier the citizens were:** For a review of this work, see J. F. Helliwell and S. Wang, "Trust and Wellbeing," *International Journal of Wellbeing* 1(1) (2011): 42–78, for a discussion of the relevant findings. Y. Tokuda, S. Fujii, and T. Inoguchi, "Individual and Country-Level Effects of Social Trust on Happiness: The Asia Barometer Survey," *Journal of Applied Social Psychology* 40(10) (2010): 2574–93.

151 **the proportion is less than 10 percent:** These stats are from Y. Algan and P. Cahuc, *Trust, Growth and Well-being: New Evidence and Policy Implications* (North Holland: Elsevier, 2013), and *World Happiness Report*, which can be accessed at http://unsdsn.org/wp-content/uploads/2014/02/WorldHappinessReport2013_online.pdf; for a reader-friendly version, see https://psyphz.psych.wisc.edu/web/News/vancouver_sun_10-06.html.

151 **In another study:** This was an informal study conducted by *Reader's Digest* in April

1996 and subsequently covered in *The Economist* the same year (June 22, 1996). Details of the study can be obtained in the following scholarly articles: S. Knack, "Trust, Associational Life and Economic Performance," in J. F. Helliwell and A. Bonikowska (eds.) *The Contribution of Human and Social Capital to Sustained Economic Growth and Well-Being* (Ottawa and Paris: Human Resources Development Canada and OECD, 2001), 172–202; and S. Soroka, J. F. Helliwell, and R. Johnston, "Measuring and Modeling Interpersonal Trust," in F. Kay and R. Johnston (eds.), *Diversity, Social Capital, and the Welfare State* (Vancouver: UBC Press, 2006), 95–132. Results of the study can be accessed at www.rd.com/slideshows/most-honest-cities-lost-wallet-test/#slideshow=slide3, and www.ibtimes.com/most-honest-cities-world-lost-wallet-experiment-infographic-1411124 (this link provides a pictorial depiction of the results). You may consider making a prediction of the number of wallets that would be returned in each of the sixteen cities and compare your predictions against the actual results.

151 **the happier the country:** Helliwell and Wang, *Trust and Well-being.* See also Knack, "Trust, Associational Life and Economic Performance"; and Soroka, Helliwell, and Johnston, "Measuring and Modeling Interpersonal Trust."

151 **you have signed up for a study:** There are many different variants of the "trust game." For an overview of the game's setup, and for a discussion of the role of trust, see M. Kosfeld et al., "Oxytocin Increases Trust in Humans," *Nature* 435 (2005): 673–76. Some other papers that use a similar setup include: D. J. De Quervain, et al., "The Neural Basis of Altruistic Punishment," *Science* 305(5688) (2004): 1254–58; C. Camerer and K. Weigelt, "Experimental Tests of a Sequential Equilibrium Reputation Model," *Econometrica* 56(1) (1988): 1–36; E. Fehr, G. Kirchsteiger, and A. Riedl, "Does Fairness Prevent Market Clearing? An Experimental Investigation," *The Quarterly Journal of Economics* 108(2) (1993): 437–59; and I. Bohnet and R. Zeckhauser, "Trust, Risk and Betrayal," *Journal of Economic Behavior & Organization* 55(4) (2004): 467–84.

152 **95 percent . . . *don't* walk away:** See www.theguardian.com/science/2012/jul/15/interview-dr-love-paul-zak; for a review of this research, see P. J. Zak, *The Moral Molecule: The New Science of What Makes Us Good or Evil* (New York: Random House, 2013); for Paul Zak's TED talk: www.ted.com/talks/paul_zak_trust_morality_and _oxytocin?language=en. It should be noted that not all studies have found such a high incidence of "reciprocity" (the tendency to pay back trust with trustworthiness). For example, Berg et al. (1995) report that around 80 percent reciprocated trust with trustworthiness in their studies. Nevertheless, the level of reciprocity documented in the papers is far higher than what would be expected based on "classical" economic theory's predictions. J. Berg, J. Dickhaut, and K. McCabe, "Trust, Reciprocity, and Social History," *Games and Economic Behavior* 10(1) (1995): 122–42, who call it the "investment game."

152 **people who are trusted . . . reciprocate . . . trust:** Berg, Dickhaut, and McCabe, "Trust, Reciprocity, and Social History"; W. D. Creed and R. E. Miles, "Trust in Organizations," in *Trust in Organizations: Frontiers of Theory and Research* (Thousand Oaks, CA: Sage, 1996), 16–38; K. A. McCabe, S. J. Rassenti, and V. L. Smith, "Reciprocity, Trust, and Payoff Privacy in Extensive Form Bargaining," *Games and Economic Behavior* 24(1) (1998): 10–24; D. J. McAllister, "Affect- and Cognition-Based Trust as Foundations for Interpersonal Cooperation in Organizations," *Academy of Management Journal* 38(1) (1995): 24–59; K. A. McCabe, M. L. Rigdon, and V. L. Smith, "Positive Reciprocity and Intentions in Trust Games," *Journal of Economic Behavior & Organization* 52(2) (2003): 267–75; for an overview of how people reciprocate trust with trustworthiness, see H. Gintis et al., "Explaining Altruistic Behavior in Humans," *Evolution and Human Behavior* 24(3) (2003): 153–72. For a more reader-friendly overview of the various strategies leaders can use to motivate their employees (including

trusting them first), see http://99u.com/articles/32883/the-most-important-skill-for -great-leaders-trustworthiness.

152 **"trust molecule":** Although the release of oxytocin has been found to enhance trusting behavior, it's not entirely clear if being trusted necessarily releases oxytocin, although it would seem likely. For more on this topic, see M. Kosfeld et al., "Oxytocin Increases Trust in Humans," *Nature* 435(7042) (2005): 673–76; J. L. Merolla et al., "Oxytocin and the Biological Basis for Interpersonal and Political Trust," *Political Behavior* 35(4) (2013): 753–76; M. Mikolajczak et al., "Oxytocin Not Only Increases Trust When Money Is at Stake, but Also When Confidential Information Is in the Balance," *Biological Psychology* 85(1) (2010): 182–84; for a review of Paul Zak's work, see J. Conlisk, "Professor Zak's Empirical Studies on Trust and Oxytocin," *Journal of Economic Behavior & Organization* 78(1) (2011): 160–66. For a review of this literature, see M. H. Van IJzendoorn and M. J. Bakermans-Kranenburg, "A Sniff of Trust: Meta-analysis of the Effects of Intranasal Oxytocin Administration on Face Recognition, Trust to Ingroup, and Trust to Out-group," *Psychoneuroendocrinology* 37(3) (2012): 438–43.

153 **BFFs:** BFF is an acronym that stands for Best Friends Forever. (If you didn't know this, you should visit social media sites like Facebook more often!)

153 **Karma Kitchen:** For more on Karma Kitchen, see www.karmakitchen.org/index .php?pg=about.

153 **Grameen Bank:** For more on Grameen Bank, see www.grameenfoundation.org/.

153 **an incredible 98 percent:** This statistic is from S. M. Covey, G. Link, and R. R. Merrill, *Smart Trust: Creating Prosperity, Energy, and Joy in a Low-Trust World* (New York: Simon & Schuster, 2012).

153 **Zappos:** Information and details about Zappos are from T. Hsieh, *Delivering Happiness* (New York: Business Plus, 2010), 147.

154 **ranking eighty-sixth in *Fortune*'s 2014 list:** Source: http://fortune.com/best-com panies/zappos-com-38/.

154 **because of our hardwired cynicism:** For more on this topic, see I. Bohnet and R. Zeckhauser, "Trust, Risk and Betrayal," *Journal of Economic Behavior & Organization* 55(4) (2004): 467–84; C. A. Holt and S. K. Laury, "Risk Aversion and Incentive Effects," *American Economic Review* 92(5) (2002): 1644–55; E. Fehr and K. M. Schmidt, "A Theory of Fairness, Competition, and Cooperation," *Quarterly Journal of Economics* 114(3) (1999): 817–68; J. Haidt, *The Happiness Hypothesis: Finding Modern Truth in Ancient Wisdom* (New York: Basic Books, 2006). See p. 29 of the book, in which Haidt notes: "The cost of missing a cue that signals food is low; odds are there are other fish in the sea, and one mistake won't lead to starvation. The cost of missing the sign of a nearby predator, however, can be catastrophic."

155 ***The Truth About Trust:*** D. DeSteno, *The Truth About Trust: How It Determines Success in Life, Love, Learning, and More* (New York: Penguin, 2014). For journal articles on how trust involves risk-reward trade-offs, see T. K. Das and B. S. Teng, "Between Trust and Control: Developing Confidence in Partner Cooperation in Alliances," *Academy of Management Review* 23(3) (1998): 491–512. L. Strickland, "Surveillance and Trust," *Journal of Personality* 26(2) (1958): 200–215.

156 **wonderful to inhabit such a world?:** A number of papers have discussed how important trust is for well-being, including the ones mentioned at the beginning of the chapter. For a more reader-friendly perspective on the topic, see Covey, Link, and Merrill, *Smart Trust*; and S. M. Covey, *The Speed of Trust: The One Thing That Changes Everything* (New York: Simon & Schuster, 2006).

156 **tend to reciprocate the trust:** Berg, Dickhaut, and McCabe, "Trust, Reciprocity, and Social History"; Creed and Miles, "Trust in Organizations"; McCabe, Rassenti, and Smith, "Reciprocity, Trust, and Payoff Privacy in Extensive Form Bargaining"; McAl-

lister, "Affect-and Cognition-Based Trust as Foundations for Interpersonal Cooperation in Organizations"; McCabe, Rigdon, and Smith, "Positive Reciprocity and Intentions in Trust Games"; for an overview of how people reciprocate trust with trustworthiness, see H. Gintis et al., "Explaining Altruistic Behavior in Humans," *Evolution and Human Behavior* 24(3) (2003): 153–72.

157 *five* **trustworthy behaviors:** J. Gottman, and N. Silver, *The Seven Principles for Making Marriage Work: A Practical Guide from the Country's Foremost Relationship Expert* (New York: Harmony, 2015).

158 **found in a set of studies:** R. Raghunathan, and E. J. Han, "Default Social Cynicism: Asymmetries in the Fundamental Attribution Error," working paper, University of Texas at Austin, 2014.

162 **Interpersonal Trust Scale:** The items in the scale have been adapted from J. Rotter, "A New Scale for the Measurement of Interpersonal Trust," *Journal of Personality* (1967).

164 *Smart Trust:* Covey, Link, and Merrill, *Smart Trust.*

Chapter 5B: The Fifth Habit of the Highly Happy: Exercising "Smart Trust"

166 *more trustworthy than we give them credit:* Several findings that I reviewed in the last chapter provide support for this conclusion, including those from the "wallet drop" studies as well as those from the "trust game" studies.

166 **we are surrounded by negative news:** According to this article, "bad news outweighs good news by as much as seventeen negative news reports for every one good news report": www.psychologytoday.com/blog/wired-success/201012/why-we-love-bad-news. Media stories continue to be negative (or have become increasingly negative) despite lower rates of crime: http://positivenews.org.uk/2015/culture/media/17119/traditional-media-questioning-focus-negative-news-claims-radio-documentary/. Media focuses more on negative (vs. positive) news in the financial sector: https://reutersinstitute.politics.ox.ac.uk/sites/default/files/Media%20Coverage%20of%20Banking%20and%20Financial%20News.pdf. See, for a review, B. Glassner, *The Culture of Fear: Why Americans Are Afraid of the Wrong Things: Crime, Drugs, Minorities, Teen Moms, Killer Kids, Mutant Microbes, Plane Crashes, Road Rage, & So Much More* (New York: Basic Books, 2010).

166 **Coursera course:** You can see excerpts of my interview with Professor Helliwell on www.coursera.org/course/happiness.

166 **guess how many:** How many wallets would you guess would be returned? For a discussion of this "study" and implications for societal well-being, see excerpts of my interview with Professor Helliwell at https://www.coursera.org/learn/happiness/lecture/CzjbL/week-5-video-4-perceived-vs-actual-trust.

167 **when in fact . . . 95 percent do:** To do a similar informal test on yourself to see how (dis) trusting you are, visit www.rd.com/slideshows/most-honest-cities-lost-wallet-test/.

167 **I had been cheated:** Overall, it appears that we remember past negative events better than positive ones (see www.nytimes.com/2012/03/24/your-money/why-people-remember-negative-events-more-than-positive-ones.html?_r=0 for a reader-friendly review of relevant research), perhaps because negative events are more diagnostic for our survival; S. E. Taylor, "Asymmetrical Effects of Positive and Negative Events: The Mobilization-Minimization Hypothesis," *Psychological Bulletin* 110(1) (1991): 67. However, this tendency seems to become less pronounced as we age, which may be one reason why we become happier with age (particularly after fifty or so); see M. Mather and L. L. Carstensen, "Aging and Motivated Cognition: The Positivity Effect in Attention and Memory," *Trends in Cognitive Sciences* 9(10) (2005): 496–502; Deidlitz and Diener suggest that happier people have better memory for positive (vs. negative)

events, which I guess would make me an unhappy person—except that I believe I don't have better memory for all negative (vs. positive) events: I selectively have better memory for negative events in which I believe I have been *cheated*. L. Seidlitz and E. Diener, "Memory for Positive Versus Negative Life Events: Theories for the Differences Between Happy and Unhappy Persons," *Journal of Personality and Social Psychology* 64(4) (1993): 654.

167 **aren't necessarily set in stone:** The idea that people's propensities aren't set in stone is perhaps one of the more fundamental tenets of social psychology, with researchers believing that the "context" is a more powerful determinant of people's attitudes and behaviors. This belief is rooted in a number of findings, including the famous "obedience" studies conducted by Stanley Milgram in the 1960s, in which he showed that regular people like you and me, under the guise of helping others learn a task (e.g., word associations), could be persuaded to administer severe shocks to them. The so-called broken window theory, which has its basis on a set of studies conducted by Phillip Zimbardo, too, is testament to the idea that people's propensities are not set in stone. S. Milgram, "Behavioral Study of Obedience," *The Journal of Abnormal and Social Psychology* 67(4) (1963): 371–78; for a review of Zimbardo's famous studies, see P. Zimbardo, *The Lucifer Effect: Understanding How Good People Turn Evil* (New York: Random House, 2007).

168 *bastards* **to refer to such people:** This is from a TED talk by Paul Zak, which can be accessed at www.youtube.com/watch?v=rFAdlU2ETjU.

168 **"smart trust":** I decided to use this term before I came across the book by Covey and his colleagues by the same name. S. M. Covey, G. Link, and R. R. Merrill, *Smart Trust: Creating Prosperity, Energy, and Joy in a Low-Trust World* (New York: Simon & Schuster, 2012).

000 **Among the least trusting:** See ch. 5, "Power and Money," in D. DeSteno, *The Truth About Trust: How It Determines Success in Life, Love, Learning, and More* (New York: Penguin, 2014).

170 **corrupts our moral uprightness:** P. K. Piff et al., "Higher Social Class Predicts Increased Unethical Behavior," Proceedings of the National Academy of Sciences 109(11) (2012): 4086–91. For related research, see S. Côté, P. K. Piff, and R. Willer, "For Whom Do the Ends Justify the Means? Social Class and Utilitarian Moral Judgment," *Journal of Personality and Social Psychology* 104(3) (2013): 490–503; P. K. Piff et al., "Having Less, Giving More: The Influence of Social Class on Prosocial Behavior," *Journal of Personality and Social Psychology* 99(5) (2010): 771–84; for reviews, see: M. W. Kraus et al., "Social Class, Solipsism, and Contextualism: How the Rich Are Different from the Poor," *Psychological Review* 119(3) (2012): 546–72; P. K. Piff, "Wealth and the Inflated Self: Class, Entitlement, and Narcissism," *Personality and Social Psychology Bulletin* 40(1) (2014): 34–43. Paul Piff's TED talk on the topic can be accessed at www.youtube.com/watch?v=bJ8Kq1wucsk. For a particularly moving, albeit apocryphal, depiction of the greater-than-expected generosity of the poor, see www.youtube.com/watch?v=AUBTAdI7zuY (which can be accessed by Googling "How does a homeless man spend $100?").

172 **propagating a cycle of negativity:** Taking revenge, and even thoughts of taking revenge, would have lowered my own well-being as well; see M. E. McCullough et al., "Vengefulness: Relationships with Forgiveness, Rumination, Well-being, and the Big Five," *Personality and Social Psychology Bulletin* 27(5) (2001): 601–10.

173 *The How of Happiness:* S. Lyubomirsky, *The How of Happiness: A Scientific Approach to Getting the Life You Want* (New York: Penguin, 2008).

173 **mental and physical health:** For reviews, see M. E. McCullough, "Forgiveness: Who Does It and How Do They Do It?," *Current Directions in Psychological Science* 10(6)

(2001): 194–97; M. E. McCullough and C. V. Witvliet, "The Psychology of Forgiveness," *Handbook of Positive Psychology* 2 (2002): 446–55.

173 **women older than sixty-five:** J. Hebl and R. D. Enright, "Forgiveness as a Psychother-apeutic Goal with Elderly Females," *Psychotherapy: Theory, Research, Practice, Training* 30(4) (1993): 658–67.

173 **infidelity from their partners:** J. H. Hall and F. D. Fincham, "Relationship Dissolution Following Infidelity: The Roles of Attributions and Forgiveness," *Journal of Social and Clinical Psychology* 25(5) (2006): 508–22.

174 **point out two things:** Several researchers, including Lyubomirsky, have commented on these two "things"; see pp. 169–79 of Lyubomirsky, *The How of Happiness.*

174 *The Upside of Irrationality:* See ch. 5, "The Case for Revenge," in D. Ariely, *The Up-side of Irrationality: The Unexpected Benefits of Defying Logic at Work and at Home* (New York: Harper, 2010).

175 **elicit trustworthy behavior:** Many of these recommendations derived from recom-mendations for building interpersonal trust in organizations discussed in S. Vangen and C. Huxham, "Nurturing Collaborative Relations: Building Trust in Interorganiza-tional Collaboration," *The Journal of Applied Behavioral Science* 39(1) (2003): 5–31.

175 **the less they will cheat you:** C. Y. Nicholson, L. D. Compeau, and R. Sethi, "The Role of Interpersonal Liking in Building Trust in Long-term Channel Relationships," *Jour-nal of the Academy of Marketing Science* 29(1) (2001): 3–15.

175 **important determinant of liking:** In a study in which I was involved, we explored how greater liking of the company of those with similar opinions—a phenomenon called homophily—can sometimes lead to making worse financial decisions; see B. Gu et al., "The Allure of Homophily in Social Media: Evidence from Investor Responses on Virtual Communities," *Information Systems Research* 25(3) (2014): 604–17; and J. Park et al., "Information Valuation and Confirmation Bias in Virtual Communities: Evidence from Stock Message Boards," *Information Systems Research* 24(4) (2013): 1050–67. For a more general review of how similarity breeds liking, see M. McPherson, L. Smith-Lovin, and J. M. Cook, "Birds of a Feather: Homophily in Social Networks," *Annual Review of Sociology* (2001): 415–44.

175 **warmth . . . competence:** "Warmth/friendliness" and "competence/professionalism" are two dimensions along which most people judge others relatively spontaneously, and often, someone who is perceived to be high on one of these dimensions (say "warmth") is automatically perceived to be low on the other; see S. T. Fiske, A. J. Cuddy, and P. Glick, "Universal Dimensions of Social Cognition: Warmth and Compe-tence," *Trends in Cognitive Sciences* 11(2) (2007): 77–83; and J. Aaker, K. D. Vohs, and C. Mogilner, "Nonprofits Are Seen as Warm and For-profits as Competent: Firm Ste-reotypes Matter," *Journal of Consumer Research* 37(2) (2010): 224–37. In a series of studies that my coauthors Michael Luchs, Rebecca Naylor, and Julie Irwin and I con-ducted, we explored this perceived compensatory relationship (between "doing good," which is correlated with warmth, and "efficacy," which is correlated with competence) in the context of sustainability initiatives; see M. G. Luchs et al., "The Sustainability Liability: Potential Negative Effects of Ethicality on Product Preference," *Journal of Marketing* 74(5) (2010): 18–31.

175 **Warm leaders . . . more trusted:** For a reader-friendly overview of this research, see A. Cuddy, J., M. Kohut, and J. Neffinger, "Connect, Then Lead," *Harvard Business Re-view* 91(7) (2013): 54–61, which can be accessed at: https://hbr.org/2013/07/connect -then-lead.

175 **apologize are better liked:** P. H. Kim et al., "Removing the Shadow of Suspicion: The Effects of Apology Versus Denial for Repairing Competence Versus Integrity-Based

Trust Violations," *Journal of Applied Psychology* 89(1) (2004): 104. See also Y. Xie and S. Peng, "How to Repair Customer Trust After Negative Publicity: The Roles of Competence, Integrity, Benevolence, and Forgiveness," *Psychology & Marketing* 26(7) (2009): 572–89; and A. Vasalou, A. Hopfensitz, and J. V. Pitt, "In Praise of Forgiveness: Ways for Repairing Trust Breakdowns in One-off Online Interactions," *International Journal of Human-Computer Studies* 66(6) (2008): 466–80. See also J. Aaker, S. Fournier, and S. A. Brasel, "When Good Brands Do Bad," *Journal of Consumer Research* 31(1) (2004): 1–16.

176 **either party defecting:** R. Gulati, "Does Familiarity Breed Trust? The Implications of Repeated Ties for Contractual Choice in Alliances," *Academy of Management Journal* 38(1) (1995): 85–112; R. Lewick and B. B. Bunker, "Developing and Maintaining Trust in Work Relationships," *Trust in Organizations: Frontiers of Theory and Reach* (1996): 114–39; R. Axelrod, *The Evolution of Cooperation* (New York: Basic Books, 1984); P. S. Ring, "Processes Facilitating Reliance on Trust in Inter-organizational Networks," *The Formation of Inter-organizational Networks* (1997): 113–45.

176 **proactively trust others first:** D. J. McAllister, "Affect- and Cognition-Based Trust as Foundations for Interpersonal Cooperation in Organizations," *Academy of Management Journal* 38(1) (1995): 24–59.

Chapter 6A: The Sixth Deadly Happiness "Sin": Passionate/Indifferent Pursuit of Passion

183 **fill out a survey:** C. K. Hsee, A. X. Yang, and L. Wang, "Idleness Aversion and the Need for Justifiable Busyness," *Psychological Science* 21(7) (2010): 926–30. For an extension of this work to the context of overworking (and medium maximization), see C. K. Hsee et al., "Overearning," *Psychological Science* 24(6) (2013): 852–59.

184 **took the shape of a Bionicle:** D. Ariely, E. Kamenica, and D. Prelec, "Man's Search for Meaning: The Case of Legos," *Journal of Economic Behavior & Organization* 67(3) (2008): 671–77.

185 *process of working toward outcomes:* For research on how process of working toward goals can be a separate (and more reliable) source of happiness than achieving outcomes, see A. J. Elliot, K. M. Sheldon, and M. A. Church, "Avoidance Personal Goals and Subjective Well-being," *Personality and Social Psychology Bulletin* 23(9) (1997): 915–27; A. J. Elliot and K. M. Sheldon, "Avoidance Personal Goals and the Personality-Illness Relationship," *Journal of Personality and Social Psychology* 75(5) (1998): 1282–99; K. M. Sheldon, "Goal Striving, Need Satisfaction, and Longitudinal Well-being: The Self-concordance Model," *Journal of Personality and Social Psychology* 76(3) (1999): 482–97. See also C. P. Niemiec, R. M. Ryan, and E. L. Deci, "The Path Taken: Consequences of Attaining Intrinsic and Extrinsic Aspirations in Post-college Life," *Journal of Research in Personality* 43(3) (2009): 291–306. For a more reader-friendly summary of this paper, see abcnews.go.com/Health/Healthday/story?id=7658253. For a reader-friendly review of relevant topics, see D. H. Pink, *Drive: The Surprising Truth About What Motivates Us* (New York; Penguin, 2011).

187 **"they lived happily ever after":** For an insightful and useful discussion of some ways to avoid the trap of taking your partner for granted, see ch. 1, "I'll Be Happy When . . . I'm Married to the Right Person," in S. Lyubomirsky, *The Myths of Happiness: What Should Make You Happy, but Doesn't, What Shouldn't Make You Happy, but Does* (New York: Penguin, 2013). For more on the topic of nurturing intimacy in relationships, see J. Gottman, and N. Silver, *The Seven Principles for Making Marriage Work: A Practical Guide from the Country's Foremost Relationship Expert* (New York: Harmony, 2015).

187 **certain outcomes over others:** Our preferences appear to be computed subconsciously—that is, by our neural substrates—often, and perhaps always before we become aware

of our preferences. See P. Shizgal, "On the Neural Computation of Utility: Implications from Studies of Brain Stimulation Reward," in *Well-being: The Foundations of Hedonic Psychology*, D. Kahneman, E. Diener, and N. Schwarz (eds.) (New York: Russell Sage Foundation, 1999), 500–524. For an excellent review of the research on how our preferences (and consequently judgments and decisions) are shaped well before we become aware of them, see D. M. Wegner, *The Illusion of Conscious Will* (Cambridge, MA: MIT Press, 2002). For a summary of the book, see D. M. Wegner, "Precis of the Illusion of Conscious Will," *Behavioral and Brain Sciences* 27(05) (2004): 649–59.

188 **helplessness and depression:** J. M. Ozment and D. Lester," Helplessness and Depression," *Psychological Reports* 82(2) (1998): 434; M. E. Seligman, *Helplessness: On Depression, Development, and Death* (New York: WH Freeman/Times Books/Henry Holt & Co., 1975).

188 **need for consistency:** W. B. Swann, "Identity Negotiation: Where Two Roads Meet," *Journal of Personality and Social Psychology* 53(6) (1987): 1038–51.

Chapter 6B: The Sixth Habit of the Highly Happy: Dispassionate Pursuit of Passion

191 **feel *positive* about it now:** There are a variety of reasons why we grow to look upon past negative events with lower negativity and even a whole lot of positivity. Perhaps the most important reason for this is "post-traumatic growth," which typically leads to a positive transformation in how one sees oneself—as stronger and more capable. See, e.g., R. G. Tedeschi and L. G. Calhoun, *Trauma and Transformation: Growing in the Aftermath of Suffering* (Thousand Oaks, CA: Sage Publications, 1995). Other aspects of such positive transformation include improved relationships, with greater capacity for kindness and compassion, as well as the development of a richer and more satisfying set of worldviews.

191 **become less intense over time:** This phenomenon is related to something called the "immediacy bias," according to which we consider whatever is happening right now (or has occurred in the near past) as having been more intense than a similar event that happened awhile back. This may be why we are prone to saying things like, "This was the best movie I ever watched" or "That was the most horrible traffic jam" more than we perhaps should. L. Van Boven, K. White, and M. Huber, "Immediacy Bias in Emotion Perception: Current Emotions Seem More Intense than Previous Emotions," *Journal of Experimental Psychology: General* 138(3) (2009): 368.

191 **losing money . . . or failing an exam:** Findings show that memory for certain types of negative events—which evoke what's called "cold regret"—last longer. This type of regret arises from the things we wish we had done (e.g., learned how to swim, or proposed to a "soul mate"). "Hot regret," which arises from doing the things we shouldn't have (getting into a drunken brawl, proposing to a "soul mate"—and getting rejected), fades faster with time. T. Gilovich and V. H. Medvec, "The Experience of Regret: What, When, and Why," *Psychological Review* 102(2) (1995): 379–95.

193 **"affective misforecasting":** V. M. Patrick, D. J. MacInnis, and C. W. Park, "Not as Happy as I Thought I'd Be? Affective Misforecasting and Product Evaluations," *Journal of Consumer Research* 33(4) (2007): 479–89.

193 **duration and intensity of our feelings:** T. D. Wilson and D. T. Gilbert, "Affective Forecasting," *Advances in Experimental Social Psychology* 35 (2003): 345–411.

193 **than it turns out to be:** D. T. Gilbert, et al., "Immune Neglect: A Source of Durability Bias in Affective Forecasting," *Journal of Personality and Social Psychology* 75(3) (1998): 617–38. For other explorations into affective misforecasting, see T. D. Wilson et al., "Focalism: A Source of Durability Bias in Affective Forecasting," *Journal of*

Personality and Social Psychology 78(5) (2000): 821–36; and Wilson and Gilbert, "Affective Forecasting."

193 **more intense than it proves to be**: P. Brickman, D. Coates, and R. Janoff-Bulman, "Lottery Winners and Accident Victims: Is Happiness Relative?," *Journal of Personality and Social Psychology* 36(8) (1978): 917–27.

193 **compassionate and kind**: L. G. Calhoun et al., "Parental Bereavement, Rumination, and Posttraumatic Growth," poster session presented at the meeting of the American Psychological Association, Washington, DC, 2000. For a review of this and other positive growth from negative events, see R. G. Tedeschi and L. G. Calhoun, "Posttraumatic Growth: Conceptual Foundations and Empirical Evidence," *Psychological Inquiry* 15(1) (2004): 1–18.

193 **that life often throws at us**: See H. Jordan, *No Such Thing as a Bad Day* (New York: Simon and Schuster, 2001); and C. G. Davis, S. Nolen-Hoeksema, and J. Larson, "Making Sense of Loss and Benefiting from the Experience: Two Construals of Meaning," *Journal of Personality and Social Psychology* 75(2) (1998): 561. See also K. Schultz, *Being Wrong: Adventures in the Margin of Error* (London: Granta Books, 2011), for how failures often pave the way to success.

194 **or at dull office parties**: For how we savor negative experiences, see A. Keinan and R. Kivetz, "Productivity Orientation and the Consumption of Collectable Experiences," *Journal of Consumer Research* 37(6) (2011): 935–50.

194 **we have lived through them**: Tedeschi and Calhoun, *Trauma and Transformation*. For a review of this and other positive growth from negative events, see Tedeschi and Calhoun, "Posttraumatic Growth."

194 **something positive about that experience**: S. Nolen-Hoeksema and C. G. Davis, "Positive Responses to Loss: Perceiving Benefits and Growth," in *Handbook of Positive Psychology*, C. R. Snyder and S. J. Lopez (eds.) (Oxford, UK: Oxford University Press, 2002), 598–606. See also Davis, Nolen-Hoeksema, and Larson, "Making Sense of Loss and Benefiting from the Experience."

194 **lives have changed for the better**: S. E. Taylor, R. R. Lichtman, and J. V. Wood, "Attributions, Beliefs About Control, and Adjustment to Breast Cancer," *Journal of Personality and Social Psychology* 46(3) (1984): 489–502.

196 **placebo effects**: The most cited article on the placebo effect is by Beecher, which appeared in 1955. Although there are some questions about whether the original set of studies conducted by Beecher documented evidence for the placebo effect or some other effects (see, for example, Kienle and Kiene 1997), there is little doubt that the effect is believed to be prevalent, particularly in the medical domain (see Hróbjartsson & Norup 2003). That said, however, there is ongoing debate about the potency and prevalence of the effect (see Hróbjartsson et al. 2001; Moerman et al. 2002; Wampold et al. 2005; and Hróbjartsson et al. 2010). Cites: H. K. Beecher, "The Powerful Placebo," *Journal of the American Medical Association* 159(17) (1955): 1602–6; A. Hróbjartsson and M. Norup, "The Use of Placebo Interventions in Medical Practice—a National Questionnaire Survey of Danish Clinicians," *Evaluation & the Health Professions* 26(2) (2003): 153–65; A. Hróbjartsson and P. C. Gøtzsche, "Is the Placebo Powerless? An Analysis of Clinical Trials Comparing Placebo with No Treatment," *New England Journal of Medicine* 344(21) (2001): 1594–1602; D. E. Moerman and W. B. Jonas, "Deconstructing the Placebo Effect and Finding the Meaning Response," *Annals of Internal Medicine* 136(6) (2002): 471–76; B. E. Wampold et al., "The Placebo Is Powerful: Estimating Placebo Effects in Medicine and Psychotherapy from Randomized Clinical Trials," *Journal of Clinical Psychology* 61(7) (2005): 835–54; A. Hróbjartsson and P. C. Gøtzsche, "Placebo Interventions for All Clinical Conditions," *Cochrane Database of Systematic Reviews* 1(1) (2010).

196 **Consider one study:** L. Vase, M. E. Robinson, G. N. Verne, and D. D. Price, "The Contributions of Suggestion, Desire, and Expectation to Placebo Effects in Irritable Bowel Syndrome Patients: An Empirical Investigation," *Pain* 105(1) (2003): 17–25.

197 **improve your cognitive abilities, it will:** B. Shiv, Z. Carmon, and D. Ariely, "Placebo Effects of Marketing Actions: Consumers May Get What They Pay For," *Journal of Marketing Research* 42(4) (2005): 383–93.

197 **In the context of learning:** L. S. Blackwell, K. H. Trzesniewski, and C. S. Dweck, "Implicit Theories of Intelligence Predict Achievement Across an Adolescent Transition: A Longitudinal Study and an Intervention," *Child Development* 78(1) (2007): 246–63. For a review, see C. Dweck, *Mindset: The New Psychology of Success* (New York: Random House, 2006).

198 **those who hold a spiritual attitude toward life:** A. L. Ferriss, "Religion and the Quality of Life," *Journal of Happiness Studies* 3(3) (2002): 199–215; P. C. Hill and K. I. Pargament, "Advances in the Conceptualization and Measurement of Religion and Spirituality: Implications for Physical and Mental Health Research," *The American Psychologist* 58(1) (2003): 64–74; K. I. Pargament, *The Psychology of Religion and Coping: Theory, Research, Practice* (New York: Guilford Press, 2001); M. Pollner, "Divine Relations, Social Relations, and Well-being," *Journal of Health and Social Behavior* 30(1) (1989): 92–104.

198 **hold a more positive outlook:** F. Segovia et al., "Optimism Predicts Resilience in Repatriated Prisoners of War: A 37-Year Longitudinal Study," *Journal of Traumatic Stress* 25(3) (2012): 330–36. Optimism is important for resilience (the ability to bounce back after setbacks). To assess your resilience, see the resilience scale in B. W. Smith et al., "The Brief Resilience Scale: Assessing the Ability to Bounce Back," *International Journal of Behavioral Medicine* 15(3) (2008): 194–200.

198 **popular TED talk:** David Steindl-Rast's TED talk can be accessed at www.youtube .com/watch?v=UtBsl3j0YRQ (or by Googling "Steindl-Rast TED talk").

199 **"3 good things with a twist":** The exercise is adapted from the "Three good things" exercise devised by the "father of positive psychology," Prof. Martin Seligman. For a description of the "three good things" exercise, which, by the way, had a powerful effect (as many as 94 percent of those who practiced it for a mere fifteen days showed a significant improvement in happiness levels), see M. E. Seligman, *Authentic Happiness: Using the New Positive Psychology to Realize Your Potential for Lasting Fulfillment* (New York: Free Press, 2002).

Chapter 7A: The Seventh Deadly Happiness "Sin": Mind Addiction

201 **prefer Gentleman Y:** R. Raghunathan and S. Huang, "Too Hot to Handle: Post-decisional Revision of Attribute Importance in Affectively-Charged Tasks," working paper, University of Texas at Austin, 2014.

202 **across a variety of contexts:** Ibid.

202 *post hoc rationalization:* The tendency to explain judgments or decisions after (versus before) they are made is particularly intriguing in the case of "split brain" patients—patients whose right and left hemispheres cannot "communicate" with each other (because of a severed corpus callosum, the set of nerves bridging the two sides), because it attests to the nonconscious nature of post hoc rationalizations; e.g., M. S. Gazzaniga, "Organization of the Human Brain," *Science* 245(4921) (1989): 947–52.

203 **appear uninfluenced by feelings:** C. K. Hsee et al., "Lay Rationalism and Inconsistency Between Predicted Experience and Decision," *Journal of Behavioral Decision Making* 16(4) (2003): 257–72.

203 **In one study:** See study 1 of C. K. Hsee, "Value Seeking and Prediction-Decision Inconsistency: Why Don't People Take What They Predict They'll Like the Most?," *Psychonomic Bulletin & Review* 6(4) (1999): 555–61.

203 **often lead us astray:** This is the reason why Sonja Lyubomirsky, in her latest book, *The Myths of Happiness*, recommends scrutinizing, and if necessary, revising, one's lay theories about what does, and what doesn't, lead to happiness; S. Lyubomirsky, *The Myths of Happiness: What Should Make You Happy, but Doesn't, What Shouldn't Make You Happy, but Does* (New York: Penguin, 2013).

204 **five different posters:** See study 1 of T. D. Wilson et al., "Introspecting About Reasons Can Reduce Post-choice Satisfaction," *Personality and Social Psychology Bulletin* 19 (1993): 331–39.

204 **jams and college courses:** T. D. Wilson and J. W. Schooler, "Thinking Too Much: Introspection Can Reduce the Quality of Preferences and Decisions," *Journal of Personality and Social Psychology* 60(2) (1991): 181; for related research, see A. Dijksterhuis, "Think Different: The Merits of Unconscious Thought in Preference Development and Decision Making," *Journal of Personality and Social Psychology* 87(5) (2004): 586; J. W. Payne et al., "Boundary Conditions on Unconscious Thought in Complex Decision Making," *Psychological Science* 19(11) (2008): 1118–23; I. Simonson, "Will I Like a 'Medium' Pillow? Another Look at Constructed and Inherent Preferences," *Journal of Consumer Psychology* 18(3) (2008): 155–69; J. R. Bettman, M. F. Luce, and J. W. Payne, "Preference Construction and Preference Stability: Putting the Pillow to Rest," *Journal of Consumer Psychology* 18(3) (2008): 170–74.

205 **One reason "thinking too much":** Another reason why "thinking too much" lowers happiness is because it lowers our satisfaction with the eventual choice we make. When we deliberate a lot before making a decision, we invariably come to gather more information about all available options, which in turn lowers the satisfaction we derive from the eventual choice we make, because we are more aware of what we are losing out on; see Z. Carmon, K. Wertenbroch, and M. Zeelenberg, "Option Attachment: When Deliberating Makes Choosing Feel Like Losing," *Journal of Consumer Research* 30(1) (2003): 15–29; D. V. Thompson, R. W. Hamilton, and R. T. Rust, "Feature Fatigue: When Product Capabilities Become Too Much of a Good Thing," *Journal of Marketing Research* 42(4) (2005): 431–42.

205 **in our adaptive past:** (Most) emotion researchers would agree that emotions serve the adaptively useful function of quickly steering us to the "right" or "appropriate" judgments, decisions, or actions. For scholarly perspectives on the topic, see R. Plutchik, *Emotion: A Psychoevolutionary Synthesis* (New York: HarperCollins College Division, 1980); J. A. Russell, "A Circumplex Model of Affect," *Journal of Personality and Social Psychology* 39(6) (1980): 1161; N. H. Frijda, P. Kuipers, and E. Ter Schure, "Relations Among Emotion, Appraisal, and Emotional Action Readiness," *Journal of Personality and Social Psychology* 57(2) (1989): 212.

205 **startling demonstration of this idea:** N. Ambady and R. Rosenthal, "Half a Minute: Predicting Teacher Evaluations from Thin Slices of Nonverbal Behavior and Physical Attractiveness," *Journal of Personality and Social Psychology* 64(3) (1993): 431–41; Malcolm Gladwell has an eminently readable piece in *The New Yorker* on the implications of this and other related findings; M. Gladwell, "The Naked Face," *The New Yorker* 5 (2002): 38–49.

205 **In one replication:** R. W. Naylor, "Nonverbal Cues-Based First Impressions: Impression Formation Through Exposure to Static Images," *Marketing Letters* 18(3) (2007): 165–79.

206 **can be very accurate:** This is, as you may know, the main theme of Malcolm Glad-

well's best seller *Blink*. M. Gladwell, *Blink: The Power of Thinking Without Thinking* (New York: Back Bay Books, 2007).

206 **In yet another study:** G. Berns and S. E. Moore, "A Neural Predictor of Cultural Popularity," *Journal of Consumer Psychology* 22(1) (2010): 154–60.

206 **than abstract ones:** See C. K. Hsee, "The Evaluability Hypothesis: An Explanation for Preference Reversals Between Joint and Separate Evaluations of Alternatives," *Organizational Behavior and Human Decision Processes* 67(3) (1996): 247–57.

207 **connecting with others:** This may be why we seek to rationalize something as unquantifiable as "morals" or "ethics"—so that we can come across as "reasonable" people to others; see J. Haidt, "The Emotional Dog and Its Rational Tail: A Social Intuitionist Approach to Moral Judgment," *Psychological Review* 108(4) (2001): 814.

207 **heard of August Kekulé:** The information in this section has been gathered from a variety of online sources, including Wikipedia (see https://en.wikipedia.org/wiki/August _Kekul%C3%A9#cite_note-10), and from A. J. Rocke, *Image and Reality: Kekulé, Kopp, and the Scientific Imagination* (Chicago: University of Chicago Press, 2010), 60–66.

209 **the group whirled by:** From A. J. Rocke, "It Began with a Daydream: The 150th Anniversary of the Kekulé Benzene Structure," *Angewandte Chemie International Edition* 54(1) (2015): 46–50.

210 **seemingly from out of nowhere:** From the jacket cover of *Harry Potter and the Sorcerer's Stone*, in which Rowling claims that "the idea . . . simply fell into my head one day."

210 **generated by the subconscious:** See J. Kluger, "The Spark of Invention," *Time*, Nov. 14, 2013, for a reader-friendly discussion of this idea. The article can be accessed at http://techland.time.com/2013/11/14/the-spark-of-invention/3/, or by Googling "The spark of invention, Time, 2013."

210 **she was a child:** See "The Not Especially Fascinating Life So Far of J. K. Rowling," accessed from http://www.accio-quote.org/articles/1998/autobiography.html on Sept. 18, 2015.

210 **product of the subconscious:** For a reader-friendly discussion of this idea, see J. Lehrer, "The Eureka Hunt," *The New Yorker* 28 (2008): 40–45. (The article can be accessed at www.newyorker.com/magazine/2008/07/28/the-eureka-hunt, or by Googling "Eureka Hunt, The New Yorker.)

211 **our subconscious:** See Wegner, *The Illusion of Conscious Will*. For a summary of the book, see Wegner, "Precis of the Illusion of Conscious Will."

211 **something else altogether:** For a reader-friendly discussion of this idea, see Lehrer, "The Eureka Hunt."

211 **"ideas come from outer space":** Source: www.waldorfhomeschoolers.com/edison-said -ideas-come-from-outer-space-how-that-affects-your-children, accessed on September 18, 2015.

211 **insights he might have had!:** Several studies have similarly documented the role of the subconscious in generating ideas; e.g., Dijksterhuis, "Think Different." But also see the following paper for a discussion of the limits on the ability of the subconscious to generate the best ideas: J. W. Payne et al., "Boundary Conditions on Unconscious Thought in Complex Decision Making," *Psychological Science* 19(11) (2008): 1118–23.

211 *lack of self-awareness:* For an overview of the importance of self-awareness for decision making and for emotional well-being, see R. J. Davidson and S. Begley, *The Emotional Life of Your Brain: How Its Unique Patterns Affect the Way You Think, Feel, and Live—and How You Can Change Them* (New York: Hudson Street Press, 2012).

212 **"expert" meditators . . . have a thicker left prefrontal cortex:** You can check out some other cool findings that Professor Davidson has documented in ibid.

212 **is one of the biggest happiness killers:** For more on this, see ibid.
213 **completely honest with oneself:** Taylor and Brown (1991) argued in their classic paper that some degree of self-delusion may be critical for maintaining "mental health" (or well-being). However, as I mentioned in the Introduction, and as some subsequent inquiries into Taylor and Brown's thesis have revealed (e.g., Colvin and Block 1994), there is some question as to whether and to what extent self-delusion fosters mental health. The topic (of whether self-honesty or self-delusion is better for maintaining mental health) is clearly a complex one, but what can be safely said is that neither is always good. In particular, as Haidt argues in ch. 7, "Uses of Adversity," of his excellent book *The Happiness Hypothesis*, it's important to shield oneself from experiencing a degree of trauma from which one finds it difficult to recover. S. E. Taylor and J. D. Brown, "Positive Illusions and Well-being Revisited: Separating Fact from Fiction"; C. R. Colvin, J. Block, and D. C. Funder, "Overly Positive Self-evaluations and Personality: Negative Implications for Mental Health," *Journal of Personality and Social Psychology* 68(6) (1995): 1152.
214 **such as snakes:** S. Mineka and M. Cook, "Social Learning and the Acquisition of Snake Fear in Monkeys," *Social Learning: Psychological and Biological Perspectives* (1988): 51–73. R. J. McNally, "Preparedness and Phobias: A Review," *Psychological Bulletin* 101(2) (1987): 283; A. Öhman, "Face the Beast and Fear the Face: Animal and Social Fears as Prototypes for Evolutionary Analyses of Emotion," *Psychophysiology* 23(2) (1986): 123–45; A. Öhman and J. J. Soares, "'Unconscious Anxiety': Phobic Responses to Masked Stimuli," *Journal of Abnormal Psychology* 103(2) (1994): 231; A. Öhman and S. Mineka, "The Malicious Serpent: Snakes as a Prototypical Stimulus for an Evolved Module of Fear," *Current Directions in Psychological Science* 12(1) (2003): 5–9; M. Cook and S. Mineka, "Observational Conditioning of Fear to Fear-Relevant Versus Fear-Irrelevant Stimuli in Rhesus Monkeys," *Journal of Abnormal Psychology* 98(4) (1989): 448.
214 **exposed to cat fur:** J. Panksepp, *Affective Neuroscience: The Foundations of Human and Animal Emotions* (Oxford, UK: Oxford University Press, 1998).
214 **piece of art:** This is the opening example in *Blink*, Malcolm Gladwell's best seller.
215 **emotional or "hedonic" one:** The reason relying on feelings and gut instincts in contexts in which our objective is to maximize hedonic—as opposed to functional—consequences is because feelings are more *relevant* in such contexts; see Pham (1998) for findings on this topic. M. T. Pham, "Representativeness, Relevance, and the Use of Feelings in Decision Making," *Journal of Consumer Research* 25(2) (1998): 144–59.
215 **decision based on gut feel:** Payne et al., "Boundary Conditions on Unconscious Thought in Complex Decision Making."
215 **Based on feelings and gut instincts:** Somewhat surprisingly, there has been no work (to the best of my knowledge) on whether people like those (people) better who make their decisions based on thoughtful deliberation (as opposed to feelings/gut instincts).
217 **Self-awareness Scale:** Davidson and Begley, *The Emotional Life of Your Brain.*

Chapter 7B: The Seventh Habit of the Highly Happy: Mindfulness

220 **thoughts, emotions, actions, and goals:** As mentioned in the Introduction, the idea that motivations, cognitions, and emotions are intertwined is well accepted in psychology. As an example of the interlinkages among these three aspects, see R. S. Lazarus, "Cognition and Motivation in Emotion," *American Psychologist* 46(4) (1991): 352. See also, for a compatible view, N. H. Frijda, P. Kuipers, and E. Ter Schure, "Relations Among Emotion, Appraisal, and Emotional Action Readiness," *Journal of Personality and Social Psychology* 57(2) (1989): 212.
221 **unhealthy GATE webs:** S. Lyubomirsky and S. Nolen-Hoeksema, "Effects of Self-

focused Rumination on Negative Thinking and Interpersonal Problem Solving," *Journal of Personality and Social Psychology* 69(1) (1995): 176–90; S. Lyubomirsky and S. Nolen-Hoeksema, "Self-perpetuating Properties of Dysphoric Rumination," *Journal of Personality and Social Psychology* 65(2) (1993): 339–49. For a review, see S. Nolen-Hoeksema, *Eating, Drinking, Overthinking: The Toxic Triangle of Food, Alcohol, and Depression—and How Women Can Break Free* (New York: Henry Holt and Company, 2013).

221 **"habits of the highly happy":** Jettisoning the sin of chasing superiority, in particular, can go a long way toward mitigating the tendency to overthink; as Lyubomirsky notes in *The How of Happiness* (p. 119), "the practice of incessantly comparing ourselves with others is part of the wider-ranging habit of overthinking."

221 **The First Paradox of Mindfulness:** I discussed this and the other two paradoxes of mindfulness with Prof. Shauna Shapiro from Santa Clara University, and much of the information presented here is based on my conversation with her.

222 **Bare attention:** The term "bare attention" was coined by the German-born Sri Lankan Buddhist monk Nyanaponika Thera in the 1960s, and has since been used by several mindfulness scholars, including Jeffrey Schwartz, Shear and Varela, and Weick and Sutcliffe. Nyanaponika (Thera), *The Heart of Buddhist Meditation (Satipaṭṭāna): A Handbook of Mental Training Based on the Buddha's Way of Mindfulness, with an Anthology of Relevant Texts Translated from the Pali and Sanskrit* (New York: Citadel Press, 1969); J. M. Schwartz, "Mental Force and the Advertence of Bare Attention," *Journal of Consciousness Studies* 6(2–3) (1999): 293–96; J. Shear and F. J. Varela, *The View from Within: First-Person Approaches to the Study of Consciousness* (Upton Pyne, UK: Imprint Academic, 1999); K. E. Weick and K. M. Sutcliffe, "Mindfulness and the Quality of Organizational Attention," *Organization Science* 17(4) (2006): 514–24.

222 **accompanying mental activity:** This aspect of mindfulness is captured quite well by one of Jon Kabat-Zinn's definitions of mindfulness, which is: "bringing one's complete attention to the present experience on a moment-to-moment basis." J. Kabat-Zinn, *Wherever You Go, There You Are: Mindfulness Meditation in Everyday Life* (New York: Hyperion, 1994), 4.

222 **GATE web calms down:** For a description of how the mind "calms down," see M. Wittmann and S. Schmidt, "Mindfulness Meditation and the Experience of Time," in *Meditation: Neuroscientific Approaches and Philosophical Implications* (New York: Springer International Publishing, 2014), 199–209. For implications of the mind calming down, see H. Fairfax et al., "Does Mindfulness Help in the Treatment of Obsessive Compulsive Disorder (OCD)? An Audit of Client Experience of an OCD Group," *Counselling Psychology Review* 29(2) (2014): 17–27.

222 **Douglas Harding called "headless-ness":** D. E. Harding, *On Having No Head* (London: Shollond Trust, 2013). For a neat description of the "headless" experience, see chapter 4 ("Meditation") in *Waking Up* by Sam Harris. As Harris notes, the experience of merging with the object of observation is not something that you can experience by thinking about it; indeed, thinking about it will likely get in the way of experiencing it. Rather, the most reliable way to experience it is through the practice of mindfulness. S. Harris, *Waking Up: A Guide to Spirituality Without Religion* (New York: Simon & Schuster, 2014).

223 **scary or even unpleasant:** For a great example of how the mind can interpret otherwise neutral and even interesting sensations or experiences as "pain" (or for that matter, pleasure), see Davidson's description on pp. 181–83, of a student's experience in a Vipassana retreat in R. J. Davidson and S. Begley, *The Emotional Life of Your Brain: How Its Unique Patterns Affect the Way You Think, Feel, and Live—and How You Can Change Them* (New York: Penguin, 2012).

223 **negative feelings to die more quickly:** For a compatible view on how mindfulness mitigates negativity by increasing tolerance for negative emotions, see N. A. Farb et al., "Minding One's Emotions: Mindfulness Training Alters the Neural Expression of Sadness," *Emotion* 10(1) (2010): 25–33; and J. A. Brefczynski-Lewis et al., "Neural Correlates of Attentional Expertise in Long-term Meditation Practitioners," *Proceedings of the National Academy of Sciences* 104(27) (2007): 11483–88. For a good example of how the practice of mindfulness can help those with OCD (obsessive-compulsive disorder) gain control of their emotions, see J. M. Schwartz and S. Begley, *The Mind and the Brain* (New York: Regan Books/Harper Collins, 2002).

224 **mind-wandering versus not:** M. A. Killingsworth and D. T. Gilbert, "A Wandering Mind Is an Unhappy Mind," *Science* 330(6006) (2010): 932. For an audiovisual summary of the paper, see Killingworth's TED talk: www.youtube.com/watch?v=Qy5A8d VYU3k (the TED talk can be accessed by Googling "Killingsworth TED talk").

225 **behavior affects attitude:** This theoretical basis for this phenomenon is something called self-perception theory. The idea is that we infer our characteristics (attitudes, opinions, etc.) based on how we see ourselves behaving; see D. J. Bem, "Self-perception: An Alternative Interpretation of Cognitive Dissonance Phenomena," *Psychological Review* 74(3) (1967): 183. See also a discussion of a related concept, the insufficient justification paradigm, discussed in R. E. Nisbett, and T. D. Wilson, "Telling More than We Can Know: Verbal Reports on Mental Processes," *Psychological Review* 84(3) (1977): 231.

225 **something called self-perception:** Bem, "Self-perception."

226 **to make it a "happier brain":** S. W. Lazar et al., "Meditation Experience Is Associated with Increased Cortical Thickness," *Neuroreport* 16(17) (2005): 1893–97; B. K. Hölzel et al., "Mindfulness Practice Leads to Increases in Regional Brain Gray Matter Density," *Psychiatry Research: Neuroimaging* 191(1) (2011): 36–43. (The first paper can be accessed at www.jimhopper.com/pdfs/lazar2005.pdf.) For a more general discussion of neuroplasticity (more specifically, how thoughts have an impact on brain structure), see E. A. Maguire, K. Woollett, and H. J. Spiers, "London Taxi Drivers and Bus Drivers: A Structural MRI and Neuropsychological Analysis," *Hippocampus* 16(12) (2006): 1091–1101; and A. Pascual-Leone et al., "The Plastic Human Brain Cortex," *Annual Review of Neuroscience* 28 (2005): 377–401. The former paper documented that the hippocampus—the region of the brain associated with context and spatial memory—of taxicab drivers in London was significantly larger than that of the average Londoner, while the latter showed that merely imagining practicing the piano (as opposed to actually practicing it) increased the size of the motor cortex.

226 **activation of the amygdala:** Brefczynski-Lewis et al., "Neural Correlates of Attentional Expertise in Long-term Meditation Practitioners."

226 **associated with stress and worrying:** For a reader-friendly discussion of five ways in which the practice of mindfulness thickens the left PFC and thins out the amygdala, see Sarah Lazar's interview, featured in *The Washington Post*, at www.washingtonpost .com/news/inspired-life/wp/2015/05/26/harvard-neuroscientist-meditation-not-only -reduces-stress-it-literally-changes-your-brain/.

227 *default state of the mind:* Wallace is quoted as saying this in C. M. Tan, *Search Inside Yourself: Increase Productivity, Creativity and Happiness (and World Peace)* (New York: HarperCollins, 2012).

227 **perhaps even extraordinariness:** Research by Carey Morewedge and his colleagues is consistent with the idea that mindfulness leads to becoming "absorbed" in the present experience, which in turn makes one less prone to comparing it with other similar experiences and thereby to appreciate its unique aspects better; see C. K. Morewedge et al., "Consuming Experience: Why Affective Forecasters Overestimate Comparative Value," *Journal of Experimental Social Psychology* 46(6) (2010): 986–92. Other re-

search, by Zhang et al. (2014), suggests that recalling everyday activities—such as a recent conversation or three favorite songs—can boost happiness levels; see T. Zhang et al., "A 'Present' for the Future: The Unexpected Value of Rediscovery." *Psychological Science* 25(10) (2014): 1851–60. For a more reader-friendly account of the Zhang et al. (2014) study, see http://www.spring.org.uk/2014/09/why-you-should-treasure-apparently -mundane-moments-in-life.php. For a more "experiential"—and perhaps even poetic— perspective of how mindfulness can help us see the extraordinary in the ordinary, see "Seeing," a highly evocative video created by Ludwig Dietrich, at https://vimeo .com/37153340.

227 ***Waking Up:*** Harris, *Waking Up.*

227 **on a computer screen:** M. C. Potter et al., "Two Attentional Deficits in Serial Target Search: The Visual Attentional Blink and an Amodal Task-Switch Deficit," *Journal of Experimental Psychology: Learning, Memory, and Cognition* 24(4) (1998): 979.

228 **rigorous mindfulness training:** H. A. Slagter et al., "Mental Training Affects Distribution of Limited Brain Resources," *PLOS Biology* 5(6) (2007): e138. For a reader-friendly discussion of the study, see www.nytimes.com/2007/05/08/health/psychology/08medi .html?_r=0.

229 **of the left prefrontal cortex:** Lazar et al., "Meditation Experience Is Associated with Increased Cortical Thickness"; Hölzel et al., "Mindfulness Practice Leads to Increases in Regional Brain Gray Matter Density." The first paper can be accessed at: www.jim hopper.com/pdfs/lazar2005.pdf. For a reader-friendly discussion of how the practice of mindfulness thickens the left PFC (and simultaneously thins out the amygdala), see Sarah Lazar's interview, featured in *The Washington Post*, at www.washingtonpost .com/news/inspired-life/wp/2015/05/26/harvard-neuroscientist-meditation-not-only -reduces-stress-it-literally-changes-your-brain/.

229 **promotes one's mental acuity:** E. Luders et al., "The Unique Brain Anatomy of Meditation Practitioners: Alterations in Cortical Gyrification," *Frontiers in Human Neuroscience* 6 (2012): 1–9; P. Vestergaard-Poulsen et al., "Long-term Meditation Is Associated with Increased Gray Matter Density in the Brain Stem," *Neuroreport* 20(2) (2009): 170–74.

229 **in front of an audience:** P. Kaliman et al., "Rapid Changes in Histone Deacetylases and Inflammatory Gene Expression in Expert Meditators," *Psychoneuroendocrinology* 40 (2014): 96–107; for a reader-friendly summary of the paper, see http://news.wisc .edu/22370.

229 **affects heart health:** B. Ditto, M. Eclache, and N. Goldman, "Short-term Autonomic and Cardiovascular Effects of Mindfulness Body Scan Meditation," *Annals of Behavioral Medicine* 32(3) (2006): 227–34.

229 **slow down aging:** L. E. Carlson et al., "Mindfulness-Based Cancer Recovery and Supportive-Expressive Therapy Maintain Telomere Length Relative to Controls in Distressed Breast Cancer Survivors," *Cancer* 121(3) (2015): 476–84; E. Epel et al., "Can Meditation Slow Rate of Cellular Aging? Cognitive Stress, Mindfulness, and Telomeres," *Annals of the New York Academy of Sciences* 1172(1) (2009): 34–53; T. L. Jacobs et al., "Intensive Meditation Training, Immune Cell Telomerase Activity, and Psychological Mediators," *Psychoneuroendocrinology* 36(5) (2011): 664–81. For a review of this topic, see N. S. Schutte and J. M. Malouff, "A Meta-analytic Review of the Effects of Mindfulness Meditation on Telomerase Activity," *Psychoneuroendocrinology* 42 (2014): 45–48.

229 **cured much faster:** J. Kabat-Zinn, E. Wheeler, and T. Light, "Influence of MBSR Intervention on Rate of Skin Clearing in Patients with Moderate to Severe Psoriasis Undergoing Phototherapy (UVB) and Photochemotherapy (PUVA)," *Psychosomatic Medicine* 60(5) (1998): 625–32.

230 **pause before acting or reacting:** I've borrowed this way of defining response flexibility from Chade Meng Tan's excellent book *Search Inside Yourself*, p. 20.

230 **respond in a more considered way:** Findings show that expert meditators can override even the so-called startle response, which is the automatic blinking of the eye in
response to a sudden noise. If mindfulness can help control the startle response, you
can rest assured that it can help control pretty much any instinctive response that we
might have to stimuli; R. W. Levenson, P. Ekman, and M. Ricard, "Meditation and the
Startle Response: A Case Study," *Emotion* 12(3) (2012): 650.

230 **"woo woo" or unscientific:** D. Harris, *10% Happier: How I Tamed the Voice in My
Head, Reduced Stress Without Losing My Edge, and Found Self-Help That Actually
Works—A True Story* (London: Hachette UK, 2014). As Professor Davidson notes in his
book *The Emotional Life of Your Brain*, much of the scientific community has (thankfully) seemed to have evolved past that stage—a testament to which is the fact that
even hard-core atheists, like Sam Harris, are open to discussing and defining such
topics as consciousness and spirituality. As a particularly salient testament to how
"un–woo woo" the topic of meditation and mindfulness is, consider that the National
Institutes of Health (NIH) now provides substantial funding for research on meditation, and literally thousands of scholarly papers are published every year on the topic;
see p. xvii of Davidson and Begley, *The Emotional Life of Your Brain*.

230 **the blind spot:** Sam Harris uses this example frequently and effectively on p. 136 of
Waking Up.

231 **"devil" in the smoke:** http://urbanlegends.about.com/library/bltabloid-arch10.htm.

231 **through random sequences:** T. Gilovich, R. Vallone, and A. Tversky, "The Hot Hand
in Basketball: On the Misperception of Random Sequences," *Cognitive Psychology* 17(3)
(1985): 295–314.

231 **How We Know What Isn't So:** T. Gilovich, *How We Know What Isn't So* (New York:
Free Press, 1991).

231 **many of us do:** S. T. Fiske, A. J. Cuddy, and P. Glick, "Universal Dimensions of Social Cognition: Warmth and Competence," *Trends in Cognitive Sciences* 11(2) (2007):
77–83.

231 **can't be as durable:** M. G. Luchs et al., "The Sustainability Liability: Potential Negative
Effects of Ethicality on Product Preference," *Journal of Marketing* 74(5) (2010): 18–31.

232 **top of their organizations:** A. M. Grant, *Give and Take: Why Helping Others Drives
Our Success* (New York: Penguin, 2013).

232 **Novak Djokovic:** "Novak Djokovic: The Unloved Champion," *The New York Times*,
Sept. 7, 2015, accessed on Sept. 19, 2015, at www.nytimes.com/2015/09/11/fashion/
mens-style/novak-djokovic-how-to-be-a-champion.html.

232 **mindfulness can benefit its soldiers:** "Meditating Marines: Military Tries Mindfulness to Lower Stress," ABC News, Jan. 20, 2013, accessed on Sept. 20, 2015, at http://
vitals.nbcnews.com/_news/2013/01/20/16612244-meditating-marines-military-tries
-mindfulness-to-lower-stress?lite.

232 **conversation I had with him:** You can catch excerpts of my conversation with
Professor Richie Davidson at https://www.coursera.org/learn/happiness/lecture/
ADpWa/week-6-video-9-some-other-obstacles-to-mindfulness-including-logistical
-ones.

232 **silent Vipassana meditation retreat:** I went to the Vipassana Meditation Center in
Kaufman, Texas, between April 18 and April 29, 2012.

232 **memorable experiences I've had:** You can read about my experiences at the retreat
on www.happysmarts.com/About_Raj/My_vipassana_experience.

233 **five minutes a day for five weeks:** C. A. Moyer et al., "Frontal Electroencephalo-

graphic Asymmetry Associated with Positive Emotion Is Produced by Very Brief Meditation Training," *Psychological Science* 22(10) (2011): 1277–79.

233 **out of the question:** Our work life has turned so "toxic," according to Anne-Marie Slaughter, that only those who are young and childless can cope with it; see "A Toxic Work World," *The New York Times*, Sept. 18, 2015, accessed on Sept. 18, 2015, at www .nytimes.com/2015/09/20/opinion/sunday/a-toxic-work-world.html.

234 **devised three strategies:** Variants of these strategies can be found across almost all books on mindfulness, including J. Kabat-Zinn, *Wherever You Go, There You Are: Mindfulness Meditation in Everyday Life* (New York: Hyperion, 1994).

235 **going on in the mind:** This point is also made by Eckhart Tolle in his best-selling book *The Power of Now*; E. Tolle, *The Power of Now: A Guide to Spiritual Enlightenment* (New York: New World Library, 2004).

235 **good thing to observe:** See S. Hagen, *Meditation Now or Never* (London: Penguin UK, 2012).

236 **Vijay Bhat:** Vijay calls himself a cancer "thriver" (as opposed to "survivor"), and has written about his experience with cancer in a wonderful book, *My Cancer Is Me*; you can find out more about Vijay Bhat at www.mycancerisme.com/.

Chapter 8: The Road Ahead

240 *self-determination theory:* R. M. Ryan, and E. L. Deci, "Self-determination Theory and the Facilitation of Intrinsic Motivation, Social Development, and Well-being," *American Psychologist* 55(1) (2000): 68.

241 **the "abundance" route:** Although the terms "scarcity" and "abundance" don't have a history of use in academic research (for an exception, see Biberman and Whitty 1997), they have been used frequently in more informal contexts. For example, in his TED talk, Nipun Mehta, the founder of servicespace.org and Karma Kitchen, uses them in ways that evoke a set of concepts very similar to the ones I discuss here. Mehta's TED talk can be accessed at www.youtube.com/watch?v=kpyc84kamhw (or by Googling "Nipun Mehta TED talk"). Biberman and Whitty, too, use the terms in a way that is compatible with my use of them; J. Biberman and M. Whitty, "A Postmodern Spiritual Future for Work," *Journal of Organizational Change Management* 10(2) (1997): 130–38.

243 **significant proportion of the world's population:** According to one article, as high a proportion as 60 percent of the world's population does not have access to adequate water-related sanitation; see "60% of the World's Population Still Don't Have the Best Innovation in Human Health," *Slate*, Feb. 22, 2013, accessed on Sept. 18, 2015, at www .slate.com/blogs/future_tense/2013/02/22/_60_percent_of_the_world_population _still_without_toilets.html.

243 **"bottom of the pyramid":** This is a term introduced by management professor C. K. Prahalad to refer to those below the poverty line; C. K. Prahalad, *The Fortune at the Bottom of the Pyramid: Eradicating Poverty Through Profits* (Upper Saddle River, NJ: Pearson Education, 2005).

244 **have repeatedly shown:** See *Drive* by Dan Pink for a reader-friendly review of this literature; D. H. Pink, *Drive: The Surprising Truth About What Motivates Us* (New York: Penguin, 2011).

244 **climate change:** E.g., see T. L. Root et al., "Fingerprints of Global Warming on Wild Animals and Plants," *Nature* 421(6918) (2003): 57–60.

244 **species decimation:** E.g., A. P. Dobson, A. D. Bradshaw, and A. A. Baker, "Hopes for the Future: Restoration Ecology and Conservation Biology," *Science* 277(5325) (1997): 515–22.

244 **wealth inequality:** For a review, see J. Stiglitz, *The Price of Inequality* (London: Penguin UK, 2012).

244 **water scarcity:** S. Postel, *Last Oasis: Facing Water Scarcity* (New York: W. W. Norton & Company, 1997).

244 **pernicious hyperproductivity:** For an enlightening discussion of the various challenges we collectively face as a humanity and what we can do about them, see J. Sachs, *Common Wealth: Economics for a Crowded Planet* (New York: Penguin, 2008).

244 **create more harm than good:** The following famous statement made by Peter Drucker, the management guru, summarizes this sentiment better than anything else I have heard: "Nothing is less productive than to make more efficient what should not be done at all."

245 **positive psychology:** For the origins of positive psychology, see https://en.wikipedia .org/wiki/Positive_psychology.

245 **unprecedented levels of peace:** S. Pinker, *The Better Angels of Our Nature: The Decline of Violence in History and Its Causes* (London: Penguin UK, 2011).

245 **"half a century ago":** See p. 42 of S. Lyubomirsky, *The How of Happiness: A Scientific Approach to Getting the Life You Want* (New York: Penguin, 2008).

246 **"conscious" business practices:** See J. Mackey and R. Sisodia, *Conscious Capitalism: Liberating the Heroic Spirit of Business* (Cambridge, MA: Harvard Business Review Press, 2014).

246 **"room for everyone to grow":** W. C. Kim and R. Mauborgne, *Blue Ocean Strategy, Expanded Edition: How to Create Uncontested Market Space and Make the Competition Irrelevant* (Cambridge, MA: Harvard Business Review Press, 2015).

246 **110 percent more profits:** J. N. Sheth, R. S. Sisodia, and D. B. Wolfe, *Firms of Endearment: How World-Class Companies Profit from Passion and Purpose* (Upper Saddle River, NJ: Pearson Prentice Hall, 2003).

246 *biosphere consciousness:* J. Rifkin, *The Empathic Civilization: The Race to Global Consciousness in a World in Crisis* (New York: Penguin, 2009).

248 **evaluability of goals:** C. K. Hsee, "The Evaluability Hypothesis: An Explanation for Preference Reversals Between Joint and Separate Evaluations of Alternatives," *Organizational Behavior and Human Decision Processes* 67(3) (1996): 247–57.

248 **already under way to do so:** See "Why More Companies Are Ditching Performance Ratings," *Harvard Business Review*, Sept. 2015, accessed on Sept. 18, 2015, at https:// hbr.org/2015/09/why-more-and-more-companies-are-ditching-performance-ratings.

248 **over positive ones:** R. F. Baumeister et al., "Bad Is Stronger than Good," *Review of General Psychology* 5(4) (2001): 323.

249 *The Happiness Hypothesis:* J. Haidt, *The Happiness Hypothesis: Finding Modern Truth in Ancient Wisdom* (New York: Basic Books, 2006).

249 **Chip and Dan Heath:** C. Heath and D. Heath, *Switch: How to Change When Change Is Hard* (New York: Broadway Books, 2010).

249 *What Got You Here Won't Get You There:* M. Goldsmith, *What Got You Here Won't Get You There: How Successful People Become Even More Successful* (New York: Profile Books, 2010).

249 *Smart Thinking:* A. Markman, *Smart Thinking: Three Essential Keys to Solve Problems, Innovate, and Get Things Done* (New York: Penguin, 2012).

249 *Smart Change:* A. Markman, *Smart Change: Five Tools to Create New and Sustainable Habits in Yourself and Others* (New York: Penguin, 2014).

249 **hundreds of organizations:** Goldsmith mentioned this to me during our interview, which I conducted for my Coursera course. You can watch excerpts of my interview at https://www.coursera.org/learn/happiness/lecture/8Jpj3/week-6-video-13-the-7 -happiness-sustaining-strategies.

250 **more productive ones:** Markman mentioned these to me during an interview that I conducted for my Coursera course. You can watch excerpts from the interview (toward the latter end of the video) at https://www.coursera.org/learn/happiness/lecture/8Jpj3/week-6-video-13-the-7-happiness-sustaining-strategies.

253 **Third Happiness Measurement:** E. D. Diener et al., "The Satisfaction with Life Scale," *Journal of Personality Assessment* 49(1) (1985): 71–75.

269 **out of severe depression:** See M. E. Seligman, *Authentic Happiness: Using the New Positive Psychology to Realize Your Potential for Lasting Fulfillment* (New York: Free Press, 2002).

INDEX